P9-CEM-510

Failing at Fairness

Failing at
FAIRNESS

HOW

AMERICA'S

SCHOOLS

CHEAT

GIRLS

Myra and David Sadker

CHARLES SCRIBNER'S SONS
NEW YORK
Maxwell Macmillan Canada
TORONTO
Maxwell Macmillan International
NEW YORK   OXFORD   SINGAPORE   SYDNEY

Charles Scribner's Sons   Maxwell Macmillan Canada, Inc.
Macmillan Publishing Company   1200 Eglinton Avenue East
866 Third Avenue   Suite 200
New York, NY 10022   Don Mills, Ontario M3C 3N1

Macmillan Publishing Company is part of the Maxwell Communication Group
of Companies.

Library of Congress Cataloging-in-Publication Data
Sadker, Myra.
    Failing at fairness: how America's schools cheat girls / Myra and David
Sadker.
        p.   cm.
    Includes bibliographical references and index.
    ISBN 0-684-19541-0
    1. Sex discrimination in education—United States.   2. Sexism in educa-
tion—United States.   3. Women—Education—United States.   I. Sadker,
David Miller.   II. Title.
LC212.82.S27   1993
370.19'345—dc20   93–11586

Macmillan books are available at special discounts for bulk purchases for sales
promotions, premiums, fund-raising, or educational use. For details, contact:

Special Sales Director
Macmillan Publishing Company
866 Third Avenue
New York, NY 10022

Book design by Jennifer Dossin

10   9   8   7   6   5   4   3   2   1

Printed in the United States of America

Contents

At workshops we give around the country for parents and teachers, the questions we are asked most often are, "How did you discover there was gender bias in education? How did you get personally involved?" The answers take us back almost thirty years, to the 1960s when, according to surveys of that decade, most girls still believed the only careers open to them were those of teacher, nurse, secretary, and mother.

At that time there were few women and even fewer married couples in doctoral programs, and so we stood out. We attended the same classes, prepared the same assignments, read the same books—and realized we were getting two very different educations.

One 1968 meeting of students and professors in our graduate education program started a ripple effect of changes in our lives. About fifty participants, almost all men, were discussing civil rights for minorities in education. One male voice after another joined the discussion until Myra made a suggestion and waited for a reaction. But the men kept right on talking. "Perhaps they didn't hear me," she thought, so she tried again. But the discussion rambled on as if she had not uttered a word. Then a loud, deep voice boomed out, the kind of powerful voice that causes eyes to look skyward searching for Charlton Heston bringing down the tablets. All eyes turned to six-foot Mike from Utah as he slowly repeated Myra's idea. The talking stopped, there was complete silence, and then the room exploded with praise. "That's what we've been looking for! Great idea!"

As a result of Myra's good idea that was attributed to Mike, a professor assigned the task of writing grant proposals to improve education for minorities. We worked together and signed our names as coauthors. The faculty member began the next meeting with this announcement: "There's one paper that stands out," he said. "I'd like to talk with you about David's proposal. He has some ideas I think we can pursue." There was enthusiasm for our proposal, our ideas, but "our" had become "David's." "I wrote it, too," Myra said lightly so as not to appear petty. The faculty member looked surprised and concerned. "Of course when we say David, we mean you, too. You know that, don't you?"

Later in the year Myra expressed her frustration and anger in an editorial in *Tabula Rasa*, the School of Education newspaper. In an article entitled "The Only Socially Acceptable Form of Discrimination," she tried to explain how it felt to be female, invisible, and voiceless in a doctoral program. What professors could not hear in classrooms or meetings, they listened to in print. One faculty member who read the editorial was a part-time education editor for Harper & Row. He suggested that the editorial might be expanded into a book. After all, *Why Johnny Can't Read* was a bestseller. And no one had ever thought about girls in school.

Myra spent the next year searching through libraries. In 1970 there was almost nothing to be found on the education of girls—no books, articles, or studies—so she researched in classrooms, talking to children and examining textbooks. As she looked into it more extensively, the enormity of the problem became clear: School was eroding girls' potential, and nobody had an inkling that anything was wrong.

In 1973, *Sexism in School and Society* was published.[1] Written for teachers, it was the first textbook to establish the nature of sexism in school. Documenting sex-segregated courses, unfair teaching and counseling, and bias in books, it raised issues twenty years ago that remain a blueprint for the study of gender bias in education today.

During the second year of the book's life, the publishing company called with disturbing news. Not only were people no longer buying *Sexism in School and Society*, but a group of first-year purchasers had returned the book and asked for their money back. Myra was devastated. Did people hate her book so much that they were taking the trouble to wrap it up and request a refund?

Today when we give workshops on sexism in school, we often ask participants, "Why do you think people in 1973 were returning *Sexism in School and Society*?" They offer many explanations:

"The truth hurts."

"It made people mad. They—especially men—became so angry, they sent the book back."

"It was written by a woman who didn't have enough sense to use a man's name. A lot of people won't pay attention to anything a woman says."

"People didn't want to hear it, so they denied everything the book said and asked for a refund."

Although those are good suppositions, few people in our workshops uncover the real reason. Pornography stores were among the major purchasers of *Sexism in School and Society* that first year. They stocked their shelves with what they thought was a book about sex in school. Our workshop participants chuckle as they picture sleazy, raincoated figures pulling *Sexism in School and Society* from a shelf, turning to the chapter on curriculum in the hope of something sexy, and tossing the book aside in frustration. No wonder they wanted their money back!

But when the laughter stops, the parents and teachers in our workshops have come to a new awareness: Changing terms signify changing times, a stunning revolution. During the early 1970s, the word *sexism* was unfamiliar to many people. It did not mean bias or discrimination as it does today. In thirty years we have journeyed from Betty Friedan's "problem that has no name" to a realization that sexism affects every part of our lives, from what we watch on television to what we do on our jobs, from the preaching in our religious institutions to the teaching in our schools.

Throughout the history of education in America, the angle of the school door has determined the direction schoolgirls travel to different adult destinies. Sometimes the door was locked and barred; at other times it was ajar a matter of degrees. Today it appears wide open for girls to pursue the curriculum of their choice. But an open-door policy does not by itself result in fair schools. Today's schoolgirls face subtle and insidious gender lessons, micro-inequities that appear seemingly insignificant when looked at individually but that have a powerful cumulative impact. These inequities chip away at girls' achievement and self-esteem. The crucial question now is, "How do these hidden lessons shortchange girls and women as they study along with boys and men?" We have spent a quarter of a century trying to uncover the answer.

Our original research project in this long-term endeavor was to examine textbooks. Since students spend most of their school day working with instructional materials, these materials are undeniably influential. As the officially sanctioned version of the knowledge that is worthy to be learned in the classrooms, these books discuss the people who will serve as role models for our children. When we discovered pervasive sexism in textbooks, we brought it to the attention of the textbook publishers; they were surprised by our findings and vowed to reform.

Eventually we realized that there was an even more powerful hidden curriculum that surfaced in the way teachers treat children and the way children treat one another. We have spent a decade, thousands of hours of classroom observation, analyzing this secret system of interaction that is prevalent throughout a child's educational lifetime.

We have observed classrooms from elementary school through higher education. Using an objective and systematic methodology, we have collected data on patterns of classroom instruction. In the first interaction study, which lasted more than three years, trained raters observed in over one hundred classrooms of fourth, sixth, and eighth graders in Connecticut, Maryland, Massachusetts, Virginia, and the District of Columbia. They filled out thousands of observation sheets to record classroom life in the inner city, in rural schools, and in the affluent suburbs. The raters looked at classes that were racially integrated as well as those that were all black or all white. After a year of analyzing the information they had gathered, we knew we had uncovered shocking patterns of sexism in schools, irrefutable data that would have escaped us had our methods been less rigorous.

In our next two-year study, raters analyzed again, counting and classifying classroom communication, this time at the college level. We discovered that education doesn't get fairer as girls grow up. New grants helped us develop a program to train teachers to interact fairly with girls and boys and to study the treatment of sexism in the movement for education reform.

As we worked, our findings were replicated and amplified by researchers in other parts of the country. Throughout the 1970s and early 1980s scholars won grants, completed studies, delivered papers, and wrote articles. Gender equity in education had become a full-blown field of study in the midst of a knowledge explosion.

In the television classic "All in the Family," Archie Bunker's oft-intoned warning to Edith was "Stifle yourself." The 1980s, Reagan-Bush backlash years, also tried to "stifle" women's voices. With funding cut, grants terminated, projects discontinued, there was no federal support for research or the researchers. Talented women and men reluctantly abandoned their quest for gender equity in education and moved on to other occupations.

Conservative leaders declared victory and claimed that equity had been achieved. "Girls today can be anything they want" was the party line, usually conveyed through a spokes*woman*. "Sexism is a relic of the past not worth whining over" was the view of federal education officials. Despite proclamations that equity had been achieved, the cover-up was transparent: Bias persisted from the elementary grades through medical and law school.

As educators and as parents of two daughters, we have come face-to-face with this bias, personally as well as professionally. Anyone who thinks the obstacles have been eliminated should have been with us at the junior high school parent-teacher conference for our older daughter. "Robin," the teacher told us, "is adorable, such a pretty girl. But she just can't do math. Don't worry about it. A lot of girls have that problem." Robin is in medical school now, but she might not be there if we had let the school track her into the slower math group. Our younger daughter, Jackie, anguished for several years, almost overwhelmed by the self-doubt that threatens so many gifted girls. Despite the financial burden, we decided to move her to an independent single-sex middle school to help her through the most painful years of low self-esteem. Now a National Merit Finalist, she has emerged assertive and confident. If these measures had failed for either of our daughters, we would have tried repeatedly to find other solutions.

Most parents whose daughters circumvent sexist gender lessons know the need for constant vigilance. But for every girl who succeeds, too many fail or live down to expectations or settle for second best. Most educators are unaware of the subtle ways in which gender lessons infiltrate the school environment, and while sexism harms girls at school, it is a two-edged sword: It damages boys as well. Focusing on their experiences in the chapter entitled "The Miseducation of Boys," we also document the price they pay.

We hope this book will be read by girls and boys in school as well as by their teachers and parents. In delving beneath the surface of studies and statistics, we have been able to expose biased lessons, frame by frame, and reveal how sexism sabotages girls at school. We believe that understanding these crucial issues will enable people to work for change. Tomorrow's women cannot afford to be cheated out of their academic achievement and self-esteem. Society is no longer gender divided, with women working at home and men in the salaried labor force outside. Schools that fail at fairness deny boys a wide range of options and prepare girls for poverty.

At the workshops and lectures we give to eradicate sexism at school, we have been told by concerned parents and dedicated teachers about the hidden lessons that marred their own school experiences. They have described incidents of sexism that still happen in schools every day. Many of their stories collected over the past decade are here, along with strategies for nonsexist education that have been developed and field-tested in schools and homes all over America. This book therefore presents an action agenda for teachers and parents who refuse to let tomorrow's women learn less than they deserve. When schools succeed at fairness, the nation and its daughters will benefit. We can only imagine what advances will then be achieved for all.

Acknowledgments

For a quarter of a century we have been welcome guests in schools across the country. Hundreds of teachers and thousands of students have been gracious and candid as we observed their classrooms. Whether we visited as a team or watched classes separately, throughout *Failing at Fairness* we use the pronoun "we" rather than indicating "Myra" and "David" individually. No matter the setting or which one of us observed and interviewed, public and private school teachers, principals, professors, students, and parents shared their experiences willingly. Following standard ethical research practice, we have kept their names in confidence; but they know who they are, and we are grateful for their contributions.

Several individuals have been crucial before and beyond this book. As early as 1968, Louis Fischer realized the harm done by sexism in schools, and his foresight led to Myra's first textbook on this issue. In the 1970s, Shirley McCune was a national focal point for educators concerned about gender bias, and she guided us to our first grant on textbook analysis. Sue Klein's concern about subtle sexism in the classroom led to our first multiyear study on teacher-student interactions; the success of this research owes much to the dedication of Joyce Bauchner and Leslie Hergert. As director of the Women's Educational Equity Act Program, Leslie Wolfe provided sponsorship for several of our research and training projects, including our work in preparing nonsexist teachers. Her courage in the face of political pressure helped many equity advocates during very difficult times.

Individuals in state departments of education, desegregation assistance centers, and local school districts have given us opportunities and resources to transform schools into more equitable places for girls. In Maine, Jane Riley and Stephanie Irvine made a real difference, and in California, Barb Landers exerted influence that went beyond state borders. They are missed. Today, educators such as Sharon

Steindam in Virginia and Bettie Tipton and Marsha Robertson in Kentucky have never failed to open school doors for us for research and training. We also offer our gratitude to Anne Bryant for her leadership as the American Association of University Women works to bring gender equity to the forefront of the nation's education agenda.

Lynn Rosen, our agent, has been indispensable through every phase of the development of this book—as a reader of many manuscript versions and as a source of support and friendship from the initial idea to the final sentence. Erika Goldman, our editor at Scribners, has not only provided insightful comments and productive suggestions, but she has also been a pleasure to work with, always ready with encouragement and a kind word. Charles Flowers reduced problems and moved manuscripts with dispatch. We are grateful for the support of Barbara Grossman, whose commitment to this book has never wavered. Susan Bailey, Jim Cooper, Keith Geiger, Patricia Ireland, Bill Korin, Jadwiga Sebrechts, Mitchell Wendell, and Leslie Wolfe read manuscript drafts and offered suggestions; we are in their debt.

Special thanks go to our research assistants: Katharine Volker, Julia Masterson, Amy Monaghan, Alicia Ruvolo, Abigail Lewit, Kirsten Hill, and Kathryn Clark McNerney, and Leoner Jose Perez tracked down articles, helped with the production of manuscripts, and were always there when we needed them. Ethan Leonard, Terese O'Neil Noenick, and Shannon Shuemake added to their efforts by researching special topics and interviewing students in classrooms. Melinda Salata was invaluable in compiling nonsexist children's literature, and Laura Healy, Judy Leon Park, Christine Rossi, Alicia Ruvolo, Jacqueline Sadker, Claudia Seifert, Marnie Stone, Kendra Tohidloo, Katharine Volker, and Pamela Zatz stayed with us to the last minute, reading and rereading children's books. Our colleague Deborah Thompson, the staff of the Chesire Cat bookstore, and librarians throughout the Washington, D.C., metropolitan area offered helpful suggestions.

The American University library staff never learned the meaning of the word *no*. If a book was not on their shelves, they found it elsewhere and put it in our hands. No article was too esoteric to track down. Andra Powell Henderson and Sulaima Kochaji helped with the typing, and we are appreciative.

This book is dedicated to our daughters, Robin and Jackie. They have been a source of inspiration and have taught us, close to heart and home, how parents and teachers must be constantly vigilant in fighting gender bias in the classroom and beyond. This book is written with the hope that all our children will be educated in better, fairer schools.

Failing at Fairness

1
Hidden Lessons

Sitting in the same classroom, reading the same textbook, listening to the same teacher, boys and girls receive very different educations. From grade school through graduate school female students are more likely to be invisible members of classrooms. Teachers interact with males more frequently, ask them better questions, and give them more precise and helpful feedback. Over the course of years the uneven distribution of teacher time, energy, attention, and talent, with boys getting the lion's share, takes its toll on girls. Since gender bias is not a noisy problem, most people are unaware of the secret sexist lessons and the quiet losses they engender.

Girls are the majority of our nation's schoolchildren, yet they are second-class educational citizens. The problems they face—loss of self-esteem, decline in achievement, and elimination of career options—are at the heart of the educational process. Until educational sexism is eradicated, more than half our children will be shortchanged and their gifts lost to society.

Award-winning author Susan Faludi discovered that backlash "is most powerful when it goes private, when it lodges inside a woman's mind and turns her vision inward, until she imagines the pressure is all in her head, until she begins to enforce the backlash too—on herself."[1] Psychological backlash internalized by adult women is a frightening concept, but what is even more terrifying is a curriculum of sexist school lessons becoming secret mind games played against female children, our daughters, tomorrow's women.

After almost two decades of research grants and thousands of hours of classroom observation, we remain amazed at the stubborn persistence of these hidden sexist lessons. When we began our investigation of gender bias, we looked first in the classrooms of one of Washington, D.C.'s elite and expensive private schools. Uncertain of exactly what to look for, we wrote nothing down; we just observed. The classroom was a whirlwind of activity, so fast paced we could easily miss the quick but vital phrase or gesture, the insidious incident, the tiny inequity that held a world of meaning. As we watched, we had to push ourselves beyond the blind spots of socialization and gradually focus on the nature of the interaction between teacher and student. On the second day we saw our first example of sexism, a quick, jarring flash within the hectic pace of the school day:

Two second graders are kneeling beside a large box. They whisper excitedly to each other as they pull out wooden blocks, colored balls, counting sticks. So absorbed are these two small children in examining and sorting the materials, they are visibly startled by the teacher's impatient voice as she hovers over them. "Ann! Julia! Get your cotton-pickin' hands out of the math box. Move over so the boys can get in there and do their work."

Isolated here on the page of a book, this incident is not difficult to interpret. It becomes even more disturbing if you think of it with the teacher making a racial distinction. Picture Ann and Julia as African-American children moved away so white children can gain access to the math materials. If Ann and Julia's parents had observed this exchange, they might justifiably wonder whether their tuition dollars were well spent. But few parents actually watch teachers in action, and fewer still have learned to interpret the meaning behind fast-paced classroom events.

The incident unsettles, but it must be considered within the context of numerous interactions this harried teacher had that day. While she talked to the two girls, she was also keeping a wary eye on fourteen other active children. Unless you actually shadowed the teacher, stood right next to her as we did, you might not have seen or heard the event. After all, it lasted only a few seconds.

It took us almost a year to develop an observation system that would register the hundreds of daily classroom interactions, teasing out the gender bias embedded in them. Trained raters coded classrooms in math, reading, English, and social studies. They observed students from different racial and ethnic backgrounds. They saw lessons taught by women and by men, by teachers of different races. In short, they analyzed America's classrooms. By the end of the year we had thousands of observation sheets, and after another year of statistical analysis, we discovered a syntax of sexism so elusive that most teachers and students were completely unaware of its influence.[2]

Recently a producer of NBC's "Dateline" contacted us to learn more about our discovery that girls don't receive their fair share of education. Jane Pauley, the show's anchorwoman, wanted to visit classrooms, capture these covert sexist lessons on videotape, and expose them before a television audience. The task was to extricate sound bites of sexism from a fifth-grade classroom where the teacher, chosen to be the subject of the exposé, was aware she was being scrutinized for sex bias.

"Dateline" had been taping in her class for two days when we received a concerned phone call. "This is a fair teacher," the producer said. "How can we show sexism on our show when there's no gender bias in this teacher's class?" We drove to the NBC studio in Washington, D.C., and found two "Dateline" staffers, intelligent women concerned about fair treatment in school, sitting on the floor in a darkened room staring at the videotape of a fifth-grade class. "We've been playing this over and over. The teacher is terrific. There's no bias in her teaching. Come watch."

After about twenty minutes of viewing, we realized it was a case of déjà vu: The episodal sexist themes and recurring incidents were all too familiar. The teacher was terrific, but she was more effective for half of the students than she was for the other. She was, in fact, a classic example of the hundreds of skillful well-intentioned professionals we have seen who inadvertently teach boys better than girls.

We had forgotten how difficult it was to recognize subtle sexism before you learn how to look. It was as if the "Dateline" staff members were wearing blinders. We halted the tape, pointed out the sexist behaviors, related them to incidents in our research, and played the tape again. There is a classic "aha!" effect in education when people finally "get it." Once the hidden lessons of unconscious bias are understood, classrooms never look the same again to the trained observer.

Much of the unintentional gender bias in that fifth-grade class could not be shown in the short time allowed by television, but the sound bites of sexism were also there. "Dateline" chose to show a segregated math group: boys sitting on the teacher's right side and girls on her left. After giving the math book to a girl to hold open at the page of examples, the teacher turned her back to the girls and focused on the boys, teaching them actively and directly. Occasionally she turned to the girls' side, but only to read the examples in the book. This teacher, although aware that she was being observed for sexism, had unwittingly transformed the girls into passive spectators, an audience for the boys. All but one, that is: The girl holding the math book had become a prop.

"Dateline" also showed a lively discussion in the school library. With both girls' hands and boys' hands waving for attention, the librarian chose boy after boy to speak. In one interaction she peered through the forest of girls' hands waving directly in front of her to acknowledge the raised hand of a boy in the back of the room. Startled by the teacher's attention, the boy muttered, "I was just stretching."

The next day we discussed the show with future teachers, our students at The American University. They were bewildered. "Those teachers really were sexist. They didn't mean to be, but they were. How could that happen—with the cameras and everyone watching?" When we took those students into classrooms to discover the hidden lessons for themselves, they began to understand. It is difficult to detect sexism unless you know precisely how to observe. And if a lifetime of socialization makes it difficult to spot gender bias even when you're looking for it, how much harder it is to avoid the traps when you are the one doing the teaching.

Among Schoolchildren

Subtle sexism is visible to only the most astute readers of *Among Schoolchildren*, Tracy Kidder's chronicle of real-life educator Chris Zajac. A thirty-four-year-old teacher in Mt. Holyoke, Massachusetts, Mrs. Zajac is a no-nonsense veteran of the classroom. She does not allow her fifth-grade students to misbehave, forget to do their homework, or give up without trying their hardest. Underlying her strict exterior is a woman who cares about schoolchildren. Our students admired her dedication and respected her as a good human being, and it took several readings and discussions before they discovered her inadvertent gender bias. Then came the questions: Does Mrs. Zajac work harder teaching boys than girls? Does she know there is sex bias in her classroom?

These questions probably do not occur to most readers of *Among Schoolchildren* and might jolt both Chris Zajac and the author who so meticulously described the classroom. Here's how Tracy Kidder begins the story of a year in the life of this New England teacher:

"Mrs. Zajac wasn't born yesterday. She knows you didn't do your best work on this paper, Clarence. Don't you remember Mrs. Zajac saying that if you didn't do your best, she'd make you do it over? As for you, Claude, God forbid that you should ever need brain surgery. But Mrs. Zajac hopes that if you do, the doctor won't open up your head and walk off saying he's almost done, as you said when Mrs. Zajac asked you for your penmanship, which, by the way, looks like who did it and ran. Felipe, the reason you have hiccups is, your mouth is always open and the wind rushes in. You're in fifth grade now. So, Felipe, put a lock on it. Zip it up. Then go get a drink of water. Mrs. Zajac means business, Robert. The sooner you realize she never said everybody in the room has to do the work except for Robert, the sooner you'll get along with her. And . . . Clarence. Mrs. Zajac knows you didn't try. You don't just hand in junk to Mrs. Zajac. She's been teaching an awful lot of years. She didn't fall off the turnip cart yesterday. She told you she was an old-lady teacher."[3]

Swiftly, adroitly, Kidder introduces the main characters in the classroom—Clarence, Claude, Felipe, Robert, and back to Clarence, the boy in whom Mrs. Zajac invests most. But where are the girls?

As our students analyzed the book and actually examined who Mrs. Zajac was speaking to, they saw that page after page she spent time with the boys—disciplining them, struggling to help them understand, teaching them with all the energy and talent she could muster. In contrast, the pages that showed Mrs. Zajac working with girls were few and far between.

When we ask teachers at our workshops why they spend more time helping boys, they say, "Because boys need it more" or "Boys have trouble reading, writing, doing math. They can't even sit still. They need me more." In *Among Schoolchildren*, Chris Zajac feels that way, too. Kidder describes how she allows boys to take her over because she thinks they need her.

So teachers of good intention, such as Chris Zajac, respond to boys and teach them more actively, but their time and attention are not limitless. While the teachers are spending time with boys, the girls are being ignored and shortchanged. The only girl clearly realized in *Among Schoolchildren* is Judith, a child who is so alert that she has a vast English vocabulary even though her parents speak only Spanish. But while Judith is a girl of brilliant potential, she rarely reaps the benefit of Mrs. Zajac's active teaching attention. In fact, rather than trouble her teacher and claim time and attention for herself, Judith helps Mrs. Zajac, freeing her to work with the more demanding boys. Mrs. Zajac knows she isn't giving this talented girl what she needs and deserves: "If only I had more time," she thinks as she looks at Judith.

On a field trip to Old Sturbridge Village, the children have segregated themselves by sex on the bus, with the boys claiming the back. In a moment of quiet reflection, Chris realizes that in her classroom "the boys rarely give her a chance to spend much time with her girls." She changes her seat, joins the girls, and sings jump rope songs with them for the remainder of the trip.[4]

But her time spent with the girls is short-lived—the length of the day-long field trip—and her recognition of the gender gap in time and attention is brief: a paragraph-long flash of understanding in a book of more than three hundred pages. On the whole, Chris Zajac does not invest her talent in girls. But nurturing children is not unlike tending a garden: Neglect, even when benign, is withering; time and attention bear fruit. Mrs. Zajac and other caring teachers across the country are unaware of the full impact of uneven treatment. They do not realize the high academic and emotional price many girls pay for being too good.

Drawn from years of research, the episodes that follow demonstrate the sexist lessons taught daily in America's classrooms.[5] Pulled out of the numerous incidents in a school day, these inequities become enlarged, as if observed through a magnifying glass, so we can see clearly how they extinguish learning and shatter self-esteem. Imagine yourself in a sixth-grade science class like the one we observed in Maryland.

The teacher is writing a list of inventors and their discoveries on the board:

Elias Howe	sewing machine
Robert Fulton	steamboat
Thomas A. Edison	light bulb
James Otis	elevator
Alexander Graham Bell	telephone
Cyrus McCormick	reaper
Eli Whitney	cotton gin
Orville and Wilbur Wright	airplane

A girl raises her hand and asks, "It looks like all the inventors were men. Didn't women invent anything?" The teacher does not add any female inventors to the list, nor does he discuss new scholarship recognizing the involvement of women in inventions such as the cotton gin. He does not explain how hard it was in times past for women to obtain patents in their own names, and therefore we may never know how many female inventors are excluded from the pages of our history books. Instead he grins, winks, and says, "Sweetheart, don't worry about it. It's the same with famous writers and painters. It's the man's job to create things and the woman's job to look beautiful so she can inspire him." Several boys laugh. A few clown around by flexing their muscles as they exclaim, "Yes!" One girl rolls her eyes toward the ceiling and shakes her head in disgust. The incident lasts less than a minute, and the discussion of male inventors continues.

We sometimes ask our students at The American University to list twenty famous women from American history. There are only a few restrictions. They cannot include figures from sports or entertainment. Presidents' wives are not allowed unless they are clearly famous in their own right. Most students cannot do it. The seeds of their ignorance were sown in their earliest years of schooling.

In the 1970s, analyses of best-selling history books showed a biological oddity, a nation with only founding fathers.[6] More space was given to the six-shooter than to the women's suffrage movement. In fact, the typical history text gave only two sentences to enfranchising half the population. Science texts continued the picture of a one-gender world, with the exception of Marie Curie who was permitted to stand behind her husband and peer over his shoulder as he looked into a microscope. Today's history and science texts are better—but not much.[7]

At our workshops we ask teachers and parents to tell or write about any sexism they have seen in their schools. We have been collecting their stories for years.[8] A Utah teacher told us: "Last year I had my U.S. history classes write biographies about famous Americans. When I collected all one hundred and fifty, I was dismayed to find only five on women. When I asked my kids why, they said they didn't know any famous women. When I examined their textbook more closely, I saw there were few females in it. And there were even fewer books on famous American women in our school library."

Teachers add to textbook bias when they produce sexist materials of their own. One parent described her efforts to stop a teacher-made worksheet that perpetuated stereotypes of yesteryear:

> A few years ago my daughter came home upset over her grade. When I looked at her paper, I got more angry than she was. At the top of the worksheet were the faces of a man

and a woman. At the bottom were different objects—nails, a saw, a sewing needle, thread, a hammer, a screwdriver, a broom. The directions said to draw a line from the man to the objects that belong to him and a line from the woman to the objects that go with her. In our house my husband does the cooking and I do the repair work, so you can imagine what the lines on my daughter's paper looked like. There was a huge red F in the middle of her worksheet. I called the teacher right away. She was very understanding and assured me the F wouldn't count. A small victory, I thought, and forgot about it.

This year my son is in her class. Guess what he brought home last week. Same worksheet—same F. Nothing had changed at all.

When girls do not see themselves in the pages of textbooks, when teachers do not point out or confront the omissions, our daughters learn that to be female is to be an absent partner in the development of our nation. And when teachers add their stereotypes to the curriculum bias in books, the message becomes even more damaging.

In a 1992 survey in *Glamour*, 74 percent of those responding said that they had "a teacher who was biased against females or paid more attention to the boys." Math class was selected as the place where inequities were most likely to occur. Fifty-eight percent picked it as their most sexist subject. Physical education was second, and science came in third, selected by 47 percent of the respondents.[9] Women at our workshops recall remarks made by math and science teachers that years later still leave them upset and angry:

In my A.P. physics class in high school in 1984 there were only three girls and twenty-seven boys. The three girls, myself included, consistently scored at the top end of the scale. On one test I earned a 98. The next closest boy earned an 88. The teacher handed the tests back saying, "Boys, you are failing. These three pretty cookies are outscoring you guys on every test." He told the boys it was embarrassing for them to be beaten by a girl. He always referred to us (the girls) as "Cookie" or made our names sound very cutesy!

Sometimes the humiliating lessons come not from school policies, teachers, or books but from boys, the very individuals that adolescent girls most want to impress:

The New England high school was having an assembly during the last period on Friday, and the auditorium was packed with more than a thousand students, who were restless as they listened to announcements. A heavy, awkward tenth grader made her way across the stage to reach the microphone located in the center. As she walked, several male students made loud barking noises to signify she was a dog. Others oinked like pigs. Later a slender long-haired senior walked to the mike; she was greeted by catcalls and whistles. Nobody attempted to stop the demeaning and hurtful public evaluation of the appearance of these teenage girls.

Tolerated under the assumption that "boys will be boys" and hormone levels are high in high school, sexual harassment is a way of life in America's schools. While teachers and administrators look the other way, sexually denigrating comments, pinching, touching, and propositioning happen daily. Sensitive and insecure about their appearance, some girls are so intimidated they suffer in silence. Others fight back only to find this heightens the harassment. Many girls don't even realize they have a right to protest. And when they do come forward, bringing school sexual harassment into the open, it is often dealt with quickly and nervously; it is swept under the rug, turned aside, or even turned against the girl who had the courage to complain. A teacher at a workshop in Indiana told us: "In our school a girl was pinched on the derriere by two boys and verbally harassed. When she reported the incident to the principal, she was told that her dress was inappropriate and that she had asked for it."

Intimidating comments and offensive sexual jokes are even more common in college and sometimes are even made public as part of a classroom lecture and discussion. A female faculty member, teaching at a university that was historically all male, told us about one of the most popular teachers on campus, an economics professor:

> He would show slides illustrating an economic theory and insert women in bikinis in the middle "to keep the students interested." He illustrated different phases of the economic cycle by showing a slide of a woman's breast and pointed out how far away from the nipple each phase was. When a number of female students complained, the local newspaper supported the professor and criticized the "ultrasensitive coeds." That semester the university gave the professor the Teacher of the Year award.

Although sexually harassing remarks, stories, and jokes occur only occasionally in classrooms, female silence is the norm. During our two-year study of colleges, our raters found that girls grow quieter as they grow older. In coeducational classes, college women are even less likely to participate in discussions than elementary and secondary school girls. In the typical college classroom, 45 percent of students do not speak; the majority of these voiceless students are women.[10]

Breaking the Sound Barrier

Women who have spent years learning the lessons of silence in elementary, secondary, and college classrooms have trouble regaining their voices. In our workshops we often set up a role play to demonstrate classroom sex bias. Four volunteers, two women and two men, are asked to pretend to be students in a middle school social studies lesson. They have no script; their only direction is to take a piece of paper with them as David, playing the part of the social studies teacher, ushers them to four chairs in front of the room. He tells the audience that he will condense all the research on sexism in the classroom into a ten-minute lesson, so the bias will look blatant, even overwhelming. The job of the parents and teachers in the audience is to detect the different forms of egregious sexism. He begins the lesson.

"Today we're going to discuss the chapter in your book, 'The Gathering Clouds of War,' about the American Revolution. But first I'd like you to take out your homework so I can check it." David walks over to Sarah, the first student in the line of four. (In real life she is an English teacher at the local high school.)

"Let's see your paper, Sarah." He pauses to look it over. "Questions three and seven are not correct." Sarah looks concerned.

David moves to Peggy (who is a communications professor at a state college). "Oh, Peggy, Peggy, Peggy!" She looks up as everyone stares. David holds up Peggy's paper. "Would you all look at this. It is sooo neat. You print just like a typewriter. This is the kind of paper I like to put on the bulletin board for open school night." Peggy looks down, smiles, blushes, looks up wide-eyed, and bats her eyelashes. She is not faking or exaggerating these behaviors. Before our eyes she has returned to childhood as the stereotypical good girl with pretty penmanship. The lessons have been well learned.

Next David stops by Tony (who is a vocational education teacher) and looks at the blank paper he is holding. "Tony, you've missed questions three, seven, and eleven. I think you would do better on your assignments if you used the bold headings to guide your reading. I know you can get this if you try harder." Tony nods earnestly as David moves to Roy. Sarah, who missed questions three and seven, looks perplexed.

David scans Roy's paper and hands it back. "Roy, where's your homework?"

Roy (a college physics teacher) stammers, "Here it is," and again offers the blank paper that served as homework for the others in the role play.

"Roy, that's not your history homework. That's science." Roy still looks puzzled. "Trust me, Roy," David says. "No matter what you come up with, it won't be history homework. Now, where is it?"

"The dog ate it," Roy mutters, getting the picture and falling into the bad boy role.

Next David discusses revolutionary battles, military tactics, and male leaders—George Washington, John and Samuel Adams, Paul Revere, Benjamin Franklin, Thomas Jefferson, and more. He calls on Roy and Tony more than twenty times each. When they don't know the answer, he probes, jokes, challenges, offers hints. He calls on Sarah only twice. She misses both her questions because David gives her less than half a second to speak. After effusively praising Peggy's pretty paper, David never calls on her again. As the lesson progresses, Sarah's face takes on a sad, almost vacant expression. Peggy keeps on smiling.

When the scene of blatant sexism is over, many in the audience want to know how the two women felt.

"That was me all through school," Peggy blurts out. "I did very well. My work was neat. I was always prepared. I would have had the right answer if someone had called on me. But they never did."

"Why did you watch the two males get all the attention?" we ask. "If you weren't called on, why didn't you call out?"

"I tried. I just couldn't do it."

"Why? You weren't wearing a muzzle. The men were calling out."

"I know. I felt terrible. It reminded me of all those years in school when I wanted to say something but couldn't."

"What about you, Sarah?" we ask. "Why didn't you just shout out an answer?"

"It never occurred to me to do it," Sarah says, then pauses. "No, that's not true. I thought about it, but I didn't want to be out there where I might get laughed at or ridiculed."

David has taught this role play class hundreds and hundreds of times in workshops in big cities and small towns all across the United States. Each time he demonstrates sex bias by blatantly and offensively ignoring female students, and almost always the adult women, put back into the role of twelve-year-olds, sit and say nothing; once again they become the nice girls watching the boys in action. Inside they may feel sad or furious or relieved, but like Sarah and Peggy, they remain silent.

When women try to get into classroom interaction, they rarely act directly. Instead they doodle, write letters, pass notes, and wait for the teacher to notice them. In a California workshop one parent who was playing the part of a student developed an elaborate pantomime. She reached into her large purse, pulled out a file, and began to do her nails. When that failed to attract David's attention, she brought out a brush, makeup, and a mirror. But David continued to ignore her, talking only with the two males.

"I was so mad I wanted to hit you," the woman fumed at the end of the role play when she was invited to express her feelings.

"What did you do to show your anger?" David asked.

"I didn't do anything." Then she paused, realizing the passive-aggressive but ultimately powerless strategy she had pursued. "No, I did do something—my nails," she said sadly.

After hundreds of these role plays, we are still astonished at how quickly the veneer of adulthood melts away. Grown women and men replay behavior they learned as children at school. The role plays are always revealing—funny, sad, and sometimes they even have a troubling twist.

At a workshop for college students at a large university in the Midwest, one of the young women ignored in the role play did not exhibit the usual behavior of silence or passive hostility. Instead, in the middle of the workshop in front of her classmates, she began to sob. She explained later in private that as one of only a few girls in the university's agricultural program, she had been either ignored or harassed. That week in an overenrolled course an instructor had announced, "There are too many students in this class. Everyone with ovaries—out!"

"What did you do?"

"What could I do? I left. Later I told my adviser about it. He was sympathetic but said if there was no room, I should consider another major."

Silent Losses

Each time a girl opens a book and reads a womanless history, she learns she is worth less. Each time the teacher passes over a girl to elicit the ideas and opinions of boys, that girl is conditioned to be silent and to defer. As teachers use their expertise to question, praise, probe, clarify, and correct boys, they help these male students sharpen ideas, refine their thinking, gain their voice, and achieve more. When female students are offered the leftovers of teacher time and attention, morsels of amorphous feedback, they achieve less.

Then girls and women learn to speak softly or not at all; to submerge honest feelings, withhold opinions, and defer to boys; to avoid math and science as male domains; to value neatness and quiet more than assertiveness and creativity; to emphasize appearance and hide intelligence. Through this curriculum in sexism they are turned into educational spectators instead of players; but education is not a spectator sport.

When blatantly sexual or sexist remarks become an accepted part of classroom conversation, female students are degraded. Sexual harassment in business and the military now causes shock waves and legal suits. Sexual harassment in schools is dismissed as normal and unavoidable "boys will be boys" behavior; but by being targeted, girls are being intimidated and caused to feel like members of an inferior class.

Like a thief in school, sexist lessons subvert education, twisting it into a system of socialization that robs potential. Consider this record of silent, devastating losses.[11]

- In the early grades girls are ahead of or equal to boys on almost every standardized measure of achievement and psychological well-being. By the time they graduate from high school or college, they have fallen back. Girls enter school ahead but leave behind.[12]
- In high school, girls score lower on the SAT and ACT tests, which are critical for college admission. The greatest gender gap is in the crucial areas of science and math.
- Girls score far lower on College Board Achievement tests, which are required by most of the highly selective colleges.
- Boys are much more likely to be awarded state and national college scholarships.
- The gap does not narrow in college. Women score lower on all sections of the Graduate Record Exam, which is necessary to enter many graduate programs.

- Women also trail on most tests needed to enter professional schools: the GMAT for business school, the LSAT for law school, and the MCAT for medical school.
- From elementary school through higher education, female students receive less active instruction, both in the quantity and in the quality of teacher time and attention.[13]

In addition to the loss of academic achievement, girls suffer other difficulties:

- Eating disorders among girls in middle and secondary schools and in college are rampant and increasing.[14]
- Incidents of school-based sexual harassment are now reported with alarming frequency.[15]
- One in ten teenage girls becomes pregnant each year. Unlike boys, when girls drop out, they usually stay out.[16]
- As girls go through school, their self-esteem plummets, and the danger of depression increases.[17]
- Economic penalties follow women after graduation. Careers that have a high percentage of female workers, such as teaching and nursing, are poorly paid. And even when women work in the same jobs as men, they earn less money. Most of America's poor live in households that are headed by women.

If the cure for cancer is forming in the mind of one of our daughters, it is less likely to become a reality than if it is forming in the mind of one of our sons. Until this changes, everybody loses.

2

Through the Back Door: The History of Women's Education

Mention educational inequality and, for most people, race comes to mind: black children walking down a dusty road to a dilapidated school while a bright yellow bus with white children passes them by; or an urban ghetto school with iron bars protecting already broken windows, a building ravaged by poverty and time. While the record of racial injustice is at the forefront of our national conscience, history books still do not tell the story of profound sexism at school. Few people realize that today's girls continue a three-hundred-year-old struggle for full participation in America's educational system.

No Entrance

For almost two centuries American education, following European traditions, barred girls from school. Education was the path to professions and careers open only to men. During Colonial times, viewed as mentally and morally inferior, women were relegated to learning only domestic skills, though they hungered for more.

While formal histories say little, letters and diaries hint of women's desire for learning and the lack of opportunity to fulfill that desire. In the early 1700s a Virginia girl wrote to her brother who had been sent to England to study: "I find you have got the start of me learning very much, for you write better already than I expect to do as long as I live."[1] The parents of another Virginia girl, Mary Ball, searched to find a tutor for their able daughter. After four years they finally found a minister who agreed to live in their home and teach young Mary, the woman who would later give birth to George Washington.

But these were the lucky girls. Most received no education or just a few years in a dame school where they might learn to read the Bible. An analysis of documents reveals that only 30 percent of women during this time could even sign their names.[2] We know only a few of their stories. Historians tell us of a girl in Colonial Hatfield, Massachusetts, who hungered to learn to read and write. Day after day she did her chores—spinning, sewing, knitting—and then slipped away to sit on the schoolhouse steps. She looked in through the window spellbound, and with her ear to the crack in the door, she could hear the boys recite their lessons: one of generations of girls destined to be only bystanders to the education of boys.[3]

While the school door was closed, the house door was wide open. The home, serving as the girl's classroom, was where she learned the practical domestic skills for her inevitable role as wife and mother— inevitable, that is, as long as Providence took a hand and a mate was found. And, in Colonial America, there were ways to assist Providence.

To attract suitors a girl needed a graceful carriage and erect posture. Special chairs were designed to align properly the female backbone, complete with harnesses, stocks, and rigid backs. Committed to attaining that desirable graceful and erect carriage, girls were strapped into these chairs for hours. Unable to move—and usually unable to read—they just sat. A popular gift item, the restraining chair served as a harbinger of the restricted adult life to come.[4] But by the late 1700s, new ideas were brewing. When the boys left for home, girls were smuggled into school to receive an hour's worth of instruction. Some public schools actually opened their doors to girls, but with severe restrictions. In 1767 a school in Providence, Rhode Island, advertised that it would teach both reading and writing to female children. The small print noted the hours of instruction: from six to seven-thirty in the morning and from four to six-thirty in the afternoon. Each female student was charged a hefty sum for this inconveniently timed education. By tucking girls' education around the boys' regular hours, the teachers acquired needed additional income. Other elementary schools provided winter instruction for boys and allowed the girls to attend in the summer, an off-season education at a discount rate. Thus, slowly, as the concept of democracy was taking root, so was the notion that girls as well as boys should receive an education.[5]

Revolutionary Ideas

The new democracy enlarged the European view of women, for while a woman's place was still in the home, in America her role took on new dimensions. In those revolutionary times she was to nurture her children's intellectual development. America's mothers were the nation's first teachers, and it didn't take long for people to realize that before a woman could enlighten children, she had to be enlightened herself.

The current debate over "school choice" would pale in comparison to the entrepreneurial array of schools that flourished in America's early years. And some schools began to open their doors to girls, at least those whose parents were able and willing to pay. Noted educator Benjamin Rush created the Young Ladies Academy in Philadelphia to transform girls into strong and intellectually able mothers. Religious orders spread their educational philosophies in girls' schools built by Quakers, Moravians, and Catholics.

By the first half of the nineteenth century, some communities in Massachusetts began to experiment with the radical concept of high school education for girls. A high school for boys had already been established in Boston, and in the late 1820s the public demanded one for girls, too. But city leaders underestimated the interest, and there were far more applicants than spaces available. Three out of four girls were turned away. Facing growing public unrest, Boston's mayor had to explain why 75 percent of the girls applying could not attend high school, and he came up with a brilliant but painful solution: Disappointing everyone equally, he played no favorites and closed the high school. Girls who thirsted for more education would have to wait until after the election; with the mayor's defeat, their high school was finally reopened.[6]

While large cities struggled to establish separate high schools, smaller communities could not afford to build one high school for boys and another for girls. With true American ingenuity, towns and rural communities built one high school and then pretended that they had built two. Entering by separate doors, boys and girls went directly to their assigned single-sex area. Sometimes they went to different floors, or boys went to one side of the building and girls to the other. Frequently the girls were taught by women and the boys by men, so they continued to learn in their own sex-segregated worlds. But they were in the same school building at the same time—a revolutionary development!

These "mixed" schools, as they were called, stirred emotional debate. Critics worried that boys and girls learning together in one place would have dire consequences. Such a combustible mix, they warned, required close supervision. These worries only increased as, over several decades, "mixed" schools became "mixed" classrooms. Opponents to this burgeoning coeducation charged that boys and girls were headed for different destinies, and they should be educated separately for their distinct life paths. Offering girls and boys identical lessons would do little to encourage womanly interest and skill in domestic activities.

Advocates of coeducation argued that the presence of girls would refine boys' rough behavior and that these mixed schools and classrooms would develop better-educated females who, when they became mothers, could teach their own children more effectively. But the winning argument was economic: One school for boys and another for girls meant higher taxes. So coeducation came to America as the outcome of financial necessity.

Citizens discussed the sexual consequences and economic costs of coeducation, but no one evaluated the effectiveness of this new approach or the possibility that different books or teaching strategies might be needed now that girls had arrived. Coeducation happened because it was cheaper, but was it educationally better?[7]

The number of coeducational elementary and secondary schools increased throughout the 1800s. Some families rejected coeducation, however. For them the seminary became the school of choice.

Morals, Mind, Manners, and Motherhood

Picture yourself back in the 1800s, the parent of a terrific daughter. You've saved some money, and you want the best for her. She did well in elementary school, and now it is time to complete her education. The public high school is not near your home, the quality is not what you had hoped, and you have never been totally comfortable with mixed schools. You've thought about your options, and the choice is clear: a female seminary.

If the word *seminary* conjures up images of an austere, cloistered, and religious world, you are not far off at all. Historians have summarized seminary curriculum as "the three M's: morals, mind, and manners." These institutions provided protected educational environments, safe havens for high-school-age girls to learn to become fit companions for their husbands, the first teachers of their children, and the moral and spiritual cornerstone of the family. These seminaries were dedicated to the tricky proposition of expanding women's educational options while keeping their role in life limited.

To the three M's of seminary education we could add a fourth: motherhood. In 1821 when Emma Willard was struggling to establish the Troy Seminary, she wooed adherents and financial backers with her claim to "professionalize motherhood": "O how immensely important is this work of preparing the daughters of the land to be good mothers."[8] Her tactics were effective, and she built her seminary. After all, who would not support motherhood?

Willard explained to New York's Governor De Witt Clinton, "It is believed that housewifing might be greatly improved by being taught not only in practice but in theory."[9] Girls in seminaries learned the secrets of managing homes to make them healthier and more efficient. In her seminary, Willard raised domesticity to a science.

For many of these schools, the spiritual and moral development of their students was paramount. Mary Lyon established Mount Holyoke in 1837, organizing it around her evangelical beliefs. Students lived and studied in one building, along with their instructors who carefully monitored students around the clock. Bells signaled every step the girls took—prayers in the morning, classes during the day, and prayers again in the evening. Self-denial and strict discipline were considered important tools in molding devout wives and moral mothers.

Mount Holyoke provided students with an intellectually challenging program as well, including Latin, mathematics, ancient history, chemistry, and philosophy. Academic offerings of the stronger seminaries compared favorably with those of the first two years of college. Some seminaries were far less impressive, however; they avoided rigorous courses and provided instruction in traditional women's crafts instead. Some of the strongest and some of the weakest schools in America shared the name "seminary."

With help from the Quakers and Harriet Beecher Stowe, Myrtilla Miner, a white woman from New York, mounted the first organized effort to provide higher education for black women. As a result, in the 1850s the Miner Normal School for Colored Girls was established in Washington, D.C., with a curriculum that was typical of seminaries at the time. Eventually the school's mission focused on education, and it became Miner Teachers College. In 1881, Sophia Packard and Harriet

Giles, two New England missionaries and teachers, brought Bibles and schoolbooks to Atlanta, Georgia, and started the Spelman Female Seminary whose curriculum emphasized the liberal arts, practical skills, and teacher preparation. Today the former seminary is Spelman College, a highly regarded school for African-American women.[10]

Although seminaries were intended to prepare a woman for "her own sphere" as wife and mother, they opened up different paths for women to take. At Troy Seminary and Mount Holyoke, over 80 percent of the graduates entered teaching. Viewed as an extension of the home, the classroom was another setting in which to raise and guide children, and women were welcome, but once they wed, their teaching careers were over.

The seminaries undertook teacher education with missionary zeal, creating both innovative and effective teacher training programs. While male graduates of academies and colleges taught by recitation and memorization, seminaries developed more dynamic strategies and stressed reasoning and creativity. Seminary leaders such as Emma Willard and Catherine Beecher wrote textbooks on teaching methods. Seminary graduates promoted student cooperation, avoided corporal punishment, and created more humane classrooms. Female teachers did more than fill a role, they restructured a profession.

Horace Mann was a great supporter of this new breed of teacher. "That woman should be the educator of children I believe to be as much a requirement of nature as that she should be the mother of children."[11] Horace Mann had good reason to validate these recent recruits to the classroom: He desperately needed them. During the first half of the nineteenth century Mann had initiated the "common school movement" where Americans of all backgrounds could attend a public school supported not by charging fees but by tax dollars. Poor, middle-class, and wealthy children would all receive a "common education," an experience necessary to build a united nation. The supply of male teachers was insufficient to staff these new public schools, so women were welcomed, especially given the cost factor. Women could be paid significantly less than men. With more of them in the classrooms, school costs and thus taxes could be kept low.

Seminaries became a necessity and staffed the rapidly growing public school movement with well-trained teachers, but some women wanted and worked for full educational citizenship. Their efforts were rewarded in Oberlin, Ohio, where the cult of domesticity was brought to the college campus.

Knocking at the College Door

Considered a radical, even dangerous place, Oberlin was the first American college to admit both women and men. Then this higher education institution became in 1833 not only a "mixed" college but one that admitted racial minorities as well. In fact, Mary Jane Patterson, the first African-American woman to graduate from college, received her degree from Oberlin in 1862. But along with opportunities there were problems.

Daily practice mocked Oberlin's lofty ideals; religious and social restrictions were everywhere. Oberlin women experienced a distinctly second-class education; they attended the "Ladies Course," a sub-college-level program focused on gender-limited options. The ladies were closely supervised and always segregated from the men.

Older than most students who attended Oberlin, Lucy Stone saw more clearly the injustice of the college's gender restrictions. "Oberlin's attitude," she wrote, "was that women's high calling was to be mothers of the race." As a result, female students at Oberlin were "washing the men's clothes, caring for their rooms, serving them at table, listening to their orations, but [were] themselves remaining respectfully silent in public assemblages."[12] Lucy Stone was not one to accept this role. Although she found her public voice later and became a noted public speaker for antislavery and women's rights, she was not allowed to speak at Oberlin. For the graduation ceremony she was awarded the honor of preparing the commencement address. She was elated until she discovered that she was expected to author the speech, not deliver it. A male student would give the oration. She declined the "honor."

The tension between the liberating effect of education and the restricting nature of sexism soon spread beyond Oberlin's campus to other battlegrounds. When Kentucky moved to upgrade a female secondary school to a college in 1835, a Massachusetts newspaper thought that the proposed degrees, Mistress of Music, Mistress of Instruction, and the like, were inappropriate. While the "Mistress" title was often used to distinguish female degrees from the bachelor's degrees awarded men, the newspaper recommended a new genre of titles: the M.P.M. for Mistress of Pudding Making, M.D.N. for Mistress of Darning Needles, and the M.C.S. for Mistress of Common Sense. Honorary degrees included the R.W.H.H., Respectable Wife of a Happy Husband, and M.W.R.F., Mother of a Well-Regulated Family. Underlying this satire was a serious question: Should a woman's education be expanded beyond that for her role as wife and mother?[13]

As at the seminaries, women in these small, church-related colleges were closely supervised and were housed and educated separately from the men. Female students did well academically at Oberlin and Antioch, and this added to the pressure to admit them to other colleges, especially the larger, state-supported universities. After all, state universities were funded by state taxes and had a moral obligation to admit all state residents. If moral arguments did not persuade opponents, practical ones did. Few states were financially able to fund a separate state university for women. In addition, female tuition dollars would help pay the bills at the state university. As more than one cost-conscious advocate pointed out, "You can lecture to one hundred students as cheaply as fifty."

In 1858 three women formally applied to the University of Michigan, one of the largest and most prestigious state universities. Their applications were given national attention. Would the elite University of Michigan become coeducational? A committee formed to decide their fate and wrote to college administrators across the nation for advice. University presidents in the East were united in their opposition. Even Oberlin and Antioch, both already coeducational, warned of the difficulty in monitoring women and maintaining sex-segregated activities. The University of Michigan's president also voiced his opposition: "Men will lose as women advance, we shall have a community of defeminated women and demasculated men. When we attempt to disturb God's order, we produce monstrosities." Finally, the committee reached its decision: The University of Michigan would not enroll women. A local paper applauded the decision, concluding that to admit women would "unwoman the woman and unman the man."[14]

One of the major forces that ultimately opened college doors for women was the Civil War. The loss of male students, casualties of war, created economic pressures for female tuition dollars, so it was not surprising that, in 1870, Michigan finally relented. But even then women were not very welcome. Male students often jeered when females entered class, avoided them on campus, and made their lives difficult. And professors openly ridiculed women. One disgruntled professor stopped his students from removing a dog that had wandered into his class. "The dog is a resident of Michigan," he said. "Don't you know that we now recognize the right of every resident of the state to enjoy the privileges afforded the university?"[15]

Opposition to coeducation continued and intensified across the nation. The University of Rochester's story is the stuff of a television miniseries, perhaps called "Education for Ransom." Women had fought for more than thirty years to open the university's doors. The trustees finally agreed to admit them, but only if they raised $100,000 within two years to pay for additional classrooms and instructors. It was a combination of "Beat the Clock" and "Dialing for Dollars"; by the spring of 1900 they had raised $40,000. With the deadline just a few months away, the trustees reduced the target goal to $50,000. The women struggled and reached $42,000. With only weeks to go, Susan B. Anthony entered the fray. Prior to this she had kept her name out of the crusade to admit women because "feminists" were perceived as radical by many Americans, and she feared her reputation might hurt the cause. But now time was running out. She mounted a brave effort and feverishly drove around Rochester asking friends for contributions. She cashed in her own life insurance policy, a gift for her work in women's suffrage, and donated it to the cause. In the nick of time, the $50,000 goal was met, and women were admitted.

This happy result was changed, however, when the new president voiced his opposition. Encouraged by the official cold shoulder, male students responded by stamping their feet when a woman entered a classroom, physically blocking classroom doors, and mocking and jeering women whenever they appeared on campus. By 1913 the university's administration said enough was enough: A separate women's college was organized, and female students were once again isolated and had fewer educational resources. The men had their university back.

Male educators voiced many different reasons why women should not go to school with men. Some predicted that the brisk give and take of classroom debate would be softened in deference to the ladies. Other critics feared the loss of romance, arguing that if men and women learned together, the "mysterious" attraction between the sexes would evaporate. As a result, women would marry late or not at all. (In fact, there is evidence that women who graduated from college did marry later, were more particular in choosing their husbands, and may have avoided uncongenial marriages altogether.)[16] But the real reason behind such strong opposition was that education was devalued as women were included. If a woman could do college-level work, then the whole system of higher learning became less prestigious and less exclusive.

Ivy League Spinoffs

The most elite eastern colleges were slow to jump on the coeducation bandwagon. At prestigious Harvard an invisible college for women took shape. Professors taught men in Harvard Yard, then walked a few blocks to rented homes where they repeated their lectures to women— for an extra fee, of course. There were no permanent buildings for the women, an arrangement that pleased President Charles W. Eliot, an adamant opponent to their admission. The Harvard professors and their female students became known as the "Annex," and women who graduated were awarded certificates that indicated they had accomplished academic work equivalent to that of Harvard men.

In 1893 the invisible college finally achieved visibility and was named Radcliffe after a woman who had contributed funds to Harvard in 1641. Two hundred and fifty years after the gift, the college was offering a halfhearted thank-you, for women still had only limited access to the university's impressive resources. After the Harvard library closed each evening, messengers slipped in to obtain books for the Radcliffe women to study. The books had to be returned before the library opened the next morning. Burning the midnight oil was not an expression to be taken lightly at Radcliffe.

Although not equal partners, Radcliffe at Harvard and the newly opened Barnard at Columbia represented progress. In these "coordinate colleges" women moved closer to acceptance in America's most prestigious institutions. But at other colleges, such as Tufts, the coordinate college was actually a step back. Women had been admitted to Tufts in 1892; at the same time, enrollment dropped. The college president identified the admission of women as the cause. "The future of the academic department of Tufts College as a man's college depends upon the immediate segregation of the women into a separate department or college," he proclaimed. "I regard this as the most pressing education problem we have before us. . . . I have no doubt that a failure to solve it would involve imminent disaster to the College of Liberal Arts."[17] To avoid "disaster," Jackson College was founded in 1900, and women were removed from the Tufts campus. Resegregation occurred at other colleges, such as Brown and Pembroke. Wesleyan took more drastic measures: In 1912 the college reversed its open-door policy but did not segregate women; it barred them from attending at all.

A College of Her Own

Frustrated with the struggle to receive equal education at the existing universities, some women and men envisioned a bold alternative: the creation of colleges for women. These visionaries did not want a break-away branch of a male university, a less-than-equal education in a co-educational institution, or even a "near" college experience at some of the more rigorous female seminaries; they wanted "to build and endow a college for young women which shall be to them what Yale and Harvard are to young men." While still a radical idea in the 1850s, it was not new. Two centuries earlier, in the year that Harvard was founded, Lucy Downing had shared her vision of education for women with Governor John Winthrop: "I would build far off from men a college like a man's," she wrote. "And I would teach them all that men are taught."[18]

In 1855, Matthew Vassar's search for a way to immortalize himself resulted in the advancement of Lucy Downing's visionary idea. Impressed with the beautiful hospitals he had seen in Europe, Vassar decided to build one here in America that would be a lasting monument to his achievements. All this changed when his friend Milo Jewett convinced him that a great hospital in the small town of Poughkeepsie would be mostly unused, a waste of Vassar's hard-earned brewery fortune. Jewett suggested that Vassar build the first "real" college for women, one with ample resources, qualified faculty, and an endowment. Vassar became convinced that a woman's college would be an appropriate legacy—unique, necessary, and "more lasting than the Pyramids."[19] And so Vassar College was established.

As the college grew, so did its founder's commitment to education for women. When Vassar College opened in 1865, critics might have accused it of having a patronizing form of government, similar to that of the female seminaries, complete with bells, prayers, and monitors. But there was nothing condescending about the curriculum, which was undoubtedly at college level. Most of the early students were not prepared for this degree of rigor. Two-thirds arrived without the necessary academic background, and they were redirected to the preparatory department where they enrolled in high-school-level prerequisites.

In many respects Wellesley was a hybrid of Vassar's physical structure and Mount Holyoke's practices. The school was founded by Henry Fowle Durant, a successful Boston lawyer whose life changed when his young son died. Durant turned to religion, became an evangelical Christian, and sought a vehicle to spread his beliefs. As a great supporter of the Mount Holyoke seminary, Durant decided to invest his fortune in building a similar religious women's college on his magnificent country estate near Boston. He believed in the power and competence of women and appointed them not only as trustees of the new school but as the entire faculty, a courageous move at that time and, many believed, unworkable. He launched a recruiting expedition and hired women graduates from Mount Holyoke, Oberlin, Vassar, and the recently coeducational University of Michigan. Still, Durant could not fill the thirty faculty positions. Devising his own affirmative action plan, one that was more effective than many of today's attempts, Durant identified intellectually talented women who had not received an official college education and paid their way for additional schooling. When they completed their studies, they joined the Wellesley faculty.

Smith College was established in another part of Massachusetts in September 1875; it was the first women's college endowed by a woman. Sophia Smith had inherited a large fortune and turned to her pastor for advice. John Greene suggested that she establish a college for women, but one that differed dramatically from the seminary model.

At the time Smith College was planned, large institutional buildings were being criticized as sources of physical and mental stress, so Smith was developed as a college of small, intimate cottages. Also, John Greene, Sophia Smith's adviser, feared the dangerous ideas that might result from so many women confined in a large building. He worried that these isolated structures would encourage rejection of social norms and roles, or even worse. Such fears were described in 1884 by J. G. Holland, an editor at Scribners: "No consideration would induce us to place a young woman—daughter or ward—in a college which would shut her away from all family life for a period of four years. The system is unnatural, and not one young woman in ten can be subjected to it without injury."[20]

Holland feared that the seminary model, while it might protect young women from men, left them vulnerable to the advances of other women. Sophia Smith chose to avoid these potential "hot beds" by building smaller cottages, supervised by adults, to better reflect a natural family environment. Contact with the townspeople would also dissuade the students from developing radical notions and visionary ideas. But visionary ideas are difficult to contain, as M. Carey Thomas would show.

Among the first women to graduate from Cornell University in 1877, Thomas was ahead of her time. She was accepted, reluctantly, by the graduate school of Johns Hopkins, but she was barred from seminars.

After Hopkins, she set sail for Germany where she spent three years earning her doctorate. When she heard about plans to create Bryn Mawr, she wrote letters promoting herself as the president of the new college. She might have seemed the perfect candidate for the Quaker College for Women: She was a Quaker woman returning from Europe with her new doctorate and was the daughter, niece, and cousin of various members of the board of trustees. But being an inexperienced administrator, a woman, and something less than a devout Quaker all worked against her. Nevertheless, she was selected as dean and a faculty member. Several years later, when the male president died, the board saw the wisdom of her arguments, and she became more than president: She was the force that shaped Bryn Mawr.

The quality of the faculty at Wellesley, Smith, and Vassar fell far short of Thomas's expectations. At Bryn Mawr she envisioned a women's college with the standards, curriculum, and scholarship of Johns Hopkins. She recruited a largely male faculty that had been newly trained in German universities and were dedicated to academic excellence. By 1885, Bryn Mawr's faculty was comprised of highly promising scholars, including Woodrow Wilson. Promising students were also valued. Applicants who did not pass the strict entrance requirements and examinations were not accepted. Bryn Mawr's standards would not be diluted by enrolling students in a high-school-level preparation program as Vassar had done.

Carey Thomas rejected not only inferior academic standards but inferior life standards for women. She broke with the Victorian notion of a woman's sphere; Bryn Mawr women did not perform domestic chores. They wore caps and gowns to class, as did male scholars at that time. Protective buildings, guardians, and monitoring were abandoned. Bryn Mawr students enjoyed privacy and lived in buildings similar to the quadrangle design of many men's campuses.

The seven sisters—Smith, Mount Holyoke, Wellesley, Vassar, Barnard, Radcliffe, and Bryn Mawr—were founded to transform young women, but over time they themselves were transformed. Students created their own clubs, organizations, and traditions. Evangelical fervor and religious conformity were replaced by diversity of opinion and culture.

Faculty members discovered their own voice as well. They refused to serve as the eyes and spies of the administration, constantly supervising student behavior. Increasingly they recognized and confronted their own exploitation. Vassar's distinguished astronomer, Maria Mitchell, felt the pain of sexism when the college president asked for a list of faculty publications but sent the request to male instructors only. Female faculty at women's colleges were systematically paid less than males, were housed in more modest living quarters, and sometimes were even barred from participating in faculty meetings. At Smith, women faculty members of all ranks were called teachers; men were called professors. This treatment in colleges dedicated to women's advancement became a painful public reminder of the continuing inequality between women and men.

Despite this sexism, the influence of these colleges was enormous. A critical mass of educated women had been brought together to learn about their world, but many of them did not like what they saw. The women's colleges, so focused at their inception, were spinning off in new directions, unleashing forces unimagined by their original founders.

Choice: Ovaries or Algebra?

By the second half of the nineteenth century, education for girls and women had undergone a revolution. Beyond the campus, a national women's movement gained momentum; its agenda included political rights, social reforms, and economic equity. More and more women entered the labor market. Much like the 1970s, the 1870s marked tremendous progress for women and a period of conservative backlash followed.

Nineteenth-century women had proven themselves in the formerly forbidden realm of higher education. Several colleges reported that they earned higher grades than men. Since women were succeeding academically, concern about their intellectual inadequacies almost disappeared.

Some women knocked on the doors of the professional schools. Julia Ward Howe, the well-known social reformer, looked beyond college education to professional and graduate studies as "the keystone to the arch of women's liberty."[21] But opposition to women in the professions was fierce. The medical profession offered especially stiff resistance.

Although Elizabeth Blackwell worked as a teacher for years to support herself, she had always dreamed of becoming a doctor. The fact that no woman had ever attended a medical school did not deter her from applying. As she anticipated, the rejection letters piled up. Except for one—a school in Geneva, New York, accepted her. She graduated two years later, in 1849, with the first medical degree awarded in this country to a woman. Harriet Hunt was less fortunate. She had practiced medicine without a diploma for years when she applied to medical schools. At this time Hunt was forty-five and viewed by the Harvard faculty "as a dignified matron who would not enflame the sexual passions of the male students."[22] Her skills and efforts were recognized in her admission to Harvard Medical School, along with three male African-American students. Actually, her admission limited her to attendance at lectures while the African-Americans were admitted to the full degree program. When word of her impending lecture attendance spread, students protested, and she was forced to withdraw. The African-American students remained.

In 1870, Mary Hovey attempted to open medical schools to women such as Harriet Hunt. She offered Harvard a $10,000 gift (in the grand old tradition of a bribe) if it would admit women. She believed that if prestigious Harvard opened its doors, others would follow. Similar to the strategy that would be used at the University of Rochester, Hovey's "creative philanthropy" or "education for ransom" approach caused a year-long debate. Finally, Harvard refused the money and rejected female applicants. In 1891, Mary Ganett tried the same scheme with a promise of a $60,000 gift to Johns Hopkins Medical School. That was worth a two-year debate, and eventually the gift was increased to $306,000. That price was right; Hopkins saw the value of women students.

Faced with such extraordinary educational advances, opponents of education for women needed new ammunition. They found it in one of the oldest positions: Biology is destiny. Their arguments suggested that below the skin and under the skull lurked the real reasons women did not belong in higher education. Their problems were in their brains and in their ovaries.

Twentieth-century Americans are intrigued by reports on the mysteries of right brain and left brain. Imagine the popularity this topic would have enjoyed in the nineteenth century when craniology was considered a science. Liberating in its simplicity, craniology taught that brain size revealed intelligence. Since large brains required large skulls, measuring cranial size revealed a person's intellect. Craniology confirmed popular biases of the day. The brightest race was Caucasian, with a definite skull-size advantage over smaller headed Africans and

Asians. Measurements also showed northern Europeans with bigger skulls than southern Europeans, confirming another widely held prejudice. Unfortunately, childbirth stunted women's evolutionary development. Their brains would never be as big or as complex as those of men.

Because craniology reflected the prejudice of the times, it withstood problems that would have rapidly toppled a less appealing science. Errors were commonplace, measurements were taken incorrectly, male-female brains were mislabeled, women were discovered with larger skulls than very bright men; and finally, investigations showed that brain size was not related to intelligence. By the early twentieth century, craniology was on the way out, but during the late 1800s it provided opponents of women's educational progress with a biological explanation for the intellectual supremacy of males. But the anatomy lesson was not over.

Other adversaries moved to the reproductive organs to explain why women should avoid higher education. In a slim volume entitled *Sex in Education* (1873), Dr. Edward Clarke asserted that prolonged coeducation was physically dangerous to the reproductive health of females. During the teenage years girls developed their reproductive organs, and "periodicity" (menstruation) was of central importance. If young women attended school during formative adolescence, blood would be diverted from these reproductive organs to the brain. The result would be "monstrous brains and puny bodies . . . flowing thought and constipated bowels."[23] If Clarke's beliefs were reduced to a warning label, it would be: WOMEN BEWARE: HIGH SCHOOL AND COLLEGE MAY BE HAZARDOUS TO YOUR HEALTH. As historian David Tyack suggested, Clarke was forcing girls to choose between algebra and ovaries.

But Clarke had a solution to this dilemma: Replace coeducation with less demanding sex-segregated schools. Girls should attend schools that were sensitive to the needs of their reproductive organs: less study, less stress, easier curriculum, no competition, and "rest" periods during menstruation. Separate girls' education would ensure the future of the Anglo-Saxon race. To continue coeducation was to flirt with "race suicide." The vast majority of girls attending high school and colleges in the 1870s and 1880s were white, affluent, and Anglo-Saxon. Like the craniologists, Clarke accepted Darwin's belief of Anglo-Saxon superiority, and his recommendations focused on protecting the "fittest" of womanhood. The reproductive damage done to black women by long hours spent working in the fields or to immigrant women by extraordinary hours of labor in crowded factories and sweat shops did not concern him. In fact, lowering their reproductive abilities while increasing the fertility of the superior Anglo-Saxon woman was the genetically correct position, according to Darwin and Clarke.

Clarke's book enjoyed brisk sales as people debated the reproductive cost of educating females. Even advocates of coeducation worried about the health of girls. In 1889 the superintendent of Detroit's public schools pleaded for elevators because climbing stairs was "a menace to normal functional development" of women. An editorial in a college newspaper warned: "A woman . . . cannot afford to risk her health in acquiring knowledge of the advance sciences, mathematics, or philosophy for which she has no use. . . . Too many women have already made themselves permanent invalids by overstrain of study at schools and colleges."[24]

The seeds of doubt were planted. Even intellectually gifted, fiercely independent women such as M. Carey Thomas, president of Bryn Mawr, confided the fears she experienced from Clarke's thesis: "I remember often praying about it, and begging God that if it were true that because I was a girl, I could not successfully master Greek and go to college, and understand things, to kill me for it."[25] As late as 1895, more than twenty years after Clarke's work first appeared, the University of Virginia faculty concluded that "women were often physically unsexed by the strains of study."

While education put ovaries in danger, evidently it did not threaten male reproductive health. Imagine how concerned men would be if a renowned medical authority discovered an inverse relationship between college credits and sperm count. Research findings that tie law degrees to male impotence might also have a chilling effect. But according to Clarke, there were no such dangers. Men appeared to be biologically fit for every intellectual endeavor.

Like the theories of the craniologists, Clarke's arguments appealed strongly to prejudice but fell short on evidence. In 1885 the Association of Collegiate Alumnae, which later became the American Association of University Women, feared for the worse and sponsored a nationwide survey of women's health. While 78 percent of college women reported good health, only 50 percent of noncollege women made such a claim. As the decades wore on, evidence to support either Clarke or the craniologists became increasingly more difficult to find. Women of all skull sizes were doing well academically, and their ovaries remained intact. The theories could not discount reality.

Vocational Destiny

In the decades that followed the Clarke controversy, coeducation flourished and school attendance soared. But coeducation did not mean
equal education. Part of the problem can be traced to an influential reform effort to modernize the secondary school.

In 1918 the Commission on the Reorganization of Secondary Education was about to steer America on a new course of schooling. Members of the commission viewed the high school college preparation
curriculum—Latin, Greek, German, philosophy, algebra—as out of
date with the more practical needs of the country. Although schools
prepared students for college, most of them never went. It was sus-
pected that this classical curriculum contributed to the high dropout
rate as students lost interest, performed poorly, or both. The commission called for a new American high school, one more responsive to
non-college-bound students and to the real demands of the world of
work. To education's historical mission of providing students with a
classical education, a new responsibility was added—preparing youth
for the world of work. Eventually, vocational education became a new
high school track.

The aim of vocational education was progressive and forward-look-
ing, but for coeducation it meant a step backward. The adult world of
work was highly sex segregated, so vocational education courses separated students, sending girls into one sphere of study and boys into
another. Girls took home economics and business courses. Boys went
into the more profitable trades and industrial arts. Even college-bound
girls who were not enrolled in the vocational curriculum were required to take domestic science or home economics while boys took
manual training or industrial arts. For black and minority women,
home economics became vocational training, a form of preparation for
domestic work.

As the century moved on, new electives proliferated that allowed
girls and other students to skip courses like math and science. Simultaneously, classes like physics were made "girl friendly," as was shown
by San Jose, California's course offering: "The Physics of Home
Plumbing and Lighting." Physical education expanded, with sports
and athletics becoming more central for boys and less important for
girls. Even extracurricular activities were marked by sex segregation.
In clubs, boys were the "Future Farmers of America" and girls were the
"Future Homemakers." Dr. Clarke's concern for the well-being of a
woman's ovaries never restructured schools, but he probably would
have taken some solace in this resegregation of the sexes.

Woman's sphere had expanded beyond the home, but her vocational role in that world was very restricted. As late as the mid-1960s, when asked what they wanted to be when they grew up, girls' answers still fell into four categories: teacher, secretary, nurse, or mommy. Until the gender equity revolution of the 1970s, schools persisted in channeling girls and women into these limited roles.

When we ask women in our workshops to recall what it was like to be educated during the 1940s, 1950s, and 1960s, their stories come pouring out. Perhaps some of them will sound familiar:

> I still remember my high school graduation in Minnesota, May 1949. There was a big assembly, and two awards were presented for Outstanding Citizenship, one to a girl and one to a boy. The boy received a gift of $50, the girl received $25. No one thought about questioning it, least of all me—even though I had done so much more than the boy who received double my money. I was just so pleased to get the $25. When I think back now, I have lots of questions!

> In 1944 when I was in college, I asked the dean of the agriculture school if I could be admitted. He told me no girls were allowed in the agriculture school. *I accepted it!*

> I graduated from high school in Algoma, Wisconsin, in 1958. At that time only boys were allowed to take physics. It was considered inappropriate for girls.

> When I was in the ninth grade in the 1950s, we took a battery of aptitude tests. When I had my appointment with the guidance counselor to talk about the results and choose my courses, she said, "Well, Ann, you scored highest in the school on spatial relations, but you can forget that. There's nothing a girl can do with it." Then she said, "And for heaven's sake, don't tell the boys. They'll be so embarrassed to have been beaten by a girl."

> In my junior high school in the 1960s, more than anything I wanted to be a patrol. But girls were not allowed to be patrols because the winter weather was too cold, and we were told this might hurt us. Instead we were supposed to clean the school steps. Boys were not allowed to clean them. Cleaning was girls' work, even in the winter.

> For three years running, 1965 to 1968, I tried to get into the industrial arts class in our high school because I was not in-

terested in home ec. The principal told me I was not allowed to take it because I was a female. I was told the "language" used by the boys in the "shop" would be offensive to girls, and I would not "fit in."

In 1965, as a high school junior in the South, I decided to run for school office. Girls were allowed to run for secretary and vice president. We were not allowed to run for president and treasurer. Those two offices were for the boys. All of the candidates were presented to the students in an assembly in the gym. The presidential candidates—all boys—gave speeches. The girls were not allowed to give speeches. My campaign manager, a boy, gave a very brief speech on my behalf. He did not mention my grades or my leadership ability or my qualifications for the job. This is how he described me: "And here's our candidate for vice president. Look at her, folks! Isn't she beautiful?" I wasn't, but I won anyway.

In 1965 I was sixteen years old, and I wanted to study architecture at Iowa State University. My father took me to talk with an architecture faculty member about their program. All I can remember is that he said he would have to admit me but that I would never graduate. He said that girls didn't graduate in architecture at Iowa State. I didn't enter that program. Instead I received a degree in art education. Even today I still dream about being an architect. I never used my art education degree.

In 1960 I was one of two women majoring in accounting at my college. My professor said to me, "Why are you taking accounting? You'll never get to be an accountant. You should go to secretarial school." He said this to me even though I had the best grades in the whole class.

In 1967 I was a Ph.D. candidate in classics at Brown University. One of my professors told me that I was taking the place of a man in the degree program and that women were a waste of the department's time and resources. All they did was get married. Men, on the other hand, would work and use the degree.

I went to a large university in New England during the 1960s. I was called into the dean's office along with another senior, a young man named John. The dean congratulated us both on our academic performance. He told us there was one scholarship to graduate school available. Although I had a slightly higher grade point average, he decided to award the money to John who, he said, would have to support a family some day. What really gets me today, almost thirty years later, is that back then it all made perfectly good sense. Even though John came from a rich background and I came from a poor one, I agreed that the scholarship should go to John. Today I am the sole support of my two children, and I wish I had that graduate degree.

What is fascinating about these incidents from the past is how intensely women remember them twenty, thirty, and forty years later. It might have been just a phrase, a comment in class, a counseling session, a meeting in a school administrator's office, but they changed attitudes, self-esteem, career goals, and the direction of women's lives.

The Era of New Hope

In 1972, Shirley McCune of the National Education Association organized a unique gathering when she invited every American educator concerned about sexism in schools to a meeting in Warrenton, Virginia. We were two of approximately 150 people who attended. Educators, parents, and concerned citizens from across the country—we all fit easily into a single large room. But there was a sense of energy and commitment that could not be contained. People who had been working in isolation, fighting for an issue few in their towns and communities took seriously, discovered they were not alone. We came as individuals and left as part of a critical mass. By the end of the decade it seemed as if nothing could stop the growing numbers of those who saw schools as the vehicle to liberate the potential of girls. From Hawaii to Maine, sex equity in education had become a popular cause.

Congress also passed Title IX in 1972, and it seemed as if the federal government was offering both moral and legal support. Here, miraculously, was a federal law making sex discrimination in schools illegal. Under Title IX, sex bias was outlawed in school athletics, career counseling, medical services, financial aid, admissions practices, and the treatment of students. From elementary school through the university, Title IX violators were threatened with the loss of federal funds. Those committed to gender equity in education were elated. There was now a legal weapon to fight schools that refused to treat girls fairly.

Then federal dollars began to flow for sex equity research and training. In 1974, Congress passed the Women's Educational Equity Act to fund research, materials, and training to help schools eliminate sex bias. WEEA projects ranged from creating strategies to helping schools comply with Title IX to recruiting girls into math and science. In 1978, Congress broadened the Civil Rights Act to include educational services to eliminate sex bias. Under the redesigned civil rights legislation, ten sex desegregation assistance centers were created to assist teachers, parents, and students in developing nonsexist programs. By 1980 even the National Institute of Education, the federal research agency, was providing limited funding to investigate the nature of sex bias in schools. Compared to most government programs, the funds for sex equity were modest, but for those who had been working with nothing, they were a breakthrough.

More and more schools made changes. Better (but not equal) athletic programs for girls developed. Teachers took creative steps to shatter the gender lines separating home economics and industrial arts. Girls were urged to take more courses in math and science, and some schools even checked to make sure that encouraging words translated into enrollment. Teachers learned how to analyze books for sex bias and lobbied publishers for better, fairer instructional materials.

As the 1970s drew to a close, disappointments mounted. It became clear that the hope placed by educators in the power of Title IX was not to be fulfilled. The law may have been on the books, but many schools did not take it seriously. In one school only boys were allowed to take advanced math courses. In another, vocational programs remained segregated with cosmetology and secretarial courses only for women and electrical and automotive courses only for men. In another community, pregnancy was grounds for expelling teenage mothers, but teenage fathers were not expelled. Many school districts spent twenty times as much on boys' sports as girls' sports. One college awarded ten times as many scholarships to males as to equally qualified females. Complaints were lodged, paperwork piled up, delays were common, and penalties became a new mythology, for they were rarely applied. Between 1972 and 1991, no school lost a single dollar of federal funds because of sex discrimination.

The situation is much the same today. One assignment we give to our students at The American University is to visit local schools and evaluate their compliance with Title IX. A free lunch is the prize for any students who can find a school not violating the law. Our lunch fund is undiminished.

While parents and educators working for gender-fair education grew disappointed with the lack of implementation, at least the federal government's heart was in the right place. The 1980s saw a federal heart transplant as the Reagan-Bush administration took over.

Backlash—Education Style

Question: Is there a better way to shape the hearts and minds of the next generation than being a teacher? Answer: Yes. Control the Department of Education and influence what is taught across the entire country.

Feminism was a red flag that infuriated the archconservatives who took over the Education Department after the Reagan-Bush election. Many of these new educational leaders had limited formal training or no experience in education, the field they were supposed to direct, but they did have a clear picture of what they wanted, and equality for girls and women was not part of it. As political soldiers in the Reagan revolution, they conducted systematic search-and-destroy missions on all federal programs that encouraged gender equity.

Why the interest in eradicating education for female equality? Because increasing the achievement and encouraging the career potential of girls was seen as a threat to the family. For the archconservatives now in charge of education, there was only one politically correct family—the patriarchal family with a husband and father at its head. A well-educated woman of independent thought and means was a challenge to that patriarchal system. Education's new leaders had regressed more than a century for their ideas, back to the notion of the home as the only right and proper sphere for women.

High on the backlash agenda was the Women's Educational Equity Act—a program that helped enforce Title IX and encouraged the achievement of women in science, math, and nontraditional careers—and its director, Leslie Wolfe. The Heritage Foundation's 1981 "Mandate for Leadership" targeted WEEA as "an important resource for the practice of feminist policies and politics." As such it had to be crushed.

A civil service employee for more than a decade, Wolfe was attacked in magazines and on talk shows as a "radical feminist," and WEEA was denounced as a "money machine for a network of openly radical feminist groups." "We were not a very large program," Leslie Wolfe said. "In a federal budget of billions, we had $10 million to try to achieve equity for girls across the nation. But I was a feminist, and our program was getting results. We drove them crazy."

The Reagan administration reorganized the Department of Education, attempting to consolidate scores of programs into block grants, money given to the states. Once consolidated, the federal program would be gone. The plan was to consolidate WEEA out of existence. Congresswoman Margaret Heckler was instrumental in saving WEEA, but it was only a reprieve. A few weeks after the *Conservative Digest* magazine attacked Wolfe in April 1982, she was reassigned to a task force on "fraud, waste, and abuse" because, she was told, this important mission required "her high-level management skills." Protesting unsuccessfully, she spent the next three months doing nothing. "I was sitting under a sign that read WEEA IN EXILE." Three months later she returned to WEEA and an anxious staff. "People in the department were avoiding us," Wolfe says. "It was as though you could catch being fired by associating with WEEA people who had been attacked for their advocacy of women's equality. There was no vaccine. We were in isolation."

Then came the grant review process. Each year individuals from around the nation apply for WEEA funds to implement Title IX, to develop curriculum and teaching strategies to attract girls into math and science, and to encourage girls' achievement in all academic areas. A panel of knowledgeable judges decides who gets funded. Typically, one application in ten is chosen to receive support. The panel usually consists of federal employees as well as educators and equity experts from outside government. While Wolfe was on her ninety-day exile, she discovered that nominating candidates for the panel was no longer her responsibility. Review panel members now came from extremely conservative sources, including Phyllis Schlafly's Eagle Forum and Bob Jones University. These new reviewers were neither education experts nor supporters of equity. One reader reviewing proposals to help schools enforce Title IX asked, "What is this Title 'One X' I keep reading about?" Another wondered if being Native American qualified as a "disability." One project was rejected on the grounds that sex discrimination does not exist and that gender differences are the result of "the fact that boys and girls are born with certain desires." A later investigation of these field readers by the General Accounting Office found one out of five unqualified and most of the readers barely qualified. The report noted that minority field readers had been cut by 75 percent. Following their victory at WEEA, the new Reagan revolutionaries selected politically compatible review panel members for grant awards in other agencies as well.[26]

Within a year the Women's Educational Equity Act program was downgraded, its budget cut, and its staff reassigned, and Leslie Wolfe was no longer working for the government. By 1992, under President Bush, the agency's budget dwindled to half a million dollars, and the administration was still requesting its elimination.

"I was so naive," Leslie Wolfe remembers. "I kept my feminist posters up in my office when people advised me to take them down. Others were hiding when I was advertising. But I didn't want the thought police to intimidate me. If they had silenced me, they would have won."

The destruction of WEEA was highly visible and drew strong reaction from equity leaders across the country, but in countless, stealthy, less obvious ways, steps were taken to impede other gender equity programs. An effective way to do this is to fire the talented people who run the programs and replace them with less competent people or, better yet, put in place capable people who are dedicated to destroying the gender equity programs they are supposed to lead.

Education professionals who have been trained as scholars and researchers have told how unprepared they were to cope with the hardball political tactics of the right wing. In recalling her experience at the National Institute of Education during the 1980s, a woman who worked on an equity project said, "One day I was called into the office of a new Reagan appointee, an extremely conservative man. He told me, 'There is no job for you here.' I was not prepared for this. I was shocked. 'Why? What did I do?' I asked. He said, 'I don't have to give you a reason.'"

This woman did not leave quietly. She filed a sex discrimination complaint. Approximately six years later the Equal Employment Opportunity Commission (EEOC) found in her favor and denounced "a pattern" of sex discrimination at the National Institute of Education. Today she said, "It really wasn't worth it. Six years of legal work to win a few months of salary owed to me on my contract. There are no damage awards. The system is designed to make you lose. But I was just too angry to let them treat people like that."

"They were so clever," said another education professional no longer with the Department of Education. "Their tactics were right on target. They knew just how to demolish the programs we had spent years building."

Equity experts who could not be fired were reassigned. Professionals with doctorates typed, answered telephones, did nothing, were shuttled from office to office so frequently that it was hard to keep track of their phone numbers. And in state after state as federally funded programs for girls ended, talented and dedicated women and men were forced to abandon their work for equity and seek employment elsewhere, and gender equity was badly crippled.

At this time we had just completed the second year of our three-year contract to explore the treatment of girls in school. Preliminary findings were in, and we gave an interview to *The Washington Post*. The next day we opened the newspaper to see a picture of our family beside an article about our gender equity research. Our two daughters went off to school thrilled about being in the newspaper. We were pleased, too, until our first phone call. "What are you doing giving interviews?" The caller was someone from the National Institute of Education, a friend who had supported our research. "You have to keep a low profile. Here they're searching for gender equity projects so they can kill them, and there you are in *The Washington Post*."

Like Leslie Wolfe, we, too, had been naive, not calculating the intensity of the war against women's educational equity. We tried to continue our research as a covert operation, and we received some friendly NIE phone calls: "'Equity' is on a list of unacceptable words. They're doing computer searches of all grants. When they find 'equity' in your grant title, they'll eliminate your project. I'm changing 'equity in classrooms' to 'effectiveness in classrooms.' Effectiveness is not on the list."

Later we found out that "ecology" was another unacceptable word. A nationally renowned early childhood educator used the phrase "ecology of the child" in his grant description, and when the computer targeted his "liberal"-sounding research for termination, he had to fight to keep his project.

We changed our title and then the abstract describing the project, but it was too late: As antifamily radical feminists, we were blacklisted. The next calls were not friendly; our grant was to be terminated. "There must be some mistake," we protested. "We've spent two years of time, effort, and money collecting data. In the third year we're supposed to analyze all the information and come up with our findings. It will be a terrible waste to cut the contract now." "There is no mistake," we were told.

People who supported our research were outraged and called their congressional representatives. This time, fighting back worked. We took some cuts, but our contract was reinstated, and we were able to complete the research described in this book.

Susan Faludi writes, "Just when women's quest for equal rights seemed closest to achieving its objective, the backlash struck it down."[27] Just when the schools became the wedge for unleashing female potential, support was cut off. Research was terminated, funds were curtailed, and Title IX, a paper tiger, was declawed. By the 1990s, when the AAUW Report on continuing sexism in school made headlines, a Department of Education spokeswoman told this moderate group of women to stop acting like "whining feminists" and be grateful for schools that are "islands of equity."

Many of us grew disheartened while working on gender equity during this period of backlash. We had moved forward when we saw a light at the end of a tunnel, only to crash into an oncoming train. At its worst it felt as if our twenty years of effort and personal struggle had been misguided. But we were wrong to think our years of work were wasted. The Reagan-Bush administration may have cut off the flowers, but the plant had taken root. In huge cities and small towns in every part of America, parents and teachers continued to become aware of sexism in school and in countless small ways fought back. Through them the historic struggle for the full education of America's girls goes on.

3
Missing in Interaction

"Candid Camera" would have a field day in elementary school. There would be no need to create embarrassing situations. Just set the camera to take a photograph every sixty seconds. Since classroom action moves so swiftly, snapshots slow down the pace and reveal subliminal gender lessons.

Snapshot #1	Tim answers a question.
Snapshot #2	The teacher reprimands Alex.
Snapshot #3	Judy and Alice sit with hands raised while Brad answers a question.
Snapshot #4	Sally answers a question.
Snapshot #5	The teacher praises Marcus for skill in spelling.
Snapshot #6	The teacher helps Sam with a spelling mistake.
Snapshot #7	The teacher compliments Alice on her neat paper.
Snapshot #8	Students are in lines for a spelling bee. Boys are on one side of the room and girls are on the other.

As the snapshots continue, the underlying gender messages become clear. The classroom consists of two worlds: one of boys in action, the other of girls' inaction. Male students control classroom conversation. They ask and answer more questions. They receive more praise for the intellectual quality of their ideas. They get criticized. They get help when they are confused. They are the heart and center of interaction. Watch how boys dominate the discussion in this upper elementary class about presidents.

The fifth-grade class is almost out of control. "Just a minute," the teacher admonishes. "There are too many of us here to all shout out at once. I want you to raise your hands, and then I'll call on you. If you shout out, I'll pick somebody else."

Order is restored. Then Stephen, enthusiastic to make his point, calls out.

> STEPHEN: I think Lincoln was the best president. He held the country together during the war.
> TEACHER: A lot of historians would agree with you.
> MIKE (seeing that nothing happened to Stephen, calls out): I don't. Lincoln was okay, but my Dad liked Reagan. He always said Reagan was a great president.
> DAVID (calling out): Reagan? Are you kidding?
> TEACHER: Who do you think our best president was, Dave?
> DAVID: FDR. He saved us from the depression.
> MAX (calling out): I don't think it's right to pick one best president. There were a lot of good ones.
> TEACHER: That's interesting.
> KIMBERLY (calling out): I don't think the presidents today are as good as the ones we used to have.
> TEACHER: Okay, Kimberly. But you forgot the rule. You're supposed to raise your hand.

The classroom is the only place in society where so many different, young, and restless individuals are crowded into close quarters for an extended period of time day after day. Teachers sense the undertow of raw energy and restlessness that threatens to engulf the classroom. To preserve order, most teachers use established classroom conventions such as raising your hand if you want to talk.

Intellectually, teachers know they should apply this rule consistently, but when the discussion becomes fast-paced and furious, the rule is often swept aside. When this happens and shouting out begins, it is an open invitation for male dominance. Our research shows that boys call out eight times more often than girls. Sometimes what they say has little or nothing to do with the teacher's questions. Whether male comments are insightful or irrelevant, teachers respond to them. However, when girls call out, there is a fascinating occurrence: Suddenly the teacher remembers the rule about raising your hand before you talk. And then the girl, who is usually not as assertive as the male students, is deftly and swiftly put back in her place.

Not being allowed to call out like her male classmates during the brief conversation about presidents will not psychologically scar Kimberly; however, the system of silencing operates covertly and repeatedly. It occurs several times a day during each school week for twelve years, and even longer if Kimberly goes to college, and, most insidious of all, it happens subliminally. This micro-inequity eventually has a powerful cumulative impact.

On the surface, girls appear to be doing well. They get better grades and receive fewer punishments than boys. Quieter and more conforming, they are the elementary school's ideal students. "If it ain't broke, don't fix it" is the school's operating principle as girls' good behavior frees the teacher to work with the more difficult-to-manage boys. The result is that girls receive less time, less help, and fewer challenges. Reinforced for passivity, their independence and self-esteem suffer. As victims of benign neglect, girls are penalized for doing what they should and lose ground as they go through school. In contrast, boys get reinforced for breaking the rules; they are rewarded for grabbing more than their fair share of the teacher's time and attention.

Even when teachers remember to apply the rules consistently, boys are still the ones who get noticed. When girls raise their hands, it is often at a right angle, arm bent at the elbow, a cautious, tentative, almost insecure gesture. At other times they raise their arms straight and high, but they signal silently. In contrast, when boys raise their hands, they fling them wildly in the air, up and down, up and down, again and again. Sometimes these hand signals are accompanied by strange noises, "Ooh! Ooh! Me! Me! Ooooh!" Occasionally they even stand beside or on top of their seats and wave one or both arms to get attention. "Ooh! Me! Mrs. Smith, call on me." In the social studies class about presidents, we saw boys as a group grabbing attention while girls as a group were left out of the action.

Another way to observe in a classroom is to focus on individual children and record and describe their behavior for an extended period of time. Here is what we found when we watched two children for a forty-five-minute class. Perhaps you will see yourself in their behavior. Maybe you will see your son or daughter.

The fifth-grade boy sits in the fourth seat, second row. Since there are more than thirty other children in the class, getting the teacher's attention is a very competitive game. Watch how he plays.

First the boy waves his hand straight in the air so that the teacher will select him from the surrounding forest of mainly male arms. He waves and pumps for almost three minutes without success. Evidently tiring, he puts his right arm down only to replace it with the left. Wave and pump. Wave

Doonesbury

BY GARRY TRUDEAU

and pump. Another two minutes go by. Still no recognition. Down with the left hand, up with the right. He moves to strategy two—sounds: "Ooh, me. C'mon. C'mon. Pleeze. Oooooh!" Another minute without being noticed. Strategy three: He gets out of his seat, stands in front of his desk, and waves with sound effects for another thirty seconds. He slumps back into his seat, momentarily discouraged. Five seconds later there's the strategy-four effort: He holds his right arm up in the air by resting it on his left as he leans on his elbow. Three more minutes go by.

"Tom." His name. Recognition. For a brief moment he has the floor. The eyes of the teacher and his classmates are on him, the center of attention. He has spent more than nine minutes in his effort to get a half-minute in the sun. Post response: He sits for four quiet minutes. Then up shoots the arm again.

There is another student in the same class on the other side of the room, a little more toward the front. She begins the class with her arm held high, her face animated, her body leaning forward. Clearly she has something she wants to say. She keeps her right hand raised for more than a minute, switches to the left for forty-five seconds. She is not called on. She doesn't make noises or jump out of her seat, but it looks as though her arm is getting tired. She reverts to propping the right arm up with the left, a signal she maintains for two more minutes. Still no recognition. The hand comes down.

She sits quietly, stares out the window, plays with the hair of the girl in front of her. Her face is no longer animated. She crosses her arms on the desk and rests her head on them, which is how she spends the final twelve minutes of class time. Her eyes are open, but it is impossible to tell if she is listening. The period ends. The girl has not said a word.

When we videotape classrooms and play back the tapes, most teachers are stunned to see themselves teaching subtle gender lessons along with math and spelling. The teacher in the social studies class about presidents was completely unaware that she gave male students more

Doonesbury

BY GARRY TRUDEAU

attention. Only after several viewings of the videotape did she notice how she let boys call out answers but reprimanded girls for similar behavior. The teacher who taught Tom and the silent girl did not realize what effort it took to get attention. Surprised and saddened, he watched on videotape how his initially eager female student wilted and then faded from the activities of the classroom.

In our workshops for educators we call boys like Tom "star students" or "green-arms." Teachers smile with weary recognition as we describe students whose hands are up in the air so high and so long that the blood could have drained out. Our research shows that in a typical class of twenty-five students, two or three green-arm students may capture 25 percent of the teacher's attention.

Most students are not so salient. Rather, nominally involved, they are asked one or two questions by the teacher each class period. Even though nominal students don't wave arms and make birdlike noises, they do exhibit their own distinct patterns. If you were a nominal student, you can probably remember the following from your own school days: As the teacher approaches, you tense. The question is asked. Your shoulders rise, your adrenaline pumps, and your heart pounds so loudly that the teacher's voice is barely audible. You answer. Correct! You exhale with relief. The teacher's shadow and cologne move on. You've paid your dues. If the teacher asks you another question, you're likely to think, "He's picking on me."

When teachers ask students to read aloud one after the other down the row, one paragraph after another, nominal students count ahead and practice their paragraph silently. Can you remember industriously working on an impending passage only to have the student in front of you flub his, leaving you to stumble over unknown literary ground? If you can picture yourself in this scene for at least part of your school career, you were probably a nominal student.

In the typical classroom we found that approximately 10 percent of students are green-arms and 70 percent are nominal. Who's left? The remaining 20 percent, about four or five students in most classrooms, do not say anything at all. Of course some boys are shy and some girls are assertive, but we found that male students are more often stars and female students are more often stifled.[1] One researcher found that for every eight star-boys there is only one star-girl.[2]

Boys cast in starring classroom roles are often high achievers. Bright boys answer the questions, and their opinions are respected by

Doonesbury

BY GARRY TRUDEAU

the teacher. Low-achieving boys also get plenty of attention, but more often it's negative. No surprise there. In general, girls receive less attention, but there's another surprise: Unlike the smart boy who flourishes in the classroom, the smart girl is the student who is least likely to be recognized.[3]

When we analyzed the computer printouts for information about gender and race, an intriguing trend emerged. The students most likely to receive teacher attention were white males; the second most likely were minority males; the third, white females; and the least likely, minority females. In elementary school, receiving attention from the teacher is enormously important for a student's achievement and self-esteem. Later in life, in the working world, the salary received is important, and the salary levels parallel the classroom: white males at the top and minority females at the bottom. In her classroom interaction studies, Jacqueline Jordan Irvine found that black girls were active, assertive, and salient in the primary grades, but as they moved up through elementary school, they became the most invisible members of classrooms.[4]

The "Okay" Classroom Is Not

As part of our work at The American University, we supervise student teachers. At one of these supervisory sessions a young woman, one of the most talented in our teacher preparation program, confronted a sexist incident:

> The teacher flicks on the overhead projector, and a poem in the shape of a seesaw draws the third graders' attention. Another transparency and a new image, this time in the shape of a candy bar. The children giggle and whisper. More images—a kite poem, and even one looking like a giraffe. The youngsters are captivated.
>
> "What do these poems have in common?" the teacher says to open the discussion. Through skillful questions and explanations she teaches concrete poetry and motivates the children to write their own poems. "What are some topics

Doonesbury
BY GARRY TRUDEAU

you might want to write about?" The third graders are eager to share their ideas: Trucks. A cat. Dogs. TV. My doll.

"That's so dumb." A boy's comment breaks the collegial brainstorming. "I bet all the girls will draw girly Barbie dolls."

"Not me," a girl shoots back. "I'm doing a horse poem."

Not about to let sexism mar her lesson, this teacher confronts the comment. "There's nothing wrong with dolls. A lot of girls and boys like to play with them, which is nice because they learn how to take care of people that way. Not all girls like dolls, just like not all boys like football. Now me— I like teddy bears. [The children laugh.] I'm going to write my concrete poem about a teddy bear."

As the class settles down to write, the teacher walks from desk to desk giving reactions and offering suggestions.

First stop, a boy's desk (twenty seconds): "That's good. I like the way you use describing words."

Second stop, a boy's desk (two minutes; the teacher kneels so she can be eye to eye with the student): "You can't think of anything to write about? What are some of your hobbies?" (There are several more questions about hobbies, and then the boy's interest is sparked and he begins to write.)

Third stop, a boy's desk (fifteen seconds): "That's great! A deck of cards. I never would have thought of that."

Fourth stop, a boy's desk (two minutes): "Tony, this isn't right. It's not supposed to be in straight lines. A concrete poem is in the shape of something. (More discussion that is inaudible. Tony seems to have gotten the idea and starts to write.)

Fifth stop, a girl's desk (four seconds): "Okay."

"I was so nervous. I can't believe that boy's comment about the doll," the student teacher said, shaking her head as she talked with us after the lesson. "How do these kids come up with this stuff? Did I handle it well? What do you think?"

We assured the student teacher that she had handled the doll incident skillfully. Many instructors would not even have picked up on the comment, and even fewer would have challenged it. Ironically, even as

Doonesbury

BY GARRY TRUDEAU

this talented beginning teacher confronted the sexist comment of one of her young male students, she inadvertently doled out insidious gender lessons herself.

In our studies of sexism in classroom interaction, we have been particularly fascinated by the ways teachers react to student work and comments because this feedback is crucially important to achievement and self-esteem. We found that teachers typically give students four types of responses.

Teacher *praises*: "Good job." "That was an excellent paper." "I like the way you're thinking."

Teacher *remediates*, encouraging a student to correct a wrong answer or expand and enhance thinking: "Check your addition." "Think about what you've just said and try again."

Teacher *criticizes*, giving an explicit statement that something is not correct: "No, you've missed number four." This category also includes statements that are much harsher: "This is a terrible report."

Teacher *accepts*, offering a brief acknowledgment that an answer is accurate: "Uh-huh." "Okay."

Teachers praise students only 10 percent of the time. Criticism is even rarer—only 5 percent of comments. In many classrooms teachers do not use any praise or criticism at all. About one-third of teacher interactions are comprised of remediation, a dynamic and beneficial form of feedback.

More than half the time, however, teachers slip into the routine of giving the quickest, easiest, and least helpful feedback—a brief nonverbal nod, a quick "Okay." They rely more on acceptance than on praise, remediation, and criticism combined. The bland and neutral "Okay" is so pervasive that we doubt the "Okay Classroom" is, in fact, okay.

In the scene above, boys received not only more instruction but also better instruction. Two boys were praised, a response that promotes their confidence and self-esteem, and alerts them to what they do well. Through constructive criticism, another boy learned that he was not completing the assignment accurately, and he corrected his mistake. The teacher gave another boy remediation, helping him develop ideas for his poem. The only feedback given to a girl was bland and imprecise, without direction or information. "Okay" can only leave her to wonder, "How am I doing? Is my poem good? Can I make it better? Were you really listening? Tell me more, please."

In our research in more than one hundred classrooms, we found that while boys received more of all four reactions, the gender gap was greatest in the most precise and valuable feedback. Boys were more likely to be praised, corrected, helped, and criticized—all reactions that foster student achievement. Girls received the more superficial "Okay" reaction, one that packs far less educational punch. In her research, Jacqueline Jordan Irvine found that black females were least likely to receive clear academic feedback.

At first teachers are surprised to see videotapes where girls are "Okay'd" and boys gain clear feedback. Then it begins to make sense. "I don't like to tell a girl anything is wrong because I don't want to upset her," many say. This vision of females as fragile is held most often by male teachers. "What if she cries? I wouldn't know how to handle it."

The "Okay" response is well meaning, but it kills with kindness. If girls don't know when they are wrong, if they don't learn strategies to get it right, then they never will correct their mistakes. And if they rarely receive negative feedback in school, they will be shocked when they are confronted by it in the workplace.

Pretty Is—Handsome Does

Ashley Reiter, National Winner of the 1991 Westinghouse Talent Competition for her sophisticated project on math modeling, remembers winning her first math contest. It happened at the same time that she first wore her contact lenses. Triumphant, Ashley showed up at school the next day without glasses and with a new medal. "Everyone talked about how pretty I looked," Ashley remembers. "Nobody said a word about the math competition."

The one area where girls are recognized more than boys is appearance. Teachers compliment their outfits and hairstyles. We hear it over and over again—not during large academic discussions but in more private moments, in small groups, when a student comes up to the teacher's desk, at recess, in hallways, at lunchtime, when children enter and exit the classroom: "Is that a new dress?" "You look so pretty today." "I love your new haircut. It's so cute." While these comments are most prevalent in the early grades, they continue through professional education: "That's a great outfit." "You look terrific today."

Many teachers do not want to emphasize appearance. "They pull you in," a preschool teacher says. "The little girls come up to you with their frilly dresses and hair ribbons and jewelry. 'Look what I have,' they say and wait for you to respond. What are you supposed to do? Ignore them? Insult them? They look so happy when you tell them they're pretty. It's a way of connecting. I think it's what they're used to hearing, the way they are rewarded at home."

Like girls, boys in the early grades also ask teachers how they look, but teachers respond to boys and girls differently. And in these differences there is a world of meaning:

A first-grade classroom: A girl approaches the teacher and holds up the locket that is hanging around her neck. "See my new necklace?" The teacher smiles. "That's beautiful. Did your mother give it to you?" The little girls nods. "You look so pretty today."

The same first-grade classroom: A boy comes up to the teacher and points to his sneakers. "These are new," he says. "That's neat," the teacher responds. "I'll bet you can jump really high in those."

A kindergarten classroom: The teacher walks over to a boy who is playing with small, round plastic hoops. He has slipped his hand through them and holds out his arm, circled in red, blue, green, and yellow "bracelets," for the teacher to admire. The teacher finds a plastic peg that stands on the floor. "Look. Here's what you should do with these." The teacher and the boy spend the next several minutes removing the hoops from the boy's arm and putting them around the peg. "First we'll put blue," says the teacher. "What color shall we put on next? What color is that? Right, yellow. Are all the rings the same size? Let's see if any are bigger than the others."

When teachers talk with boys about appearance, the exchanges are brief—quick recognition and then on to something else. Or teachers use appearance incidents to move on to a physical skill or academic topic. In the scene just described, the teacher used the bracelet incident to teach about size, shape, and color. In another exchange, a little boy showed the teacher his shiny new belt buckle. Her response: "Cowboys wore buckles like that. They were rough and tough and they rode horses. Did you know that?"

When teachers talk to girls about their appearance, the conversations are usually longer, and the focus stays on how pretty the girl looks. Sometimes the emphasis moves from personal appearance to papers and work. When boys are praised, it is most often for the intellectual quality of their ideas. Girls are twice as likely to be praised for following the rules of form. "I love your margins" is the message.[5]

The Bombing Rate

"How long do you wait for students to answer a question?" When we ask teachers to describe what they do hundreds of times daily in the classroom, their answers are all over the map: One minute. Ten seconds. Five seconds. Twenty-five seconds. Three seconds.

Mary Budd Rowe was the first researcher to frame this question and then try to answer it. Following her lead, many others conducted wait time studies and uncovered an astonishingly hurried classroom. On average, teachers wait only nine-tenths of a second for a student to answer a question. If a student can't answer within that time, teachers call on another student or answer the question themselves.[6]

When questions are hurled at this bombing rate, some students get lost, confused, or rattled, or just drop out of the discussion. "Would you repeat that?" "Say it again." "Give me a minute. I can get it." Requests such as these are really pleas for more time to think. Nobody has enough time in the bombing rate classroom, but boys have more time than girls.[7]

Waiting longer for a student to answer is one of the most powerful and positive things a teacher can do. It is a vote of confidence, a way of saying, "I have high expectations for you, so I will wait a little longer. I know you can get it if I give you a chance." Since boys receive more wait time, they try harder to achieve. As girls struggle to answer under the pressure of time, they may flounder and fail. Watch how it happens:

"Okay, class, get ready for your next problem. Mr. Warren has four cash registers. Each register weighs thirteen kilograms. How many kilograms do the registers weigh altogether? Linda?"

The teacher waits half a second. Linda looks down at her book and twists her hair. She says nothing in the half-second allotted to her.

"Michael?"

The teacher waits two seconds. Michael is looking down at his book. The teacher waits two more seconds. Michael says, "Fifty-two?"

"Good. Exactly right."

Less assertive in class and more likely to think about their answers and how to respond, girls may need *more* time to think. In the real world of the classroom, they receive less. For female achievement and self-esteem, it is a case of very bad timing.

DIFFERENT WORLDS

This chapter began with time-lapse photography, a series of frames frozen to reveal the hidden meaning in snapshots of classroom life. If the camera were to go beyond the classroom and take pictures throughout the school, here is what they would reveal:

Snapshot #1   An all-girl line and an all-boy line thread through the hall to recess.

Snapshot #2   Leaving the library, a single caterpillar line crawls along—its first half all female, its second half all male.

Snapshot #3   An anti–Noah's Ark line travels through the hallway two by two, without a single male-female pair.

Snapshot #4   At a long rectangular lunchroom table a group of fifth and sixth graders eat lunch together, black and white, Hispanic and Asian. Every child is male.

Snapshot #5   Another group of fifth and sixth graders eat lunch together. This table is also racially mixed, but the

gender barrier does not break down. The group is
all girls.

The camera leaves the building and, still snapping a picture a minute,
pans the playground.

Snapshot #6   A large all-male soccer game is in play. It stretches
out to take over most of the schoolyard.

Snapshot #7   Several girls and a few boys climb on the jungle
gym and play on the swings.

Snapshot #8   A few girls jump rope at the edge of the schoolyard.

Snapshot #9   In an adjoining grassy area four girls crouch by a
puddle to sail paper boats.

If you look again at the photos but substitute white and black for male
and female, the segregation screams out. There are two separate, alien,
unequal nations, two separate societies that are walled off by gender
but left undisturbed. A racial inequity would be unacceptable, but a
gender inequity is not even noticed. We must freeze the action to even
see the divisions. A separate boy world and a separate girl world is just
education as usual. Many of us were schooled in these gender-divided
worlds, and it didn't seem to hurt us. Or did it?

Boy Bastions—Girl Ghettos

Raphaela Best spent four years as an observer in an elementary school
in one of Maryland's most affluent counties. She helped the children
with schoolwork, ate lunch with them, and played games with them in
class and at recess. As an anthropologist, she also took copious notes.
After more than one thousand hours of living with the children, she
concluded that elementary school consists of separate and unequal
worlds.[8] She watched segregation in action firsthand. Adult women remember it well.

A college student recalled, "When I was in elementary school, boys
were able to play basketball and kick ball. They had the side of the playground with the basketball hoops." Another college woman remembers more formal segregation: "I went to a very small grammar school.

At recess and gym the boys played football and the girls jumped rope. All except one girl and one boy—they did the opposite. One day they were pulled aside. I'm not exactly sure what they were told, but the next day the school yard was divided in two. The boys got the middle and the girls got the edge, and neither sex was allowed on the other's part."

A third grader described it this way: "Usually we separate ourselves, but my teacher begins recess by handing a jump rope to the girls and a ball to the boys." Like the wave of a magic wand, this gesture creates strict gender lines. "The boys always pick the biggest areas for their games," she says. "We have what's left over, what they don't want."

"When it's recess time," an elementary school girl observed, "the boys run to the closet and get out the balls and bats and mitts and other stuff."

"Does the teacher ever say anything about the boys taking all the balls?" we asked her.

"Never."

"Would you like to play ball in the big area of the playground?"

"Sometimes I would like to. And sometimes girls do play kick ball, but mostly not. This is just the way it is in our school."

Every morning at recess in schoolyards across the country, boys fan out over the prime territory to play kick ball, football, or basketball. Sometimes girls join them, but more often it's an all-male ball game. In the typical schoolyard, the boys' area is ten times bigger than the girls'. Boys never ask if it is their right to take over the territory, and it is rarely questioned. Girls huddle along the sidelines, on the fringe, as if in a separate female annex. Recess becomes a spectator sport.

Teachers seldom intervene to divide space and equipment more evenly, and seldom attempt to connect the segregated worlds—not even when they are asked directly by the girls.

"The boys won't let us play," a third grader said, tugging at the arm of the teacher on recess duty. "They have an all-boys club and they won't let any girls play."

"Don't you worry, honey," the teacher said, patting the little girl's hair. "When you get bigger, those boys will pay you all the attention you want. Don't you bother about them now."

As we observed that exchange, we couldn't help but wonder how the teacher would have reacted if the recess group had announced "No Catholics" or if white children had blatantly refused to play with Asians.

Raphaela Best observed the children over four years, and the walls of gender segregation grew higher and more entrenched. In the first grade little boys hid out in the restroom. By the second grade the boys' restroom had become the site of club meetings. Grade three saw the emergence of a highly structured all-boy organization, the Tent Club, with its own rules, rituals, and secrets. By the fourth grade the Tent Club was a force to be reckoned with, one that dictated peer relationships and popularity; it even challenged the authority of the teacher and principal. But not once did an educator ever think to challenge the fairness of the all-male club.

Raphaela Best found the lunchroom to be another area of increasingly formal segregation. In the first grade boys and girls sat together, talking and playing. By second grade they sat at the same table, but it was as if an invisible line had cut it in half, with girls on one end and boys on the other. By the third grade the boys burst into the cafeteria at a dead run to claim their male-only table.

Barrie Thorne, a participant observer in elementary schools in California and Michigan whose students are mainly from working-class families, captured the tiny incidents that transform integrated classes into gender-divided worlds:[9] Second-grade girls and boys eat lunch together around a long rectangular table. A popular boy walks by and looks the scene over. "Oooh, too many girls," he says, and takes a place at another table. All the boys immediately pick up their trays and abandon the table with girls, which has now become taboo.

Although sex segregation becomes more pervasive as children get older, contact points remain. School life has its own gender rhythm as girls and boys separate, come together, and separate again. But the points of contact, the together games that girls and boys play, often serve to heighten and solidify the walls of their separate worlds.

"You can't get me!" "Slobber Monster!" With these challenges thrown out, the game begins. It may be called "Girls Chase the Boys" or "Boys Chase the Girls" or "Chase and Kiss." It usually starts out one on one, but then the individual boy and girl enlist same-sex peers. "C'mon, let's get that boy." "Help, a girl's gonna get me!"

Pollution rituals are an important part of these chases. Children treat one another as if they are germ carriers. "You've got cooties" is the cry. (Substitute other terms for different cultures or different parts of the country.) Elaborate systems are developed around the concept of cooties. Transfer occurs when one child touches another. Prepared for such attack, some protect themselves by writing C.V. (cooties vaccination) on their arms.

Sometimes boys give cooties to girls, but far more frequently girls are the polluting gender. Boys fling taunts such as "girl stain" or "girl touch" or "cootie girl." The least-liked girls, the ones who are considered fat or ugly or poor, become "cootie queens," the real untouchables of the class, the most contaminating females of all.

Chasing, polluting, and invasions, where one gender attacks the play area of the other, all function as gender intensifiers, heightening perceived differences between female and male to an extreme degree. The world of children and the world of adults is comprised of *different* races, but each gender is socially constructed as so different, so alien that we use the phrase "the *opposite* sex."

It is boys who work hardest at raising the walls of sex segregation and intensifying the difference between genders. They distance themselves, sending the message that girls are not good enough to play with them. Watch which boys sit next to the girls in informally sex-segregated classrooms and lunchrooms; they are the ones most likely to be rejected by male classmates. Sometimes they are even called "girls." A student at The American University remembers his school lunchroom in Brooklyn:

> At lunch our class all sat together at one long table. All the girls sat on one side, and the boys sat on the other. This was our system. Unfortunately, there were two more boys in my class than seats on the boys' side. There was no greater social embarrassment for a boy in the very hierarchical system we had set up in our class than to have to sit on the girls' side at lunch. It happened to me once, before I moved up the class social ladder. Boys climbed the rungs of that ladder by beating on each other during recess. To this day, twenty years later, I remember that lunch. It was horrible.

Other men speak, also with horror, of school situations when they became "one of the girls." The father of a nine-year-old daughter remembered girls in elementary school as "worse than just different. We considered them a subspecies." Many teachers who were victims of sexist schooling themselves understand this system and collaborate with it; they warn noisy boys of a humiliating punishment: "If you don't behave, I'm going to make you sit with the girls."

Most little girls—five, six, seven, or eight—are much too young to truly understand and challenge their assignment as the lower-caste gender. But without challenge over the course of years, this hidden curriculum in second-class citizenship sinks in. Schools and children need help—intervention by adults who can equalize the playing field.

The first step is for parents and teachers to question education as usual. A Milwaukee teacher recalls when she finally understood she was questioning too little and accepting too much:

> As I walked my assigned area of the playground on a recent Monday, I looked at the boys playing basketball on the far end and the girls huddled or walking in small groups along the side. No one was fighting or swearing, so I figured it was a good day. And then I caught myself. No, all was not well because I knew that some of the girls huddled in the groups liked to play basketball. So why weren't they playing? And what was I doing about it? Why did I allow a "might-makes-right" playground where the boys decided where they would play and with whom, which in practice meant no girls on the basketball or soccer teams. What was the hidden message I was giving to the girls on the playground? That the boys decide, and that's that?[10]

Male Magnets

We are often asked to talk to classes about sexism in school. In one recent visit to a sixth grade, a thoughtful African-American girl talked about how baffled she was by boys. "What thoughts go on inside their heads?" she asked. Her classmates began to giggle until they realized her question was completely honest. "No, I mean it. I know they don't think like I do. Something different goes on inside their heads, but I can't figure out what it is." Her sincerity drew in others:

"Yeah, guys are totally different. They're like aliens."

"When I go to the movies and something sad happens, I cry. But a guy doesn't cry. It's not that they have *different* feelings. They don't have *any* feelings."

"I don't think that's true. They have feelings, they just don't let anyone know it."

"Girls are strange, too. We don't get them at all," one boy said, getting the boys into the discussion.

A popular African-American male student addressed his reaction directly to the girls in the classroom: "You don't talk about normal things like we do. All you talk about is hair, and makeup, and what to do if you get your period."

Several students glanced up quickly to catch our reaction to this taboo topic. But the boy was not after shock effect; he was being honest, too. We were struck by the confusion of these eleven-year-olds. They did not understand one another because they had so little opportunity to really interact. We asked the sixth graders to look around their classroom and see if they noticed anything that might lead to miscommunication and misunderstanding. The classroom was arranged in eight groups of four. Half the class was minority, and Asian, Hispanic, and African-American children sat with one another and with white children in the groups. The students were surprised to see that not a single group was integrated by gender.

We have found that sex segregation in the lunchroom and schoolyard spills over into the classroom. In our three-year, multistate study of one hundred classrooms, our raters drew "gender geography" maps of each class they visited. They found that more than half of the classes were segregated by gender. There is more communication across race than across gender in elementary schools.

We have seen how sex segregation occurs when children form self-selected groups. Sometimes the division is even clearer, and so is the impact on instruction.

The students are seated formally in rows. There are even spaces between the rows, except down the middle of the room where the students have created an aisle large enough for two people standing side by side to walk down. On one side of the aisle, the students are all female; on the other side, all male. Black, white, Hispanic, and Asian students sit all around the room, but no student has broken the gender barrier.

The teacher in this room is conducting a math game, with the right team (boys) against the left team (girls.) The problems have been put on the board, and members of each team race to the front of the room to see who can write the answer first. Competition is intense, but eventually the girls fall behind. The teacher keeps score on the board, with two columns headed "Good Girls" and "Brilliant Boys."

The gender segregation was so formal in this class that we asked if the teacher had set it up. "Of course not." She looked offended. "I wouldn't think of doing such a thing. The students do it themselves." It never occurred to the well-meaning teacher to raise the issue or change the seats.

Here is another segregation episode, this one involving affluent independent school students during a swimming lesson.

> The pool is divided by a rope into two lap lanes. No one has tested the children or divided them by ability to make faster and slower lap lanes, but all the girls are in one lane and all the boys in another. Although many of the girls swim as fast or faster than the boys, gender alone created the division.
>
> A male teacher and a female teacher supervise the swimming. The male teacher stands at the end of the pool directly in front of the boy lane. He gives boys suggestions and advice as they come across the pool: "Good stroke, Tom." "Sean, watch your breathing." "Michael, don't forget to kick." "Tim, bend your arm forty-five degrees, like this." The boys find these comments helpful, so they call out questions and clamor for more attention. "Is this it?" "Look at my stroke and tell me if it's good." The female teacher comes over to the male side of the pool to help answer the avalanche of male requests.
>
> Meanwhile, the girls talk to each other, splash, jump up and down to keep from getting cold. Finally, too bored to wait for more directions, several start swimming to the other end of the pool. Others follow. Not a single girl has received instruction on how to improve her performance.

In our research we have found that gender segregation is a major contributor to female invisibility. In sex-segregated classes, teachers are pulled to the more talkative, more disruptive male sections of the classroom or pool. There they stay, teaching boys more actively and directly while the girls fade into the background.

The Character(s) of the Curriculum

At a workshop on sexism in the curriculum, we asked participants, "Have you ever read the book *I'm Glad I'm a Boy! I'm Glad I'm a Girl!?*" Since most of the teachers, principals, and parents had not read it, we showed it to them. *I'm Glad I'm a Boy! I'm Glad I'm a Girl!* is for very young children. One page shows the jobs and activities that boys can do, and the following page shows what is appropriate for girls.[11]

The book announces that boys can be doctors and shows a large male cartoon character with a stethoscope around his neck.

"What do girls do?" we asked the audience.

"They're nurses," the parents and educators chorused as one. They may not have read this book, but they seemed to know the plot line. A little girl nurse pushing a wheelchair is drawn on the page.

"Obviously a case of occupational stereotyping with the girl receiving less of every kind of reward including money, but do you notice anything else?" we asked. Most of the people were puzzled, but a few spotted the subtlety: "Look at how little the girl is." When we showed both pages at once, the boy doctor, a cartoon version of Doogie Howser, towered over the girl pushing the wheelchair.

The next page shows boys as pilots. "What are girls?" we asked.

"Stewardesses," the audience called back. A cartoon girl with a big smile and a short skirt carries a tray of drinks. The audience chuckled as several people remarked, "Look, her underpants are showing." "A little cheesecake for the younger set," someone joked as the next picture emerged, a boy drawn as a policeman.

"What are girls?"

This one had the group confused. "Mommies?" "Criminals?" "Crossing guards?" "Meter maids?" They found it. A tough-looking female figure is shown writing out a ticket for an obviously miserable motorist caught in a parking violation. "She looks as if she's had a steroid treatment," a teacher joked. "She's very big this time." The images continued: boys as those who eat, and girls as the ones who cook; boys as the builders of homes, and girls as the ones who clean them. The picture accompanying the caption about cleaning is that of a smiling cartoon girl pushing a vacuum cleaner. She and the cleaning machine are drawn very large because there is so much work to do. This image upset the audience. "Oh, no," several groaned. Others hissed and booed.

The next caption identified boys as the ones who fix things.

"Girls break things," the audience chorused back. But this time the author had outsmarted them. "Break" was too active. The parents and educators tried other stereotypes: "Girls clean things?" "Play with things?" "Buy things?" "Girls cry over things?"

"These are great responses, but they're all too active."

"Girls watch boys?" an astute parent suggested. She was on to something. Several studies have shown that in basal readers the activity girls are most often engaged in is watching boys in action. They look at boys play baseball, admire them as they perform magic tricks, wave good-bye from behind windows as boys leave for adventure. But in this case even "watch" was too active. The audience was stumped.

"Girls are things!" a young woman burst out. She had actually outdone the author, so we displayed the page: GIRLS NEED THINGS FIXED. The smiling stationary figure is holding the wheel of her doll carriage in her hand. She isn't doing anything with the wheel, she is just standing there beside her tipped-over vehicle, clearly in need of male help. The audience groaned, but the pictures went on with boys shown as inventing while girls are described as using things boys invent. Accompanying this description is an illustration of a girl lying in a hammock and reading, thanks to a lamp invented by a boy. "Who invented the cotton gin?" we asked. Several people from around the room answered, "Eli Whitney." Like Alexander Graham Bell and Thomas Edison, this name is one of the staples of American education. "Has anyone ever heard of Catherine Littlefield Greene?" The parents and teachers were silent.

We told the story of the woman who, after the death of her husband, Nathaniel, who had been a general in the Revolutionary War, met Eli Whitney. A Yale-educated tutor, Whitney devised a model for the gin while working at Greene's Mulberry Grove Mansion. But his design was flawed; although seeds were pulled from the cotton, they became clogged in the rollers. It was Kitty Greene who came up with the breakthrough idea of using brushes for the seeds. The concept of the machine was so simple that copycat gins sprang up on other plantations. To pay for lawsuits during the fierce battle for patent rights, Kitty Greene sold her estate. It wasn't until seven years later that Eli Whitney won full title to the cotton gin.[12]

"Why wasn't the patent taken out in both names?" a history teacher asked. It was an excellent question, and in the answer is an important lesson for children. At a time when it was unseemly for women to write books (many female authors took male names), it was especially unlikely for a lady to patent an invention. Textbooks tell the story of the names registered in the patent office, but they leave out how sexism and racism denied groups of people access to that registry.

The caricature of gender roles isn't over, and the picture book moves from inventions to politics, showing boys as presidents and girls as their wives.

"Is this some kind of joke?" a teacher asked. "When was it written?" We threw the question back at the audience.

"The 1920s?" someone called out.

"No, they didn't have stewardesses then. Or meter maids. I think it was the 1950s," another teacher suggested.

Most of the group were stunned to learn that the book was published in 1970 and was in circulation in libraries and schools for years afterward. Few teachers would read a book like this to children today, and if they did, the phone lines would light up in most communities. Twenty-five years ago, books like this were commonplace, and it is a sign of progress that today they are considered outrageous.

"This book is so bad, it's good," a kindergarten teacher said. "I want to show it to my class. A lot of my kids fly on planes and see male flight attendants, and one of my children has a mom who's a doctor."

We agreed that the book with its yesteryear sexism was a good teaching tool. We have shown it to students in every grade level. They have often read it critically and identified the stereotypes, but not always.

In a school in the Midwest, a large group of students gathered to learn about sexism; they sat in the auditorium as we read the book. At first the reaction was as expected—friendly laughter and surprise at the broadly drawn typecasting. But then the tone changed, and the laughter took on a hard, nasty edge. When the picture of the girl as cook appeared, there was applause. Next came the girl with the vacuum cleaner, and the clapping got louder. "All right!" "Yes!" Protected by the safety of numbers, some of the boys began to voice their approval of the unequal gender roles. "We like it like that," another shouted. "Clean, girl, clean," a group of boys began to chant. It got louder, like a cheer at a football game. Several students laughed, others looked uncomfortable. Many of the girls glanced around and then looked down nervously. For a few seconds there was a scary feeling in the room. We closed the book, the chanting stopped, and the mood was broken. We had to decide how to respond.

In this case we moved to a lecture about the goals of a democracy and the importance of equal opportunity for all people, regardless of race, religion, or gender. We spoke of how wrong and hurtful it was to put down or make fun of any group. The students stared ahead, once again quiet and well mannered, as if listening to a sermon in their place of worship. But were we getting through? We had no idea.

"Thank you for saying those things," said a girl who stopped us as we were leaving. "This isn't the first time the boys have acted like that. It's not everybody, just some. And it only happens when they get in a large group. No one, not even the teachers or the principal, has really taken them on. I'm glad you did it."

Balancing the Books

Few things stir up more controversy than the content of the curriculum. Teachers, parents, students—all seem to be aware intuitively that schoolbooks shape what the next generation knows and how it behaves. In this case research supports intuition. When children read about people in nontraditional gender roles, they are less likely to limit themselves to stereotypes. When children read about women and minorities in history, they are more likely to feel these groups have made important contributions to the country. As one sixth grader told us, "I love to read biographies about women. When I learn about what they've done, I feel like a door is opening. If they can do great things, maybe I can, too."

A few years after Betty Friedan wrote *The Feminine Mystique*, parents began to take active notice of gender treatment in schoolbooks. The more they looked, the more worried they became. Throughout the 1970s, parents and educators conducted studies to document objectively how men and women were portrayed in the curriculum. Sanctioned by school and society, the curriculum was the first aspect of school that researchers investigated for sexism. It was easy to investigate, and there was no need to use time-lapse photography to stop the action. The messages were already frozen on the textbook pages.

In their 1975 study *Dick and Jane as Victims*, The Women on Words and Images studied 134 elementary school readers from sixteen different publishers and found the following ratios:[13]

Boy-centered stories to girl-centered stories	5:2
Adult male characters to adult female characters	3:1
Male biographies to female biographies	6:1
Male fairy tale stories to female fairy tale stories	4:1

Lenore Weitzman and Diane Rizzo identified the elementary books that were used most widely between 1967 and 1972. In second-grade books, girls and women were portrayed in fewer than one-third of the illustrations. By the sixth grade the numbers of portrayals had declined to one-fifth. Minority females, portrayed half as frequently as minority males, were truly invisible.[14]

Weitzman and her colleagues next turned their attention to award-winning children's literature, Caldecott winners from 1953 through 1971. These picture books, chosen as the best of the year by the American Library Association, had eleven times as many boys and men pictured as girls and women. When the researchers counted animals, really people dressed in feathers and fur (Sylvester the donkey, Mickey Mouse), the ratio became a staggering ninety-five to one. In one-third of the award winners, there were no women at all.[15] Imagine parents of the 1950s and 1960s dutifully reading award-winning bedtime stories to their children and offering them a womanless world. Picture-book lessons in female invisibility were reinforced daily by the textbooks in school.

When girls and women were included, they were typecast. They looked in mirrors, watched boys, cried, needed help, served others, gave up, betrayed secrets, acted selfishly, and waited to be rescued. While men were involved in 150 different jobs, women were housewives. When they took off their aprons and discarded their dishtowels (the actual costume of the textbook housewife), they worked outside the home only as teachers and nurses.[16]

Children's literature and school texts routinely included derogatory comments about being female.[17] For example:

> From the *Lippincott Basic Reading Series*: "Women's advice is never worth two pennies. Yours isn't worth even a penny."
> From Harper & Row's *Around the Corner*: "Look at her, Mother, just look at her. She is just like a girl. She gives up."
> From Scott Foresman's *Ventures*: "We are willing to share our great thoughts with mankind. However, you happen to be a girl."

And this poem from the Caldecott award-winning *Mei Li*:

> "We keep a dog to watch the house.
> A pig is useful too.
> We keep a cat to catch a mouse.
> But what can we do with a girl like you?"

The negative publicity over sexist books jolted publishers. By the mid-1970s many had responded with guidelines so that texts would be fairer and more inclusive. Scott Foresman, Ginn, Macmillan, McGraw-Hill, Harper & Row, and several others pledged recognition of women and minorities, and an end to stereotypes and sexist language. Their guidelines offered recommendations to authors and illustrators on writing gender-fair books.[18]

Double Jeopardy

We wanted to see how well the newer books were working, so during the spring of 1992 we visited sixteen fourth-, fifth-, and sixth-grade classes in Maryland, Virginia, and Washington, D.C., and gave students this assignment:

> In the next five minutes write down the names of as many famous women and men as you can. They can come from anywhere in the world and they can be alive or dead, but they must be real people. They can't be made up. Also—and this is very important—they can't be entertainers or athletes. See if you can name at least ten men and ten women.
>
> At first the students write furiously, but after about three minutes, most run out of names. On average, students generate eleven male names but only three women's. While the male names are drawn directly from the pages of history books, the female names represent far greater student creativity: Mrs. Fields, Aunt Jemima, Sarah Lee, Princess Di, Fergie, Mrs. Bush, Sally Ride, and children's book authors such as Beverly Cleary and Judy Blume. Few names come from the pages of history. Betsy Ross, Harriet Tubman, Eleanor Roosevelt, Amelia Earhart, Sojourner Truth, Sacajawea, Rosa Parks, Molly Pitcher, and Annie Oakley are sometimes mentioned.
>
> Several students cannot think of a single woman's name. Others have to struggle to come up with a few. In one sixth-grade class, a boy identified as the star history student is stumped by the assignment and obviously frustrated:
> "Have you got any girls?" he asks, turning to a classmate.
> "Sure. I got lots."
> "I have only one."

"Think about the presidents."

"There are no lady presidents."

"Of course not. There's a law against it. But all you gotta do is take the presidents' names and put Mrs. in front of them."

In a fourth-grade class, a girl is drawing a blank. She has no names under her Women column. A female classmate leans over to help. "What about Francis Scott Key? She's famous." The girl immediately writes the name down. "Thanks," she says. "I forgot about her."

As we are leaving this class, one girl stops us. "I don't think we did very well on that list," she says. "It was too bad you didn't let us put in entertainers. We could've put in a lot of women then. I wrote down Madonna anyway."

Given a time line extending from the earliest days of human history to current events, and given no geographic limits whatsoever, these upper-elementary schoolchildren came up with only a handful of women. The most any single child wrote was nine. In one class the total number of women's names given didn't equal ten. We were stunned!

Something was very wrong—was it with the new textbooks? We decided to look at them more closely. During the summer of 1992 we analyzed the content of fifteen math, language arts, and history textbooks used in Maryland, Virginia, and the District of Columbia. When we counted pictures of males and females, we were surprised to find that the 1989 language arts textbooks from Macmillan and D.C. Heath had twice as many boys and men as girls and women. In some readers the ratio was three to one. A 1989 upper-elementary history textbook had four times as many males pictured as females. In the 1992 D.C. Heath *Exploring Our World, Past and Present*, a text for sixth graders, only eleven female names were mentioned, and not a single American adult woman was included. In the entire 631 pages of a textbook covering the history of the world, only seven pages related to women, either as famous individuals or as a general group. Two of the seven pages were about Samantha Smith, the fifth-grade Maine student who traveled to the Soviet Union on a peace mission.[19] While we felt that Samantha Smith's story brought an interesting message to other students, we wondered why Susan B. Anthony didn't rate a single line. No wonder students knew so little about women. Given the content of their history books, it was a tribute to their creativity that they could list any female names at all.

Researcher Adrienne Alton-Lee investigated classrooms in New Zealand to discover the effect of sexist curricula on children. Observing during a unit on the Middle Ages, she found that students were bombarded with three to four male names every minute of class discussion, but a female name was mentioned only once every six minutes. At the end of the unit, interviewers asked what women did during the Middle Ages. Here's a sample of what the students said:

> SAM: They used to . . . aw . . . can't remember now, they used to um . . . um . . .
> INTERVIEWER: What about the women?
> SAM: Walk up and down the castle trying to act beautiful. (Laugh)
> INTERVIEWER: Trying to act beautiful, you think?
> SAM: Trying to act so smart.
> INTERVIEWER: Do they?
> SAM: Some of them would show off.
> INTERVIEWER: Sorry?
> SAM: Some of them did show off.
> INTERVIEWER: Did show off, did they?
> SAM: Yeah.
> INTERVIEWER: What for?
> SAM: I don't know. . . . If they were so good they used to comb their hair so nice and . . .
> INTERVIEWER: Yes?
> SAM: And they used to walk up and down, they thought they were great.
> INTERVIEWER: 'Cos they thought they were great?
> SAM: Yeah, they thought they were great. And people used to go, "Wow, you're so beautiful."[20]

The interviews made it clear that when women were left out of the curriculum, the students knew nothing about them. Even worse, without real knowledge, the children filled in the gaps with stereotypes and distortions. The result was a twisted view of half the people and their history.

When a sexist curriculum is compounded by sexist teaching, the damage increases exponentially. In a third-grade language arts classroom, the children were sitting on a carpet, clustered around the teacher who was putting cartoon characters on a felt board. At first glance it was a charming scene, but after looking more closely we could see how biases in curriculum and instruction merged to put girls in double jeopardy.

TEACHER: What is a noun? (More than half the class waves their hands excitedly.)

TEACHER: John?

JOHN: A person, place, or thing.

TEACHER: Correct. (She places a large cartoon dragon on the felt board.) What part of the definition is this? Antonio?

ANTONIO: A thing.

TEACHER: Good. (She places a castle on the felt board above the dragon.) What part of the definition is this? Elise?

ELISE: A place.

TEACHER: Okay. (She puts a tiny princess in front of the dragon. The face of the princess is frozen in a silent scream.) Here is a person. Now, what is a verb? Seth?

SETH: An action word.

TEACHER: I'm glad to see you remember your parts of speech. (She posts a cartoon of an enormous knight riding a horse.) What are some action words that tell what the knight is doing? Mike?

MIKE: Fight?

TEACHER: Right. What else?

PETER (calling out): Slay.

TEACHER: Good vocabulary word. Any others? Al?

AL: Capture.

TEACHER: Excellent verbs. What is an adjective? Maria?

MARIA: A word that describes something.

TIM (calling out): Adjectives describe nouns.

TEACHER: Good, Tim. (The teacher posts a minstrel strumming a lute. A large bubble is drawn, cartoon style, showing that the minstrel is singing the words "Oh, she is beautiful.") What is the adjective in this sentence? Donna?

DONNA: Beautiful.

TEACHER: Now we are going to see how parts of speech can be used in stories. Each one of you will write your own fairy tale about how the brave knight slays the dragon and rescues the beautiful princess.

For the next twenty minutes the children write their stories as the teacher and a student teacher, placed in the classroom as part of her training program, circle the room and assist. Then:

TEACHER: You have written wonderful stories. I want each and every one of you to get a chance to read them out loud. All the girls should go to Miss McNeil [the student teacher]. If you talk very softly and don't bother anyone, you can read your stories in the hall. The boys will stay in the classroom with me.

This lesson lasted only an hour, but it taught far more than parts of speech. The children learned that Middle Ages men were creative and bold. They wrote songs and fought dragons. They worked as minstrels and knights. Women in the Middle Ages were tiny, beautiful princesses who could not take care of themselves; no other role was shown.

As the lesson progressed, the students were funneled into a narrower vision of the world. First they heard and watched as the teacher validated stereotypes, and then—and this was where the psychological backlash turned truly vicious—they were taught to make those stereotypes their own. The children created their *own* stories about the pretty passive princess and the big brave knight. They read their stories, their versions of the stereotypes, to one another. If the teacher had schemed to indoctrinate the children in the stereotypes, she could not have done it more brilliantly.

But of course there was much more going on. Donna, Maria, Elise, and the other third-grade girls were not called on as often as John, Antonio, Seth, Mike, Al, Tim, and the other male students. Like the active knight on the felt board, many of the boys in the class were active, too. When the teacher did not call on them, they called out and were praised for their assertive effort. During the entire lesson, no girl called out. Like the passive little princess, their voices were also frozen and unheard. When boys answered, the teacher took the time to offer evaluations in the form of praise. Indifferent and imprecise reactions—"Uh-huh," "Okay," or no comment—were reserved for the girls.

The sexist messages continued. When the teacher divided the class, she did it by gender. The girls were allotted second-class space and an inexperienced assistant. There was also a parting shot: The female children were told to read their stories quietly so that no one would even know they were there. The boys were left in control of the classroom and instructed by the real teacher.

The teacher, a female who could have served as a role model for the girls, both accepted and facilitated the male dominance of the classroom. She herself had been a victim of years of sexist schooling and had no idea that she collaborated with a system that stunts the potential of female students. The girls, knowing no better, did not realize that little by little, lesson by lesson, day by day they were being robbed. The student teacher was also indoctrinated into the sexist curriculum and instruction. She would be licensed to teach the following year, and it is quite likely that she will teach gender-biased lessons in a classroom of her own.

Every day in America little girls lose independence, achievement, and self-esteem in classes like this. Subtle and insidious, the gender-biased lessons result in quiet catastrophes and silent losses. But the casualties—tomorrow's women—are very real.

4
The Self-Esteem Slide

When viewing an exhibit of photographs, we were drawn to one particular image, that of a six-year-old girl. She had climbed arduously to the top of a tall playground slide, and there she stood on her sturdy legs, with her head thrown back and her arms flung wide. As ruler of the playground, she was at the very zenith of her world. The image aroused us because the camera had captured a proud and perfect time, and for too many girls such times are short-lived.

Poised between preschool and adolescence, the girl in the photo is full of energy, self-reliance, and purpose. She feels confident about what she can do and who she can become. Girls in lower and middle elementary school have a strong sense of self-esteem, the result of internal self-evaluation as they interact with the world. Self-esteem is not only a vital sign of mental health, it is also a connection to academic achievement and a direct link to career goals and hopes for the future.

Barbara Kerr, who studies the underachievement of gifted women, highlights the "I can do it" assurance of girls in the middle elementary grades. She says they are "like birds in spring . . . in their most colorful phase."[1] Ready to try anything, their daily routine is the unexpected. They think they can be archeologists, detectives, clowns, authors, bungee jumpers—consecutively or maybe all at once. Side by side with their brothers, these spunky girls rush forward eagerly to seek new challenges to test their mettle. Their world is wide and packed with possibilities. They love their lives, but they do not want to hold back time. They choose to keep going and to keep growing. They cannot see ahead to the mind- and body-altering changes yet to come.

Like the tightening of a corset, adolescence closes around these precocious, authoritative girls. They begin to restrict their interests, confine their talents, pull back on their dreams. As they work on blending in with other girls, they move toward the end of their colorful phase.

For both girls and boys, adolescence is a time of confusion as their bodies and lives go through jarring transformations. But for most males the change is for the better. When boys describe what happens to their bodies, images of size, growth, strength, and physical prowess predominate. Boys learn they can do more, and they are in charge: "You get to be in control. . . . If you're a boy, you don't have to worry about girls beating up on you. You're bigger than the girls."

Compared to most boys, girls are now smaller, weaker, slower, not as good in sports, no longer in control. In a society where thin is beautiful, suddenly they grow fat on their chest, waist, buttocks, thighs. They move "from self-confidence to self-consciousness."[2]

If the camera had photographed the girl on the slide half a dozen years later, at twelve instead of six, it would have captured a very different pose: Her arms would no longer have been open, leaving her vulnerable as she embraced the world; she would have been looking at the ground instead of the sky; her sense of self-worth would have been an accelerating downward spiral.

The transition from elementary to middle school may be the most damaging period of a girl's young life. In 1990 the American Association of University Women conducted a national survey to learn how boys and girls from ages nine to fifteen viewed themselves, their present and future lives. The study sample included three thousand children in grades four through ten in twelve locations nationwide. When the results were tallied for the many different questions asked by the researchers, one stood out from the rest: A self-esteem gap separated boys and girls as they entered adolescence. As these boys and girls matured, the gap became a divide, a vast gulf that revealed troubling differences in how males and females felt about themselves.[3]

In response to the statement, "I'm happy the way I am," 67 percent of the boys responded affirmatively in elementary school, but by the time they reached high school, only 46 percent agreed with the statement, a self-esteem slide of 21 points. For girls the slide was a free-fall, especially between elementary and middle school, with a total drop of 31 points. While 60 percent of girls said they were happy about themselves in elementary school, 37 percent answered affirmatively in middle school, and only 29 percent in high school.

A loss of self-esteem by girls was revealed in other questions on the AAUW survey as well. Girls were less likely than boys to agree with the statement "I like most things about myself." They were more likely to say, "I wish I were somebody else," and to admit, "Sometimes I don't like myself."

The self-esteem of Hispanic girls fell the most steeply, a total drop of 38 points. In elementary school 68 percent of Hispanic girls said they always felt happy about themselves, but this sense of contentment faded, and by high school only 30 percent said they were always happy with themselves. The number of Hispanic girls who agreed with the statement "I feel good about myself when I'm with my family" tumbled an eye-opening 41 points—from 79 percent in elementary school to 38 percent in high school.

For African-American females, higher levels of self-esteem emerged in elementary school: 46 percent said, "I like most things about myself." Their sense of self-worth continued to grow, and by high school 50 percent agreed with that statement. In elementary school 59 percent of African-American girls considered themselves "important," a percentage that climbed to a healthy 74 percent by high school. African-American males also exhibited a solid sense of self-esteem, one that put them ahead of black girls in general happiness and confidence in their ability to do things.

At the time of puberty, girls are experiencing many changes at once. They are caught in bodies that swell and expand in puzzling ways, and when they look ahead to options that are mysteriously shrinking, they must also deal with the shift to middle school. It is a larger, more complicated place and, many critics charge, harshly out of touch with the needs of adolescence. In this more chaotic and alienating school, with new rules and unchartered social norms, it is easier to become both physically and emotionally lost.

Typically, boys reach puberty after they have made the shift to middle school, so they can cope with one change at a time. The trauma experienced by girls in dealing simultaneously with the metamorphosis of puberty and the adjustment to a new, more difficult school can be seen as a major contributor to the shattering of their fragile self-esteem.[4]

The Short-Circuit

One of the important reasons boys maintain their self-esteem is that they feel capable of "doing things." According to the AAUW survey, in elementary school 55 percent of boys said they were always "good at a lot of things." This declined to 48 percent in middle school and to 42 percent in high school. For girls the drop was far more precipitous: 45 percent of girls in elementary school said they were always "good at a lot of things," 10 points behind the boys. Girls' belief in their ability to do things tumbled an extraordinary 16 points between elementary and middle school and then declined another 6 points to 23 percent in high school. Boys' faith in their competence to "do things" was strongly and directly linked to their higher levels of self-esteem.[5]

One reason for this self-esteem gap is that males have more confidence in their athletic ability, four times as high for adolescent boys as girls. Also, girls do not think adults expect them to be able to do things because throughout school they are interrupted in attempts to accomplish things on their own.

The short-circuiting begins early. It was first documented by Lisa Serbin and Daniel O'Leary when they were analyzing early childhood and kindergarten classes two decades ago. Teachers, Serbin and O'Leary found, gave boys extended directions on how to accomplish tasks for themselves. When it came to girls, teachers were less likely to offer explanations and directions as to how to do things but instead would do *for* them. For example, children went up to the teacher's desk to staple handles onto party baskets. When a boy didn't spontaneously work the stapler, the teacher showed him. When a girl didn't spontaneously staple, the teacher took the handle and the basket and stapled it for her.[6]

The short-circuit syndrome hasn't changed in twenty years. Marta Cruz Janzen has been studying gender lessons in the kindergarten classroom of the 1990s. She visited a class of Hispanic children, seven boys and eight girls, several times over the course of a year. At the beginning of the year both boys and girls went to the teacher aide for assistance. Whenever girls wanted to view tapes on the VCR in this classroom, a male aide agreeably set it up for them. When boys wanted to watch a video, he explained to them how to insert the tape, turn on the machine, rewind the tape when the video was finished, and put the tape away. At the end of the year, girls still went to the aide to play their tapes, but the boys operated the VCR by themselves.[7]

The short-circuiting is found on all levels of education. We saw it again and again in the classrooms when we began to explore schools for subtle sexism. Here's how it looked in the upper-elementary and middle school grades:[8]

A fourth-grade girl doesn't know how to put a disk into the computer. She raises her hand for help. The teacher stops at her desk for a few seconds and puts the disk in for her.

A sixth-grade girl is having trouble working out a math

problem. The teacher takes the pencil out of her hand and quickly does the problem for her.

In an eighth-grade science lab, a girl can't adjust her microscope. The teacher asks a boy to show her how to do it. He goes over and adjusts it.

In none of these cases were the girls ignored, but they were dismissed. Most experienced parents and teachers know it is quicker and easier to take over and do something for a child than to show the child how to do it. But quicker isn't always better. Giving careful explanations over and over is not a quick fix. It is an investment of time, effort, patience, and teaching talent.

After years of being short-circuited by adults, girls eventually learn to short-circuit themselves. Losing faith in their skill, they hang back while boys take over. In her year-long observation of gifted girls in a southeastern middle school, researcher Linda Kramer watched how short-circuiting was internalized. In one example a class of gifted students had taken a field trip to a government building, and the city clerk was explaining the computer system.

> CITY CLERK: Right now we're fixin' to boom! This whole area is growing so we need systems like this. (The boys crowd around, asking questions and touching the computer. Nancy and Cindy stand outside the group, next to the observer, and listen politely.)
>
> NANCY (whispering to the observer): Why's he doing this? I'm not going into computer sciences. I want to be a dentist or a nurse . . . one that takes care of babies.
>
> OBSERVER: Why do you think the guys are so interested?
>
> NANCY (shrugging): I don't know. I guess because they're more skilled.
>
> OBSERVER: Oh, really? Why?
>
> NANCY: I don't know. They're just better than girls at this.[9]

We once had a poster that read: GIVE ME A FISH AND I EAT FOR A DAY. TEACH ME TO FISH AND I EAT FOR A LIFETIME. When a teacher or a parent does *for* a girl instead of teaching her *how* to do for herself, education is turned off. Independence and self-esteem are short-circuited as well.

Women in our workshops remembered being short-circuited, having things done for them in school and throughout their adult lives. Sometimes it was little things, as in the case of the woman who said,

"If I didn't show instant expertise, my husband would grab the hammer from me when we hung pictures. Now it's gotten to the point that I don't even try. I automatically hand the hammer and nails to him. Today, at forty-something, I'm not sure I know how to hang a picture straight because I've never done it."

Another woman, Bonnie, a science teacher at a technical school in Maine, recalled the following:

> I graduated from an all-female college, Wellesley, where I was very comfortable as a biology major in classroom laboratory situations. Graduate school for me was at Cornell Medical College, which in 1972 was only 10 percent female. Ph.D. candidates like myself were also in the minority.
>
> In my physiology lab group there were four males and two females. The other female and I were extremely passive throughout the semester, letting the males set up and perform the experiments while we watched.
>
> Now I am a biology professor, and I am still suffering the effects of not having participated in that lab. Now, twenty years later, when I have to conduct labs for my students and do demonstrations on my own, I am still unsure of myself.

Sometimes the short-circuit is a split-second action that deprives a girl or woman from doing something on her own, but when it is more systematic and thorough, when girls are blocked from instruction or experience in an entire domain of accomplishment, then the impact—both intellectual and psychological—is more devastating. Emilie, a woman in her forties, will never forget a particular birthday:

> I thought the most exciting time of my life would come the day I turned sixteen. Two years earlier my brother had turned sixteen. I remember the anticipation he felt about obtaining his driver's permit. I watched him leave in the evenings several weeks before his birthday to practice parking and "city driving" with my dad. I envied him that special time and could taste the freedom he would soon have because he could *drive!* But I knew my time would come.
>
> Before my birthday there was no mention of driving lessons, but I believed with all my heart that on my birthday I would be presented a schedule of upcoming driving classes. On the day of the party, that special envelope was not there. I asked when I would start my lessons. The answer: "Not for at least two years." "But why? My brother was six-

teen when he received his permit." The answer: "You're just a girl. He is a boy and needs it."

I received pearls instead. "That's what a girl needs." I went to my room and put my fist through a window. Shortly afterward I began to display symptoms of asthma. A little later my pearls broke. To this day I have never gotten my driver's permit.

"Help Me, God. I'm a Girl."

"Suppose you woke up tomorrow and found you were a member of the other sex. How would your life be different?" During the past decade we have posed that question to hundreds of students across the country. The question fascinates them; their answers reveal the value they place on each gender as well as on themselves.[10]

Girls' reactions run the gamut when it comes to changing their gender. Many would rather stay girls. As an eleven-year-old said, "Being female is what I'm all about. It would be confusing to be a boy." Still, girls are intrigued at the thought of becoming boys, at least for a little while. "I don't think being a boy would be that bad," said twelve-year-old Hannah. "I would not want to be a boy permanently, but I would like to try it for a week to see how it feels. If I liked it, I would stay longer."

Other girls embrace their new roles enthusiastically; they see many advantages. "When I grow up, I will be able to be almost anything I want, including governor and president of the United States," wrote twelve-year-old Dana. "People will listen to what I have to say and will take me seriously. I will have a secretary to do things for me. I will make more money now that I am a boy." Anita said, "I would feel sort of more on top. I guess that's what a lot of boys feel."

For boys the thought of being female is appalling, disgusting, and humiliating; it is completely unacceptable. "If I were a girl, my friends would treat me like dirt," said a sixth-grade boy from a rural school. "My teachers would treat me like a little hairy pig-headed girl," said Michael from an urban classroom. The essays of desperate horror continue:

"If I was a girl, I would scream. I would duck behind corners so no one would see me."

"I would hide and never go out until after dark."

Many choose the final exit: "If I were turned into a girl today, I would kill myself."

Between 1988 and 1990, almost eleven hundred children in Michigan wrote essays about what life would be like if they experienced a gender change. Forty-two percent of the girls found many good things to say about being male: They would feel more secure and less worried about what other people thought, they would be treated with more respect, they looked forward to earning more money at better jobs. Ninety-five percent of the 565 boys saw no advantage at all to being female. Only 28 boys saw any benefits. Some of the reasons offered by this 5 percent were sincere. They talked about not being punished as much, getting better grades, not needing to pay for dates, and not getting hurt in fights. But the advantages were often phrased as stereotypic put-downs: "crying to get out of paying traffic tickets" and getting out of trouble by "turning on the charm and flirting my way out of it."

Sixteen percent of the Michigan boys wrote about fantasy escapes from their female bodies, with suicide the most frequent getaway selection:

"I would *kill* myself *right away* by setting myself on fire so no one knew."

"I'd wet the bed, then I'd throw up. I'd probably go crazy and kill myself."

"And I would never wake up again and would be heading over to the cemetery right now and start digging."

"If I woke up tomorrow as a girl, I would stab myself in the heart fifty times with a dull butter knife. If I were still alive, I would run in front of a huge semi in eighteenth gear and have my brains mashed to Jell-O. *That would do it.*"

"No cat liked me. No dog. No animal in the world. I did not like myself."[11]

When we analyzed the hundreds of essays students wrote in response to our question, we found similar themes. Boys took imaginative, desperate measures to get out of being girls. A twelve-year-old wrote: "To have my boy body I would walk off a cliff. I would bungee jump without a bungee cord off the tallest mountain." Stephen, also twelve, said he would "walk around the world on hot coals," and Jesse offered to "jump out of a plane into a glass of milk to get my boy body back."

As girls move into adolescence, being popular with boys becomes overwhelmingly important, the key to social success. They look to males for esteem, hoping to see approval and affirmation in their eyes. But if the attitudes expressed in the male stories of gender changing are any measure, girls are seeking comfort in a carnival mirror, one sending back an image so grotesque and misshapen that its distortion is startling. Although we have read hundreds of boys' stories about waking up as a girl, we remain shocked at the degree of contempt expressed by so many. If the students were asked to consider waking up as a member of a different religious, racial, or ethnic group, would rejection be phrased with such horror and loathing?

When we talked with students about these essays, we tried to understand why the boys made such disparaging comments about girls, why their stories were marked by such jolting themes of revulsion. Part of the reason appeared to lie in boys' perception of the female body as fragile, limited, and incompetent, especially in athletics and sports. More than one in four elementary school boys regards athletics as the best thing about being male, and almost three-quarters dream about being sports stars when they grow up. Twenty-eight percent say their first career choice is to become an athlete or a sports star.[12] One regret that repeatedly emerged in fifth- and sixth-grade boys' essays of gender change was loss of the ability to play sports. Boys said: "Being a girl sucks. Now instead of basketball I have to play boring jump rope." "Now that I'm a girl, they won't let me play football. But I'll play it anyway. I'll play in a dress if I have to." Eleven-year-old Keith told how becoming female meant losing the most important fantasy of his life: "So many times I wish I was still a boy because of all my dreams to become a baseball player. But now they've perished into the night, and I'm just a little old bag lady sitting in a cardboard box. And whenever I go to a baseball game I cry my eyes out because my dreams have been lost forever."

While a female body represents loss of sports, a male body means access. Fifth- and sixth-grade girls who imagined they had turned into boys said: "People would call me slugger instead of sweetie." "When the boys play ball, they never pass to the girls, but if I was a boy, I would probably get the ball thrown to me all the time." "At school the boys would say 'Nice shot' if I scored a goal and not 'Ewwwww, busted by a girl.'" "I would get to play with a *real* basketball instead of a *beach* ball like girls in our class use now."

With boy bodies some of the girls allowed themselves a new dream, that of becoming a professional sports star. In her essay, "Cool, I'm a Boy!," sixth grader Maddy said, "I've always wanted to be a boy so I could play professional hockey." And twelve-year-old Melissa wrote: "I feel that being a girl is fun and I love it, but if I were a boy, I could fulfill my dream to become a star in the NBA."

As middle school students grow older, the focus on sports ability broadens to a more general admiration for boys' physical advantages. Twenty-nine percent of boys and 34 percent of girls chose physical advantage as the reason boys were lucky. In contrast, both boys (21 percent) and girls (41 percent) considered physical characteristics to be disadvantageous.

Even the sense of being attractive, fundamental to female self-esteem, is diminished during middle school. In elementary school 31 percent of white girls said they always liked the way they looked. This feeling of being pretty took a 20-point dive to 11 percent in middle school; in high school it remained level as only 12 percent said they were satisfied with their appearance. Between elementary and middle school, pride in appearance took a 26-point plunge for Hispanic girls, from 47 percent to 21 percent. Another 10-point drop occurred between middle school and high school when only 11 percent of Hispanic girls always liked the way they looked. While African-American girls took more pride in their appearance, they also expressed more concern about pregnancy.

For girls, adolescence means pregnability. For some, menstruation is a moment of triumph, a signal of maturity. For others, it is humiliating, even scary. Now girls are restricted in where they are allowed to go. According to the AAUW survey, 13 percent of boys and 22 percent of girls cited personal freedom as the reason boys were lucky. Hispanic girls were especially aware of restraint and confinement. Twenty-eight percent said sexism or the greater freedom boys had was "a bad thing about being a girl."[13]

Awareness of the physical changes girls go through—and the vulnerability that accompanies these developments—became the topic of discussion when we talked about the gender-switching essays with a racially diverse and unusually forthright eighth-grade class.

The students have just finished writing their essays. Three black males have written a group rap poem instead and ask if they can say it out loud. Nelson, one of the best-liked students in the class, ambles to the front of the room and reads what it would be like to wake up as a girl:

Wake up in the morning
I'm the opposite sex.

Look at your private parts and check.
Sit up and cry.
I'll do anything but die.
Would my friends tease me?
I have to sit down and pee.
Oh no I lost my hairy chest,
And I'm stuck with a big breast.
I'll hide my hair in my hat
Push in my breasts so they are flat.
I'd have to wear pink underwear
And spend forever with gook in my hair.
Would I like it, no or yes?
What if I get PMS?
Would my name be Sue or Chrissy?
On the 28th day would I act all pissy?
I hate playing with girls' dolls.
Turn me back so I can have balls.

Soft-spoken and smiling, Nelson has given a humorous rather than a hostile rendition, and by the end of the poem the class is laughing and clapping. The students sneak furtive glances at the teacher to catch her reaction to some of the vocabulary, but even she is smiling—although a little uneasily.

"Is this really what you think it would be like to be a girl?" we ask.

"Yes!" several of the boys shout, putting their thumbs skyward in a victory sign.

"Being a girl can't be all bad. What are some of the advantages?" We start a list on the board. Several girls shout from different parts of the room:

"Going shopping."
"Going to the mall."
"Talking on the phone."
"Looking gorgeous."
"You get to wear better clothes—boy clothes and girl clothes."

The initial burst of enthusiasm is over, and the room grows quiet. Then a Hispanic girl raises her hand and says softly, "You get to bring new life into the world. I would never want to give that up."

No boy has yet offered an advantage, so we call on a group sitting together toward the back of the room to name one good thing about being female. "Nothin'," they say. "There's nothin' good at all."

"Not a single thing?" we probe.

"Well, you don't get into as much trouble," one boy finally volunteers. "The girls just bat their eyelashes, and we get blamed for everything."

We ask for the disadvantages. This list grows more quickly, and it is much longer. Both males and females contribute:

"Going through labor."
"Getting pregnant."
"Getting periods."
"PMS."
"Cooking and cleaning."
"Sexual harassment."
"Getting raped."
"Not getting respect."
"People don't pay as much attention to you."
"Weaker."
"Smaller."
"Not as good in sports."
"Can't be a professional football star."
"Can't be president of the United States."
"Sex discrimination."
"Don't have as much freedom."
"Don't have as much fun."
"Have to worry about your hair."
"Have to wear bras."
"High heels."
"Have to put on makeup."
"Diet all the time."
"Don't get as many jobs or make as much money."
"Have to spend all your money to look pretty."
"Have to go through too many changes."

"Did any of you write your essays about these?" we ask. An Asian boy raises his hand and reads his paragraph about the work it takes to maintain the female body: "I'd have to douche, wear tampons, shave my legs, and wear heels. I'd buy a Thighmaster, but every day I would grow more cellulite."

Other boys laugh, but Nelson, coauthor of the rap poem, is now serious. "I think the worst thing is that you're vulnerable," he volunteers. "In this school boys are always touching girls. They bump into them in the halls and touch their behinds. If you're a girl, you've got to worry about being sexually harassed or raped. I couldn't stand it if people messed with me like they do with girls."

"Do you feel that way?" we asked the girls. Almost all of them nodded. "What do boys do that frightens or embarrasses you?"

"They say things like 'Look at that juicy behind.'"

"They snap our bras in gym."

"Sometimes they squeeze breasts."

"They say mean things, like if you're not developed, they say, 'You're about as curvy as that blackboard up there.'"

"They say, 'You're so fat and ugly. Get outta my face.'"

"They say, 'Your bra is showing.'" The blonde who volunteers this comment turns beet red. "I never wore that bra again."

"Like Nelson said, they bump into us in the hallway, and they pinch us and touch us."

"Did any of you write your essays about these things?"

The girls nod.

"Would you read them?"

Thirteen-year-old Latoya volunteers: "I think my life and relationships would be totally different. People would respect me more. As it is now, I think people look at me and see a target. I also bet my mother would let me do more on my own—walk to my friends' houses, ride my bike where I want. She is very worried that when older men see a young girl like me, they see me as an easy target."

"Let me read mine," says Charlene. She saunters to the front of the room, smiles, and reads: "I wouldn't mind being a boy. I'd order *Playboy*. Knock the shower down. Buy beer. Get a car. Have parties. Have a body-building workout. Talk dirty. Pig out. Walk like an ape. Nobody would dare fool with me. I wouldn't have to deal with date rape. I wouldn't mind it for a change."

Several girls laugh and cheer. Others raise their hands to read, but the bell rings. As we leave, a slight girl, an immigrant from Vietnam, runs to catch up with us. "I'm the only child in my family, and my father wishes I was a boy. I worry, but I never have anybody to talk to. It helps to speak about these things in class. I'm glad we did it."

Self-Censored

The image of these eighth graders stays with us because the students were so honest, candid, and outspoken. More often it is hard for adolescents to speak their minds. Girls are especially reticent. As their self-esteem declines, so does their ability to express their ideas and opinions in school.

In our studies of classroom interaction, we document the silence of girls from grade school through graduate school; and in the AAUW survey, students report that girls are quieter, more hidden. Almost half of the boys, 48 percent, but only 39 percent of the girls said they speak up in class. The gender gap was wider on the question of arguing with teachers. Almost twice as many boys as girls, 28 percent versus 15 percent, said they always argued with teachers when they thought they were right.

Between 1986 and 1990, Lyn Mikel Brown and Carol Gilligan interviewed nearly one hundred girls between the ages of seven and eighteen at the single-sex Laurel School in Cleveland, Ohio.[14] Over the years they listened as these girls learned to censor themselves. Younger children spoke in clear, strong, authentic voices. As they moved up in grade, their voices became modulated, softened, sometimes obliterated. Lively, outspoken, and able to express a range of feelings at seven and eight, they became more reticent as they grew older; they monitored themselves and one another with adult prescriptions for "good girl" behavior: "Be nice," "Talk quietly," "Be calm," "Cooperate."[15] As Jesse explained, "You should be nice to your friends and communicate with them and not . . . do what you want." While Jesse harbored strong feelings and felt the need "to get my anger out of me," she was "terrified" that speaking her feelings would "cause a ruckus,"[16] disrupt the peace and quiet, anger others, or make them turn away and withdraw their love and attention. So she concealed her feelings.

As the Laurel School girls grew older, they began to mask and deny their feelings with the phrase "I don't know." When Judy was interviewed at nine, she used "I don't know" four times. Her interview at ten years of age, one of comparable length, was riddled with the phrase. When the interviewer asked Judy if there was a way to talk over problems before they exploded, Judy stumbled and was disconnected from the feelings she had concealed within her: "I don't know. It's just like if—I don't know, it's like—I don't know. I can't even begin to explain it because I don't even know if I know what it is. So I can't really explain it. Because I don't know. I don't even know, like in my brain or in my heart, what I am really feeling. I mean, I don't know if it's pain or upsetness or sad—I don't know."[17]

Girls who have spent years submerging their honest feelings, afraid to speak them aloud, eventually become confused; they begin to wonder whether their feelings are real. Neeti, a quiet, pretty girl of Indian descent who was popular and had good grades, was shocked to discover that by fifteen she couldn't write an answer to the essay question "Who am I?" This was her explanation for not being able to respond: "The voice that stands up for what I believe in has been buried deep inside me."[18]

The girls in Linda Kramer's study of a southern rural middle school had been singled out as gifted. As a result they went to extraordinary lengths to blend in, even denying and consciously hiding their special gifts. These girls felt that to survive they had to censor what they did and said, literally silencing themselves:

OBSERVER: I hear you are an excellent singer.
ELLEN: No. Not really. Not excellent.
OBSERVER: Miss Hunt told me you sing well.
ELLEN: When I was in fifth or sixth grade, I had a lot of nerve. See, I didn't care what people thought of me then, because . . . I don't know. But when I was in fifth grade I sang "Tomorrow" in front of the whole school. And if I had any way of changing it, I would.. . . .
OBSERVER: Because of that song?
ELLEN: I guess being up there by myself, people think it's weird. The boys think so. . . . I think I'd rather have friends and things than really be that good.[19]

One way to get noticed was to be called on in class. For a gifted girl, being asked a question was a no-win proposition: If she got it wrong, she looked dumb. But if she got it right, then people would dislike her for being too smart. One of the gifted girls was so nervous about this that she prayed every night that the teacher would not call on her.

When we speak with girls about what they do to avoid talking in class, they share their creative strategies: They take inconspicuous seats in the back of the room or in the corners. They check where the teacher never looks and then sit there. They raise their hands tentatively, halfway. If it looks as though the teacher might actually call on them, they change their raised arm to a yawn, a stretch, or some other movement. They use the once-in-a-while approach to classroom interaction: Consciously self-regulating their speech, they answer every now and then so that the teacher will think they are making an effort.

Astute adults understand the connection between speaking up and self-esteem. Parents at our workshops have said that they worry when their children are quiet, shy, silent, or withdrawn: "I wish she'd come out of her shell." "Why doesn't she talk more?" "She's like a little mouse. Nobody even knows she's there." After a workshop in the Midwest, one woman told us how she consciously worked on regaining her own voice as part of her journey toward self-esteem: "I wanted to talk in class so badly, but I just couldn't get up the courage to hear my own voice. How I envied those who seemed to shout out whatever was on their minds. I rehearsed my comments, filtered them so carefully that by the time I was ready to raise my hand, the discussion had moved on—and I was left behind."

This woman told us how she had sat silently through year after year of elementary, middle, and then high school. By the time she got to college, she knew she had to find her voice to save her sense of self. With the help of a supportive boyfriend, she developed a plan to make at least one comment in each of her classes. Whether it was an answer, a question, a piece of new information, or a personal anecdote didn't matter. She just had to say something: "At first I was terrified. I thought I would say something stupid, and the professor would get angry—or just be amazed at my dumbness. The other students would laugh at me or resent me. But none of that happened. Nothing at all happened really, except that each time I talked, it got a little easier. And the more I talked, the more I realized I had good ideas and the more I liked myself."

Losing Their Minds

Winners of the Westinghouse Talent Search from across the country go to Washington where, as part of their program, they have the chance to interview professionals in different fields. Most of these academic superstars request meeting with mathematics and science experts. But Ashley Reiter, 1991 National first-place winner for her mathematics research, wanted to discuss sexism in school, so she talked with us. A

soft-spoken young woman of extraordinary perceptiveness, she remembered middle school as a smart girl's torture chamber. "No one
would speak to me," she said. "I wouldn't even go into the cafeteria for
lunch. Long tables stretched the length of the whole room, but wherever I sat, people acted as if I wasn't in the right place. It wasn't so
much cliques as a long social scale, and I couldn't figure out where I
was supposed to fit. So I just decided it was easier not to go."

"What did you do about lunch?" we asked.

"I skipped it. I would go to the library. Or I scheduled meetings—I
was in a lot of activities—and ate a sandwich then. It was definitely not
cool to be smart in seventh and eighth grade, especially for a girl.
Some kids thought they would lose their reputation just by speaking to
someone smart."

With the help of supportive parents and special programs that recognized her gifts, Ashley struggled through adolescence. Today she is
a young woman of poise, apparent assurance, and outstanding
achievement. But just below the surface, the scars are still there. Ashley defied the social consequences and refused to hide her intellectual
talent, but too many other girls cope with middle school by appearing
dumb, learning less, and giving up academic achievement.

Ashley was accurate in her assessment that the cafeteria visibly signals the middle school social register. Victoria, one of the girls in
Brown and Gilligan's Laurel School study also knew the agony of being without a place to sit at lunch. She referred to herself as a "leftover
in the Laurel School cafeteria."[20]

Donna Eder and Stephen Parker spent several years observing and
interviewing 190 sixth-, seventh-, and eighth-grade girls in a midwestern middle school.[21] They found the cafeteria the most interesting time
to watch and listen to adolescents. In the sixth grade there were few
stable cliques and only modest differences in social status. But by the
seventh grade each girl's lunchroom seat was a clear sign of her social
standing. Popular girls would reserve seats for one another and prevent undesirables from invading their table: "This seat is saved. I'm
sorry, but you can't sit here."

The event that ultimately determined where each girl sat was cheerleading tryouts. Most sixth-grade girls dreamed of becoming cheerleaders. Forty-four tried out for the sixteen available positions. During
practice the coach explained the criteria for selection: poise, personality, appearance, smile, and sparkle. On those rare occasions when an
overweight girl was chosen, she was told to diet. But even more important than a slim shape was a bubbly personality. The girls were in-

structed to continue smiling no matter what. But not any smile would do—it had to look natural. One candidate didn't make the squad because the coach thought her smile looked forced.

After tryouts in the fall of seventh grade, those fortunate few who were chosen sat together at the cheerleaders' table. They were joined by their close friends and some members of student government. By eighth grade the table had expanded to include several male athletes. Theirs was the lunch bunch to watch, the group everyone else talked about and envied.

Most girls desperately wanted to be well liked and popular. For many, achievement in the social arena became far more important than academic attainment. Those who failed to gain social success said their other contributions were ignored: "If I was popular when I won that contest, everybody would have been jumping around and saying, 'Oh! Natalie won! Natalie won!' But it wasn't like that. Since I wasn't popular, everybody just kind of thought, you know, like 'Big deal!'"[22]

In interviews girls described what it took to get into the popular crowd: being pretty or cute, wearing the right clothes, having a bubbly personality, being a cheerleader or the friend of a cheerleader. Not mentioned were the following qualities: independence, courage, creativity, honesty, achievement, intelligence. In fact, brains were a barrier.

In her observations and interviews with gifted girls, Linda Kramer documented the ingenious measures they took to cloak being bright.

> LYNN: Some people say, "Look at the brain! She knows all the answers." Some of these people could be just as smart as us if they'd study. They just don't want to take the time.
> OBSERVER: Are you sure studying is the only reason?
> LYNN: (Pause.) I don't know. I try to be nice to everyone. I don't want to be a brain. I try to have fun.[23]

Over and over during interviews these very bright sixth-, seventh-, and eighth-grade girls denied their intelligence. "We are not 'brains,'" they would say, "We're 'normal.'" As Lynn's comment shows, they attributed their spot in the gifted program to studying hard. The gifted boys were different; they were "real brains." Gifted girls were like everybody else; they just worked a little harder. As Debbie, another of the girls, explained, "Tom and Bob [gifted boys] don't have to try as hard. Their whole life is brains. . . . Their talk is scientific notation."[24]

The gifted girls in this study were successful at hiding their intelligence. Kramer found that teachers were readily able to identify gifted boys but were often surprised to learn a girl was considered particularly smart. "I have trouble looking at these girls as gifted," one teacher admitted. Another commented, "Gifted girls aren't superstudents in math. They tend to do well in language." After a pause she added, "I guess it's okay to do well in language." The general consensus among the teachers was that gifted girls were "just like all little girls growing up."[25]

In this lack of perception, the teachers in Kramer's research were similar to teachers everywhere. Study after study has shown that adults, both teachers and parents, underestimate the intelligence of girls.[26] Teachers' beliefs that boys are smarter in mathematics and science begin in the earliest school years, at the very time when girls are getting better grades and equal scores on the standardized tests. Many adults think that boys possess innate mathematical and scientific ability. Girls can also achieve, they believe, but they have to try harder. These perceptions persist throughout every level of education and are transmitted to the children. Girls, especially smart girls, learn to underestimate their ability.

Beliefs shape behavior and create a chilly climate in the classroom. Teachers at our workshops described how it happens: A young woman who did her student teaching in Wisconsin said, "A lot of my female students complained about a science teacher who persisted in referring to them as 'dizzy' or 'ditzy' or 'airhead.' He often told the class, 'You can't expect *these girls* to know anything.'" A Louisiana educator told us about a science teacher who called the boys "Mr." or "Professor" but called the girls by their first names, if they were lucky, or "Blondie."

Educators who are aware of subtle sexism often tell of their frustration with parents who are not. A middle school principal described a father, a college math professor, who came in for a conference. "He was worried that the math program wasn't rigorous enough for his son, but he never called or came in to talk about his daughter even though she was a much better math student." A Vermont teacher said, "At my last parent-teacher conference, a mother praised her daughter for being a real 'go-getter.' She said that her daughter wanted to be a doctor. I was shocked when she went on to say that she told her daughter to try being a nurse first, and then if she liked it, she could become a doctor."

One mother who was consciously trying to raise a daughter with nontraditional attitudes found herself backing off when her socialization program actually began to work:

> In a toy store my daughter won't walk down the pink-purple aisle with the Barbie dolls. She says, "Yuck." She won't

have anything to do with ballet or anything frilly, and won't choose anything feminine as a Halloween costume. Her current ambition is to be a paleontologist when she grows up.

My reaction to this is interesting to me. I have written graduate papers on several aspects of sexism and spent years as a teacher trying not to perpetuate sex stereotypes. I provided my daughter with a variety of toys—dolls, building blocks, and cars—when she was younger. But now just writing this gives me a knot of fear in my stomach because I see her as a social misfit. She would rather play with boys than girls. I don't know whether to push her to make more girl friends or to stay out of it and leave her be. I love her the way she is. I just worry that she'll be hurt.

Some adults maliciously stunt girls, but most are unaware of how attitudes and expectations slip, inadvertently and subconsciously, into behavior that creates a self-fulfilling prophecy. The signals are unobtrusive but powerful.

When teachers criticize the academic performance of boys, they include suggestions that soften the blow: "I'm afraid you didn't do too well on that math test. I know you can get it. Just turn off that TV and study a little more." In this brief comment, male students receive a crucial communication: "You failed because of lack of effort. You are capable. If you try harder, you will succeed. The situation is under your control." When girls' academic performance is inadequate, they are told, "I'm afraid you didn't do too well on that math test." Missing is the vote of confidence, the attribution to effort, the suggestion that girls have the brain power and can do it if they try a little more.

When boys do well, adults say, "Great job on that exam. Straight A! You're really good in science." Again, the intimation is subtle but potent. Boys learn that they achieve because they are smart. When girls do well, they are also praised: "Great job on that exam. Straight A!" But an important piece of the message is missing—the attribution to ability. The girl does not learn she did well because she is intelligent.

Children pick up on these subtle cues and internalize the attitudes of adults. When boys achieve, they attribute their success to ability. "I'm pretty good in math," they will admit. When they fail, they attribute it to lack of effort. If they receive a low test grade, they don't think it's because they're stupid: "I can't believe it," they say. "I guess I studied the wrong stuff. I should have done better than this."

When girls bring home the A, they attribute their success to effort. "I really worked hard on this," they say to themselves. When girls get bad grades, they attribute failure to lack of ability: "I'm just not smart in math [or science]," they conclude.

When children internalize success and externalize failure (the male approach), they are able to tackle new and challenging tasks with a mastery orientation, one that perseveres in the face of difficulty and leads to future achievement. Children who attribute success to effort and failure to lack of ability (the female approach) exhibit "learned helplessness." When confronted with difficult academic material, they do not persist. "I think I can't," they say—and give up.[27]

Recent research clarifies the connection between self-esteem and academic achievement, especially in math and science. Girls and boys who enjoy science and math consider themselves more important, like themselves more, and feel better about their schoolwork and family relationships. They are also more likely to hold professional career goals. Thirty-one percent of girls in elementary school say they are good in math. By middle school, only 18 percent think they are mathematically capable.[28] When girls lose confidence in their ability to learn math and science, they avoid these subjects. When they believe they can't succeed, they become less willing to attempt new science and math tasks. As they have fewer and fewer experiences with math and science, they become less capable. As their competence withers, so does their self-esteem, and the vicious, connected cycle continues: attenuation of self-confidence that leads to loss of mental ability and results in the diminishment of self-confidence. The order of this downward spiral is crucial. The plunge in confidence comes first and is followed by the drop in achievement. It is during middle school that the fabled gender gap in math emerges and gets greater in science. The brightest girls suffer the most. In Lewis Terman's famous studies of gifted men and women, boys' IQs fell 3 points during adolescence. Girls dropped an eye-opening 13 points.[29]

By the end of middle school smart girls report they are more worried and afraid, and less encouraged and appreciated, than they were in elementary school.[30] Many see these changes as a form of adult betrayal:

> Until I was in junior high, my dad was my best friend. We read together and played chess together. He was proud of my intelligence, and he showed it. Then when I entered junior high, he began to show ambivalence toward my achievements. He still said "Great" when I got good grades, but he began asking me about boyfriends and praising me for looking pretty. Somehow this made me feel bad, but I

never could express it. I was just frustrated with him and felt betrayed. He just wanted me to be like the other girls.[31]

A woman who attended one of our workshops remembered how the academic part of her self-esteem was stripped away:

> I was an only child, and my father took me along to all of his political events, chess club meetings, and to his office. The only time I was permitted to stay up late was when he wanted to explain an especially interesting article, usually some sort of political analysis. I was encouraged to study, and my parents' greatest dream was that I would be the first in the family to go to college, a dream I would fulfill but not until many years later.
>
> Only as I grew closer to puberty did I realize that many people had a very different sense of how a girl should be educated. When I was asked what I wanted to be when I grew up, my answers—a doctor, a scientist—always generated a chuckle or two. As I edged closer to my twelfth birthday, the key question became, "What type of man would you like to marry when you grow up?" I remember a great feeling of indignation coming over me. How dare they think that of me! Didn't they know that I was every bit as smart as their sons?
>
> As time went on, I became painfully aware that less intelligence was expected of girls, both by the adult world and eventually by the girls themselves.

Poised on the edge of adolescence, girls struggle to keep their balance, retain their authenticity and vitality, and move on to emerge as secure and capable adults. But now so many pitfalls surround them: physical vulnerability, the closing of options, the emphasis on thin, pretty, and popular, the ascendancy of social success over academic achievement, the silencing of their honest feelings, the message that math and science are male domains, the short-circuiting of ability that renders them helpless, the subtle insinuations that boys are really the smart ones (they just don't try). Girls who succumb to these messages are at emotional and academic risk, in danger of losing not only their confidence and their achievement but the very essence of themselves.

The girl who once lay claim to the top of the slide does not go into the playground anymore. She has left behind childish things along with a large measure of self-esteem. No longer is she at the peak of her world, in charge of all she surveys. Instead she walks cautiously, wary of the traps around her. She moves on to high school with all its promise, but she begins the journey on very shaky ground.

5

High School: In Search of Herself

At the entrance to the young adult section of our local library is a poster with pictures of Stephen King, S. E. Hinton, and Spike Lee. In bold letters below the pictures is the announcement THEY SURVIVED HIGH SCHOOL. The verb "survived" is apt, because adolescence leaves an indelible mark. In his insightful book *Is There Life After High School?*, Ralph Keyes describes these pressures. He writes about "innies," students with prestige and popularity, and "outies," those at the bottom of the social status ladder.[1]

Keyes's question about life after high school is rhetorical, of course, but many adults carry high school around with them always. It is a unique, eccentric, and insulated social system, a pressure cooker where teenagers rush from one class to another, shoved into close quarters with twenty-five or thirty others their age they may love, hate, care little about, or hardly know at all. It has its own norms, rituals, vocabulary, and even its own way to tell time—not by the minute and hour but, as sociologist Edgar Friedenberg has pointed out, by periods.[2] As the setting for the adolescent search for identity, high school is, Kurt Vonnegut wrote, "closer to the core of the American experience than anything else I can think of."[3] There is life after high school, but what we do as adults is powerfully shaped by those years.

Looking-Glass Girls

In the central drama of adolescence, high school is when girls begin their quest to develop an adult identity. They see each small incident enlarged as if it were a life-shattering event,[4] and they experiment with different roles in ways that bewilder their parents. As one mother told us:

> My daughter comes home from school exhausted. She doesn't say much usually, but yesterday she couldn't stop talking. First she was so happy because the cast names were up for the play and she got a part. Then she learned that this girl was spreading rumors about her, and she was upset and angry. Next she got her chemistry test back and bombed it. She was depressed and wouldn't talk to anybody. After school she and a group of her friends went to McDonald's; they were so happy and having the best time. I can still see her face as she asked me, "How is it possible to have so many different feelings and be so many different people in such a short time? Sometimes I don't even know who I am!"

As adolescent girls struggle to reconcile different aspects of their personalities, they look to parents, teachers, classmates, and friends for reactions. Girls use these reactions as a yardstick to measure themselves, pooling and reflecting them in a process Charles Horton Cooley called "the looking-glass self."[5] By high school the mirror held up by peers is the one girls look into most to learn who they are and what they can become.

In his classic study *The Adolescent Society*, James Coleman found that in the 1950s high school boys wanted overwhelmingly to be remembered by peers as "top athletic stars"; second choice was "brilliant student," and third was "most popular." Girls wanted to be remembered as a "leader in activities," closely followed by "most popular." "Brilliant student" ranked a distant third.[6] For boys, athletics was mentioned again and again as the gateway to high school status. When girls were asked how they reached the leading crowd in school, they referred to appearance and personality: "Wear just the right things," they said. "Money, clothes, a flashy appearance. Date older boys, get fairly good grades, but don't be too smart. Flirt with boys. Be cooperative on dates."[7]

When Ralph Keyes interviewed adults who had attended high school during the 1970s, he found that being popular was still a top priority for girls and that even famous personalities were haunted by memories of high school rejection. Actress Ali McGraw remembered never having a date in high school. Author of *The Feminine Mystique*, Betty Friedan recalled going out infrequently, mostly with "misfits like myself."[8] When writer Nora Ephron was asked what she wished she had been like in high school, her answer was immediate:

> Beautiful, feminine, popular with the boys, popular with

the girls. . . . The one thing I would like to get across about my whole feeling regarding high school is how I was when I was fifteen: gawky, always a hem hanging down, or a strap loose, or a pimple on my chin. I never knew what to do with my hair. I was a mess. And I still carry that fifteen-year-old girl around now. A piece of me still believes I'm the girl nobody dances with.[9]

Ephron not only described what it felt like to be fifteen and awkward, she also told how she improved her popularity by dating boys who weren't too bright. She took her most important step toward status when she stopped raising her hand so that classmates wouldn't realize she knew the answers. She told Keyes:

"It made a tremendous difference."

"You were asked out more?"

"Oh, yeah. Instantly." She grimaced. "I realize the kind of patheticism of it—(a) that I stopped raising my hand, (b) that I felt I had to, and (c) that it worked."[10]

In today's adolescent society many girls still think that being bright is in conflict with being popular. To go to the prom with the right date, to be a cheerleader, to be chosen as most popular, to be elected class officer—such is the stuff of high school dreams. High academic success is not always congruent with these new priorities. The assertive style that leads to intellectual achievement does not mesh with the passive noncompetitive role many boys desire and expect. Since the ultimate social failure is to be seen as a female nerd or brain, too many girls opt out of advanced mathematics and science courses, critical decisions that may later prevent access to careers in science and technology. High school girls who avoid these courses are making their first career move, and most of them don't even know it.

Since competing with boys—and winning—can result in being home alone on Saturday night, some girls put the brakes on academic success and cloak or camouflage their talent; not trying hard in school is just one step away from "playing dumb." One high school senior we spoke to admitted, "When a girl asks me what grades I got last semester, I answer, 'Fair, only one A.' When a boy asks the same question, I act surprised. 'I can't believe it, I got an A!'" Other girls told us that they hid out in class and never volunteered so classmates wouldn't know how smart they were. One senior explained that she spent years faking intellectual mediocrity. "I never pretended to be a potato, but I didn't want people to think I was a brain, either," she said. "When I qualified as a National Merit Semifinalist, I felt as though I had blown my cover. So I went around saying that I just got lucky on the test; it could never happen again. After I said it often enough, the other kids seemed to believe it."

On dates, girls introduce topics of interest to boys, then listen intently, the epitome of the good audience. Years after graduation, women remember high school in terms of social success and failure. Ironically, when girls shy away from academic success, they relinquish the very behavior—the achievement orientation—that leads to high self-esteem.

Today just as when Coleman wrote *The Adolescent Society*, the most reliable route to popularity for girls is looking pretty. Teenage boys agree that good looks are important for a girl and even claim that pretty girls have better personalities.[11] For today's adolescent girls, "pretty" is synonymous with "thin."

> The fifteen-year-old girl looks to the right and left, as if checking for passing cars on a busy street. Seeing that no one is around, she slips outside the dressing room and hurries to look at the prom dress in the large mirror outside. She surveys her appearance critically and pushes the dress down over her hips several times as if to erase them. "I've been starving myself for weeks," she mutters. "I can't believe I'm still so fat." The tag on the dress she is wearing says size three.

> "Allison has such a pretty face," one mother told us after a shopping expedition. "But I can't stand to see her try on clothes. It's pathetic. If only she would lose weight. I don't think I can shop with her anymore. She's so sensitive, and all we do is fight about it."

Different versions of these scenes are played out across the country, especially before prom or homecoming dances. The obsession with being thin takes many forms: girls who skip breakfast or lunch or dinner, or all three; girls who exist on diet drinks and popcorn; girls whose most predictable and reliable daily activity is checking their weight on the scale morning and night.

The obsession with thinness is a recent phenomenon. In earlier times a full figure was thought to be beautiful; ample breasts, belly, and buttocks signified health and fertility. During the 1950s, girls and women worked to achieve the hourglass shape. In that time of "mammary madness," girls bought falsies and stuffed bras with tissue and cotton. Cinch belts and crinoline skirts were also part of the hourglass image. Today the ideal of the curvaceous woman has been replaced by a "tubular" shape, a more linear form that is taller, leaner, and without a noticeable bust or hips. During the past twenty years the featured models in fashion and women's magazines have become ever thinner and now weigh a shocking 23 percent less than the average woman.[12]

Girls pore over the pictures in these magazines, studying the images as a primer for their own appearance. Surrounded by pictures of lithe, lean, long-legged beauty, the adolescent girl confronts a terrible irony. To mature normally she gains weight, especially in the bust and hips. The "fat spurt" is one of puberty's most dramatic physical changes. It adds an average of eleven kilograms of weight, an accumulation of body fat that is part of normal development and important for reproduction. Leg length as a proportion of total height decreases throughout puberty, especially for girls who mature early. But the shape of the girl *before* puberty, the form left behind during normal maturation, is the image that society says is beautiful.

It is troubling but not really surprising that models in magazines are bone-thin. More shocking is the discovery that subliminal lessons in female weight loss emerge in the books that children read at school. In third-grade texts published between 1900 and 1980, boys do not change in terms of shape or weight, but over that span of eighty years little girls lost weight and grew relentlessly thinner.[13]

It is a devastating dilemma. To mature normally is to become less attractive at the very age when beauty is most essential to popularity and self-esteem. During the 1980s, women presented in the media as beauty images, such as *Playboy* centerfolds and Miss America contestants, were 15 percent or more below the weight expected for their age and height.[14] For too many girls the message is clear and the course of action terrifying.

Girls and women discuss losing weight the same way boys and men talk about sports. Weight loss, a female preoccupation nationally, originally affected only white adolescent girls, but more recently it has expanded to include upwardly mobile minority girls as well. The number of adolescent girls who are trying to lose weight increased from one-third in the 1960s to two-thirds in the 1980s. It is estimated that at any given time approximately one-half to three-quarters of adolescent girls and three-quarters of adult women are on a diet.[15]

Persistent, chronic dieting puts an enormous stress on teenagers, one that takes a toll in physical well-being and the energy needed to learn in school. In one classic study of hunger, a group of men reduced their food intake by half. After six months the men became apathetic, depressed, prone to outbursts of anger, and unable to function well in work or social situations; in some cases their behavior was characterized by psychotic levels of disorganization.[16] Many teenage girls put themselves on equally or even more stringent weight-reduction programs.

The dramatic rise of clinical eating disorders among adolescent and young adult females is alarming. Morbidly afraid of being fat, high school and college students suffer from bulimia in which they have episodes of binge eating and then vomit or abuse laxatives to stop their bodies from absorbing food. An even more dangerous disorder, the self-starvation syndrome of anorexia nervosa, plagues adolescents whose images of their bodies are so disturbed that they adamantly refuse to maintain weight. From 90 percent to 95 percent of bulimics and anorexics are girls and women. According to the American Anorexia and Bulimia Association, these disorders afflict a million females and take the lives of 150,000 yearly.[17] While some are troubled by eating disorders as early as elementary school, for most girls adolescence marks the beginning of social starvation.

In a 1989 survey, 63 percent of secondary school teachers said that eating disorders were a problem at their school.[18] Teachers have told us at workshops that eating disorders are becoming more noticeable and troubling. They described monitoring the high school cafeteria for lunches left uneaten. A business teacher from a rural high school in Ohio described how he walks around the lunchroom to talk to the girls, urging them to eat something. "How do you expect to do well in your schoolwork if you don't eat?" he asks. "You'll never have enough energy to pass the test that's coming up next period." A health teacher said that parents have begun calling her secretly, asking her to check on whether their daughters are eating lunch. "So many of them don't touch anything on their plate," she said. "Maybe they nibble on a few raisins, but that's all." A teacher from an elite independent school told of a mother who taught her daughter and a group of middle school friends a "trick" so they could still enjoy food and not get fat. The "trick" swept through the class like a contagious disease as girls learned how to vomit their snacks and lunches. Kristen Golden of the Ms. Foundation for Women put the problem this way: "Suddenly they need diets, even surgery. It's incredible. It's not 'If you study, you can do this.' It's 'If you mutilate yourself, you, too, can look like this.'"[19]

While many teachers are becoming more aware of eating disorders, too often they don't know what to do about them. Naomi Wolf, author of *The Beauty Myth*, described herself when she was a schoolgirl afflicted with anorexia:

> At thirteen I was taking in the caloric equivalent of the food energy available to the famine victims of the siege of Paris. I did my schoolwork diligently and kept quiet in the classroom. I was a wind-up obedience toy. Not a teacher or principal or guidance counselor confronted me with an objection to my evident deportation in stages from the land of the living. . . .
>
> An alien voice took mine over. I have never been so soft-spoken. It lost expression and timbre and sank to a monotone, a dull murmur the opposite of strident. My teachers approved of me. They saw nothing wrong with what I was doing, and I could swear they looked straight at me. My school had stopped dissecting alley cats, since it was considered inhumane. There was no interference in my self-directed science experiment: to find out just how little food could keep a human body alive.[20]

Low self-esteem and negative body image set the stage for depression in teenage girls. While males show more symptoms of depression in early childhood, by adolescence the pattern is reversed. In a study of Oregon high school students, girls were twice as likely as boys to exhibit depressive symptoms, and in a Canadian high school study, the ratio was three to one. Higher self-esteem and achievement orientation protect boys from depression. Deprived of this buffer, many girls feel "helpless, hopeless, and stressed." Anxious and withdrawn, prone to feelings of failure and self-devaluation, depressed adolescent girls see little reason to enjoy life or feel optimistic about what lies ahead.[21]

Go Fetch!

In 1992, in Michigan, 1,808 students were interviewed about what it was like to be male or female at school. In elementary school 45 percent of the students said girls and boys were treated differently in school. By high school this number had risen 31 points to 76 percent.

Evidently the different treatment had a chilling effect on girls. In elementary school 3 percent of males and 15 percent of females said they wanted to be the opposite sex. By high school the male percentage was the same, but almost one-quarter of the girls said they wished they were the other gender. To learn more about their impressions of the different treatment depending on gender, a difference that became greater as they grew older, we went to talk with students in one of the most elite magnet high schools for mathematics and science in the United States.

"Have you noticed any differences in the ways males and females are treated in this school?" we ask the class of bright, talented students. "Or have you felt any sexism yourself? The question is for males as well as females. Take about ten minutes to describe your experiences, and then we'll talk about them."

Several students begin to write furiously. "Ten minutes," one girl murmurs. "I need days." Others, mainly boys but some girls, stare ahead stone-faced and write nothing. As we walk around the room, we stop by one all-male table. Several boys are slumped at an angle, their legs stretched across the floor and their arms folded.

"Can we help?" we ask.

"I'm thinking," one boy mutters. "I don't have a pencil," says another. We put one on his desk, but he makes no move to pick it up. As we turn to leave, we hear someone whisper, "Just what we need—politically correct BS from liberal Democrats."

"Five more minutes to write, " we announce. The hostile male table is still in position—slouched, sprawled, arms folded. But they are the minority and aren't able to set the tone in the room. Most of the students have written something; they look interested and are ready to respond.

A girl sitting toward the front begins to read her statement: "I had a sexist gym teacher last year. He was constantly putting down the girls in my gym class. He would say things like, 'You!' pointing to a girl, 'Get out of the way! Mark actually is trying to make a basket.' He hardly ever called the girls by name, and no matter how hard we tried, he used to say we were lazy."

A white male agrees and adds, "Male gym teachers pick boys to demonstrate things, and they expect more of boys.

But P.E. is the only class where I've ever seen anything sexist. I've never experienced any sex discrimination myself."

"I've seen it in computer science and math class," another boy volunteers. "Girls aren't pushed to go to higher levels. It's partly the teacher's fault, but a lot of it is peers. Guys say girls can't do these things, so it discourages them."

Two Hispanic boys are sitting together, and one raises his hand. "Usually boys and girls are treated the same, but some teachers seem to joke more when a girl, usually a blond, does something wrong."

"Yeah," the boy next to him agrees. "Sometimes a male teacher will joke with me or other boys about girls being slow to understand technology. I remember once a teacher made a face behind a girl's back while he explained repeatedly how to do something on a computer."

"I've seen those faces," a serious Asian girl says. "In one of my science classes a certain male teacher made rude remarks about my intelligence. He assaulted me verbally, but there are other science teachers—I've only heard of this, I haven't seen it—who favor girls depending on the length of their skirts."

This comment strikes a chord. Several students begin talking at once:

"I know who you mean. I've heard about him."

"No, it's not true. I had him last year, and he never acted like that."

"Well, my best friend had this particular science teacher last year. She didn't understand the material the entire year, but she wore low-cut blouses and escaped the course with a B."

"A lot of people talk about this," a boy volunteers. "If an attractive girl flirts with a male teacher, he'll let her get away with just about anything."

"Those are just rumors," several students call out.

"It is true! It happened to me," another girl says. "In my chemistry class I felt that if I wore a short skirt or a low-cut blouse—low-cut for a fifteen-year-old—I'd get more attention and help. He massaged girls' shoulders while they were taking tests. Believe me, that massage was anything but relaxing. He looked down their blouses and up their skirts. I heard he had to apologize to one girl."

"I really resent these generalizations," another girl says.

"Once a final grade of mine was rounded up to an A. The overwhelming reaction from other students, especially males, was, 'What did you do? Wear a short skirt?' The teacher gave it to me because he knew I was working hard and had come in for tutoring often—not because I'm a girl. I think those short skirt stories are a put-down of my and other girls' intelligence."

Almost everyone in the room has something to say about science teachers and short skirts. But the discussion is becoming a free-for-all, so we intervene and try to paraphrase: "It sounds as though at least some of you think there is a sexist culture here."

"Yes!" "Definitely!" Several girls from the all-female table begin talking at once. "The worst place is the lounge," Betsy, a slight girl with long brown hair, says. "There's usually a group of guys who start talking and making rude comments about girls. I would never go in there alone."

"What do they say?" we ask.

"They usually say things like, 'Go fetch!'" She snaps her fingers. "Get us something to eat. Go fetch a Coke." She snaps her fingers again. "Come do sexual favors for us." She turns beet red but is determined to make her point.

Several boys object: "That's just some guys. Most of us don't act like that."

One boy, the only African-American male in the class, says, "It's mostly people wearing these jerseys." He points to the shirt he and several other boys are wearing that signify they are athletes. "I think it's tough to be a girl here. I don't get to say what I want around certain people. You have to choose your words carefully if you're a minority. And here girls are like a minority."

Another boy, also wearing an athletic jersey, objects. "I think a lot of this is blown out of proportion and there's a double standard. I had a calendar with girls in bathing suits in my locker. I was called a male chauvinist pig. But girls have calendars of guys, and nobody says anything."

Another boy agrees. "You don't dare say anything anymore. You can't even tell a girl she looks good without her getting upset. Girls are so sensitive, and boys are running scared."

A teacher appears at the door. "Where's my geoscience

class? The period ended a few minutes ago. You're supposed to go to your next class."

"Geoscience!" several students groan. "We need to stay here and talk," Betsy protests. "Geoscience is forever. This is going on now."

The class begins to gather their books. A few students exit quickly through the rear door, but most walk up front. A group of girls gathers around us, reluctant to go. There is so much more they want to say. Several boys stand just outside the female circle and listen.

"This guy asked his girlfriend to go fetch a soda," Betsy says. "And she did it. That's what annoyed me most. I asked why. She said, 'He can talk to me that way. He's my boyfriend.'"

"Guys say things but they don't mean them," another girl says. "It's just when they're in a group they show off."

"That's true," another girl says. "I see certain guys that are friends of mine going around pinching girls' behinds. Some girls just laugh, other girls tell them to stop, but no one ever really gets mad. But I know that a lot of the girls do not appreciate the advances. When it happens, I don't do anything because I feel it is ultimately up to the other females to tell them to stop."

"It's just testosterone poisoning. It'll go away when they grow up."

"No, it doesn't. Look at that Tailhook scandal."

"It sure is bad now," a blond girl says. "They say things that make me feel awful."

"What things?" we ask.

Several girls begin talking, clearly upset and angry.

"Get down on your knees and give me a blow job."

"I need sex. Come with me now."

"My balls itch. Come over and scratch them."

"It's a joke, but if you don't brush it off, they'll take you seriously."

"What can you do about the boys who say these things? Is there someone you can go to?"

"Oh, no. We could never tell. They would know it was us. They would make our lives miserable," Betsy says.

The girl standing next to Betsy agrees: "You have to just let it go. Just say, 'Sure,' whatever . . ." She tosses her head as if to show the triviality of the boys' behavior. "But I have a friend who freaked out when those guys said gross things. Now they totally hate her here. She doesn't even want to come to school."

Slowly the students file out, late to geoscience. The last one to leave is a boy from the outer circle. He stands stiffly and awkwardly, looking at us through thick glasses. "I want you to know I would never treat a girl like that. I don't think a lot of boys would. But you have to understand there's a fear of being sexual and a fear of being not sexual. It's a mass of confusion."

As we gather up our books and notes and the essays the students have written, an undergraduate from the university who came with us says, "I didn't know what would happen today, but I never expected this."

"We're shocked, too," we admit. "We expected to talk about textbooks and teaching." As we are about to leave the room, Betsy comes back. She is out of breath, pale, and a little shaken.

"You know that story I told you about the boy who told his girlfriend to fetch and get him things? Well, he heard about what I told you. He and his friends—a group of them—were waiting for me at my next class. They blocked me and said, 'Go fetch, Betsy. Do sexual favors for us, Betsy.' They stood in the hallway in a line in front of me so I couldn't get by."

"That's terrible. What can we do to help?"

"Oh, it doesn't bother me. I just take it as a joke." Betsy manages a faint smile.

"It's not funny, and you look upset."

"Yeah, it kind of hurts. But I can handle it. I have friends who'll help me. Besides, it'll die down. This is Friday. By Monday they'll probably have forgotten all about it. At least I hope so."[22]

In 1980 the Massachusetts State Department of Education conducted the nation's first study of sexual harassment in school. Educators surveyed racially diverse students from urban, suburban, and rural schools across the state. They found that girls experienced sexual harassment in both academic and vocational schools. Ranging from verbal insults to rape, peer harassment was rampant. A 1986 Minnesota survey of predominantly white, middle-class juniors and seniors enrolled in a vocational school found that 33 percent to 60 percent of the girls, but only one out of 130 male students, had experienced sexual harassment.[23] In 1992, conversations with 150 girls and boys in California high and middle schools revealed that almost every student had watched, experienced, or participated in some form of sexual harassment.[24]

"What's happening to you?" the September 1992 issue of *Seventeen* asked its readers. The magazine's survey queried whether secondary school students had been touched, grabbed, pinched, or cornered against their will during the past year and whether they had been subjected to comments, notes, pictures, gestures, jokes, or pressure to do something sexual.[25] According to Nan Stein, director of the Wellesley-based project that analyzed the survey results, thousands of responses poured in from every section of the country and from every racial and ethnic group. She said that letters came in envelopes marked URGENT and PLEASE READ. Typically written on blue-lined notebook paper, they told chilling stories about daily, accepted sexual mistreatment at school: snapping girls' bras, lifting up or pulling down skirts, touching, pinching, poking at girls' bodies with fingers or pencils, comments and jokes about parts of their bodies, bathroom graffiti depicting them in obscene sexual acts. Sometimes the letters described actual physical assault and even rape.

Bernice Sandler, former director of the Project on the Status of Women at the American Association of Colleges, has been investigating the sexual climate in schools for years. Although she began her research in colleges and universities, she is now concerned about what happens in secondary and even elementary schools. "Sexual persecution," she said, "starts at a very early age. In some elementary schools there is skirt flip-up day; in others girls refuse to wear clothes with elastic waistbands because the boys pull down their slacks and skirts. In junior high schools boys tape mirrors to the tops of their shoes so they can look up girls' dresses. Groups of boys in some high schools claim tables near the line where food is purchased. Whenever a female student walks by, they hold up a card with a number on it: one for an unattractive girl and ten for a superstar. In other schools there is 'Grab a Piece of Ass Week' or lists circulate, such as 'The Twenty Sluttiest Girls in School.'"

In 1993 the American Association of University Women published *Hostile Hallways*, a national survey of middle and high school students conducted by Louis Harris and Associates. The conclusion: Harassment is rampant in schools across America, with 81 percent of girls and 76 percent of boys reporting they have been subjected to some form of unwanted sexual behavior. More than two-thirds of students say they have been the target of sexual jokes and gestures, and 11 percent report being asked to do something sexual other than kissing. Sixty-five percent of girls and 42 percent of boys say they have been grabbed, touched, or pinched in a sexual way.

While boys experience unwanted sexual behavior, girls are far more likely to have been harassed repeatedly and at younger ages. Minority girls are especially likely to be targets, with 42 percent of African-Americans and 40 percent of Hispanics reporting sexual harassment by grade six or earlier as compared with 31 percent of white girls. Girls are also far more likely than boys to report feeling embarrassed and upset, self-conscious and scared as a result of the experience. Thirty-three percent of girls and 12 percent of boys were so troubled after being harassed sexually they did not want to talk in class or even go to school.

In a boys' bathroom in Minnesota's Duluth Central High School, vulgar graffiti described sophomore Katy Lyle as having intercourse and oral sex with boys and animals. Anonymous phone calls frequently disturbed Katy's home, and she was tormented by teasing in the school building and on the school bus. When she told the principal, Katy had the feeling he was wondering what she had done to deserve these degrading slurs. Although she had never even had a serious boyfriend, she began to wonder, too. Her behavior changed. She became quiet, withdrawn, and cried often. She dreaded going to school.

When Katy's mother found out what was causing the drastic change in her daughter's behavior, she phoned the school immediately. Eighteen months and fifteen complaints later, the graffiti had not gone away. According to Duluth School District attorney Elizabeth Storaasli, the "graffiti was considered a building maintenance problem at the time." It was only when the Lyles spoke with a representative from the Program for Aid to Victims of Sexual Assault that they realized "building maintenance" was the wrong term. What they were dealing with was sexual harassment. Finally, after a formal complaint was filed with the Minnesota Department of Human Rights, the walls were painted and the ugly words were at last removed. This case was prepared for court and eventually reached a settlement that clarified school sexual harassment policies: Katy was awarded $15,000 for mental anguish, the first time a high school girl received damages for sexual harassment by male students.[26]

Unlike organizations in the workplace, schools rarely distribute and explain their policies to students. And unlike workplace harassment, which is more likely to occur behind closed doors, school harassment is generally in public—in hallways, stairwells, the cafeteria, the gym, on the school bus, and even in classrooms.[27] Part of an escalating climate of inappropriate language, crude behavior, and violence at school, school harassment is also the result of a high school gender gap in attitudes toward sexual coercion. Even more than college males, high school boys are likely to blame the victim for causing rape. These boys believe that "women secretly want to get raped" and "only bad girls get raped."[28] School teachers and administrators rarely intervene because they do not realize the damage done or because they are afraid to confront the perpetrators. So harassment continues, uninterrupted and unchallenged.

While peer-to-peer sexual harassment is most prevalent, occasionally the perpetrators are educators who are supposed to be safeguarding the school.

A high school girl in Maine is the target of daily crude and suggestive remarks by her science teacher. When she complains to her guidance counselor and asks to transfer out of the class, the request is denied. She is told to learn to handle it because it will give her practice in dealing with the real world.

In Indiana teachers watch as a principal makes suggestive remarks to students. He stares directly at the chests of two high school girls. "Are those real," he asks, "or are they Memorex?" When a high school girl asks if she can use this principal's car to transport supplies to another building, as a boy had done the previous day, he responds, "I'll let you use my car, and then you can use me."

In the cafeteria a teacher teases girls about their bodies and their boyfriends. He tickles them and massages their shoulders, sometimes letting his hands brush across their breasts. When they tell the guidance counselor this makes them feel uncomfortable, they are told that the man is just being "friendly" and that the behavior is "harmless."

In Montana a Latin teacher stands by the desk of a high school girl and sways back and forth, rubbing his genitals across her upper arm. Although she complains to the prin-

cipal, nothing is done and she eventually drops the course.
Since there is only one Latin teacher in the high school, she
is no longer able to take Latin.[29]

According to Nan Stein, music teachers, coaches, driver education
teachers, and extracurricular club advisers, those who spend time with
students in private settings, are most likely to become involved in sexual abuse or harassment. These teachers are often extremely popular
with students and sometimes are very skilled at identifying cooperative
victims. One California teacher started the school year with a self-
esteem questionnaire; female students with low scores become candidates for seduction. Of 220,000 teachers in California, 145 lost their
licenses between 1985 and 1990 because of sexual misconduct with
students. It is difficult to get any clear idea of the number of sexually
deviant teachers nationally, however, because most cases never get reported and teaching licenses are rarely revoked.[30]

Proving sexual harassment charges is like walking through a legal
mine field, so superintendents and school boards frequently make
arrangements for accused teachers or administrators to leave quietly.
They ask for a voluntary letter of resignation and offer in return a letter of reference. While this transaction "passes the trash" and rids the
school system of trouble, a mobile molester is created, one who takes
his teaching credentials and his letters of reference to another unsus-
pecting school system. This scenario is almost what happened in the
case of Andrew Hill, a sports coach and economics teacher at North
Gwinnett High School in Gwinnett County, Georgia. But high school
student Christine Franklin didn't allow him to leave quietly. Instead
she took him to court.

In 1986, when Christine Franklin was a high school sophomore,
Hill began to make inappropriate remarks, asking her about her sexual experiences with her boyfriend and whether she would consider
having intercourse with an older man. Three different times he interrupted classes she was attending and requested that she be excused; he
took her to a private office and forced her to have intercourse. Although other students complained to teachers and the principal about
Hill's behavior, the school did not take action. In fact, the school's
bandleader tried to talk Christine out of pursuing the matter because
of negative publicity. Finally, when Hill resigned with the understanding that all charges against him would be dropped, the school closed
its investigation. But Christine persisted and filed for damages in federal court under Title IX, the law which prohibits sex discrimination in

schools that receive federal financial assistance. The case eventually reached the Supreme Court. In February 1992 the Court ruled that compensatory damages were available under Title IX, and this decision should significantly enhance the power of this law.[31]

Girls exhibit the same symptoms as women who are persecuted by sexual harassment: They become withdrawn and fearful, feel intimidated, and may display the physical symptoms of illness. They often transfer out of courses or programs and sometimes drop out of school altogether. But schoolgirls are doubly endangered by harassment. They are at an age of confusion when they are struggling to define their sexual identity. Sexual harassment can stunt and twist their normal development. Without the range of knowledge or experience that comes with maturity, female children are even more powerless and more defenseless than adults. When a student is harassed by peers in public, observers as well as the victim feel threatened and intimidated. All students, those victimized and those who watch, lose faith in grown-ups and in the ability of the school to safeguard and protect them. When the offender is a teacher, counselor, or principal, the betrayal and the trauma are even more devastating.

Body Over Mind

More than a million teenage girls became pregnant every year. The Alan Guttmacher Institute says that approximately 44 percent of all teenage girls in the United States and 63 percent of African-American teenage girls will become pregnant at least once.[32] According to the Children's Defense Fund, in 1989 one of every seventeen females between the ages of fifteen and nineteen gave birth, the highest rate since 1973. The number of fifteen-year-olds with sexual experience increased from 19 percent in 1982 to 27 percent in 1988. And there has been a mind-boggling 33 percent increase in childbearing among those ten to fourteen years old.[33] One-third of teen births in 1970 were to unmarried girls, but that figure has now doubled: A shocking two-thirds of adolescents who became mothers are single parents.[34]

Among girls from different cultural backgrounds, the birth rates vary greatly. In 1989 one of every twenty-one white females and almost one of every nine black females between fifteen and nineteen years of age gave birth. Approximately one in ten Latinos in that age range gave birth, with girls of Mexican and Puerto Rican origin most likely to become mothers.[35]

But no matter the racial or ethnic background of the girl, certain characteristics remain constant: Economic and educational poverty set the stage for adolescent pregnancy. When poor girls who are failing at school look to the future, they do not see positive life options and bright prospects. Living in dire circumstances, they are left with desperate choices. These teens are five to six times more likely to bear children than are the more affluent girls who are succeeding at school.

To learn more about the lives of single adolescent mothers, *Washington Post* reporter Leon Dash moved into Ward 8, the area of Washington, D.C., with the highest rates of poverty and adolescent birth. School officials and counselors in that ward frequently admonished students that getting pregnant would ruin their lives, but since the girls saw their lives as already limited, the warnings had little effect.

Dash found it difficult to uncover the reasons why these girls became mothers. He came away from early interviews with a picture of naive, uninformed youngsters whose cynical boyfriends had taken advantage of them. But after months of interviews, the stories shifted. He learned that some of the girls were more afraid of birth control than of birth. Others bore children because they feared they were infertile. Some saw having babies as a woman's most important role, her primary purpose for being on earth. Others harbored terrifying histories of emotional, physical, and sexual abuse. All their stories had similar patterns of school frustration, failure, and neglect.

Most of these young mothers had enjoyed their early school years, but by the fifth or sixth grade they were in academic trouble and by middle school were trapped in a cycle of failure. Kept back once, twice, even three times, they knew or were told they would not finish high school. Special education services were never provided. Without any hope of academic achievement, dropping out of school was a relief, and motherhood became a rite of passage, an arena where some measure of success became possible.[36]

For eleven months Constance Willard Williams interviewed black unmarried mothers in Massachusetts, thirty girls between the ages of fifteen and eighteen. They had never been told explicitly to become pregnant, but these adolescents were, Williams concluded, "socialized to motherhood."[37] Most of them had been raised by an earlier generation of young single mothers, and most had unmarried sisters, cousins, and friends who were having babies. Many had suffered school failure.

Mae, for example, an eighteen-year-old mother with two children, had hated ninth grade in the Boston high school she called a "zoo." When she got pregnant, "that was just a good old excuse to get out of there," she said.[38]

All thirty of the girls interviewed claimed they had not intended to become pregnant—some denied it even after months of missed periods—but all except one wanted to give birth to and raise their child. Babies were a source of love, someone who would not abandon them. Others identified having a baby as a way to become independent, responsible, grown-up. Almost half of the teenagers chose becoming a mother as the single event that made them feel good about themselves. This role brought them, they felt, the acceptance, credibility, and status that had previously eluded them. Cher, whose mother "spoiled" her by buying things when she was pregnant, said, "When I became pregnant they listened more to what I had to say. 'She's pregnant now, listen to her.' I don't think it really hit me at first, but at the hospital when I had him, I told myself, *wow*, I'm a mother! I was happy; I was excited; I was really totally excited. I was shocked; I was surprised. Like wow, I really have a baby. I just gave birth to a baby!"[39]

In North Carolina, Helen Rauch-Elnekave, a pediatric psychologist, provided emotional and educational help to sixty-four adolescent mothers in a Teens with Tots program. Four of these girls were white and sixty were black; they ranged in age from twelve to seventeen. The average age at first intercourse was thirteen, and fifteen was the average age at first birth.

Through structured interviews Rauch-Elnekave learned their stories. Some told of horrifying abuse. A twelve-year-old had been raped by her mother's boyfriend. A sixteen-year-old mother bore an ear-to-ear scar on her neck where her boyfriend had slit her throat. Some had been so abused that they were left hostile, sullen, and uncommunicative. But others were optimistic: Motherhood provided a niche and gave purpose to their lives.[40]

Like other researchers, Rauch-Elnekave discovered the complexity of motives behind the decisions of these girls. She found that in their subculture becoming an adolescent mother was not an exception but the norm. The more she listened, the more she began to question whether pregnancies were really unintended. In their peer groups many adolescents felt pressure to become pregnant. Three-quarters had unwed teenage friends who had given birth or were pregnant, and although the majority of families were angry or upset, one-third were happy that their daughters were going to have babies. One fourteen-year-old said her mother was so excited that she ran to the phone to tell her friends the good news.

These adolescent girls said in interviews that their favorite subject was math, an atypical choice. Intrigued, the pediatric psychologist traced their standardized test scores from local school systems and found the records for thirty-nine of the girls. The majority were well below grade level in reading and language skills. Despite their school-related deficiencies, which sometimes emerged as early as the second grade, only two had ever received special education services. Rauch-Elnekave tested one adolescent, a shy, quiet girl who lived with her baby, six siblings, and an alcoholic mother in a housing project. Although the girl's academic skills were several years below grade level and she had informed teachers that she could not understand the work, nothing was ever done. When Rauch-Elnekave asked school officials why this girl had never been tested or given special help, the counselor said no teacher or parent had ever asked. Unidentified and untreated learning disabilities causing failure at school could be, Rauch-Elnekave concluded, a hidden but powerful motive for teen pregnancy and birth.[41]

In schools across the nation the learning problems of girls are not identified as often as those of boys, and girls are less likely to receive special education services. Educators and parents have always assumed that more boys are in these special programs because they need an academic boost. Studies now show that girls may be just as desperate for help but are not noticed.

Researchers analyzed standardized test scores in a large sample of students and found only slightly more boys than girls with reading problems, a ratio of 1.2 to 1.0. But when teachers selected children from this sample to enroll in special reading programs, they chose boys two to four times more often than girls. Typically, the boys they referred had behavior problems and were hard to manage in the regular classroom.[42] Nationally, by the time females are diagnosed for special education, they are functioning at a much lower level and are more impaired than boys who receive assistance.[43] The topsy-turvy result is that many males are sent out of the regular classroom for special education they do not need while quieter girls are left to fend for themselves. Too often these quiet girls just give up.

Michelle Fine spent a year observing and interviewing students in a New York City public high school, one that serves predominantly low-income blacks and Hispanics from central Harlem.[44] About six months into her study, new pregnancies became evident in the school. The girls who were going to become mothers held highly traditional notions of what it meant to be female. Fine said those planning to carry the babies to term were not girls "whose bodies, dress, and manner evoked sensuality and experience."[45] Instead, she noticed, they were quiet and passive in their classes. In her research field notes, Fine captured a picture of an eleventh grader, Patricia, who represented these forgotten girls: "She says nothing all day in school. She sits perfectly mute. No need to coerce her into silence. She often wears her coat in class. Sometimes she lays her head on her desk. She never disrupts. Never disobeys. Never speaks. And is never identified as a problem."[46] Two-thirds of the students in the school where Fine observed never made it to graduation. Quiet students like Patricia just slipped through the cracks and disappeared.

While more boys than girls drop out of high school initially, by age twenty-five slightly more males than females have earned their high school degree.[47] Unlike boys who drop out, when girls leave, they rarely return.[48] There are many reasons that girls drop out—academic failure, the need to earn money or to care for siblings at home—but giving birth is the single largest cause. The costs are very high. Nearly three-fourths of adolescent mothers who are seventeen or younger will not finish high school. Without education they have little hope of finding jobs that will support them and their children. In 1990 the average yearly income of a male dropout twenty to twenty-four years of age was only $8,349, but female dropouts earned a measly $3,109. More than 70 percent of single white mothers and more than 80 percent of single black mothers are raising their children in poverty.[49]

Many girls who were ignored in school and had no academic options hope that having a baby will give purpose to their lives. But the adolescent girl is searching for her own personal identity, and this makes it all the more difficult for her to attend to the daily needs of a young child. Understanding less than older mothers about how children are supposed to develop, teenagers talk less to their children and show them less warmth. As their children grow older, they exhibit more behavior and learning problems. By the time their daughters reach adolescence, this next generation of teenage girls is primed to continue the cycle of pregnancy and poverty by becoming single mothers themselves.[50]

The Separate Worlds of High School

For most of the twentieth century an imaginary line sliced through the courses of study offered by the nation's high schools. In this curricular divide, home economics was a female field, preparing girls for their roles as wives and mothers, while shop was reserved for boys. Women today remember when they made baking powder biscuits and sewed aprons in school while their brothers built circuits and made lamps and tie racks. Those who challenged the status quo came up against rules, rejection, and ridicule. A woman from New Jersey remembered what happened when she questioned this gender-divided curriculum:

> In 1952 my friend Nancy and I signed up for woodworking shop. When we arrived the first day of class, we were blocked at the door. "You're just here to meet boys," the teacher told us. The whole class of boys laughed us out of the room.
>
> I took copper craft instead. Although I was allowed to stay in that class, the teacher humiliated me at every opportunity. I still feel embarrassed whenever I remember being sent to the closet to look for elbow grease while the male teacher laughed. I still have the copper candy dish I made in that class. I keep it as a reminder.

While official policy rarely barred girls from mathematics and science, many educators actively counseled girls not to take these courses. A math teacher from Ohio told this memory of high school days:

> In 1962 I switched to a new high school. Since it was the middle of the summer, there were no counselors in the building and my new principal helped me with registration. I wanted to sign up for physics, but the principal would not allow it. His comment was that a girl had no need for physics.
>
> Today I am a secondary math teacher. I never took college physics because, without high school physics as a background, I did not feel prepared. There was only one girl in my high school graduating class who took physics. Her *father* had interceded.

When girls gained access to "male" courses, they often encountered blatant hostility and discrimination that spilled over into the classroom. Another woman, also a math teacher today, recalled this experience:

Here's how my 1960s high school chemistry class was taught: Boys were seated by the male teacher on the side of the room with the teacher's desk. Girls were seated on the far side of the room. Girls were told to be quiet and not cause trouble and they would not fail the class. When "dangerous" experiments were conducted, the boys went into the lab while the girls watched through the windows.

Women considered incapable of learning math and science when they were girls, written off by both teachers and parents, bear the scars even today, remnants of blatantly sexist schooling. In every section of the country, wherever we give workshops, we hear their stories. A college administrator in Maine remembered her own experience:

Your workshop brought back memories I had suppressed for years. I had a male ninth-grade algebra teacher who didn't care whether girls learned math. I received an A in the course but learned precious little. As a tenth grader I landed in a geometry course with another male teacher who felt girls didn't need math, so he didn't work very hard at teaching us. As the course went on I became more and more confused, and my grades began to show it. Until then I had been a straight-A student. I was so upset that at least once a week I had to excuse myself from the class. Week after week I ran straight for the girls' room and threw up. No one ever noticed or helped.

Today I hold a master's degree, but I never took math again. For me math class was so hard, it made me sick.

Male Courses—Male Careers

Today gender lines guarding male domains—mathematics, science, computer technology, athletics, and vocational education—are vanishing, but harmful remnants remain. "Math class is tough," said the new Teen Talk Barbie, in modern-day echo of the frustrations many women felt as schoolgirls thirty and forty years ago. After interviewing thousands of children, Mattel selected 270 sayings that reflected how girls feel, and they put those words in the mouth of the 1992 Barbie, the first one to talk since the 1970s. Each one of the hundreds of thousands of dolls in toy stores said four things selected from this pool of 270 comments.

The national flap over Barbie's "Math class is tough" faux pas is a symptom of the inroads females have forged in this formerly male preserve. *The Washington Post* dubbed the doll "Foot-in-Mouth Barbie," and the American Association of University Women warned that this was precisely the kind of role model girls did not need.[51] Math teachers around the country registered their dismay. "We've been working so hard at closing the gender gap and fighting math anxiety for girls," an Illinois teacher told us. "This is the last thing we need." When we talked with the college administrator in Maine, the woman who had spent tenth grade throwing up over math, her reaction was thoughtful: "Math class is tough, but Barbie shouldn't admit it unless Ken does, too. [He doesn't.] We can always look on the bright side." She paused and laughed. "At least Barbie doesn't say, 'Math makes me vomit.'"

Girls are now learning the lesson that math matters, and the imaginary line once dissecting the curriculum is fainter, more permeable— but still there. Boys and girls take almost the same number of mathematics courses, including algebra and geometry, but then their roads diverge, with more boys studying calculus and more girls dropping out.

While girls are staying with math longer, it is often a matter of endurance without enjoyment. More anxious and less confident about their math ability, girls perceive the subject as cold, impersonal, and with little clear application to their lives or to society. While math has a masculine aura for both genders, boys especially view the subject as very male. Those girls who agree are more likely to fail.[52]

When computer technology joined the school curriculum, the subject found a home in math departments, and computers became part of the landscape of the male domain. Through out-of-school experience, boys learn to connect with computers. Boys more than girls go to computer summer camps, especially the more expensive ones for older students. At home a father typically teaches computing, and he usually spends more time with his son, taking care to link computers with future careers. In a study of students who had not received computer instruction in school, more than 60 percent of boys but only 18 percent of girls had a computer at home. And when boys and girls play computer games, for education or recreation, they manipulate mainly male figures in adventures involving technology, sports, and war.

These lessons learned outside school shape in-class performance. Boys are more aggressive when it comes to grabbing space at a classroom computer, and they often fail to share with girl classmates. They are the ones who monopolize the spaces in the school's computer room at lunch and before and after school, and they take more computer courses in high school and college. When boys study computers, they learn to program. When girls study computers, it is often for word processing.

"While there is no sign on the computer room door announcing NO GIRLS ALLOWED," says Jo Sanders, coauthor of *The Neuter Computer*, "females place it there mentally themselves." After years of watching the male-computer connection, girls feel they don't belong. But when parents and teachers make special efforts to involve female students, they find converts. "Subtlety does not work," says Sanders. "You have to transmit the message loud and clear that girls and computers belong together." She advocates organizing girls' computer committees and clubs and scheduling special times for girls to use the computer room. In schools where Sanders and her colleagues have intervened, female computer use has skyrocketed, sometimes surpassing that of boys.[53]

For more than four decades researchers have been asking students to "draw a scientist." In the 1950s high school students uniformly saw a scientist as a middle-aged or older man wearing glasses and a white coat and working alone in a lab. Forty years later, little had changed. In the most recent "draw-a-scientist" study, 100 percent of the boys and 84 percent of the girls are still drawing men. Students attribute to scientists an additional set of characteristics—weird, sinister, crazy, nerdy—the very images adolescent girls, worried about appearance and popularity, want to avoid at all costs.

In middle school, boys claim science for their own while girls regard it as a neutral. But by high school both girls and boys agree that science has moved out of the neutral zone. Of all the subjects on the curricular landscape, physical science is the most male of all.

As with computers, boys are prepared to enter this male domain before they even arrive at school. From their earliest years they play more with toys that call for tinkering and exploring. They are more likely to make something out of junk, read science articles and books, talk about science with a friend, and have a science-related hobby.

By the time they take advanced courses in high school, boys and girls enroll along a gender divide, with females electing advanced biology and males choosing physics and advanced chemistry. A 1991 survey by the Council of Chief State School Officers reported that in first-year physics 60 percent of the students are male. Male enrollment is 70 percent in second-year physics. When girls look inside science classrooms, they see male teachers as well as students; less than one-quarter of high school science classes are instructed by women.

As girls go through high school, most become estranged from subject matter they see as alien. These girls participate less in science class, allow boys to take over the lab equipment, and watch male students conduct scientific demonstrations. As in the case of math, they do not understand the usefulness of science to society or to themselves. Many girls say that science makes them feel stupid.[54]

Teachers and researchers are finding that simple changes can make a world of difference. Girls become more sure of themselves when they are allowed to read about and experiment at home before discussing and doing a demonstration in class; this technique puts them on an even footing and lets them catch up with science lessons that males have learned outside school. Collaborative work and "interest enhancers" (puzzles, and mystery and fantasy devices) also involve girls. When teachers bring women who work as scientists into the classroom, the impact is powerful and shows girls that science also belongs to them. And when teachers humanize science, showing that it is relevant and accessible, boys like it better, too.[55]

Although constructive teaching strategies are now available, sexist instruction still predominates. Gail Jones and Jack Wheatley analyzed thirty physical science and thirty chemistry classes, a total of 1,332 students. They found that boys spoke more often and in louder, more confident tones. In contrast, girls received less praise and appeared to be "self-conscious and quiet." Sometimes sexism is more blatant. After investigating eighty-six classrooms in twenty-one independent schools, University of Michigan researchers found that coeducational physical science classrooms were the locus of the most sexist teaching. For example, in one class a male teacher was describing an experiment involving liquids. He talked mainly to the boys. When a girl in the front row asked for information on using the graduated cylinder, the teacher ignored her. She repeated her question. Clearly impatient, the teacher threw the water in the graduated cylinder at the girl while the primarily male classroom laughed. Later the teacher told the researcher that "girls weren't suited to 'do' science."[56]

A more subtle form of discrimination occurs when teachers or counselors kill with kindness. A Massachusetts guidance counselor told of math teachers, usually male, who seemed genuinely worried about girls' ability to handle the stress of advanced courses. But their proposed solutions were destructive. Her latest encounter was with a math teacher who said, "Things get intense in my class. I can't have girls getting all upset, emotional, and run-down. Do they really need this class?"

Sometimes it is counselors who harm when they mean to help. Feeling sorry for girls who find their math and science courses difficult, they literally excuse them, a dismissal less likely to be offered to male students. There is a cost in taking the easy way out, but high school girls don't realize it until later. A woman now in her early twenties remembered feeling relieved when her high school guidance counselor agreed to get her out of math and science. Today she knows enough to be sorry:

> I consider myself an educated person with a college degree in journalism. But I have never taken physics, chemistry, or mathematics beyond trigonometry. I didn't like those courses, and my guidance counselor said it was okay not to take them because I wouldn't need them. During college I was still able to "beat the system" because basic math and science met requirements for graduation. Today I am so embarrassed. I am ignorant of the elements of the earth and the mathematical principles that most people assume I know.

The majority of females who took the 1990 Scholastic Aptitude Test said they planned to work in the social sciences. In large numbers they turned away from careers in the physical and computer sciences and in engineering. When girls self-select out of math, science, and computer technology, they are making decisions that will affect the rest of their lives. Without the right high school courses, science courses in college are out of reach; and without college courses, females are filtered out of careers that remain overwhelmingly and solidly male.[57]

In high school the career connection is also made through sports. School athletics has a long history of helping boys build stamina, courage, leadership, loyalty to the team, self-confidence, and the drive to win. Educators also recognize sports as a vehicle for shaping boys into the men who will lead society. What benefits boys is good for girls, too—the building of character, career skills, and self-esteem. But historically females have been barred from sports; until very recently they were taught in segregated classes with poorer equipment and fewer resources.

Since the passage of Title IX in 1972 through the 1990s, girls' participation in interscholastic sports increased from 300,000 to 1.8 million, and the involvement of college women expanded by almost 600 percent. Despite extraordinary strides, the participation of boys in school sports remains almost twice that of girls. When schools stop to analyze the situation, they find entrenched financial disparities. The school system of Montgomery County, Maryland, is one of the few that has investigated these disparities. According to its 1992 study, $900,000 is spent on girls in major sports compared to $1.6 million on boys.

An ironic casualty of Title IX is the female coach, an important but vanishing role model for girls. As male and female athletic departments merged, coaches of girls' teams began to receive more money, more men were hired. In 1970 more than 90 percent of girls' teams were coached by women. By the middle of the 1980s, only 17 percent of coaches were female.[58]

But the voices of today's students and teachers tell of more than missing female leadership. They describe high school gyms and playing fields that remain mainly male:

> A rural school district in Wisconsin still has the practice of having cheerleaders (all girls, of course) clean the mats for the wrestling team before each meet. They are called "Mat Maidens."

> In my tenth-grade physical education class, a male physical educator teaches football. At the beginning of the six-week period, he separates the class into girls and guys. (Officially he is not supposed to, but he does it anyway.) He teaches the same skills—passing, running, receiving—to everyone, but the girls use a Nerf football and the guys have a real football. When we come to the end of the six weeks, the girls are still working on skills using the Nerf football, but the guys are playing real games using a real football.

> I went to school in the late 1980s. I never got to play a base during four years of high school physical education. The boys relegated the girls to the outfield because they said we made mistakes and the team wouldn't win. I think P.E. class was the most gender biased in high school.

> In 1992 our school district scheduled "Boys' Night Out" with a program featuring speeches by a player from the University of Wisconsin–Green Bay Phoenix Basketball Team. I called the school to ask if this was really only for boys, and

the response was "No girls will be turned away if they are really interested in basketball." I was also informed that girls had their own night out—featuring makeup, hair, and fashions.

In our local high school, boys' sports teams receive much more attention and money from the school system, the student body, booster clubs, and the community. The boys' baseball team members get shoes and jackets each year and play on the best-maintained grounds. I was on the girls' softball team. We received no clothes and nobody took care of our fields. Cheerleaders did not cheer for us. We were a good team, but when we played, the bleachers were mostly empty.

Nowhere is the link between what students study in high school and where they work after graduation more direct than in vocational education. While there are pockets of change in states such as Kentucky, this field is still stuck in stereotypes. Enrollment figures tell part of the story. According to the U.S. Department of Education, girls outnumber boys in home economics, health, and the clerical and secretarial side of business. Boys outnumber girls in agriculture, trade and industry, and technical fields.[59]

The woman who saved the copper candy dish to remind her of being ousted from wood shop also has shelves and an apron. The shelves were built by her daughter, and the apron was sewn by her son in middle school. "They are symbols of a changing time," she observed.

But in these changing times many attitudes are still unchanged. Vocational educators around the country have told us about the struggles of girls in nontraditional fields, and a high school student, originally from Vietnam, told the following story:

> I took a full-year shop class in high school. I was the only girl in the class, that is, the only girl by the end of the year. There was another girl at the beginning, but the two of us were— well, I wouldn't exactly say harassed, but it's true. After just a few days the other girl transferred out of the course. I'm quite stubborn, so I stayed in the course the entire year. The boys literally pushed me around, right into tables and chairs. They pulled my hair, made sexual comments, touched me, told sexist jokes. And the thing was that I was better in the shop class than almost any guy. This only caused the boys to get more aggressive and troublesome.

After a while I got past the breaking point, and I started fighting back. When they tried to shove me, I bumped them and sent them crashing. But eventually this got me an extremely bad reputation for being a bitch (pardon my term). Throughout the entire year no teacher or administrator ever stopped the boys from behaving this way.

Composing Herself

In *Writing a Woman's Life*, Carolyn Heilbrun observes:

> It is a hard thing to make up stories to live by. We can only retell and live by the stories we have read or heard. We live our lives through texts. They may be read or chanted, or experienced electronically or come to us like the murmurings of our mothers, telling us what conventions demand. Whatever their form or medium, these stories have formed us all; they are what we must use to make new fictions, new narratives.[60]

High school boys have many narratives to choose from, but the library of stories about girls contains a limited number of volumes. We decided to see the impact of this omission by trying out our elementary school challenge with older students.

"You have five minutes," we tell the history class of high school seniors. "Your challenge is to name twenty famous U.S. women from the past or present—no sports figures, no entertainers, and only presidents' wives who are famous in their own right. Do you think you can do it?"

The class stares back at us as if we have insulted their intelligence. As honor students in a competitive high school, several have already passed advanced placement history tests. "It's not as easy as it sounds," we warn.

"Oh, c'mon. It's a cinch," a boy in the front mutters.

"Do we get anything if we win?" another asks.

"How about putting up a prize?" an African-American

boy jokes. "Give a prize, and I'll name as many as you want."

"I'm ready," says a girl from the middle of the room. "Start timing."

At first the students write quickly, but after a minute or two several are squirming in their seats and looking around at one another self-consciously.

"I can't believe I can't do this," a girl whispers loudly. "This is so embarrassing."

"Time's up," we announce. "Please put your pencils down. How many of you have listed twenty women?" Not a single hand goes up. "Nineteen?" Still no hands. "Eighteen? Seventeen? Sixteen?" At this point a single Asian-American girl comes forward and at our request reads her list: "Eleanor Roosevelt, Harriet Tubman, Betsy Ross," she begins.

"I've got them," several students call out. "I could only think of three, and she just named them," a girl admits.

"Geraldine Ferraro."

"Oooh," several students groan. "We forgot about her."

"Emily Dickinson, Zora Neale Hurston."

"Authors! Do authors count?" A student in the back is exasperated. "I could've gotten a lot more if I had thought of authors."

"Why do you think you had so much trouble naming women?" we ask after the girl has finished her list.

"Women didn't do anything," a boy says.

"Nothing?" we probe.

"Cooking." "Cleaning." "Having babies." Boys call out from around the room. One male student offers the following definitive statement: "From the dawn of human times to almost the present day women have been irrelevant in history. They have been on the sidelines. Except for the suffrage movement they haven't done anything. I don't mean to upset people, it just happens to be the truth." But the comment is upsetting. "What do you expect?" one girl retorts. "There was discrimination. Women lived in men's shadows."

"Look around the classroom," we suggest. On one wall hangs a large picture of all the presidents. Another poster, about the signing of the Constitution, features a roomful of white men in colonial garb. There is a battle scene in front of the room, again all male. We recommend that the students count the figures; they find more than three hundred males but only eleven women. Pocahontas, Harriet Tubman, and Sojourner Truth are on display as "Multicultural Heroes." The remaining eight are on a current events bulletin board where a newspaper clipping shows women becoming more involved in politics.

The students are surprised. They had not been aware of the disparity.

A girl in the back of the room who hasn't said anything yet raises her hand. "But did women really do anything worthwhile? I mean, like Mark says, maybe we were irrelevant."

The comment is honest, and the class waits for our response. It is a question we have heard before, and therefore we have brought material with us: On the teacher's desk we display books about the lives of girls and women, and on the chalk tray leaning against the board are biographies of outstanding women. As the students help us mount the posters of women that we have brought, a girl whose parents are from India comes up to us. "I'm very glad to know this," she says, speaking softly, barely above a whisper. "I hardly know any famous women, and it makes me feel bad, as though I can't do anything. I like science, but this is the first time I've seen books about women scientists. Can I please borrow the book about Barbara McClintock? I want to learn more."

We have offered this challenge about famous women to hundreds of students in high schools around the country. We can count on the fingers of one hand the number who have been able to meet it. On average, students can list only four or five women from the entire history of the nation. Sometimes we opened the playing field to the history of the world. Even then, few students were able to name twenty women or fifteen or even ten. Omission of half of humanity leads not only to ignorance but to boredom and apathy as well. A study of 1,174 students from three junior high schools and four high schools revealed that fewer girls than boys cite social studies as their favorite subject. More girls than boys say it is the course they like least of all.[61]

Students know little about women because their books tell them little. There are more than a thousand pages in Prentice-Hall's 1992 *A History of the United States* by Daniel Boorstin and Brooks Mather Kelley. The history of the nation unfolds against a backdrop of illustrations with four males for every female. Less than 3 percent of that history is about women. Only eight women in these thousand pages have as many as twenty-five lines (about a paragraph or two) written about them: Abigail Adams, Jane Addams, Rachel Carson, Dorothea Dix, Eleanor Roosevelt, and Harriet Beecher Stowe. The remaining two women in this history of the United States—Queen Elizabeth and Queen Isabella—are European. As though in defiance of the laws of biology, founding fathers gave birth to our nation.[62]

In Addison-Wesley's *World History: Traditions and New Directions*, five times more men than women are pictured. Another large volume, this 1991 review of the world offers approximately 2 percent of its attention to women. The index lists 596 men and 41 women, only four of whom are American: Ida Tarbell, Susan B. Anthony, Elizabeth Cady Stanton, and Gertrude Stein. Susan B. Anthony and Elizabeth Cady Stanton are mentioned together in a single sentence. Altogether, American women are covered in less than one page of this 819-page book.[63]

At first glance we did not realize this history book's staggering gender tilt because we were fooled by the "cosmetic factor." The text includes fifteen very visible half-page boxes called "Spotlight on People." Eight of these boxes spotlight men, and the other seven, women. A committee that selects textbooks might easily be blinded by the spotlight and miss the main show: the massive omission of half the human race.

When one of our graduate students called Addison-Wesley to ask why women were left out of the history of the world, the representative was courteous but puzzled. She referred to Addison-Wesley's policy of inclusiveness and said that since the book was not a social history, the authors had no choice but to record events as they occurred. But our student pressed the point and offered examples: In a section on electoral reform in England, eight sentences discussed the extension of suffrage to most adult men, but the struggle for women's voting rights was taken care of with the following sentence: "Women, however, did not win the right to vote until 1918." Concerned, the representative said she would "check into" the problem.

History is not the only subject area that ignores women. Recent studies of music texts indicate that almost 70 percent of music-related figures are male. When women appear in the text, they are singing or playing the piccolo, the maracas, or the flute. Men play a variety of instruments: saxophone, trombone, trumpet, bassoon, clarinet, double bass, and others. They also conduct groups of musicians.[64]

Science is a special problem. One study compared chemistry texts currently in use with those published during the early 1970s. Only two of the seven books that were analyzed showed improvement; on several measures, the remaining books actually got worse. Another recent study of five new science texts reveals that from two-thirds to three-quarters of drawings are of males. Not one of the five books analyzed included a drawing of a female scientist. All of the books used body outlines to show the position of organs within the body; in four of the books, all the outlines were of the male body. The message is powerful: The male body is the norm.[65]

Books read in school are all the more important because their stories do not remain anchored on the page. They take on life when they become topics for discussion. Figures from a history book can stimulate a classroom controversy, as a high school sophomore described to us:

> Just yesterday in class I was in this discussion group and we were talking about King Ferdinand and Queen Isabella, and one guy asked who was more powerful, the king or the queen. I, being the only female in the group, said "Queen Isabella." Even though King Ferdinand didn't do much, they said he dominated because he was the man. There I was trying to argue my point against three guys who think a woman's place is in the kitchen. Then—I don't know how it happened—but we got off on this tangent. They brought up things about teenage pregnancy and said it was all our fault for not being protected. They began to say mean things about girls and to call them disgusting names, and those things hurt.

When New Zealand researcher Adrienne Alton Lee studied the impact of the curriculum, she discovered the subtle ways stories about men insinuated themselves into the hearts and minds of schoolchildren, causing them to devalue women. Observing a unit about cultural differences in New York City, she gathered a systematic record of how a curriculum that focused overwhelmingly on males eventually became embedded in the thought processes of students. She found that girls and women were only 2.4 percent of the total number of people mentioned by the students or the teacher in the classroom. The teacher described men such as Henry Hudson and Peter Stuyvesant as bold and fearless. On the few occasions when women were mentioned, they were demeaned. For example, in a discussion about jobs in New York City, one of the few career paths suggested for women was prostitution.

During interviews with students, Alton Lee detected insidious and disturbing patterns: Students had no knowledge about women and no mental images of them, either. When the teacher or text used a supposedly generic term such as "mankind" to refer to all people, the students pictured males. And even when the teacher or the text talked about "people," the children, both boys and girls, still saw only men. In fact, females often identified with males. When Mia, a bright and independent girl, talked about the early settlement of New York, she made a "leap of gender" and saw herself as a male settler. She was not conscious of this identification with males until the interviewer pointed it out:

> MIA: Indians came before . . . and you sort of think of them being first there because they're before us.
> INTERVIEWER: And do you feel, when you say *us*, do you mean that the people who came to settle New York after the Indians were people like us?
> MIA: Mm. Mm. (Nods.)
> INTERVIEWER: How were they like us?
> MIA: Well, they didn't wear, um, war paint and carry weapons around. They just sort of had— They wore clothes like us, sort of (laugh) civilized clothes.
> INTERVIEWER: When you say *us*, do you think of women or men?
> MIA: I think of men, really. . . . Yeah, that's right! *I only think of the men.* I don't think of the women.[66]

A girl who is struggling to hold on to her bold dreams of what she can achieve in life after high school will find little to inspire her in the school curriculum. If she cannot empathize with the women she studies, she is left to deny the experience of being female, to submerge part of herself, to bury her story, and like Mia, "only think of the men."

"Am I Just Imagining Things?"

Girls who resist the ever-tightening constraints of gender, who want to claim all of the curriculum, and who try not to deny their intelligence are the most hurt and bewildered of all. The value of their own experience is stolen so insidiously, they are not sure how or even *if* it is actually happening. While many are aware of isolated events that threaten or offend, these incidents are like tiny pieces of a large puzzle that cannot be comprehended until it has been completely assembled. We meet these girls in every high school we visit, and we listen to their stories and questions:

> I have a teacher I respect so much because he is smart. When he asks a question, he challenges my mind. I thought he would respect my intelligence, too, but he calls me the class "model" and says things like, "What music are you listening to? Is there a short circuit up there?" It's like he's trying to make me think I'm an airhead.

> In my science class the teacher never calls on me, and I feel like I don't exist. The other night I had a dream that I vanished.

> People are always surprised to learn I have a 4.0 and I'm a National Merit Finalist. Their image of me is "that *blond* girl who used to go out with Scott." Why can't they understand there's more to me?

> I had just learned I got into Stanford. Instead of congratulating me, several boys began to tease me. They said, "In California, 90 percent of the girls are pretty. The other 10 percent go to Stanford." They were just kidding around, but since I'm not very attractive, the way they did it hurt.

> I have teachers who behave as if I'm an ornament and less able to achieve than guys. They don't seem to take girls seriously, and they treat us in a semimocking way. Is how I look more important than how I think?

> It seems to me teachers treat girls in one of two ways. They either ignore them and choose to interact with boys, or they treat girls as sex objects by being especially nice to the ones they find attractive. I think this hurts all girls emotionally.

> I have a teacher who calls me "airhead" and "ditz." I used to think I was smart, but now I don't know. Maybe I'm not. What if he's right? The more he treats me like an airhead, the more I think maybe I am.

As these girls, the bright women of tomorrow, are taught to devalue themselves, they also begin to doubt the validity of their senses, the very reality of their own experience. "You mean there's evidence that teachers treat boys and girls differently?" Westinghouse Talent Search

Winner Ashley Reiter asked us when she learned about our research. "I thought something was going on in my classes, but I wasn't sure. I began to wonder, 'Is this really happening, or am I just imagining things?' Thank God there's proof!"

Denied their history, discouraged from taking crucial courses that lead to key careers, concluding that the appearance of their bodies may be worth more than the quality of their minds, realizing they are not the gender of choice, and doubting their intelligence and ability, high school girls make the journey from adolescence to womanhood. They pay a steep price for their passage.

6
Test Dive

From middle school to medical school, girls and women face a testing gender gap that denies them the best educational programs and prizes. Lower test scores block females in disproportionate numbers from the finest colleges and the most prestigious graduate schools and professions. This gender gap is especially startling because of the early advantage girls hold, but around middle school their scores begin a steady decline. It is one of the costliest falls suffered in education, yet few people notice. Females are the only group in America to begin school testing ahead and leave having fallen behind. That this dive has received so little national attention is a powerful reminder of the persistence and pervasiveness of sexism in school.

The only test where the female drop-off has received publicity is the Scholastic Aptitude Test (SAT), recently renamed the Scholastic Assessment Test, which is required for admission to most colleges. On this critical exam, boys typically receive scores that are 50 to 60 points higher. In fact, this gender gap is so predictable it has become an accepted feature of the educational landscape. Few people talk about the SAT gender gap; fewer still are angry or upset. We cannot help but wonder if the reaction would be different if females were in the SAT driver's seat, and males watched as their college choices vanished in a trail of dust left by high-scoring young women.

As we investigated these testing troubles, we discovered it is far more than an SAT issue. Critical tests at every level of education short-circuit girls and women. The more we researched, the more concerned we became. We were surprised by what we found, but unlocking the information was not easy.

When we requested male and female scores from the companies that produce America's tests, we struck a bureaucratic wall. While a few companies were cooperative, others demanded detailed, written explanations of our intentions. We felt as if we were violating some official government secrets act. Some companies claimed they kept no record of test scores by gender, while others stated flat out that they had the information but would not release it. The persistence of our graduate students, who tenaciously refused to be put off by outright refusal or evasive answers, and the cooperation of organizations such as FairTest in Cambridge, Massachusetts, were critical to uncovering the information presented in this chapter.

Reversal of Fortune

Five-year-old Jessica came home from kindergarten smiling broadly, eager to share her latest achievements. Her mother, an attorney, was curious:

"What did you do in school today?"

"I learned to bubble."

"You blew bubbles? Did you have fun?"

"I didn't blow bubbles. I bubbled. I practiced filling in the little test bubbles with my pencil. You know, not going outside the lines and coloring in the whole bubble."

Jessica attends a school in Washington, D.C., but her lesson could have been in almost any school in America. The typical student, in Jessica's terms, bubbles three times every year. Some students undergo as many as twelve standardized tests annually, and each year more states require still more tests—enough to support a billion-dollar-a-year industry.

When standardized test scores from schools around the country are collected and analyzed, they provide a national picture of American education, one that brings into focus academic success and failure. This school portrait reveals the extraordinary reversal of fortune experienced by many girls and women as their initially promising test scores falter and tumble.

Among the nation's many test "photographers," one of the best known is the National Assessment of Educational Progress. Often called the "Nation's Report Card," the NAEP has been taking academic snapshots of America's students since 1969. Funded by the federal government, the National Assessment tests nine-, thirteen-, and seventeen-year-olds in several different subjects. Unlike the SAT exam, which develops academic pictures of only the college-bound, the National Assessment offers information on a sample of all students during elementary, middle, and senior high school. It is through this and other national tests that we learn how well girls begin their school careers and what happens with each year's promotion to a new grade.

Girls begin school looking like the favored sex. They outperform boys on almost every measure. Most people are aware of their verbal advantage and their reading and writing skills. Fewer realize that in these early years girls also surpass boys on math and social studies tests; in fact, they surpass boys on every standardized test in every academic area except science, where boys hold a slight advantage. If tests offer the nation a school photograph, they depict elementary school girls as capable and looking toward a promising future.[1]

Female test scores begin to descend around middle school when the girls are overtaken by the boys. Girls' test scores continue their downward slide throughout the rest of their education. In science, the small lead enjoyed by elementary school boys widens in middle school and is further expanded in high school. The longer girls stay in school, the further behind they fall, especially in the critical areas of mathematics and science.[2]

The National Assessment of Educational Progress displays a familiar school picture, one with a commonly accepted gender divide: boys overtaking girls in math and increasing their superiority in science, and girls maintaining an advantage in reading and writing.[3] But not all tests draw this widely accepted division. In fact, the most important tests paint a much more depressing portrait.

In October of their junior year, college-bound students take a scaled-down version of the SAT called the Preliminary Scholastic Assessment Test, or PSAT. This test also gives students an opportunity to win college scholarships. The results of the PSAT are used to select winners of the prestigious National Merit Scholarships, and many states and colleges also use PSAT scores in awarding scholarships of their own. For example, a student from Maryland who scores well on the PSAT will find tuition to any Maryland college or university reduced by $3,000. So high scores on this test can be both a boost for a student's self-esteem and an economic windfall.

Modeled on the SAT, the PSAT serves as an early indicator of the winners and losers in the great SAT contest soon to follow. The test is similar to the SAT, with both math and verbal questions, but it is much shorter. Timing is vital for success on both the PSAT and the SAT. Students have only a minute or less to spend on each question. They must move quickly to attain a strong score.

The PSAT is the first national peek into the future. For girls it is a frightening preview. Boys score so much higher than girls on the PSAT that two out of three Merit semifinalists are male. PSAT results are like a fire bell in the night, and the developer of the test, the Educational Testing Service (ETS), knows it. ETS tackles this disturbing problem head-on; it rigs the scoring in an attempt to reduce the gender gap. ETS counts the PSAT verbal score twice and the math score only once. By giving twice the weight to verbal performance, traditionally an area of female strength, ETS officially recognizes the impact of gender-based scoring differences. All this effort still does not result in equal male and female performance. While eighteen thousand boys reach the highest PSAT categories, only eight thousand girls attain them. (See Figure 1.)

Doubling verbal scores reduces but does not eliminate the gender gap because boys outscore girls on *both* the verbal and the math sections of the PSAT. Without this adjustment, the dramatic male lead in mathematics would create an even greater difference. But the PSAT is only the opening act. The main event—the SAT—is only a few months away.[4]

Handicappers would have to spot girls about 60 points to make the

FIGURE 1

Number of males and females scoring in the top categories on the 1991 PSAT

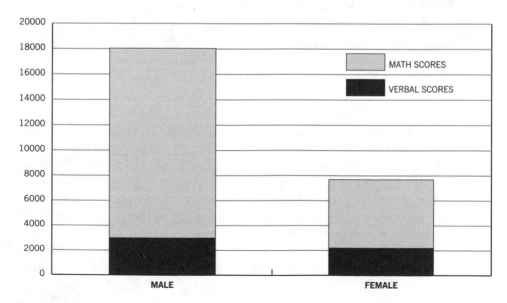

SAT an even bet. Most Americans are not surprised to learn that males typically outscore females by approximately 50 points on the math section. The fact that boys also surpass girls on the verbal section is less well known. Actually, males' verbal SAT scores add another 8, 10, or 12 points to their overall testing lead. In the public mind the smaller male lead on the verbal section has become misconstrued as a female advantage. It's not. The SAT is a clean male sweep, one for which the lower-scoring girls pay dearly.

The SAT is one of life's memorable markers. Twenty or thirty years after the SAT scores arrive in the mail and the envelope is opened, people recall the wave of pain or joy or bewilderment the information brought. Test scores label students, put a value on intellect, classify brain power, expose the unseeable—just how smart someone really is or isn't. Most believe these test scores are a truer reflection of their real intelligence than report card grades.

Boys looking into the SAT mirror see in it an image bigger than life. Girls see less than is really there. After taking the SAT, they may wonder if their excellent school grades were given for hard work rather than real intelligence. Or perhaps their higher grades were only the teacher's "thank you" for their quiet, cooperative behavior. After all, report card grades are just the teacher's opinion. The SAT, on the other hand, is objective, scientific, national. Girls are persuaded by the impressive SAT printout that compares them to a million of their peers that the scores are tangible proof of their worst fear: They really aren't as smart as they had hoped. They begin to think that maybe they don't deserve to get into that selective college after all.

The SATs send an even more devastating message to minority girls. With the exception of Asian-American test takers, minority students do not perform as well on the SATs as white students, a fact as well known as it is troubling. Less well known is that within each racial or ethnic group, minority girls consistently score behind minority boys. For example, girls whose families are originally from Asia, Mexico, or Puerto Rico score approximately 50 points lower than boys from these areas. Girls of Latin American origin face the largest gap on the SAT: Boys score an average of 62 points higher. For Native Americans the gender gap is 46 points, and for African-Americans the gap is narrowest at 19 points. Regardless of ethnic or racial background, all American girls share a common bond: a gender gap in test performance that leaves them behind the boys.

Although the SAT receives the most publicity, it is not the only college admission test. In many areas, especially the Midwest, more than a million students take the American College Testing Program, the ACT. This test is described not as an aptitude measure but as an assessment of academic achievement. It evaluates students in four areas: English, mathematics, the natural sciences, and reading. To create questions directly measuring what students learn in school, ACT test makers analyze textbooks and interview teachers. Since girls attain better grades in class work, many anticipate that they should achieve similar success on the ACT.

Girls do perform better on the ACT than on the SAT. They score almost a full point higher than boys on the English section of the ACT, but on the rest of the test, boys are ahead, from a small lead in reading to more than one full point on both the math and science sections. Even on a test designed to mirror school learning, boys' composite scores are higher and the gender gap persists.

While almost all college-bound students engage in an academic duel with either the SAT or the ACT, a smaller group confronts an additional challenge, the achievement tests. Unlike the SATs, these one-hour, multiple-choice exams gauge not general aptitude but academic accomplishment in more than a dozen subject areas, from mathematics to science, from foreign language to history. The most selective colleges and universities require students to take three achievement tests along with the SAT. One would expect that girls would do better on these tests, which, like the ACT, are based on class work. They don't.

The achievement tests are a male landslide. In 1992 boys registered higher scores on eleven of the fourteen achievement tests. Girls performed better on only three. While boys typically overshadowed girls by more than 30 points, the girls averaged only 4 points higher on the three tests. In 1992 the largest gender gap was in physics (62 points), but the year before it had been in European history (60 points). In fact, males led in almost all fields: the sciences, social sciences, math, and even most languages. Boys averaged 46 points higher in chemistry and 33 points higher in biology. On the two math achievement tests, the size of the gender gap was consistent: 37 points in Math I and 38 points in Math II. In American history the gap was 25 points; in Latin, 28; in French, 12; in Hebrew, 8; and in Spanish, 3. (See Figure 2a.) Girls were in the driver's seat on only three tests: German (3 points), English composition (3 points), and literature (6 points).

When the achievement test results arrived in our office, we began recording the scores and graphing the gender gap. One of our graduate students, a young woman from England, watched with growing amazement as the bar graph emerged. Soon a cluster of graduate students, all female, gathered to watch as the size of each gender gap was recorded. "This is unbelievable," whispered one. The others nodded silently, at last realizing why their own scores had not lived up to expectations. The size of the gender gap on achievement tests was shocking new information even to students studying for graduate and doctoral degrees.

After students are admitted to colleges, the importance of tests is not diminished. College and university women realize that standardized tests hold the key—or shut the door—to graduate programs, professional schools, future careers, and economic prospects. In these times of runaway college grade inflation, graduate schools have learned to accept extraordinarily high grade point averages with a great deal of skepticism, relying on standardized tests to assist graduate admission and scholarship decisions.

The test most often required for entrance to graduate and doctoral programs is the Graduate Record Examination, or GRE, an older sibling of the SAT and one that bears a remarkable family resemblance. The GRE has three sections: verbal, quantitative, and analytical. As in the SAT, 200 is the lowest possible score and 800 is perfect. And as in the SAT, on all sections women score lower than men.

FIGURE 2a

Gender Gap: Male Point Advantage on 1992 Achievement Scores

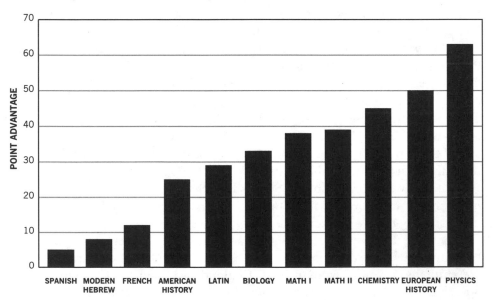

As test takers grow older, the gender gap grows wider. In 1987–88, the last year the Educational Testing Service published information on GRE scores, males scored a jolting 80 points higher than females on the quantitative math section, a substantially larger advantage than they enjoyed on the SATs. Men scored 21 points higher than women on the verbal section and 26 points higher on the analytical section. Although the SAT gender gap is substantial, the 127-point male lead on the GRE is larger still. And as on the SAT, there are performance differences among racial and ethnic groups. As of 1988 most minorities continued to score below the GRE average, a gap ranging from 200 to more than 500 points. The one exception was Asian-Pacific Americans; their total score was only slightly below the average, but their math score was the highest of any group. Within each of these racial and ethnic groups, males continued to outperform females. For whites, Native Americans, as well as students from Mexican and Puerto Rican backgrounds, males enjoyed more than a 100-point advantage. Smaller gender gaps were registered by African-Americans (79 points) and Asian-Pacific Americans (59 points).

The size of the gender gap on the GREs was a shock, and it made us even more curious to see the scores on the GRE subject area tests.

FIGURE 2b

Gender Gap: Female Point Advantage on 1992 Achievement Scores

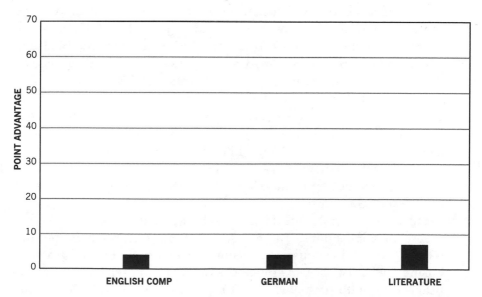

Like the SAT achievements, the GRE offers in-depth assessments in subjects from sociology to engineering, from geology to literature, and these tests are required for admission to many graduate programs. Did the gender gap on the SAT achievements reappear in the GRE subject fields, or perhaps even increase? We can only speculate. Although we made several requests, we were not allowed to see these scores.

Persuading testing companies to release scores posed a constant challenge. The last reported results for the basic GRE were in 1988, and we therefore requested more recent scores for this exam. After repeated phone calls, we were finally allowed to listen over the phone to a summary of more recent GRE test scores but only if we agreed not to publish them. We are honor-bound not to print what we heard, but the information we received did not make us optimistic about options for women.

Standardized tests are also crucial in the competitive race for access to professional schools, including law, medicine, and business. Only a few points on these tests can mean the difference between acceptance and rejection, scholarships and a future of debt. These professional tests differ in content and approach, but they share a common thread: Women score lower than men on all of them.

As law has become a popular professional choice, college graduates flock in increasing numbers to testing sites for the Law School Admission Test (LSAT). The LSAT measures logical and analytical reasoning, reading comprehension, and writing. Although there is no separate math section, there is a gender gap. The LSAT has been scored on a scale from 10 to 48. In 1991 men averaged 33.3 and women 32.4, typical of the modest but persistent male advantage on this exam. Like so many standardized tests, the LSAT is out of step with the grades that men and women receive in college. A man with a C average in college registered a 29 on the LSAT, while a woman with the same C average attained only 25.7. A man with an A– grade point average typically scored 38.8, while the A– woman's score was 37.1. At every level, when women and men earned the same grade point average, the female applicant to law school had her chances diminished by a lower LSAT score.

During the past decade, business schools have also seen a hefty increase in applications. The Graduate Management Admission Test (GMAT) is used in admission decisions by almost a thousand graduate business schools. The GMAT includes reading comprehension, English usage, and math problems, and it reports scores on a scale ranging from 200 to 800, with 500 the average. In 1991 women were below the midpoint, averaging 477, while men were above, at 504.

The most challenging graduate-level exam is the Medical College Admission Test (MCAT), which runs from 8:30 A.M. to 5:00 P.M. The $140 admission fee buys 221 questions in verbal reasoning, physical sciences, biological sciences, and writing skills. Although most of the questions are multiple choice, two thirty-minute essays are also required. On a scale ranging from 3 to 45, the typical female score is 22.5 while the average male score is more than 24. In the fight for limited medical school openings, especially at the most prestigious schools, each point is critical. The MCAT, the LSAT, and in fact the vast majority of these tests act as unseen trip wires, making women stumble just as they are about to cross the threshold into America's elite and lucrative professions.

While writing this chapter, we often found ourselves wishing there was a Consumer's Guide to Tests, one that would inform the public about the gender gap. There isn't, but it is possible to make some comparisons. To do this we obtained the last year of available test scores (1987–88 for the GREs, 1991 and 1992 for all others) and converted

FIGURE 3

Gender Gap: Male Percent Advantage on Graduate School Admission Tests

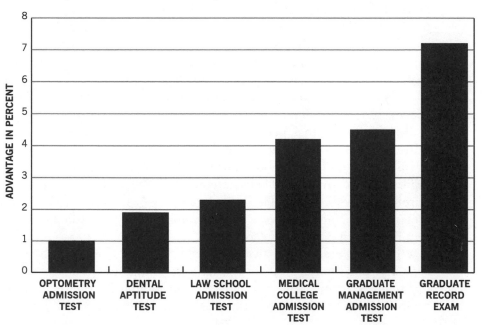

these scores into percentages. Comparing these percentages enables us to measure the size of the gender gap on each test. (See Figure 3.) Women who apply to graduate and doctoral programs using the GRE face the greatest test obstacle, while women applying to optometry school score only slightly below male applicants. Women striving for admission to America's most advanced or competitive graduate and professional programs continue to be harmed by the gender gap in standardized testing. In many ways it is gifted girls and women who are hurt the most.

Visible Ceiling

The test ceiling first materializes in preadolescence when talented girls compete for a limited number of openings in special summer programs for the gifted. Tests are often the tollgate to these elite programs. In New Jersey's selective summer enrichment program in science and social science, PSAT scores determine who will be admitted and who will be denied. It is not unusual to have sixty-five boys but only thirty-five girls chosen to participate. Johns Hopkins University's prestigious Center for Talented Youth (CTY) selects participants based on SAT scores earned by fifth, sixth, and seventh graders. At every level more males than females pass the admission test. In 1992 a total of 5,882 males but only 4,612 females qualified. Ironically, many of these programs offer classes on how to improve test scores, lessons that high-scoring boys have already mastered.[5]

But if failure brings penalty, success is suspect. When girls are admitted to elite programs and schools, their achievement is questioned, trivialized, and dismissed. One girl who was accepted to a top magnet high school for math and science confided: "When I got in here, the parents of boys who didn't make it were very upset with me. They said, 'You got in because you were part of a quota. They had to have a certain number of girls so they took you.'"

When scholarships are awarded, girls are once again sent the message they don't belong, this time with a price tag attached. More than one hundred scholarship programs rely on standardized tests to select recipients. Few are more prestigious than the National Merit Scholarship Program, which awards over eighty-five hundred college scholarships based on PSAT scores. There is a temptation to rename these winning students National Magnet Scholars since they attract interest and dollars from so many colleges.

Although we already knew that girls do less well on both the PSAT and the SAT, we were interested in learning how many girls were admitted to the magic circle of National Merit Semifinalists. The National Merit Corporation in Evanston was pleased to tell us that more than fifteen thousand students annually make the semifinalist round, and about half of them win scholarships. We learned that the National Merit Board awards two thousand of these scholarships, and the rest come from corporate and college sponsors. What we did not learn was how many girls qualified. When we asked how many girls and boys were identified as semifinalists, we were transferred to another office. Then another office. Then a third office. Finally, the public information office told us that they didn't have that information, but we persisted. After all, every test contains a box that the student checks to indicate male or female; in the stressful world of standardized testing, this may be one of the few questions most students answer with confidence.

"Don't you ask students to indicate their gender?" we asked.

"Well, yes," the information officer responded, "but we don't use that information. The College Board does in New York. Perhaps they can help you."

The College Board, awash in statistics, was also stumped by our question. "We really aren't equipped to do research here. All that information is in Princeton at the Educational Testing Service."

The people at ETS were friendly and acknowledged that they did have gender information: "Colleges buy our mailing lists to send out recruitment information. They ask for the sex of each applicant so that they can properly address their recruitment letters. But we really don't track how well males and females do in qualifying for the National Merit awards. We do publish the names of the finalists, so you could count how many males and females there are."

"But there are over fifteen thousand names each year. That's a lot to count."

"Yes, I know. And some of the foreign names are difficult to sort out. Sorry."

Our next call was to FairTest, the Cambridge, Massachusetts, organization that tracks test statistics, numbers that seem to elude the test makers.

"You were rubberwalled," said Bob Schaffer of FairTest. "They redirect your calls from one place to another, bouncing you from office to office until you tire out and give up. Of course they have that information. They just hide it. I have the numbers here. Last year girls did the best in a long time, with about thirty-seven percent becoming semifinalists. Typically, boys win at least sixty percent of the semifinalist slots. There're always a few percent unaccounted for. They have that information, they just run you into walls made of rubber instead of stone."[6]

High test scores unlock scholarship dollars at 85 percent of the private colleges and nearly 90 percent of public institutions, and they can result in state grants as well. In Wisconsin, for example, scores on the SAT or ACT exams as well as grade point averages are used to select All-State Academic Scholars. More than a hundred students receive $1,500 scholarships each year based on their grades and test scores. Even with grades thrown into the mix, the majority of Wisconsin winners, from 60 percent to 65 percent, are male. Actually, the inequity is really more extreme than it appears since boys make up only 35 percent to 40 percent of the students nominated by teachers for these awards. FairTest and others charge that such results, which are not atypical, prove test bias.[7] Not everyone is ready to blame the exams, but as more people learn about the inequitable distribution of scholarship dollars, opposition is growing to the practice of using standardized tests to decide who will win awards. New York State is a case in point.

New York offers an impressive twenty-six thousand academic scholarships each year. In 1988, using SAT and ACT scores, New York awarded 72 percent of its Empire State Scholarships and 57 percent of its Regents Scholarships to boys. The American Civil Liberties Union and others charged that this method of awarding scholarships was discriminatory, and federal judge John Walker agreed, writing: "SAT scores capture a student's academic achievement no more than a student's yearbook photograph captures the full image of her experiences in high school."[8] This decision legally limiting the use of standardized tests for scholarship awards is likely to spark other court cases in other states. While the legal process runs its course, boys will continue to garner the lion's share of scholarships, and girls will continue to lose out.

Scholarship dollars provide a tangible ledger sheet of the cost paid by girls and women because of the gender gap in standardized tests.[9] Less tangible but perhaps even more damaging is the psychological price. Low scores are mentally locked away, rarely revealed. A woman in one of our graduate courses finally gained enough confidence in her academic ability to share her SAT secret with her classmates:

I took the PSAT when I was a sophomore in high school. I scored a 710 combined. My parents had always been proud of how bright I was—until those scores arrived. They never thought I was smart again.

I remember I had a date that weekend with a boy I really liked. He asked me what I got on the PSAT. I told him 710, and he said, "That's great! What did you get on the math?" I was so humiliated, I made up a score.

Poor test performance can be hidden from others but not from the test takers themselves. A low score is a lifelong brand, a never-ending reminder of intellectual weakness; it is a stop sign, quietly directing students away from prestigious programs and demanding careers and steering them instead on a path of lower expectations and fewer choices. It is a path more likely to be traveled by gifted and competent women.

Students who remember SAT scores with the greatest pain are the girls at the top of the class. A high school girl with an A+ grade point average typically scores 83 points lower than a boy with an A+ average. The more talented and competent the girl, the greater the gender gap. Perhaps that is why test results hit smart girls like a bombshell. Lower-than-expected scores direct girls away from the highly selective colleges, and later on they are an obstacle to elite graduate and professional schools.

Donna, a woman who attended one of our workshops in New England, wrote about her experience with tests and how this rerouting process takes place:

Ever since I can remember, I wanted to be a lawyer. In high school I joined the prelaw club, and in college I was president of the law and government society. I worked hard in college, and my grades were very good. I felt so lucky. Half my friends didn't know what they wanted to be, while I felt I always knew.

But deep down I had a fear. My SAT scores were not good, and by my second semester in college I had already started to worry about the LSATs.

I first took the LSAT as a junior. It was a disaster. I convinced myself that my score would rise when I retook the test as a senior, but I was still very nervous. I pulled out all the stops. I took dozens of practice tests as well as the Stanley Kaplan preparation program, and I studied all the time.

But it wasn't like my courses in college where if I worked hard enough I could succeed. The more I studied, the more terrified I became. On the day of the test I was the first one there, more than an hour early. That only made it worse. I went to the ladies' room, looked in the mirror, and realized I had rushed so much I hadn't even washed all the shampoo out of my hair. That was a bad sign.

My LSATs never improved. My grades were good enough to get me into law school, but my LSAT was bad enough to keep me out of the top schools and eventually the top jobs. The LSAT didn't stop me from becoming a lawyer—I wanted it too much. But I know the test slowed me down and hurt my career. I work as hard as it takes, and I'm sure I could compete with the best students in the best law schools. I just never had the chance.

Like Donna, many women have personal stories of how tests altered their lives. They are bewildered and sometimes resentful. When they went through school, they did what good girls were supposed to: They followed the rules, were conscientious about their studies, finished their homework, and received good grades. Then the standardized test score knocked the wind out of their plans. They attended less prestigious schools, abandoned hopes for a scholarship, decided against further education, and even gave up career goals completely.[10]

Invisible Scores

Despite the enormous cost of the testing gender gap, most people don't even know it exists. The *USA Today* headline on August 27, 1992, read: SAT SCORES SHOW SIGNS OF RECOVERY, a story echoed in hundreds of the nation's newspapers. The upbeat accounts reported that the average SAT verbal score had increased 1 point since 1991, while the average math score had improved 2 points. Optimistic news stories portrayed the 3-point gain as a milestone on the road to educational recovery. Local papers touted neighborhood high schools' SAT averages as if they were sports scores. Most articles lamented the continuing poor performance of minority students, and a few even turned to the past, recalling that between 1969 and 1991 SAT scores nationally had tumbled 60 points. The 1992 upturn, a modest 3 points, might signal the end of this national embarrassment.

The source of these stories was a twenty-one-page news release issued by the sponsors of the SAT. In this news release were analyses of scoring differences between urban and rural, and majority and minority students; there was no discussion of the gender gap.[11] But tucked in the end of the report was a chart of male and female scores which revealed that since 1969 boys' scores had dropped a substantial 50 points while girls' scores had skidded a whopping 65. The chart also disclosed that in 1992 girls trailed boys by 52 points. This information was not picked up by the media, however; the gender gap was a nonstory in newspapers across the country.

Hidden from public view, this gender gap has evolved into a major educational mystery. Girls enter school with a standardized testing advantage, yet their lead mysteriously vanishes. Girls are winners on report cards and later on college transcripts, yet the boys attain higher scores on the standardized tests. Why the contradiction?

Designing Tests

"The tests are biased!" critics charge, an accusation fueled by the somewhat shady history of test development. Standardized tests were not widely used until World War I, when the army found itself inundated with new recruits. To sort and categorize this immense number of soldiers, the army turned to the new profession of psychology and produced the Army Mental Test. This test was destined to play an important role in college admissions because in a few short years it was reborn as the nation's first SAT.

It was not college that motivated the army to measure intelligence but the need to match soldiers with appropriate jobs. Unfortunately, the Army Mental Test was so culturally biased that upper- or middle-class white, native-born Americans won all the intelligence points— and all the good jobs. The passage of time has made these questions as alien to us today as they must have appeared to the immigrants who tried unsuccessfully to answer them seventy-five years ago:[12]

| The Percheron is a kind of | goat | horse |
| | cow | sheep |

"There's a reason" is an "ad" for a	drink flour	revolver cleanser
The number of a Kaffir's legs is	two six	four eight
The Pierce Arrow car is made in	Buffalo Toledo	Detroit Flint
Five hundred is played with	rackets cards	pins dice

Test results confirmed the popular prejudice of the day: Certain races and groups were bright, and others were less intelligent. In fact, the father of the Army Mental Test, Carl Campbell Brigham, believed that Americans of Nordic ancestry were genetically brighter than others and as one traveled south through Europe, intelligence levels dropped off. According to Brigham, by the time Africa was reached, the intellectual gene pool had just about run dry. Brigham's insights extended to Jews, whose intelligence he concluded was highly exaggerated. He viewed the arrival of Africans as "the most sinister development in the history of the continent." Brigham wrote, "The really important steps are those looking toward the prevention of the continued propagation of defective strains in the present population."[13]

After the war, Brigham took his views to Princeton where he became a professor. He might never have been heard from again if it had not been for the trouble at Columbia University. Early in the century almost half of the students attending public school in New York City were children of immigrants, many of them Eastern European Jews. By 1915 a substantial portion of those students had found their way to the door of Columbia University, and the Ivy League school felt besieged, trapped by its own geography. The dean feared that the refugee scholars might frighten away Columbia's typical undergraduates— polished students from "homes of refinement." Could heaven rescue Columbia from this alien threat?

Heaven sent a savior in the form of a new admissions test, a more effective filter to weed out immigrants. Reenter Professor Brigham of Princeton, who fashioned the Scholastic Aptitude Test from his experience developing the culturally biased Army Mental Test. Not surprisingly, immigrant applicants performed miserably on the SAT, and far fewer were admitted to Columbia. As the "old" Columbia reemerged, Harvard, Yale, Princeton, and others also came to rely on the new test for "discriminating" admissions. Although the College Board and the

Educational Testing Service are quick to disown the prejudices of their founder, today's test critics use this history of prejudice to fuel their contemporary suspicions and concerns.

The Educational Testing Service maintains that today's SAT is a far cry from the past and in fact helps colleges evaluate applicants more fairly. Since high schools across the country differ in difficulty, SATs are needed to unmask school inequalities. They offer colleges a common yardstick to measure applicants and help to determine if an A average at one school is equivalent to an A average at another. The SATs also give some students (those with a low grade point average) a second chance to show they can do college work. Used this way, the test can be viewed as a force for fairness.

But critics claim that the ghost of Professor Brigham still haunts the exam. While today's SATs have eliminated the blatant discrimination of the past, the charge is that subtle bias endures. After all, the primary purpose of the SAT is to predict how well high school applicants will perform in college courses, a task the test does not do very well. Each year the SAT misleads with an optimistic forecast of future male performance in college and an underprediction of the grades to be earned by women. As we have seen, high school boys and girls receiving the same grades in the same courses do not have the same SAT scores. The female scores are typically 30 to 40 points lower. In short, the SAT overpredicts the college performance of male high school students while the potential of high school females is underestimated and devalued.

Critics blame sophisticated test biases for this underprediction.[14] For example, boys answer more questions correctly when these include male characters; girls achieve more on questions with female characters or an equal number of males and females. While many SAT questions do not include people, those that do are more likely to represent the male world. For example, a recent group of SAT reading comprehension questions mentioned forty-two men but only three women. One of the three was anthropologist Margaret Mead, whose research was criticized throughout the passage.

Even themes and topics can be more "male friendly," and this affects scores, as the reaction of a gifted high school girl shows:

> On the PSAT, the question that was supposed to be easiest on the analogies was a comparison between football and a gridiron. I had no idea what a gridiron was. It shook me that this was supposed to be the easiest question, and I had trouble concentrating on the rest of the test.

Males excel not only on questions dealing with sports but also on test items about measurement, money, science, dates, and wars. Girls surpass boys when the questions concern personal relationships, aesthetics, civil rights, women's rights, abstract concepts, and topics traditionally thought to interest women. For example, on recent SAT exams, boys were more successful on analogies about finance and war—choice (C) in the first question and (B) in the second:[15]

Dividends : Stockholders
  (A) investments : corporations
  (B) purchases : customers
  (C) royalties : authors
  (D) taxes : workers
  (E) mortgages : homeowners
Mercenary : Soldier
  (A) censor : author
  (B) hack : writer
  (C) agent : performer
  (D) fraud : artist
  (E) critic : soldier

But girls scored better when the questions related to aesthetics—choice (D) in the first question and (B) in the second:

Pendant : Jewelry
  (A) frame : picture
  (B) cue : drama
  (C) violin : music
  (D) mobile : structure
  (E) poetry : prose
Sheen: (Select the antonym)
  (A) uneven in length
  (B) dull finish
  (C) strong flavor
  (D) narrow margin
  (E) simple shape

Phyllis Rosser, a leading SAT critic, is convinced that the road to scoring equality is paved with questions that avoid gender imbalance. She says, "Standardized tests would be much fairer if items girls do poorly on were eliminated or revised. If boys were scoring lower, they would waste no time rewriting the test."[16] Most test developers claim they are already hard at work filtering out questions likely to be friendlier to one gender than the other. But critics claim that more male items penetrate this filter and remain on the exam.[17] And some educators and test designers reject the whole idea of rewriting questions to expunge themes or references related to gender. Marcia Linn of Berkeley warns that the process of purging offensive words and themes could reduce questions to the lowest common context, one of bland and neutered words and people.[18]

While critics and test makers debate the problem of bias in question content, some studies show that even if the words are right, the format is wrong. The very approach and design of standardized tests favors males. Boys do better on multiple choice questions, the kind used on standardized tests. But girls perform best on essay questions, more difficult and time-consuming to grade and rarely found on these exams. Also, boys perform better in the beat-the-clock pressure cooker created by timed tests such as the SAT, while girls are more likely to succeed when the test is not timed.[19]

At the center of all this controversy, test producers maintain that their exams are fair, accurate, and improving. ETS is revising the SAT, but critics who have seen revision samples say there is far more similarity than difference. The major change in the verbal section is the replacement of antonym questions with more sentence completions and reading passages. On the math section more than 80 percent of the items will be identical, but there will be some opportunity for students to write in their own answers instead of always selecting from multiple choice options. FairTest calls the planned alterations "trivial."[20] In fact, the clearest change may be in name only. Dropping "aptitude" because the term implies innate, unchanging ability, the exam's new name is Scholastic Assessment Test. The one-hour achievement tests are also being renamed "SAT-II." The only change in those tests is a more frequently administered writing component in the English composition test.

Overall, even the ETS doubts that improved tests will dramatically alter the gender gap because the gap is not a function of the test but a function of the different educational experiences boys and girls receive. For example, boys still take more high school mathematics and science courses, and this imbalance contributes to higher male test scores. More girls than boys now take college admission tests, which means that less-qualified girls are now taking the test and lowering the average score of all females. And virtually every test company has a review panel to expunge biased words and problems. ETS suggests that the lower female scores are not a sign of test unfairness but rather the signal of a real educational problem. From the point of view of ETS, test critics are misguided; they are attacking the messenger because they do not like the message.[21]

Grade Inflation

While girls are behind boys on standardized tests that measure achievement, females are ahead when it comes to report card grades. This paradox is one of education's most persistent puzzles. In our search for answers, one of our visits was to a Virginia high school.

"Do you think there is any favoritism in the way teachers evaluate and grade boys and girls?" we ask the students.

This question hits a raw nerve, and several boys are ready to tell their stories. A seventeen-year-old senior says: "In my organic chemistry class, the girls are definitely graded easier than the boys. Last week the teacher returned a lab report with low grades, and some girls were upset and practically in tears. He let them go back and redo it again, and they got the points back. When boys get mad, they get confrontational. I would never have been able to get those points back from my organic chemistry teacher. I think that teachers will bend and cater to the sensitivities of females."

"I agree," another male student says, getting into the discussion. "I think that boys get more attention in class, but they also get checked more closely. When a male and a female student slack off, grading is tougher on the guy."

A tenth-grade Asian-American girl says, "I have found that teachers will help girls and tell them the answer. If boys don't know the answer, they will be made to solve it themselves."

Ben, sitting in the back row, raises his hand, then says: "That's right. It happened again last week in calculus. I was working on a problem, and I asked the teacher for help. He said, 'You can handle this. Figure it out yourself.' Then a girl asked for help on the same problem. The teacher went over to her desk, took her pencil, set up the problem for her, started the computations, and then let her do the last step. And I was still sitting there trying to figure it out."

"That made you angry?"

"I was burned. I struggled with that problem and never did get the right answer. And that girl not only got help but she got credit for getting it right. She ended up with a higher grade."

"Who got the better education," we ask, "you or that girl?"

Ben looks startled. This is a new angle on his story, and he takes his time thinking about it. A little less sure but still concerned that he is a victim, Ben responds, "Maybe I did end up learning more about how to do the problem—but my grade sure didn't show it."

Ben still felt the injustice in his situation, but now he had a new view of the problem: The higher grade awarded to the girl had a price tag, and the teacher's favoritism may not have been a favor after all. As the short-circuited student, the one who had the work done for her instead of doing it herself, she learned less.

School counselors and teachers are familiar with the classroom compromises made by girls. A former high school mathematics teacher and college counselor at a prestigious all-girls school outside Washington, D.C., reported that in 1992 twenty-one of the sixty-seven seniors at her school received National Merit recognition. This is the largest percentage of test success enjoyed by girls in any high school in America.

"Looking at the entering scores of those students, you would not anticipate that one in three would graduate with national honors," she said. "They entered as good students, but they graduated as the best. The difference is that we don't trade passivity for good grades. We expect our students to take calculus and physics and computer science. We expect them to participate actively in class discussion, to take tough courses, and to do well."

But this school is the exception. Most teachers face classes filled with both boys and girls vying for the teacher's attention. In the whirlwind pace of classroom interaction, the good behavior of girls can be a lifesaver tossed to the teacher. Without their active cooperation, classroom dynamics might spin out of control. Many teachers share this fear, and they often return the favor by giving well-behaved girls special consideration. Researchers report that teachers evaluate cooperative girls as more intelligent than others, and they give them higher report card grades. While many boys have discovered the secret to higher standardized test scores, good girls have broken the code for better classroom grades.[22]

Good grades for good behavior is a compromise worked out in the earliest school years. Linda Grant observed elementary school teachers in midwestern and southern classrooms. Over the course of several years she concentrated on how teachers evaluated girls, and she found they measured female students by blending good behavior with academic achievement. Here's what the teachers in her study said about their high-achieving white female students—the ones they rewarded with the best grades.

> I knew about an hour after the year began that [Clarissa] was going to be a top student. She does everything neatly and on time and obeys rules and sets a good example. She reads beautifully, gets along with everybody.

> I have no doubt that [Sheila] will stay in [gifted track classes]. She's always careful and cooperative. She works very hard and is equally strong in reading and math. Pleasant. All the students like her. All the teachers, too.

But Audra was a different story. Although compliance and competence were still connected, it was not a positive association:

> All I can say is that it's good we're living in an era of women's lib. She wants to be a broncobuster, can you imagine that? She wears jeans all the time—always too big—and her hair's a mess. I don't think I could get a comb through it even if she would stand still long enough for me to try. I just don't know what will become of her. On top of everything else, she never seems to listen to what I say.[23]

Author and teacher Raphaela Best has suggested that many girls enter school socialized for docility. Elementary teachers rely on that cadre of dependable female citizens to orient new students, handle chores, and even help the teacher manage discipline problems. "If they talk," one teacher instructed her newly assigned female monitor, "give them one warning, then send them back to their desks."[24] One of our graduate students remembered being sent to the back of the room to sit with the misbehaving boys. "I was devastated," she said, "until the teacher explained that this wasn't for punishment but to quiet the bad boys." In many classrooms female students are made exemplars of appropriate academic and social behavior. And when report cards are sent home, girls are rewarded for their meritorious service.

The Bubble Bursts

"She gets unbelievable grades," the proud parents exclaimed, unaware that the A's may be most unbelievable to the girl receiving them. When grades and standardized test scores diverge and part company, girls reject the validity of grades, which are likely to be higher, and believe test scores, which are likely to be lower, as the true measure of intelligence.

Self-doubt afflicts even the most intellectually talented young women. Karen Arnold studied students graduating at the top of their class. For the past decade she has tracked high school valedictorians and salutatorians, forty-six women and thirty-five men selected from schools throughout Illinois. When these students graduated, they reported equal estimations of their own intelligence. But by their sophomore year of college the women had lowered their opinions of their own intellect while the men had not. By the time these top students were college seniors, not a single female valedictorian still thought her intelligence was "far above average" even though most were planning to enter graduate and professional schools. But 23 percent of the male valedictorians still put themselves in this top category. Although the women continued to earn high grades in college—slightly higher than the men, in fact—they saw themselves as less competent.[25]

Fewer women than men in this valedictorian study found their way into prestigious professions. In increasing numbers they abandoned careers in science, mathematics, and medicine. A decade of interviews reveals that even top-graded high school women harbor deep-rooted questions about their intellectual ability, and this uncertainty affects their future.

These academic superstars did not lower their self-assessments and aspirations until college, but many girls hesitate and falter much earlier. When Lyn Mikel Brown and Carol Gilligan interviewed girls at the Laurel School, they discovered that as early as age ten, female students were questioning themselves and relinquishing their opinions.[26] At about the same age that Brown and Gilligan were hearing the "I don't know" refrain in interviews, the National Assessment of Educational Progress exam in science was recording the very same female response. Unlike most multiple choice tests where students must select the one correct response from several possibilities, this test also offered the unusual opportunity of choosing "I don't know." Filling in the oval for "I don't know" was the only obviously incorrect choice. After all, a lucky guess gave students full credit while "I don't know" was hopeless, equivalent to raising a white flag and surrendering. Girls more than boys selected "I don't know" and abandoned any chance of getting credit for the question. Although the process for responding was a bit different on this test, the outcome was the same: Girls scored lower than boys.[27]

Only a few short years before the National Assessments, there is not even a hint of the dive girls are about to take. Female students sail into elementary school with great expectations. Their scores on standardized tests confirm their confidence. Like Jessica at the beginning of this chapter, young girls are pleased at their ability to "bubble," and they are even more satisfied with the test results bubbles bring. But by upper-elementary school, standardized tests, especially in math and science, may find Jessica choosing incorrect responses or neatly filling in the bubble for "I don't know."

Bubbles usually ascend, but as girls grow older, their test bubbles pull them down, lowering their self-esteem and educational horizons. When Jessica sets off for college, she will take more than her suitcase and stereo; she will also carry with her the extra burden of self-doubt.

7

Higher Education: Colder by Degrees

Like tourists in a foreign country, the small group obediently trailed behind their guide and listened to the history of the land. They asked questions about everyday life, food, housing, and recreation. But this tour was not a vacation and the foreign culture was not Europe, Africa, or Asia; it was a college campus in the United States.

In the competition for a dwindling supply of students, colleges market themselves aggressively with videotapes, personal phone calls, and the ubiquitous campus tour. Along with information about distinguished faculty and successful graduates, each student guide also spices the tour with college lore: "On this spot John F. Kennedy gave his famous speech calling for nuclear disarmament." "British soldiers occupied this building during the revolution." "The statue of John Harvard [or Nathan Hale at Yale] is actually an actor posing. We don't know what he really looked like." Most of the guide's anecdotes concern men because the arrival of women on campus is a relatively recent event. In fact, many of the women who attended college since World War II still remember their own struggle for fair treatment:

> During the 1940s I applied for admission to the University of Wisconsin. I never thought I would run into a problem because I had been a good student in high school. A professor told me that my application was incomplete because I had failed to include a letter from my husband giving me permission to attend classes. When I complained to the admissions office that I didn't think a twenty-six-year-old woman needed permission to attend class, they said that requiring permission letters from husbands was a good policy.
>
> In 1968 my friend Mary and I were education majors at the

University of Florida. One evening Mary had to do some research on a legal question for one of her education courses. She returned from the law school library in tears. "What happened?" I asked. She told me that when she walked through the library, all the men sitting at tables shuffled their feet loudly. Laughing, they continued to stomp and shuffle until she left, humiliated. "Mary," I said, "didn't you know that girls aren't supposed to go into the law school library? Whenever a girl enters, it's a tradition for the guys to shuffle their feet until she goes away."

I registered for a calculus course my first year at DePauw. Even twenty years ago I was not timid, so on the very first day I raised my hand and asked a question. I still have a vivid memory of the professor rolling his eyes, hitting his head with his hand in frustration, and announcing to everyone, "Why do they expect me to teach calculus to girls?" I never asked another question. Several weeks later I went to a football game, but I had forgotten to bring my ID. My calculus professor was at the gate checking IDs, so I went up to him and said, "I forgot my ID but you know me, I'm in your class." He looked right at me and said, "I don't remember you in my class." I couldn't believe that someone who changed my life and whom I remember to this day didn't even recognize me.

Patricia Ireland, president of the National Organization for Women, is the student who dropped out of calculus at DePauw. To this day she regrets abandoning her studies in mathematics. What Ireland and other women learned the hard way was that although they paid the same tuition, the college world they lived in was different from the one attended by their male classmates.

The Divided Campus

Graduation day is a family milestone, official recognition of full and active partnership in the American Dream. Parents crowd the bookstore to buy sweatshirts and baseball caps emblazoned with school insignia. Even the car shows its colors with a college decal affixed to the window, proclaiming to all the world previous accomplishments and future promise. Amid all this celebration it is easy to forget that little more than a century ago higher education was mainly a man's world.

In the late 1800s college was the place to be for rich young men; it was a source of social polish and a rollicking good time. Informal sporting events and athletic competitions were harbingers of today's lucrative college football and basketball seasons. Fraternities created a world without adult rules, a haven for males in their late teens and early twenties who drank, gambled, and talked about loose women. While a few focused on academics, most worked at fitting in and getting along, the marks of a successful student. In the vernacular of the 1800s, working to win the approval of the professor by class participation was ridiculed as "sticking your neck out" or "fishing." Cheaters were shielded by fraternities and secret societies, and peer loyalty was the measure of integrity.[1]

The first women to enter this male-ordered campus were venturing into unmapped terrain. True pioneers who defied conventions to settle in hostile territory, they were not greeted with open arms or the hospitality accorded welcome guests. At the University of Michigan after the Civil War, women could not join the campus newspaper or college yearbook staffs. Michigaum, the prestigious honor society, closed its doors to females and kept the portals shut throughout the century. Cornell's response to the newcomers was undisguised disgust, and the school excluded them from clubs and social activities. Even speaking to women on campus was an infraction of fraternity rules. At Wesleyan, male students beat other men who talked to women.

When they graduated, these pioneering women cultivated new careers. Many worked in elementary schools or the recently created high schools. By 1918, 84 percent of the nation's teaching force were women, and in this profession they could earn more than unskilled men and could support themselves. Like Jane Addams and her Hull House colleagues, some women became settlement workers in the new profession of social work, while others studied to become doctors. As this wave of college women surged into emerging careers, they often abandoned the traditional life-style of marriage and motherhood.

Many college administrators were not ecstatic about these new students. At Stanford, 102 men and 98 women graduated in 1901, but the women received more honors and awards. In 1904, Stanford corrected the problem by setting a quota for future enrollments of three males for every female admitted, a policy maintained until 1933.[2] But the rate of women flooding the nation's colleges could not be halted. In 1870, two out of three postsecondary institutions turned women away; only thirty years later, more than two out of three admitted them; and by 1900, 19 percent of college graduates were female. But as their numbers increased, they became more conventional and less courageous.

The early twentieth century witnessed a second generation of college women who were wealthier, less serious, and more conforming. Rather than blaze new career trails, many of these women saw college as a four-year dating game, a prelude to married life. Social activities became central as they formed their own clubs, originally called female fraternities. Barred from leadership positions in the main campus organizations, they created their own newspapers, honor societies, and athletic teams, although these lacked the power and prestige of male clubs and awards.

The choice of their academic major reinforced patterns of campus apartheid. Women enrolled in literature, the new social sciences, health courses, and the liberal arts, which were particularly popular for those preparing to become teachers. The new field of home economics was created in the late 1800s and grew in popularity through the early part of the twentieth century. Although viewed as the epitome of the status quo, home economics included pioneering courses on the role of women in society, a precursor of today's women's studies programs. On the other side of the campus, men claimed the hard sciences and professions ranging from engineering to agriculture. The curricular lines were drawn, and men and women walked into different classrooms. In coeducational colleges, vocational goals dictated the courses that students chose, and social pressures channeled women and men into different careers.[3]

Women began to realize that their organizations and academic pursuits were not as prestigious as the men's, and they therefore sought to gain prestige by dating the "right" men. Money fueled the dating game: The men financed the cars and entertainment while the women invested in appearance. So much was spent on clothes and makeup that in 1946 one campus reporter observed: "At coeducational colleges the girls generally dress to the teeth . . . [using] all the bait they can for the omnipresent man."[4] College women were judged not by their academic achievements or career goals but by the number and quality of suitors. Wealthy men from the right families and the right fraternities were the most sought-after prizes.

Throughout much of the twentieth century, pursuing men rather than careers made good economic sense. In 1947, for example, 86 percent of male college graduates but only 36 percent of female graduates earned $3,000 or more a year. While 23 percent of college-educated men earned more than $7,750 a year, only 1 percent of women with college degrees earned that much. Most females graduated with teaching degrees and earned not only less than other professionals but also a third less than other teachers who happened to be born male.

From club to classroom, from social status to postgraduation economics, the signs of a second-class college education for women were everywhere. Some women found their limited higher education intolerable and rebelled. In 1919 a young woman arrived at DePauw College anticipating an "intellectual feast." She wrote: "I looked forward to studying fascinating subjects taught by people who understood what they were talking about. I imagined meeting brilliant students, students who would challenge me to stretch my mind and work. . . . In college, in some way that I devoutly believed in but could not explain, I expected to become a person."[5] Instead she discovered fraternity life and football games. Margaret Mead had come up against her first anthropological insight: the male college culture.

After misspent efforts to join a sorority and fit in, Mead was transformed into a college rebel and transferred to Barnard. There she fought not to get into a sorority but to save Sacco and Vanzetti and to destroy the barriers that separated and subjugated women on campus. In the end she provided the college community with the intellectual feast she had so fervently sought.

The trickle of female pioneers fighting for admission to male universities in the 1870s eventually became a tidal wave. A century later most remaining holdouts, including many Ivy League schools, finally capitulated and opened their doors. Today, women are the majority, 53 percent of the nation's postsecondary students, and the barriers once separating the sexes seem to have been demolished. But appearances deceive. The brick walls have been replaced with those of glass; the partitions are so transparent that they are all but invisible. The campus remains a divided one; it channels women and men into different educations that lead to separate and unequal futures.

The "hard" sciences are still housed on the male side of the glass wall. Almost 70 percent of today's students who major in physics, chemistry, and computer science are male. Engineering tops all of these, however, with 85 percent of bachelor degrees going to men. The overwhelmingly male majority extends beyond the hard sciences and engineering to theology (75 percent male), philosophy (64 percent), agriculture (69 percent), and architecture (61 percent).[6]

But it would be a mistake to view the male campus only in terms of academic courses because the heart of extracurricular life beats there, too. Male athletes enjoy an impressive array of "perks," including special meal allowances, exclusive living arrangements, lucrative scholarships, and at all too many institutions, academic dispensation when studies and game schedules conflict. This side of the campus also has valuable real estate, precious land that was turned over to fraternity row. In fact, this is the part of the campus where the lion's share of financial and educational resources are invested.

On the other side of the glass wall, the "soft" sciences and humanities are taught to classes populated mostly by women. On this second campus, females receive 90 percent of the bachelor degrees in home economics, 84 percent in health sciences, and 67 percent in general liberal arts. Here women are awarded three out of every four degrees in education and foreign language, and two out of three in psychology, communications, and the performing arts. On the women's side of the glass wall, class schedules are less likely to include advanced courses in mathematics, science, and technology. If graduation requirements insist on science courses, women typically opt for biology rather than physics or chemistry. Science, after all, is what many worked hard to avoid in high school. Although they pay the same tuition, study in the same libraries, reside in the same dorms, and receive diplomas with the name of the same college, the female students are less likely to take the courses that lead to lucrative and prestigious careers.

Women who move on to graduate and professional schools, where they earn half as many doctorates as men, also discover the divided campus:[7] Men receive 75 percent of the doctoral degrees in business and 91 percent of those in engineering, but women acquire more doctorates than men in education. Despite this, three out of every four professors are male, and nine out of ten are white and non-Hispanic. Even prestigious Ivy League schools, the ones with their pick of the most talented women, seem unable to find them. Only 10 percent to 13 percent of Ivy League faculties are female, and they earn on average almost $14,000 less annually than their male colleagues.[8] Nationally, 68 percent of male faculty members have tenure, while only 45 percent of the women enjoy this lifetime job security. It is no secret among faculty members who is valued, vested, and rewarded. Through comments, attitudes, and behavior, the message is clear that female faculty members have second-class citizenship on campus; and this message filters down to the students.

If students somehow miss the salary and tenure subtleties, the power of numbers overwhelms. Ninety-eight percent of the engineering faculty is male. While this is the most extreme imbalance, in every field students see mainly male professors: more than 60 percent in the humanities, 75 percent in business, fine arts, and the social sciences, and 83 percent in the natural sciences. Again, women are best represented in education, but even here, where they claim almost 58 percent of the doctorates, they are only 45 percent of the faculty.[9] Female students who are looking for role models, counselors, and mentors must search long and hard. With Hispanic and African-American women comprising only 1 percent of the faculty, students who are both minority and female receive an even stronger signal of their place on campus. Lacking role models and missing the mentoring connection, college women are less likely to pursue graduate work. The process becomes a continuing cycle: Mainly male professors prepare men to become the faculty of the future, and the campus remains divided and unequal.

Every now and then the glass wall separating the two campuses is almost visible. For example, when we visited the school of education at one university, we entered a building and turned right. If we had turned left, we would have arrived at the physics department and met a faculty that was 100 percent male. As we observed students entering the building, it was like watching gender-segregated lines in elementary school: Those who turned left for physics were male, those who turned right for the school of education were female.

Sometimes the differences between the two campuses is as simple as turning right or left in a building, but other differences can be observed in a different school: the community college. These two-year institutions offer a less expensive education, but they are also less prestigious. As the prestige factor dips, the proportion of women rises: Women hold 47 percent of community college faculty positions and comprise 57 percent of the students.[10]

While females are more likely to attend community colleges, they are less likely to find themselves at the most highly selective schools. Harvard may not be able to list by name the students who will be admitted next year, but it does know that only 40 percent of them will be women. Since females face occupational and income barriers, they will probably earn less than men and therefore will have less to donate to the university. From this perspective, admitting more men who will earn more money may be seen as good business practice. So economic discrimination becomes grounds for admissions discrimination, which in turn leads to further economic discrimination.

Although there are now more female applicants to college, most Ivy

League schools also seem hard-pressed to locate acceptable female candidates.[11] Only Columbia University accepts approximately equal numbers of female and male students. The frightening possibility of women comprising the majority of the student body can be reason enough to tinker with the admissions machinery.[12] In 1987, officials at the University of North Carolina noted that more than half of their new students were women. They recommended placing more weight on SAT tests and less on high school grades in order to achieve the "desirable" balance.

Although sex segregation on campus has become a way of life, there are times when students attend classes in equal numbers. The glass walls come down in general subjects required of everybody, courses such as English and political science. In these classrooms, parallel campuses converge, and all students sit in the same rooms, read the same texts, and are taught by the same professors. But even as men and women share the same space, they receive substantially different teaching.

In a Silent Voice

At the highest educational level, where the instructors are the most credentialed and the students the most capable, teaching is the most biased. We discovered this during a two-year grant in which we and a staff of trained raters observed and coded post-secondary classrooms. When we analyzed the data, we discovered how hidden lessons, rooted in elementary school and exacerbated in high school, emerged full-blown in the college classroom. Drawn from our research files, the following classroom scene offers more than a discussion of the Constitution; it shows how earlier subtle sexism has evolved and intensified.

> The course on the U.S. Constitution is required for graduation, and more than fifty students, approximately half male and half female, file in. The professor begins by asking if there are questions on next week's midterm. Several hands go up.
>
> BERNIE: Do we have to memorize names and dates in the book? Or will the test be more general?

PROFESSOR: You do have to know those critical dates and people. Not every one but the important ones. If I were you, Bernie, I would spend time learning them. Ellen?

ELLEN: What kind of short-answer questions will there be?

PROFESSOR: All multiple choice.

ELLEN: Will we have the whole class time?

PROFESSOR: Yes, we'll have the whole class time. Anyone else?

BEN (calling out): Will there be an extra-credit question?

PROFESSOR: I hadn't planned on it. What do you think?

BEN: I really like them. They take some of the pressure off. You can also see who is doing extra work.

PROFESSOR: I'll take it under advisement. Charles?

CHARLES: How much of our final grade is this?

PROFESSOR: The midterm is 25 percent. But remember, class participation counts as well. Why don't we begin?

The professor lectures on the Constitution for twenty minutes before he asks a question about the electoral college. The electoral college is not as hot a topic as the midterm, so only four hands are raised. The professor calls on Ben.

BEN: The electoral college was created because there was a lack of faith in the people. Rather than have them vote for the president, they voted for the electors.

PROFESSOR: I like the way you think. (He smiles at Ben, and Ben smiles back.) Who could vote? (Five hands go up, five out of fifty.) Angie?

ANGIE: I don't know if this is right, but I thought only men could vote.

BEN (calling out): That was a great idea. We began going downhill when we let women vote. (Angie looks surprised but says nothing. Some of the students laugh, and so does the professor. He calls on Barbara.)

BARBARA: I think you had to be pretty wealthy, own property—

JOSH (not waiting for Barbara to finish, calls out): That's right. There was a distrust of the poor, who could upset the democracy. But if you had property, if you had something at stake, you could be trusted not to do something wild. Only property owners could be trusted.

PROFESSOR: Nice job, Josh. But why do we still have electors today? Mike?

MIKE: Tradition, I guess.
PROFESSOR: Do you think it's tradition? If you walked down the street and asked people their views of the electoral college, what would they say?
MIKE: Probably they'd be clueless. Maybe they would think that it elects the Pope. People don't know how it works.
PROFESSOR: Good, Mike. Judy, do you want to say something? (Judy's hand is at "half-mast," raised but just barely. When the professor calls her name, she looks a bit startled.)
JUDY (speaking very softly): Maybe we would need a whole new constitutional convention to change it. And once they get together to change that, they could change anything. That frightens people, doesn't it? (As Judy speaks, a number of students fidget, pass notes, and leaf through their books; a few even begin to whisper.)

A visit to the typical college class, which is a stop on the campus tour that most parents never make, shows that students behave as if they, too, are visitors. While 80 percent of pupils in elementary and secondary classes contribute at least one comment in each of their classes, approximately half of the college class says nothing at all. One in two sits through an entire class without ever answering a question, asking one, or making a comment. Women's silence is loudest at college, with twice as many females voiceless. Considering the rising cost of college tuition, the female rule of speech seems to be: The more you pay, the less you say.

At the other end of the college speech spectrum are the salient students who monopolize the discussion. Their hands shoot up for attention even before the professor finishes the question. Others don't bother to wave for recognition; they blurt out answers, sometimes way off the mark, before other students formulate their ideas. As in the class we described, these aggressive, Jeopardy-like players are usually male. In our research we have found that men are twice as likely to monopolize class discussions, and women are twice as likely to be silent. The college classroom is the finale of a twelve-year rehearsal, the culminating showcase for a manly display of verbal dominance.

Studying classrooms at Harvard, Catherine Krupnick also discovered this gender divide, one where males perform and females watch. Here were the most academically talented women in the nation, and even they were silenced. When they did speak, they were more likely to be interrupted. Males talked more often, and they talked longer.

When the professor as well as most of the students were male, the stage was set for women to be minor players, a virtual Harvard underclass.[13]

Bernice Sandler and Roberta Hall found that professors give males more nonverbal attention as well. They make more eye contact with men, wait longer for them to answer, and are more likely to remember their names. The result, Sandler and Hall concluded, is a "chilly classroom climate," one that silently robs women of knowledge and self-esteem.[14]

When females do volunteer comments, the impact of years of silence and self-devaluation becomes evident. In our class scenario above, Angie showed this loss. Like many women, she has learned to preface her speech with phrases like "I'm not sure if this is what you want" or "This probably isn't right but . . ." These female preambles of self-deprecation are a predictable part of the college classroom. In our coding system we called them "self-put-downs." In class after class we were disheartened at how many times women compromised superb comments: "I'm not really sure," "This is just a guess," "I don't know, but could the answer be . . ." Or like Judy they spoke in such a soft and tentative manner that their classmates don't even bother to listen.

When we asked college women why they neutralized the power of their own speech, they offered revealing explanations:

> I do it to lower expectations. If my answer is wrong, so what? I don't lose anything. I already said it might be wrong.

> I don't want to sccm likc I'm taking over the class or anything. If I disguise that I know the answers, then the other students won't resent me.

> I say I'm not sure because I'm really not sure. I'm not certain that I'm following the professor, and I'm just being honest about it.

> I didn't know I was talking like that.

The last one is the reaction we hear most frequently. Self-doubt has become part of women's public voice, and most are unaware it has happened.[15] This pattern of uncertain speech is reminiscent of the standardized science test taken in elementary and middle school, the exam where many girls selected the "I don't know" option rather than take a guess at the correct response. By the time these schoolgirls become college women, the "I don't know" option, the only one guaranteed not to garner any points, has insinuated itself into speech, a tacit acknowledgment of diminished status.

We also found that one-third of the college classrooms that contain both males and females are characterized by informally sex-segregated seating, patterns formed by the students themselves. The salient students, usually male, are well versed in the concept of strategic seating; they choose places where they can be spotted quickly by the professor. Those who want to hide, the silent students, who are more likely to be female, prize the corners, the unobtrusive areas, and the anonymity that grows with distance. It is as if a transparent gender divide was erected within the classroom.

While not as stark, the parallel with the sex segregation of elementary school is obvious. And teachers continue their patterns, too. The subtle bias in teacher reactions that we detected in lower grades resurfaces in college. Professors usually respond to student answers with neutral silence or a vague "Okay." But when praise is awarded, when criticism is leveled, or when help is given, the male student is more likely to be on the receiving end. In the class scene we described, Mike was challenged to improve his answer and then rewarded for the correction. In fact, the professor praised three male students: Ben, Josh, and Mike. Women's comments never received the professor's stamp of approval. At best they were merely acknowledged, at worst interrupted or ridiculed. So, like boys in elementary school, men in college receive not only more attention from the professor but better attention as well.

The professor in the previous example did not intervene when Ben poked fun at women and at Angie's comment, but he did not say anything sexist or sexual himself. But many professors do. At Iowa State, 65 percent of female students said they had been the target of sexist comments, and 43 percent said professors flirted with them. At Harvard University, almost half the women graduate students reported sexual harassment. This is how women described the incidents:

> He came into class, looked directly at me, and announced to everyone, "Your sweater is too tight." I felt terrible. The next week he whispered to me, "You look like you had a tough night." I just dropped his course and had to go to summer school.

> One day this professor requested that I come to his office to discuss a paper. When I arrived, he escorted me to a chair and closed the office door. He walked over to me, put his hands on either side of my face, and told me I was a very beautiful woman. Then he kissed my forehead. We never discussed any of my academic work. . . . I disregarded his constant requests to visit his office and hurriedly left his class. I received my lowest grade in his course.

Joseph Thorpe, a professor at the University of Missouri, knows just how bad it can get. He sent questionnaires to over one thousand women who were recent recipients of psychology doctorates and were members of the American Psychological Association. Thorpe found that many students had been propositioned by their professors. Most of these overtures were turned down, but almost half said they suffered academic penalties for refusing. The survey also revealed that one in every four or five women studying for their psychology doctorates was having sex with the teacher, adviser, or mentor responsible for her academic career.[16]

"These figures seem terribly high," we said in an interview with Thorpe. "Do you think they're inflated?"

"I think they underpredict what's going on," he said. "The study did not interview any of the women who dropped out, the ones who became so emotionally devastated that they never finished their programs. If we knew those numbers, the figures would be higher. In fact, for subgroups in our sample, the numbers were higher. When we looked at the responses from single, separated, or divorced female students, the sex-with-adviser rate climbed to 33 percent."

Senior professors are overwhelmingly male and critically important. These professors distribute funds in the form of assistantships and fellowships. They can offer coauthorships on publications crucial to a fledgling career. With the right phone calls, they can land prestigious jobs for their students. Male students are more likely to be part of this mentoring relationship, but when women are mentored, the dynamics sometimes become sexual.

With grades and professional careers at stake, female students may feel vulnerable and powerless to object.[17] If a professor is a senior faculty member and distinguished in his field, it becomes even more difficult. When one of our students at The American University told us of harassment she was experiencing in a course, we urged her to bring charges. "It's useless," she told us. "This professor is a nationally known scholar. When I said I was going to report him, he laughed. 'No one would believe you,' he said. 'Do you know how many awards I have won? I'm like a god on this campus.'" This young woman did not report the professor; she dropped the course instead.

The alienation of female students on the male campus emerges even in the quiet alcoves of the university library. Surrounded by books with few if any females, women continue to learn they are worth less.

Out of Sight, Out of Mind

The first grant we ever received was to investigate sex bias in college books. In the late 1970s, we spent more than a year examining the twenty-four best-selling teacher education textbooks. We read each line, evaluated every photo, and assessed the books from cover to cover—from the table of contents to the index. Twenty-three of the twenty-four texts gave the issue of gender equity less than 1 percent of book space. One-third never mentioned the topic. Those least likely to include girls and women were the books about how to teach mathematics and science courses. Not one of the twenty-four texts provided teachers with strategies or resources to eliminate sexism from the classroom.

Using these college texts, tomorrow's teachers would actually learn to be more sexist. One book offered a lengthy rationale for paying female teachers less than male teachers. Another author advised prospective teachers to stock their classroom libraries with twice as many books about males as females. The author explained that "boys will not read 'girl books' but girls will read 'boy books.'" An educational psychology text offered this helpful tidbit to increase teacher efficiency: "If all the boys in a high school class routinely get distracted when a curvaceous and provocative coed undulates into the room to pick up attendance slips, tape the attendance slips to the outside of the door."[18]

A science textbook explained that girls "know less, do less, explore less, and are prone to be more superstitious than boys." Another education text emphasized the impact of technology with a fascinating analogy: If it were not for recent technological breakthroughs, "all women over twenty years of age in the United States would have to be telephone operators to handle all the phone calls." A reading textbook offered recommendations for bringing parent power into the classroom: "Some fathers could help the third-grade boys make birdhouses easier than the teacher could; some mothers could teach sixth-grade girls how to knit; many mothers would be glad to drive a carload of children to the airport, to the museum, or to the public library."[19]

Adding to the stereotyped narrative was the male world presented by the books. From the photographs to the index listings, education was pictured as populated and experienced by boys and men. One text highlighted seventy-three famous educators, seventy-two of whom were male. Another text featured the work of thirty renowned educators, all men. The message to tomorrow's teachers, most of whom are women, was clear: Even in this female profession, it is the men who deserve to be remembered.

To turn this picture around, we developed a set of nonsexist guidelines, suggestions for publishers interested in creating fairer college texts. Several publishers distributed our guidelines to their authors. A few publishers actually sent our research findings to the authors of the textbooks we had critiqued and requested that they "repair" their work in future editions.

Considering the job done, we turned our attention to classroom interaction, but in 1991 we were jolted back into the world of college books. The second edition of our own teacher education textbook had just been published, and we were sent an advance copy. We had taken special care to integrate women and minorities throughout the narrative of the book, but the outside of the book was something else. Without our knowledge the publisher had chosen a vibrant multicultural photograph, but it included four times more boys than girls. A call to the publisher cleared up the matter. It was all a "terrible mistake"; the photograph had been chosen to reflect cultural diversity, but the publisher, sensitive to racial representation, had not noticed that girls were left out. We began calling other publishers about their guidelines. Here is a typical exchange:

"Guidelines? What guidelines?"

"The nonsexist guidelines you agreed to follow over a decade ago."

"Over a decade ago. That's way before I arrived here. I don't remember seeing any nonsexist guidelines."

Many college textbooks have withstood the winds of change. From philosophy to psychology, from history to the sciences, students may still learn about a world of male accomplishment and female invisibility. Centuries of recorded history parade before today's college students, but women continue to make only a rare appearance. For example, a classic text in English literature survey courses is the two-volume *Norton Anthology*. Here the culture's great works are collected, and the literary canon is offered to the next generation. Norton has introduced students to centuries of literature: Chaucer, Shakespeare, Milton, Byron, Shelley, Keats, Matthew Arnold, T. S. Eliot; the showcase of male literary accomplishment is extensive. The 3,450 pages of the initial 1962 edition were expanded to 5,000 pages in the 1986 (fifth) edition, where the preface discusses efforts to reflect "contemporary culture." Less than 15 percent of these new pages included women writers. In fact, the percentage of women in the *Norton Anthology* was greater in 1962 than in 1986.[20]

Women in higher education are frequently aware that their lives are left out of books, and they feel excluded from a recorded culture that is not their own. As one student said: "In history we never talked about what women did; in geography it was always what was important to men; it was the same in our English class—we hardly ever studied women authors. I won't even talk about math and science. . . . I always felt as though I didn't belong. . . . Now I just deaden myself against it so I don't hear it anymore. But I really feel alienated."[21]

Centuries of bias cannot be undone in a single chapter or insert, but authors and publishers try nonetheless. The results of their efforts to rectify imbalance can be seen in chapters or boxes called "Women and Art," "Female Authors," "Famous Women Scientists," or "American Diversity: Founding Mothers." This last title came from a popular 1991 political science textbook that offers information about women's contributions during the revolution.[22] The authors tell how the "daughters of the revolution" boycotted British goods, wrote political pamphlets, were leaders in the fight for independence, and fought in the Revolutionary War disguised as men. In fact, the only Revolutionary War veteran buried at West Point is a woman who took full advantage of the absence of pre-induction physicals and joined the Continental army. The "Founding Mothers" represents a step forward, but it is only one page long, which is the problem with boxes and chapters. The student is left with a fragmented world view: Males are the main story and women are a sideshow, confined to a brief insert, anecdote, or biographical summary.

Sometimes women do not even make sideshow status. The controversy over generic male pronouns and nouns is a case in point. Some professors and students say that words such as "he" and "mankind" exclude women, while others charge that all the fuss is a tempest in a teapot, a case of semantic hypersensitivity. But studies show that words are powerful indeed. When a career or job is described using male pronouns, females find the job less appealing than when neutral terms are used. When a job applicant is referred to as a "girl" instead of a "woman," she is seen as less tough, less dignified, and of course less well paid.[23]

Despite studies showing that when "man" is said, in the mind's eye man is seen, many college texts persist in using these deceptive generics. Some authors even resort to creative strategies such as asking readers to imagine that inclusive language has been used, as if saying makes it so.

> Note that we have not made a distinction between the sexes. The theory is intended to apply to adolescent boys as well as adolescent girls. We have used the masculine gender in this report for convenience; it should be considered a neutral, general usage.[24]

When textbooks exclude them, some women develop their own defense. We were discussing generic words with our class when one of our students, Paul, showed us a copy of *Everyone Wins: A Citizen's Guide to Development*, a book about protecting the environment.[25] "This book belongs to my friend Connie at Portland State," he told us. "I want you to see what she did." As we leafed through the text, we saw how Connie had laboriously crossed out all the *he* and *him* pronouns and replaced them with *she* and *her*. "Connie felt as though the book was talking to someone else," Paul said, "so as she read through it, she included herself."

We asked our students to analyze the content of their textbooks to see how widespread sex bias was in the books read at our own university. They found psychology, economics, and sociology textbooks that rarely even mentioned a woman's name. One art book included 245 photographs, but only 18 depicted women. Other studies have also noted the slow pace of textbook change, but not all textbooks are frozen in time; several contain nonsexist language and include males and females in relatively equal numbers. Why such extremes? Unlike elementary and high schools, postsecondary schools do not have committees to evaluate and select books. At the college level, professors choose their own texts and call it academic freedom. For students, it's *caveat emptor*.

The Girls Next Door

When I entered college in North Carolina in the 1960s, I was given my official women's rule book, a thirty-four-page tome filled with guidelines and expectations for all coeds. (Female students were "coeds"; male students were "gentlemen.") The following are some of the rules:

- No beer in the dorm, even to use as a hair rinse, as was the custom of the day. Men, of course, could have as much beer in their rooms as they wished.
- No smoking while walking on campus since this was considered "unladylike" conduct.
- No visiting a boy's apartment unless there was another couple present.

- No dates outside the town line unless you were "signed out" to do so. Male students could go wherever they pleased.

The rules went on and on. I don't believe male students had a rule book. To be fair, I should note that by the time I graduated in 1970, the rule book had been shortened to pamphlet length.

In the 1970s when students reinvented dorm life, they abridged and then discarded the rule book completely. Almost overnight single-sex dorms seemed out of date and coeducational living became the arrangement of choice. Researchers found both positive and negative sides to these new coed dorms. Men told fewer off-color jokes, drank less, and talked with women more; women became more outgoing and were more likely to attend university events. Cross-sex friendships flourished as residents went to classes, meals, and university activities together. But there were problems as well as benefits. While men studied more, women in coed dorms took their academic work less seriously, held lower career aspirations, and dropped out of school more often. And stories of unwanted teasing and touching became increasingly frequent.[26]

Stories that surfaced in the 1970s have become commonplace on today's campus. A survey of Cornell students found that four out of five women experienced sexist comments and 68 percent received unwanted attention from men. At the Massachusetts Institute of Technology, 92 percent of the women reported receiving unwanted sexual attention. At the University of Rhode Island, seven out of ten women said they were sexually insulted by men. Sexual harassment can occur anywhere on campus, but students are especially vulnerable when it happens where they live.[27]

My dorm at Stanford is composed of fifty men and women who reside on two coed hallways. We are all freshmen. Last week several of the girls, including me, discovered that the men on the second floor had posted in the men's room a "rating and ranking" sheet of the second-floor women. The ranking was obviously based on the relative physical attractiveness of the girls in the dorm and was accompanied by various and sundry disgusting comments. Naturally, many of the second-floor women were upset by this list. . . . I decided that this was something so fundamentally wrong, I couldn't ignore it.

As the week progressed, I began to discuss "the list" with some of the second-floor men, explaining my objections. I felt that the list was dehumanizing and humiliating . . . immature and childish, a remnant of middle school days. How could these guys whom we'd been living with for eight months think of their closest friends in such superficial terms? How could they degrade us in that way? And most of all, how could they be sitting in front of me and defending themselves instead of apologizing for their actions?

Eventually a male resident adviser decided to hold a house meeting to discuss the problem in a more formal setting. This meeting became a battle between me and the ten to twelve men on the second floor who could find nothing wrong with their "list." Amazingly enough, throughout the entire argument not one of the other second-floor women who had initially been so angered . . . had the strength to help validate my arguments with her support. In fact, several were so afraid to become embroiled in an argument that they pretended they knew nothing about the list. The men who were not part of the ranking and who I knew were opposed to it . . . didn't attack my position, but they certainly were not willing to put themselves on the line to defend it. After this confrontation and for the next few days, however, many of the women in the dorm . . . came to me separately and thanked me for standing up for them and myself, and for trying to explain how disturbing and upsetting the situation was.

In this case, words created a psychological betrayal, shattering the veneer of honest communication. When the betrayal is physical instead of verbal, it is far more threatening:

I was driving home from a bar with five guys who lived in my dorm. Most of them were drunk (I wasn't). I was sitting on the lap of one of my friends. He kept trying to touch me on my inner thighs or my buttocks. I was squirming and telling him to stop, but he ignored me. The other guys kept laughing. One kept grabbing my breasts while another whispered in my ear that I should go to his room tonight. I felt like Jodie Foster in *The Accused*. I was trapped in a car with no way to escape.

The young woman from The American University who described this incident to us said that the "guys were just messing around," and nothing else happened; but she felt "frightened, helpless, and violated." She said, "When I tell people the story, they say that being with five drunk guys is just asking for trouble. But they don't understand. These guys were my *friends*." Another college student also described the frightening transformation of someone she considered a friend, the man who lived next door.

> John and I were friends in the same dorm. Just friends. He knew I had a boyfriend and that I saw him as a friend. One day I was in his room talking with him. We were always hanging out in each other's rooms, listening to music and watching TV. When I got up to leave, he blocked the door, grabbed my arms, and forcefully kissed me. I was shocked. I didn't know what to do. I mean, this was a pretty good friend of mine acting like this. He picked me up and threw me down on his bed. . . . He started kissing me and saying how much he wanted to make love to me. I said no. I was completely pinned down. I have never felt so lacking in control in my own life. I realized that something I didn't want to happen could—and I didn't have any say in the situation. He didn't care about my feelings. I must have said no about a thousand times. I kept struggling, and I finally convinced him to stop. . . .
>
> To this day (and I know this for sure because he lives next door to me) he doesn't feel as if he did anything wrong. I still haven't been able to make him understand how he affected me that day. Almost being raped . . . I can only begin to imagine what I would have felt like if a rape had really happened.

Baffled by the way her trusted friend treated her, this young woman keeps playing the incident over and over in her mind, trying to understand why it happened. But these terrifying experiences are not even distant possibilities in the minds of new students as they unload their cars and move into their dorms. And most parents, as they wave goodbye, have no inkling of the alarming extracurricular activities their tuition dollars may be buying.

The Years of Living Dangerously

During the 1980s fraternity and sorority membership grew, and by the 1990s over a million students were part of the resurgence of Greek associations on campus. Fraternities often set the social rhythm of undergraduate life because they have more and bigger houses for parties; sometimes they have the only location on campus.

Walk through the typical campus and you are far more likely to see a fraternity house than a sorority house. When we asked college students why fraternities were more likely to claim campus real estate, we often heard a rendition of the bordello story, which goes something like this: "It's an ancient law here in [the District of Columbia, St. Louis, Boston, or the city of your choice]. When three or four women rent or buy a house together, it's considered a brothel. Back then it was called a bordello. That's why sorority houses are illegal. It has nothing to do with campus inequality, it's just these stupid, outdated bordello laws."

The longer history of fraternities and their greater wealth and influence, not bordello laws, have created the real estate gender gap. But we have heard this explanation at so many different colleges and universities, it qualifies as campus mythology.

Nationally there are more than twice as many fraternities as sororities. And on the typical campus, sorority row is a weak reflection of its male counterpart. On some campuses the sorority house is big enough only for meetings and parties; no one lives there. On others, there are no sorority houses, just dorm areas where sorority sisters live together. In many cases there is not even dorm space; all that is available is a meeting room in a university building.

This less well-appointed sorority life still produces enthusiastic supporters. As one woman said, "Living like sisters creates a lifelong bond. The sorority gave me friendship and support." Both fraternity and sorority members are quick to point out that they raise money for charitable causes and do good work for children, the poor, and the homeless. But it is the social activities—and scandals—that gain public attention, and these usually take place on the male side of the campus.

Fraternity row is home to an all-male society, one separate from the rest of the world where secret rituals bond new brothers into a surrogate family. Here the stage is set for life's last fling before the onset of work and family responsibilities. Alcohol, parties, good times, and close friendships characterize fraternity life. But along with horseplay and harmless fun, there exists a menacing, darker side:

> The theme for Dartmouth's winter carnival was *Camelot*, so
> a group of fraternity brothers built a snow sculpture for the

event—a woman's breast pierced by a sword and captioned GUINEVERE—THANKS FOR THE MAMMARIES, ARTHUR.[28]

At Middlebury, the 1988 toga party was hosted by one of the biggest fraternities on campus. As part of the decor, the torso of a female mannequin was hung from the balcony and splattered with red paint to look like blood. A sign underneath suggested the female body was available for sex.[29]

One fraternity sponsored a campus scavenger hunt. Points were awarded to those who could produce photocopies of female genitalia.

A fraternity on a New England college campus hosted "pig parties." Females from a nearby state teacher's college were imported, and the date of the one voted ugliest was the winner.

At UCLA a fraternity manual, forgotten in an apartment, found its way into a campus magazine. The fraternity's history, traditions, and bylaws were included, as well as a series of songs the pledges were supposed to memorize. Many of the lyrics described sexual scenes that were shockingly graphic, unbelievably bizarre, and revoltingly sadistic. For example, one song recounted the life of a Mexican girl named Lupe who performed any sexual act imaginable. She first had intercourse when she was eight years old, and even in death, "while maggots crawl[ed] out of her decomposed womb," the smile on her face signaled that she still wanted more sex.[30]

When fraternity members are involved in these pranks and songs, they create a mind-set that turns women into objects, animals, prey. Then the college campus becomes a setting of very real danger.

The young woman, newly arrived on campus, was seeking acceptance from her classmates. She looked forward to attending the fraternity party, a beginning event in her college social life. At the party she was encouraged to drink, and eventually she passed out. The brothers had a name for this practice: "working a Yes out." She was carried upstairs, stripped, and raped by a number of men. They lined up outside the door and took turns, an approach called "pulling train." Several times she regained consciousness and pleaded for them to stop. The university learned of the incident and punished those involved. Several were required to do community service projects. Some additional reading and writing projects were also assigned for the fraternity members involved. The woman who was gang-raped left without graduating.[31]

The police had a difficult time piecing together the sordid details. A gang rape was reported at the Pi Kappa Alpha house at Florida State University, and a witness alleged that a visiting brother from Auburn University helped dump the body of the unconscious woman at a neighboring fraternity house. Even though they were charged with obstructing justice, all the brothers kept their pledge of secrecy. Although two were on trial facing life sentences, no one would cooperate with the police.[32]

Campus rape is more common than college officials care to admit, and they are far less well equipped to deal with it than most parents realize. According to national studies, approximately one in four college women says she has been forced into having sex, and one in six reports having been raped.[33] While most people think of rape as an assault by a violent stranger, in nine out of ten college incidents, the sex is forced by a friend or acquaintance. Victims experience a maelstrom of emotions: shock, disbelief, fear, and depression. They also agonize over every nuance of their own behavior and are likely to find themselves at fault: "How could I have been so wrong about him?" "What did I do to lead him on?" When the perpetrator is a "friend," college women are not even sure they have a right to call the ordeal "rape."[34]

While the victim is at a loss to figure out how it happened, the perpetrator fits a predictable profile. Socialized into the aggressive male role, he believes that women tease and lead him on, that they provoke and enjoy sexual encounters and later cry rape falsely. To these men it is not rape at all but part of a game men and women play. More than one in every three college men believes that a woman who says "no" to sex really means "yes," or at least "maybe." According to one study, a shocking 30 percent of men admitted they would rape a woman if they thought they could get away with it.[35]

Drugs and alcohol trigger sexual violence. Intoxicated men are more likely to be violent, and intoxicated women are less able to resist. This dangerous situation is viewed very differently by females and males. When asked, "If a woman is heavily intoxicated, is it okay to

have sex with her?" only one in fifty women agreed. But one in four college men said that an intoxicated female was an appropriate target for
sex. In addition to alcohol or drugs, location and date can be danger
factors. Women who find themselves in a man's living quarters, at his
party, or even in his car are more vulnerable.[36] So are women who go
out with athletes.

Basking in status and popularity, male athletes are like campus no-
bility. In athletic events and on television, their physical exploits garner glory, network dollars, and alumni contributions. But off the field,
physical exploits of a different nature can bring disgrace. The National Institute of Mental Health found athletes involved in one out of every
three sexual assaults nationally. At Maryland's Towson State, athletes
are five times more likely than others to be involved in gang rapes. A
major southern university found that 27 percent of its athletes had
threatened women into having sex against their will. In just one year,
from 1989 to 1990, at least fifteen gang rapes were reported, involving
fifty athletes. No one knows how many gang rapes went unreported.[37]

> Meg Davis called them her friends; she "buddied" with
> them. In the spring semester her "friends," all on the uni-
> versity's football team, sexually assaulted her. For three
> hours, seven to nine men took turns. She blacked out as she
> was being sodomized. Back at the dorm, she showered un-
> til the hot water ran out. "I felt so dirty. Even so, I didn't call
> what happened to me rape. These were guys I knew. It
> wasn't until I went to a women's center in town that some-
> one explained I'd been gang-raped."[38]

After fraternities, athletic teams are most likely to be involved in gang
rapes. Whether called "brotherhood," as in fraternity houses, or "teamwork," as in sports, the mind-set generated by male bonding can sup-
press independent thought and morality. A director of a rape treatment
center described the impact of this bonding: "There has never been a
single case in all the gang rapes we've seen where one man tried to
stop it. . . . It's more important to be part of the group than to be the
person who does what's right."[39]

At Carleton College in Northfield, Minnesota, women took matters
into their own hands. As one woman said, "I had been on the campus
for five weeks when I was raped. The college knew this man was a
rapist, and they could have prevented this from happening."[40] After
hearing the evidence, Carleton suspended the male offender for less
than a year. When he returned to campus, he harassed the woman who

had reported the rape. She and others sued the college, and then they did something else. On the wall of the women's bathroom at the university's library, as a warning to other women on campus, they posted an unofficial list of the names of Carleton men who had raped.

Colleges are not always slow to respond. Many institute special programs to sensitize the campus community, but when these programs are evaluated, the results are surprising. Female participants become more sensitive to the problem even before the training begins. Just responding to questions about rape on a survey changes their attitudes, heightens their level of concern, and causes them to become more sympathetic toward rape victims. Once in the program, they place even more importance on stopping college rape. But males respond differently. Traditional educational programs have little impact on their attitudes, and evaluation results show that many who continue to believe pro-rape myths blame the victim. These starkly different reactions to rape prevention reveal not only a profound gender gap in perception but also a fundamental difference in campus entitlement and power.[41]

From the Classroom to the Boardroom

Dorothy Holland and Margaret Eisenhart spent four years interviewing college women as they progressed from their freshman year through their senior year. Some of the women attended a predominantly white institution while others were enrolled in a historically black college. At first the researchers were surprised that so many arrived on campus with clear and ambitious career goals, but after a while they found a gradual but persistent drop in professional aspirations.

Paula, for example, was a straight-A high school student who planned to major in biology en route to becoming a doctor. But as her grades dropped, she switched majors, first to nursing and then to education. By her sophomore year Paula was less sure of her professional future than when she had first set foot on campus. Her social goals, on the other hand, were coming into sharp focus. "Since I've been here, I've changed my mind about a thousand times. . . . And, like right now, I feel like . . . just not working would be the greatest thing in the world—just taking care of children and not studying." Paula eventually majored in the social sciences, enrolled in a management training program at a department store, and got married. A few years after graduation, she viewed the world of work this way: "[My husband and I] want to have successful careers . . . his is a career, where I feel mine is a job. So my career goals are for his career more than mine. . . . I'm trying to be there to help [him] when I can."[42]

Even today, when the Cinderella myth is supposedly shattered, many women experience a campus climate reminiscent of an earlier time when courtship was more important than careers. Saturday night dates, bars, mixers, and parties are campus events that often conflict with and eventually become more important than demanding academic majors and high grade point averages. As the social world replaces the academic one, many women willingly revise and scale down their career goals. They plan for future employment that they think will mesh more comfortably with the demands of wife and mother.

While black colleges show impressive academic results, females in these schools are caught in a disturbing undertow that erodes their professional progress. African-American women actually lose assertiveness in college as heightened social pressure pushes them toward sex-stereotyped careers. Just as these women are increasing their academic capability, they are being "romanced" away from lucrative future professions.[43]

While many college women envision compromised careers, others refuse to prepare for second-class employment. They are delaying romance, breaking glass walls, and taking aim at glass ceilings.

In 1970 women represented only 9 percent of medical students. Today they are 39 percent. Forty-three percent of today's law students are female, compared to less than 4 percent just thirty years ago.[44] While these numbers suggest stunning progress, they tell only part of the story. Women entering professional schools may find a world more hostile than their undergraduate college or university campus. For women, higher education gets colder by degrees.

> I had been to a women's college and never had to think about things like whether someone was treating me differently because I was a woman. . . .I don't think I'd ever really considered the issue of gender until I got here.

> For the first time in my life I felt I was hurting partly because I was female. . . . I never had any of the problems that women talked about until I got here.[45]

The "here" these women described was Yale Law School during the 1980s, but their experiences could have occurred at any number of law schools across the country. College valedictorians and members of Phi Beta Kappa, they were among the nation's brightest and best, but at Yale they felt inadequate. It didn't take long for women who thought they had finally arrived to realize they hadn't made it after all.

> [My friend] and I took this U-Haul across country . . . so I drive the U-Haul up to the front steps of the law school. I had my pink tennis shoes on and this bright pink shirt, and I think I had a Walkman on . . . and I kind of bop up and say, "Hi, where's the housing office?" . . . There . . . were these three law students just kind of sitting on the stairs, and they looked at me and said, "This is Yale." And I said, "I know. Where's the housing office?" And they said, "This is Yale Law School." . . . They all looked me up and down just like, "Oh, God, someone on the admissions committee made a mistake."[46]

To these women, the law school was a Hollywood set, a male soundstage. Ties and jackets were issued by wardrobe. Men wore them everywhere. The set designers had created a dimly lit library, appointed in dark leather from upholstery to book covers. Somber-looking portraits of men stared down from the walls. As one woman said, "How male the place was made me leap. . . . It's not just the individual people, it has to do with how the classes were conducted, the look, the ties, the jackets, the pictures. . . . I used to read *he* as *she* in all my casebooks. It made a tremendous difference. It was the only way I felt engaged and included."[47]

To prepare for classes, men formed study groups, and women were excluded. At parties, men rated females on their physical attributes, a scale one woman found to be more offensive than the fraternity rankings she had been subjected to as an undergraduate at her state university. One female student was accused of attaining her position as a research assistant by warming a professor's bed. While these attitudes offended and alienated, the women focused on the classroom as the "crucible" of their criticism. It was there that they "learned silence."

> I was very, very quiet, very reserved, and felt even more pressure in the small group than I did in large classes because of the lack of anonymity. I basically felt inadequate in all classroom settings, unable to make comments or to project myself into the conversation, often unable to think as

quickly as I thought others did, to come up with insightful or relevant things to say. . . .

I remember the second small group meeting. It was the first time I was called on. I hadn't spoken. It was an easy question, and I just couldn't answer it. I couldn't think to do it, and that became a pattern. . . . I felt as though I were missing some gene or protein. Everyone else could spew forth arguments, which I couldn't do.[48]

Other women began their classes by trying to get involved in the discussion, but gradually and for different reasons they dropped out of speaking roles:

When I got here, I decided I was going to knock 'em dead. I felt I'd been let in for suspicious reasons, so I was extra conscientious. I took class notes on white paper and reading notes on yellow. I raised my hand in [class]. I felt I was working hard to get to this point. Others seemed to do it naturally. . . . [Now] I definitely speak a lot less. . . . I wasn't made to feel that what I was saying was necessarily worthwhile. Very often I felt like—I don't know why I was feeling this way—but like I was wasting the class's time.[49]

In two classes, I feel like the professors kind of ignore my points because I'm a woman. In one course, they [the professors] kind of like "uh-huh" and go on, and then somebody else would say the same thing and we'd get into a discussion about it, and it was always when a man said the same thing.[50]

Frozen in an icy climate zone, an extreme macho culture that they had never experienced, twenty Yale women formed their own group to fight alienation, loneliness, self-doubt, and their sense of being silenced. Members of the women's group encouraged one another to participate in classes they saw as "laboratories for the release of aggression." One of their stunning successes occurred in a large classroom setting. A tally of the previous day's speakers was sixteen to zero, male to female. The women were determined to break the sound barrier. The next day there was a forest of female hands. When one was called, she spoke and then recognized another woman; it was like passing the baton. There was a "tipping effect" as other women in the group, and also some of the men who had been quiet, began to participate.

As the women discovered they could do it the "Yale-male way," some began to question the script. They described classroom exchanges as "nonconversation" where people didn't talk *to* one another but rather *at* one another, as if performing before an audience. In fact, students acted as if they were in competition, trying to make points at one another's expense. While women found they were capable of taking a position in these classroom battlegrounds, they got more out of discussions where people listened and responded.

> The classrooms in which I felt the most at ease, I think, were those in which we were deliberative in our style. People deliberated before they spoke. It slowed the pace down. There was a feeling of sensitivity to others when everybody was thinking about what they were saying.[51]

While these women were describing Yale, the climate is chilly, to varying degrees, at many law schools around the country. Men still comprise 73 percent of law school faculty members and 85 percent of the full professors. Women are concentrated in the lowest ranks. Of the 178 law school deans, more than 93 percent are male. Gender differences in employment are also striking. In 1991, seven times as many male graduates as female graduates from Yale were scheduled to clerk for a federal appellate court, although women were 40 percent of the graduating class.[52] The typical female lawyer in 1983 earned 89 percent of a male lawyer's income; by 1991 that had dropped to 75 percent. And it is not just money that talks; attitudes are conveyed in other ways as well. In a 1989 California state bar survey, 88 percent of female attorneys reported subtle but pervasive bias, and 62 percent believed that they were still not accepted as peers by men in the legal profession.[53] So the women at Yale and at other law schools leave a chilly educational climate to enter a cold profession. But they are not alone.

Along with law school, women are now entering medical school in record numbers, but this is not a totally new development—female students attended medical school in ancient Egypt, more than thirty-five hundred years ago. But change can be slow, and the ways of ancient Egypt are not necessarily the ways of America. In 1855, the *American Medical Gazette and Journal of Health* reported as follows:

> Shakespeare conceived Caliban, fable invented the Amazons, stories and song have conferred eternal infamy upon

> Lucrezia Borgia, Catherine, and Messalina, and I have seen
> children with two heads. But no monster of them all is so
> disgusting as this unsexed woman, who has forsaken the
> needle for the scalpel and would have more pleasure in saw-
> ing off a man's leg than in mending his breeches.[54]

The history of medical sexism may be one reason that women in the 1970s knocked more loudly on the doors of law and business schools; it took another decade before they made real inroads into the nation's schools of medicine. In fact, the profession has been extremely effective at deflecting the aspirations of medically-minded women. Nursing, a socially valuable but far less lucrative career, helped keep the more prestigious physician field an exclusive male preserve. But by the 1980s, women had arrived in schools of medicine. They found a cold reception.

The chill began in the admissions office. In interviews for the limited number of medical school openings, women were often asked to respond to illegal questions about marriage plans and children. Men heard only the appropriate sets of questions, the ones about academic achievement, medical interests, and career goals.[55]

Women who survived the admissions hurdle came face to face with financial reality: At least four out of every five students go into debt as they prepare to become doctors. But the weight of the debt falls unevenly. While almost 80 percent of female students struggle financially, for male students the figure is closer to 58 percent. Women and minorities both report that their families are less likely to offer psychological support or financial assistance and are more likely to have mixed feelings about medical careers. A daughter attending medical school may be seen as losing time in a career decision that delays marriage and children. As a result, female medical students report greater loneliness, role conflict, and depression. Katherine Kris, a Harvard psychiatrist, concludes, "The expectation [is] that they must choose between their identities as professionals or as women."[56]

The daily medical school climate only adds to this isolation and role confusion. In 126 medical schools, there are 123 male deans. About four out of every five professors are male, and at the highest level, full professor, more than 90 percent are men. While all women go about their studies in a distinctly male environment, minority women confront even more alien demographics. In addition to being overwhelmingly male, about 97 percent of medical school faculties are white and non-Hispanic.[57]

Male medicine has educated generations of doctors who view the female as "the other body," less central and important to their training. Medical textbooks reinforce these lessons. Males are presented as the anatomical standard, while females are the exceptions, the anomalies. Of eight anatomy textbooks widely used in medical schools during the 1980s, male subjects were shown in 64 percent of the illustrations while females were represented in only 11 percent (neutral representations comprised the remaining 25 percent). Textbook illustrations of the male anatomy were captioned with labels like ABDOMINAL MUSCLES and CIRCULATORY SYSTEM, subtly teaching that the physiology of men is the norm.

Anatomical equality was almost reached in only one textbook topic, where male figures totaled 48 percent of the illustrations and female figures were 45 percent. That singular area of equity was reproduction. Only here did women gain their own bodies because it is here that their anatomical destiny is clear. Gynecology textbooks expanded on the anatomy-as-destiny theme, with narrative expressing more concern for the patient's husband than the patient. One gynecology text actually advised that a woman "allow her male partner's sex drive to set their pace, and she should attempt to gear hers satisfactorily to his."[58] Journals also reinforce sexist lessons with articles like "The Medical Care Abuser" about obnoxious, irritating, difficult-to-diagnose patients, 75 percent of whom are female.[59] Where texts and journals leave off, the peer culture kicks in. Medical students share with one another mnemonic strategies to help memorize facts, and these devices can pack a sexist wallop. For example, the first letter of each word in a simple phrase is also the first letter of each of the twelve cranial nerves. To remember the nerves, simply memorize: "Oooh, oooh, oooh, to taste and feel a girl's vagina, A H."

According to Adrian Fugh-Berman, who described her personal experiences as a medical student in the 1980s, sexism was in full flower at Georgetown Medical School. On the very first day her anatomy instructor noted the large breasts on an elderly cadaver and said she "must have been a Playboy bunny." The instructor then cut the breasts off and tossed them into a thirty-gallon trash can marked "cadaver waste." With this quick comment and casual gesture he started the class off with a message of contempt for women's bodies.[60]

The next problem came when Georgetown required interviews for students interested in an elective course on sexually transmitted diseases. There was just one catch—only male students were invited to interview. When three women requested admission interviews, they were barred from the course and told that male patients objected to females attending. (The reverse of this, female patients objecting to male medical students, seems never to have been an issue.) Although a survey showed more than 90 percent of the male patients would not object to women, the medical school was slow in deciding whether to admit females to the course. While Georgetown pondered, all electives were postponed. Tempers flared as the entire class was put into a holding pattern. Eventually the elective was canceled and a new one instituted, but women admitted to the new course were not allowed to examine male patients.

The controversy over the Georgetown curriculum did not end there. The content of the human sexuality course also became an issue. Only two of eleven lectures in the course focused on women, and the topic of homosexuality never mentioned lesbians. The medical students were taught that male sexual aggression, even male hostility, was normal and that a woman's inability to reach orgasm was not a real medical problem. Female sexual dysfunction was attributed to women joining the work force. Medical students were advised that if a husband had a sexually transmitted disease, the wife's gynecologist should be contacted directly. In this way the wife would receive treatment without being informed of the reason. No such strategy was recommended for dropping the husband from the communications cycle. When a group of female students joined forces to protest the sexist content of the curriculum, they were met with peer hostility, obscene notes, and telephone calls. Some were even threatened with rape.

While sexism at Georgetown Medical School was spotlighted, it was not alone. One national study ranked the risks of sexual harassment for female medical students: There was a 10 percent chance of harassment from peers, 20 percent from physicians, and 25 percent from patients. Other studies suggest that these are conservative figures. At the University of Wisconsin Medical School, almost half of the women reported sexual harassment from peers, and at the University of California Medical School in San Francisco, 73 percent of women serving as residents in internal medicine said they were subjected to sexual harassment.[61]

Women who emerge from a less-than-cordial medical school climate confront a profession geared to male standard time. With four years of medical school behind them, doctors are scheduled to spend the next several years refining their skills in a residency. But for many women this is also an ideal time to start a family. Although only about 25 percent of residency programs have maternity policies, many women, running out of options, plan to have children during their residency training—and to have them quickly. Eighty percent of female physicians report a maternity absence of only a few weeks, with almost no interruption in their practice.

Female physicians who successfully negotiate conflicting professional and family responsibilities in their training enter a medical profession where the glass ceiling is a well-entrenched tradition. Even the most successful female physicians have discovered that an M.D. is no defense against sexism. At Stanford University's medical school, Frances Conley is a member of a select minority: one of the nation's first female brain surgeons and a tenured full professor. But in 1991, Dr. Conley resigned to protest the impending appointment of a department chair she characterized as sexist. She complained of demeaning treatment, being called "honey," and having her legs fondled under the operating table. Her story revealed that even a full professor at one of the nation's leading medical schools is vulnerable, and it sparked similar complaints from female physicians nationwide. Her resignation was eventually withdrawn when Stanford began taking her charges seriously.[62]

For Kathryn Anderson, who was up for promotion to chief of surgery at Children's Hospital in Washington, D.C., the outcome was less satisfactory. After she had served ten years as vice-chair of surgery, the search committee chose an outside candidate to become chief, accusing Dr. Anderson of being "aggressive" and "abrasive." She left the East Coast to become chief of surgery at Children's Hospital in Los Angeles, but not before initiating legal action against her former hospital for sex discrimination. Anderson, one of three female chiefs of surgery in the country, said, "The characteristics of a good surgeon are those characteristics of a good leader, somebody who can take charge, somebody who is forceful and strong. The question is the kind of word you use to describe a type of behavior in one group of individuals versus another. For a man, 'assertiveness.' For a woman, 'abrasiveness.' 'Forceful,' perhaps, for a man, 'obnoxious' for a woman."[63]

Medicine need not be hostile territory for women, and reform would benefit us all. Female physicians bring talent and skills that enhance patient care. Studies show women doctors listen more carefully to patients, elicit a clearer picture of their symptoms, and are more likely to involve patients in medical decisions. Their performance in gynecology and obstetrics is, not surprisingly, particularly strong. Even the nation's research agenda has been influenced by female physicians. Dr. Bernadine Healy, the first woman director of the National Institutes for Health, responded to the lack of medical research on women by creating the Office for Women's Health, to ensure that their physical problems also received NIH attention and research dollars.[64]

As some sexist practices tumble, others emerge. Female physicians are now discovering new glass walls: Women practice in the less prestigious and less profitable medical areas. Few women become dermatologists, surgeons, ophthalmologists, or any of the score of high-priced specialists. But one in every three women physicians becomes an internist, one in four enters pediatrics, 17 percent go into family practice, 13 percent find their way to obstetrics and gynecology, and 12 percent become psychiatrists. The economic consequence of joining these female fields becomes clear during the first four years of practice. The average male physician earns $153,600 during these early years, while the average female doctor earns 60 percent of this wage, $92,800. During her entire career, the typical female doctor is unlikely to earn more than 65 percent of the prevailing male wage. Although medical salaries are among the highest, the financial gender gap is among the widest. The impact of a new health care system on the economic gender gap is yet to be seen.

Business school enrollments exploded in the 1980s, ignited in large part by tens of thousands of women seeking new opportunities as entrepreneurs, managers, and executives. For many the shortest route to business success had three letters: MBA. But sometimes even the shortest route can be very long. A woman with a master of business administration degree from one of the nation's top twenty business schools in 1990 averaged $54,749 a year, which is a fine salary but still 12 percent less than the $61,400 earned by a man graduating with the same MBA. One reason for the difference is that not all MBAs are equal.[65]

A female applicant would be wise to think carefully about which business school to attend because when it comes to women, they have vastly different track records. Among the nation's top twenty business schools, the gender gap in first-year wages for students graduating in 1990 was the smallest for those graduating from Berkeley (2.6 percent), Michigan (4.6 percent), Dartmouth (5 percent), and Stanford (7.3 percent). The salaries of females graduating from Cornell's business school actually averaged 1.2 percent more than those of newly minted male MBAs, a unique phenomenon. The five business schools whose women graduates lagged behind the most were Rochester (15.2 percent), Columbia (18.6 percent), UCLA (22.8 percent), Virginia (24.1 percent), and MIT (32.5 percent). Despite an immediately shocking salary differentiation, none of these schools offered tuition discounts to women whose degrees seemed to be worth a good deal less on graduation day.[66]

As graduation from college or professional school becomes but a memory, work too often turns into a sex-segregated reality. The gender divide begins immediately. During job interviews, women are rated as more qualified than men when they apply for traditionally female jobs, and males receive more favorable evaluations when they interview for "gender-appropriate" careers. Today, women are still only 17 percent of the nation's architects, 9 percent of the clergy, 8 percent of the engineers, 3 percent of the technicians, and 10 percent of the dentists (up approximately 3 percent during the past decade). On the women's side of the glass wall, females comprise 83 percent of librarians, 86 percent of elementary school teachers, 88 percent of speech therapists, 95 percent of registered nurses, and 99 percent of kindergarten and preschool teachers, dental hygienists, and secretaries.[67]

But when glass walls break and women and men work alongside each other, it is like returning to school. The ordinary business meeting offers testimonial to how well lessons have been learned. If we could videotape the typical meeting, freeze it in time and record the dialogue, we would more likely hear the voices of men.

Men dominate workplace conversations just as they controlled classroom discussion. They speak with confidence in declarative sentences. They interrupt others, especially women. They jump in with answers to questions, even those that aren't addressed to them. As if in counterpoint, women speak less at meetings and defer to men, and the phrasing of their contributions is often tentative. And the more men there are at a meeting, the more uncertain and powerless the women become. At work they have mastered the fine art of the muted voice. This is not surprising: It is a lesson they have studied for twelve, sixteen, or more years at school.

There are other inequities as well. The videotape of our hypothetical meeting would likely show men, with their papers spread across the table, sprawled into women's space. By taking over territory, they make nonverbal statements about power, and these are reinforced by the use of touch. Men touch women more often than women touch men. A pat on the back on one level is a friendly gesture of camaraderie. But on another level it signifies power, for we touch things and people we think we can control.[68]

Each of these gestures alone has little impact, but taken together and occurring repeatedly, they create a workplace culture of male dominance and one that is more likely to support and promote men. In a 1993 survey, six out of ten women who work for Congress reported they were taken less seriously than men and were paid less professional attention. Two out of three said they were paid less money, too. As one House aide put it, "Women start at the bottom and rise to the middle. . . . Men start in the middle and rise to the top." And on Capitol Hill as in the workplace nationally, 34 percent of women are affected by sexual harassment. But just like girls at school who face repercussions when they report an incident, women at work, fearing retaliation, often do not come forward.[69]

Sexist lessons transform girls into second-class students. These same lessons resurface at work, where women are listened to less, promoted less, and paid less. Only when their silence is broken in the classroom will women be heard in the boardroom.

8

The Miseducation of Boys

To all the world boys appear to be the favored gender, heirs apparent to society's rewards. They are the recipients of the lion's share of teacher time and attention and the featured figures in most textbooks. Sitting atop high standardized test scores, they haul in the majority of scholarship dollars, claim more than half of the openings in the most prestigious colleges, and are destined for high salaries and honored professions. Few would consider boys "miseducated," but gender bias is a two-edged sword. Girls are shortchanged, but males pay a price as well.

While boys rise to the top of the class, they also land at the bottom. Labeled as problems in need of special control or assistance, boys are more likely to fail a course, miss promotion, or drop out of school. Prone to take risks, they jeopardize not only their academic future but their lives as they dominate accident, suicide, and homicide statistics. In fact, because the educational failures of boys are so visible and public, schools invest extra resources on their behalf, and yet the catastrophic results continue. Girls suffer silent losses, but boys' problems are loud enough to be heard throughout the school.

> Sitting in the back of the social studies classroom to supervise one of our practice teachers, we have a student's-eye-view of events. A group of eighth-grade boys storms into the room, careening off desks and one another as they make their way to their places. By the time the noise subsides and the new teacher begins her lesson, the last row has been claimed entirely by males.
>
> When the teacher tells the class to divide into geography groups, six are formed: three all-male and three all-female. The all-girl groups work quietly to complete their maps while the boys talk loudly, joke, and roam around the room.

About five minutes before the class ends, they slam their books closed and stuff them into bookbags, any pretense of work over. Shouting above the racket, our student teacher tries to give the homework assignment, but only lip readers have a chance of hearing it. The boys in the back are already shoving one another on their way out the door.

When we ask the cooperating teacher, the veteran who is helping our novice, about the boys in his class, he pulls no punches: "They're sloppy, noisy, immature. I don't know the reason, but compared to boys, the girls are a pleasure to teach. Actually, these boys are not bad. When I was teaching in Baltimore, we were warned about being hit or shot. Here the boys are difficult but not dangerous. We just try to keep them calm and working."

Raised to be active, aggressive, and independent, boys enter schools that seem to want them to be quiet, passive, and conforming. In an uneasy compromise, many walk a tightrope between compliance and rebellion. To keep the balance, schools go the extra mile for males and give them more resources and attention. For some this isn't enough, however. They fail, are left behind, and never make it to graduation. Others become stars. They climb to the head of the class only to discover increasing pressure and the steep price of success.

Starring Boys

When teachers are asked to remember their most outstanding students, boys' names dominate the list. Teachers say males are brighter, better at science and math, and more likely to become the nation's future leaders. When students are asked to choose outstanding classmates, they also name boys. But boys are also on another roster. When teachers remember their worst students—the discipline problems, the ones most likely to create a classroom disturbance or to flunk out of school—they still list boys.[1] As one teacher at a workshop put it, "Boys at school are either in the process of becoming the Establishment or fighting it. Either way, they are the center of attention."

While boys stand out, girls blend in, do their work, wait their turn, and become the supporting cast. But the main parts, the starring roles of hero and villain, are usually reserved for the boys. Training for stardom begins at home. An elementary school principal in Connecticut described an interview she had with a mother and her young son, a new kindergarten prospect:

> There they were both in my office, the mother sitting across the desk with her son on her lap. As I was explaining the kindergarten program, I watched the boy squirm. He began tapping his mother on the arm to get her attention. She asked him to wait, but he only tapped harder. I began to hurry my explanation, but I wasn't fast enough. Finally the little boy grabbed his mother's chin, pulled it down to him, and said angrily, "I need you *now!*"
>
> That image sums it up for me. Many boys come to school the center of attention, the pride and joy of the family. Then the shock hits: They're not the center anymore. As one of many, they must wait, learn to take their turn, and follow the rules. They come to school the Prince of Everything, and here they lose their royal standing.

Arriving at school as the entitled gender, boys decide which is the best lunchroom table and take it. During recess they claim the schoolyard as their own. In the classroom, attention is the prize. Boys start by raising their hands, but if the teacher does not call on them, the more assertive literally call on themselves, shouting out the answers, sometimes even interrupting the teacher midsentence. But not every boy can be at the head of the class. Only a few rise to the very top. We watched two boys fight for star status in a suburban elementary school:

> Twenty-eight students file into the room, hang up their coats, and take their seats. The teacher, a nine-year veteran of the classroom, reviews the day's agenda. Math is first on the schedule.
>
> It is then we meet Jim and Matt, without being formally introduced. With the teacher's first question their hands shoot up. First Matt answers, then Jim, as each competes to be the center of attention. Hands waving, they edge out of their seats. Jim sits on his knees, gaining a full six inches and a visible advantage over Matt. The next question goes to the now-elevated Jim, stirring Matt to even greater heights—

literally. He stands beside his chair and waves his arm. "Settle down, guys, and give someone else a chance," the teacher says. Several other students are called on, but within a few minutes the "Matt and Jim Show" returns. When the teacher writes difficult problems on the board, the questions no one else can answer, she turns to her two male stars for answers. "Matt and Jim will be great mathematicians when they grow up," the teacher comments as math class ends and she erases the problems from the board.

Evidently, Matt will grow up to be a great historian as well, for he dominates social studies, too. With Jim less involved, Matt has the floor all to himself. During language arts, the class works in small groups on stories for a school newspaper, and the achievements of Jim and Matt are featured in several articles. The last class before lunch is science, and Matt is called up for a demonstration. As he stands in front of the room and reads the results of the science experiment, the other students dutifully copy his calculations into their notebooks.

During lunch we review our observation forms. Although almost evenly divided between boys and girls, males in this class have benefited from a more active learning environment; but Matt and Jim were in a class of their own. Matt received more of the teacher's time and talent than anyone else, with Jim coming in second. Calling these two boys future mathematicians, the teacher further distanced them from the rest of the class. At the end of three hours, Matt and Jim have answered almost half of the teachers' questions, leaving the other twenty-six students to divide up the remainder of the teachers' attention. Nine students, six girls and three boys, have not said a single word.

Warmed by the academic spotlight, students like Matt and Jim reap school rewards. In the elementary grades their future careers are the talk of the teachers' room. By high school, prestigious colleges and scholarships loom on the horizon. But school life can be marred by clouds even for stars. Since their performance is head and shoulders above the other students, boys like Matt and Jim no longer compete with their classmates; they are vying with each other. These superstar students, who are more likely to be male, face ever-increasing pressure and cutthroat competition in their fight to get to the top—to win state honors, the most lucrative scholarship, a place at an Ivy League college. From Jim's vantage point, although ahead of his classmates, he just can't seem to catch up with Matt. Frustration and despair often haunt and depress smart boys who find themselves "runners-up" in the competition for top prizes.

Star students are not the only ones who capture the teacher's attention. When schools are not able to meet their needs, some boys cross the line and go from calling out to acting out. On the classroom stage these males take the bad boy role, sometimes using it as a passport to popularity. Interviewing elementary school students, researchers have found that the most admired males are those ready to take on the teacher. Here's how two fourth graders described these popular boys:

> MARK: They're always getting into trouble by talking back to the teacher.
> TOM: Yeah, they always have to show off to each other that they aren't afraid to say anything they want to the teacher, that they aren't teachers' pets. Whatever they're doing, they make it look like it's better than what the teacher is doing, 'cause they think what she's doing is stupid.
> MARK: And one day Josh and Allen got in trouble in music 'cause they told the teacher the Disney movie she wanted to show sucked. They got pink [disciplinary] slips.
> TOM: Yeah, and that's the third pink slip Josh's got already this year, and it's only Thanksgiving.[2]

If teachers were asked to "round up the usual suspects"—the class clowns, troublemakers, and delinquents—they would fill the room with boys. Teachers remember these boys for all the wrong reasons. In fact, so pervasive is the concern over male misbehavior that even when a boy and a girl are involved in an identical infraction of the rules, the male is more likely to get the penalty. Scenes like this one are played out daily in schools across America:

> Two seniors, Kyle and Michelle, arrive at their high school English class fifteen minutes late. The teacher stares at them as they enter the room. "Kyle, do you need a special invitation? Is it too much to ask that you get here on time? Never mind. Sit down and see me after class. (Pause; voice softens.) And Michelle, I'm disappointed in you."

In most cases when boys get tougher discipline, however, it is because they deserve it. Their disorderly conduct sets into motion a chain reaction with steep costs and lasting impressions. When men at our workshops looked back on their school days, some of their most unpleasant memories were of the tough disciplinary incidents they experienced. A man who is now a high school teacher in New England said: "I was in fifth grade, and it was the first time I had a male teacher. This teacher would treat the girls almost like princesses, but when the boys were disciplined, it was very physical and very rough. He would grab us by the hair and slam our heads down on the desk."

Ann, a student teacher in a Maryland middle school, is already learning the disaster potential of problem students, mainly male. Observing her class, we keep track of which students she calls on, what she says, and where she moves in the room. When we show her our notes, she sees that most of her questions went to six boys sitting at two tables near her desk.

"I know I usually call on those boys up front. I put them there so I can keep an eye on them."

"Did you realize that more than half of the questions you asked went to those six boys?"

"I didn't think I was talking with them that much, but I do use questions to keep them on task."

"Were they on task?"

"At the beginning, but toward the end they weren't paying attention."

"What about the other twenty-four students, the rest of the class? How were they doing?"

Ann looks confused. "I don't even know," she says. "I was so concerned about that group of boys, so worried they would act out, I didn't pay much attention to the rest of the class."

Ann was devoting her energy to boys at the bottom, the ones with potential to undermine her authority and throw the class into turmoil. So powerful was their influence, they determined where she walked, whom she questioned, and even how the room was arranged and where students sat.

Boys at the bottom and boys at the top are magnets that attract a teacher's attention either as a reward or as a mechanism for control. Teachers hope their male stars will become tomorrow's corporate presidents, senators, and civic leaders, but they do not hold high hopes for the boys at the bottom. Instead they fear those males could become involved in very serious trouble. Both groups are taught very different lessons and socialized into distinct aspects of the male role in America. Whether they are first or last, those boys pay a price.

Frozen Borders

At a time when girls are questioning the status quo and revising old rules, schoolboys seem locked in the past. From leisure activities to courses and career planning, inflexible codes channel them into rigidly defined roles.

Researchers watched as a woman played with a baby she had just met. When told the baby was a boy, she selected a rubber hammer from a pile of toys in the room. When the baby became restless, the woman played with him even more.

The researchers next observed another woman who came into the room to play with the same baby, but this time the woman was told the infant was female. From the pile of toys in the room she selected a doll. When the baby became restless, she tenderly soothed and cuddled it. Altogether, thirty-two women were observed, and in each case their style of caring differed depending on whether the baby was presented as male or female.[3] It appears that from their very first days, children learn the gender boundaries of their worlds.

While blankets camouflage an infant's gender, children three or four years old need more creative disguises. Resourceful researchers videotaped two youngsters engaged in rough play, their sex camouflaged by snowsuits. Adults were asked to rate the aggression level of one child who was throwing snowballs and hitting the other. Although viewers all watched the same videotape, they were given different gender information. Some groups were told both children were boys, others that both were girls, and still others that one was male and the other female. When observers thought a boy was hitting a girl or a girl was hitting anyone, they rated the scene negatively. But when viewers believed that one boy was hitting another, they did not disapprove of the fight. In fact, the scene of male violence was accepted by viewers as a typical case of "boys will be boys."[4]

While girls are encouraged to cooperate and compromise, males grow up in a rougher world. Parents, particularly fathers, are more likely to punish sons with physical force. From movies like *Rambo* and *Mad Max*, for example, boys learn that the best and fastest way to resolve conflict may be a kick or a punch. As they grow older, feet and fists are no longer enough, and weapons work their way into adolescent lives. From bar to battlefield, from post office to fast-food chain, male violence is a threat away from exploding. And as violence becomes a part of too many boys' lives, empathy and caring are in danger of being extinguished.

When a group of researchers interviewed boys from kindergarten through fourth grade in schools in Ohio and Pennsylvania, they heard voices that were sensitive and caring in the younger grades. Boys were willing to admit feelings of fear and vulnerability. Trying to adjust to a new room, one confessed, "I can't see the whole room in the dark . . . and when the garage door goes up, it sounds like a dragon. So I just shut my eyes and hold my pillow." Another described the anxiety he feels just before falling asleep: "At night I get all scared and I think I see smoke, and I get under my covers and I get all scared." When the interviewer asked what he did to keep from being frightened, he answered, "I hug my stuffed animals."

The boys also talked about how much they valued friendship. One said, "A friend is someone who's willing to do something if you ask him to . . . like if it was a tie in a vote, then he would give in and say, 'Well, you can have it this time.'" Some boys described caring for make-believe companions instead of real-life friends. A first grader described a whole classroom of imaginary friends passed on to him by his sister. They lived behind a secret door in his house, and he was their teacher. "They like to learn," he said, "and I like to help them."[5] But according to researcher Linda Tillman, this sensitive side is forced underground as the boys grow older. They learn to be careful about showing how deeply they care.

Male children who care for younger brothers and sisters become less aggressive and more nurturing in their relationships. But while parents encourage empathy in daughters, caring boys may be seen as too gentle. Psychologist Phyllis Berman videotaped forty-eight male and female two- and three-year-olds as they pretended to take care of their dolls. The parents, a sophisticated group of professionals, praised the girls with comments such as, "You're such a good mommy," but they failed to encourage similar nurturing behavior in boys.[6]

Males as well as females benefit from the experience of caring for others, and if these opportunities are denied, boys may lose touch with their own emotions. When researchers asked girls and boys to recall whether they had felt afraid, sad, disgusted, or guilty in the last month, most males denied experiencing these reactions. But when the boys were asked to keep a daily diary of their feelings, guilt, sadness, disgust, and fear all appeared in their personal accounts. Since expressing emotion is something girls are supposed to do, boys often deny their feelings—but they don't go away.[7]

Repressed emotions can explode with horrifying results. Newspapers describe with alarming frequency stories about recently separated men who murder their wives, fired employees who kill coworkers, and despondent males who take their own lives. These are men whose vocabularies lack emotional words but are filled instead with phrases of pressure: "something's gotta give," "I'm not gonna take it anymore," and "pushing it to the limit." While some men explode, others collapse inward, acquiring the habit of stony silence. Wives ask, "What's bothering you?" and children plead, "What's wrong, Daddy?" to no avail. These men have hidden their emotions so well, they no longer know what or where they are.

While boys learn the lessons of emotional amnesia and encase themselves in a tough shell, girls are not limited to such traditional and restrictive standards. Females are allowed to explore a range of behavior without excessive peer or parental concern. Girls who love sports and hate dresses were once indulgently called "tomboys," but the term is now used almost exclusively by adults. Girls' roles have expanded so dramatically that the concept makes no sense to the new generation.[8] But the world has changed far less for boys. Parents and teachers at our workshops tell us what happens when boys take even small steps beyond the rigid male borders:

> When my second-grade son asked to march in the Memorial Day parade, we were thrilled. Then he announced he wanted to twirl a baton. My husband's eyes almost popped out of his head, and he did everything he could think of to discourage him.

> On our son's ninth birthday, his uncle took him to a toy store to pick out a gift. Gary chose a walkie-talkie set. His uncle refused to buy it because it was pink.

> One of the students in my third-grade class would not take his backpack out of the closet. Day after day he would carry books home, but he never used that backpack. When I asked

him why, he finally admitted that the other boys would laugh
at the "101 Dalmatians" printed all over it.

By adolescence the pressure of conforming to the male role has become relentless; one high school student we interviewed called it a
prison. Tony attends an East Coast private school where he said five
rules must be followed by boys who want to fit the "standard" male
code of behavior: Be a good student but not too good—any better than
B+ is a nerd. Play three varsity sports—or two with weight training.
Party and get drunk. Brag about sexual accomplishments and refer to
girls as bitches in casual conversation. And never show your feelings.

But as coeditor of his school's literary magazine, Tony said he was
constantly surprised by the depth of the emotional side so many boys
were hiding. "Tough guys and jocks hand in these incredible poems.
They're usually seniors who will never see anyone again—or they
make it anonymous. They're so afraid if they mess with their macho
appearance, people will think less of them." As a student active in the
drama program, Tony had already experienced this lack of regard as
well as a great deal of hazing. "Guys will come up to me and say, 'You
do drama, right? So you're a fag, right?' And they call all the boys who
try out for plays DQs. We even call ourselves that—the Drama Queers."

Of all the cruel epithets boys hurl at one another, none is more devastating than being called a "girl," "woman," "sissy," "fag," or "queer."
So boys work hard to purge themselves of any taint of femininity. Parents, teachers, and other adults also draw gender lines, training boys
to avoid toys, games, or behavior associated with girls.[9] Again and
again participants in our workshops described how that distancing
takes place.

> As a young boy I was slow to learn how to throw a baseball.
> One day in his haste to have me learn, my father yelled at
> me, "You throw like a girl!" There was such a negative twist
> to that statement. I still hear it in my mind whenever I go to
> throw a ball. Needless to say, I never did learn how to throw
> very well.

> I was student teaching in Washington, D.C., when Jim, one
> of my third graders, came in crying. He said that Brian
> called him names because he was wearing a pink shirt.
> When Jim began to cry, my supervising teacher scolded him:
> "Stop crying, Jim. Be a man!"

> The elementary school class was about to play dodge ball,

and the teacher had divided the teams by gender. He named the boys' team the Tigers, and the girls were called the Fairies. Then he looked over at the boys' team and gave a warning: "This is a game where you learn to move fast. If you are so slow that a girl can hit you with the ball, you will go over to their team. Then you will be a fairy."

Studies show that adults worry about cross-sex behavior for both boys and girls, but parents and teachers believe girls will grow out of male behavior while boys will carry female traits into adulthood.[10] Fearing boys who play with dolls or who try on makeup or jewelry will become homosexuals or transsexuals, adults watch them with intense concern and preoccupation:

> It was my first year teaching, and there was one four-year-old boy who was the talk of the school. We had a dramatic-play area, and whenever this boy went there, he would put on women's clothes. Every teacher who saw this (some came especially to see it) said it was queer. On the playground this boy would be a "hairdresser" and do my hair. Over the course of the year he changed; he played more with the boys and stopped assuming female roles. What I thought was so peculiar was that although the boy changed, the teachers never stopped talking about the time he acted female.

When boys cross the gender line, public humiliation can follow, as one teacher from a workshop in New England remembered:

> A young boy, maybe four years old, was interested in his mother's bright, sparkly clothes and jewelry. He thought they were beautiful and interesting . . . so different from anything he had.
>
> One day he walked past his mother's closet, saw the beautiful clothes, and decided to put them on. It happened to be Thanksgiving and the whole family—grandparents, cousins, aunts, and uncles—were downstairs. What a nice surprise it would be for everyone, he thought, if he went downstairs in the beautiful clothes.
>
> Well, the boy went downstairs and stood in the middle of the floor. A dress, shoes, jewelry, even lipstick covered his small frame. On his face was a large smile; he was so proud of how he looked.
>
> His father jumped out of his chair, grabbed the boy, and

hit him over and over, calling him a faggot and a sissy. That
happened forty years ago, and I'll never forget it.

During her four years as a researcher in an elementary school,
Raphaela Best observed as male children learned the lessons of boyhood. In order to be accepted by his peers, by second grade a boy had
to "root out anything in his own actions, feelings, and preferences that
could be viewed as remotely female. . . . Whatever females did, that
was what boys must not do."[11] As they learn they are the more valued
gender and that female activities are to be avoided at all costs, boys begin to disparage girls. As we showed in Chapter Four on female loss of
self-esteem, when males were asked to write essays about how their
lives would be different if they found when they woke up that they were
members of the opposite sex, 95 percent saw no advantage to being a
girl. For many, suicide was a preferred option.[12]

Boys' feelings of misogyny, if allowed to develop unchecked, can
bear bitter fruit in adulthood. Men who view women as worth less or
as objects of scorn and submission may act on those beliefs. Each year
approximately 2 million wives are physically assaulted by their husbands and more than 100,000 women report they have been raped. Almost one-third of all female murder victims are slain by husbands and
boyfriends.[13]

The idea of waking up a girl is not only a gender step down, it is a
prison that restricts physical activity. And as any playground shows,
action is essential: Males are seen climbing jungle gyms, running the
base paths, and knocking into one another with reckless abandon as
they accumulate their boyhood quota of scratches, scabs, and stitches.
During four years spent as a researcher in an elementary school,
Raphaela Best watched boys collect wounds as if they were medals of
masculinity. She described two third graders who seemed to view
themselves as Evel Knievels in training. The woods behind their homes
became a stunt course; their minibikes were their chariots.

This is how one of the participants, Paul, described the adventure:
"Well, I was burning [rubber] and I went over [a hill] when I hit— Well,
I had an accident and hit a tree. Then I got up, and Derek did it. . . . I
thought he had broken his leg. . . . That was fun. One back tire was off
the ground. Man, that was fun." When the teacher said she was worried that the activity could result in injury, the boys shrugged it off and
told her that they loved the action. Danger was part of the fun. As Paul
carefully explained to the teacher, "It's like my granddaddy says, 'If a
boy doesn't have a couple of scars, he'll never be a man.'"[14]

Gradually, chaotic play is organized into athletic games complete with rules and goals. As they compete, boys rank one another. The fastest, strongest, and toughest take a high place in the male pecking order; the rest are left with less status and scars that cannot be seen. To defend themselves, weaker boys may band together and look to one another for sustenance and support. But rejection is a thin base on which to build friendship. In Raphaela Best's study, Ronnie, a third-grade outsider, said of the other rejected boys, "They think I like them, but I don't." Kenny, another member of a low-status group, told the teacher, "Do you hear them out there? They're waiting for me. They think I'm their best friend, but I'm not. I don't even like them."

Those at the top of the male pecking order are almost always skill-ful athletes. Sports becomes the native language of schoolboys: "Did you see the game last night?" "What position do you play?" "Who do you think will make the Superbowl?"

"All boys love baseball," Zane Grey observed. "If they don't, they're not real boys." When one former college basketball player was asked to recall how he became involved in sports, he looked puzzled. It wasn't something you "got into," it was something you did naturally, without thinking, "like brushing your teeth." Sports and masculinity nourish each other; it is a lesson boys learn early.[15]

Field of Broken Dreams

The principal of the Indiana high school obviously enjoyed showing off his school. He took us on a tour of the new computer center, the science labs, and a vocational training area. Then he began to smile broadly.

"This is our jewel," he said.

We turned a corner, he opened a door, and we entered the gym. It was enormous. Thousands of seats terraced up all sides, and the ceiling was at least four stories high. The gym was almost as big as the entire rest of the school.

"It's incredible, but why so large?" we asked.

"Intimidation," the principal responded.

"Intimidation?"

"When the other teams come here, to this small town,

they expect a small gym. This place intimidates the hell out of them. The whole town comes out and screams for our boys. This is the town's entertainment center, our sports cathedral."

In the 1950s, James Coleman studied adolescents in Illinois. He asked high school boys to select how they would like to be remembered. The choices were "most popular," "athletic star," or "brilliant student." The preferred option was "athletic star," selected by 44 percent of the teenage boys. When asked who they would like to have as a friend, an "athlete but not a scholar" was the choice of 56 percent of the boys, while "scholar but not an athlete" was chosen by fewer than 20 percent.[16]

More recent studies show that sports remains a focal point of school life and growing up male. The large sign in the hallway of a Maine middle school captures it all, a visible reminder of the connection between athletics and masculinity:

> Feel like being a State Champ—
> Join the Boys' Track Team and
> *Dominate*.
> Or maybe you would rather sit on the couch and become *fat* and *lazy*. Maybe you don't have the berries to work and win. We're looking for a *few good men*.

Aggression, repressed in the classroom, is harnessed by coaches, put to work on the athletic field, and released against the opposing team. In a middle school study, interviews with students showed how this happens. One football team member who was especially aggressive described how physical violence pleased his coach: "Yeah . . . I really socked that guy. Man, I threw him down on the concrete. Did you hear Coach James yelling 'Way to go, Orville?'" Another boy complained about a teammate who was trying to pick a fight. "Knock his socks off in practice" was the coach's advice.[17] So the playing field becomes a legitimate arena for fighting, hostility, and competition.

Boys endure pain and suffer through long hours of practice because sports offer many rewards—self-esteem, leadership, teamwork, and the satisfaction that comes from playing hard and well. A select few move from satisfaction to stardom. Even in the elementary grades talented athletes rise to the top of the popularity charts. But boys who fumble the ball are not so fortunate. A group of researchers observed and interviewed children in two elementary schools for three years. In both schools the most popular boy in each grade was also the best athlete. Those who were clumsy and awkward were picked on, ridiculed, and called "fag" and other names suggesting they were like girls. Travis, a fifth-grade student described Wren, an unathletic classmate, as "a nerd. He's short and his ears stick out." Nikko said about Wren: "When he sits in his chair, he crosses one leg over the other and curls the toe around his calf, so it's double-crossed. . . . It looks so faggy with his 'girly' shoes."[18]

Boys like Wren become school pariahs and isolates. But those who are tough and good at sports achieve social success, sometimes in spite of themselves: According to fifth-grade Nick, "Craig is sort of mean, but he's really good at sports, so he's popular." And Ben said, "Everybody wants to be friends with Gabe, even though he makes fun of most of them all the time. But they still all want to pick him for their team and have him be friends with them because he's a good athlete, even though he brags a lot about it. He's popular."[19]

By middle school boys' sports becomes the most salient and prestigious of all school-sponsored activities. While girls have teams, they pale in comparison to the visibility and status of male sports. Studying the routes to popularity in middle school, researcher Donna Eder found there were never more than twenty-five spectators at girls' games, but boys' football games were a community draw, sometimes attracting as many as five hundred people.[20] By high school, male athletes, proudly wearing their lettered school sweaters or jerseys, stand out in school hallways and at parties.

Every boy's dream of being a sports star can turn into a nightmare. A few boys win social status and fame for their athletic exploits, but most boys are found on the sidelines. Aside from the few who reap rewards from the playing field, the rest are destined to fail and have to learn to live with disappointment. Men in our workshops remember the humiliation of failing to measure up:

> I will never forget gym class in high school. I looked down when they picked the teams. I used to imagine I was somewhere else, anywhere but this place of rejection. The teacher picked the two best players to be the captains. Then they picked the members of their teams. The best boys got picked first, then the average, then the worst. By the time they got to the worst players, the ones they picked last, I just wanted the choosing to be over. When they came to me, they would sometimes choose nobody instead. One would say, "You can have him." Then the other would say, "No, I don't want him.

You take him." The argument would go on for what seemed like infinity.

Others recall developing ingenious devices to mask athletic incompetence:

> I hated being picked last for basketball games, so I developed this neat trick of spinning a basketball on my fingertip. As they were choosing teams, I'd just casually start spinning the ball. It was impressive. It wasn't until the game started that they realized I couldn't shoot a basket if my life depended on it.

Others describe exerting themselves beyond reason and good health to fulfill the male sports role:

> When I was in the eighth grade, I attended a middle school just outside New York City. We all took tests of strength, and almost everyone beat me, even some girls. I went to a health club and began working out. Weight training became a five-year obsession. I always had to be bigger and stronger than everyone, no matter how much I hurt myself. I'm twenty years old now. I can't lift anymore, I can't play tennis or racquetball anymore. I can't throw a ball, and I have worse joints than most fifty- or sixty-year-olds. But at least I was stronger than those kids in my high school gym class.

A story in a widely read magazine tells of a high school football star about to catch a game-winning pass. Students were going wild, tasting victory. But their joy was cut short by a shout from the stands. "Take him out!" yelled the principal. The students groaned as their star player was removed. His sin: He had "failed to make the academic standing required of athletes in all self-respecting schools." The article appeared in *The Saturday Evening Post* in 1912.[21] Eighty years later, *The Washington Post* ran an article with a similar theme, "Academics Stall Athletics," describing how poor scholastic performance blocked talented sports stars from playing.[22]

For most of this century, schools have struggled to balance academics and athletics. Some high schools and colleges build status and reputation on the backs of teams who climb into the national rankings; and for athletes who might never otherwise see the inside of a college classroom, physical talent becomes the magic key to a college degree. But lack of academic preparation can be the Achilles' heel of an otherwise promising athlete.[23] Seduced by their star status, many high school athletes lose touch with reality and dribble away the future.

One star basketball player from Washington, D.C., remembered that in junior high school he didn't realize professional teams selected players from college teams, so he never thought about college. He spent his first three years in high school in a world of basketball games and practice. Before long he was caught up in the excitement of joining a major college sports program, a promising match between an African-American student aspiring to higher education and the University of Maryland hoping to benefit from the talents of a local athlete. The only obstacle to this blissful union was academics. The boy's high school average had fallen below a C, and he had not enrolled in the demanding courses required for college admission. Late in his high school career he got a tutor and enrolled in more core courses. He studied, took the SATs again and again, but never met the minimum test score requirement, which sabotaged his chances for a college education. "I didn't take most things seriously in high school," he said. "If I had it all to do over again, I'd just buckle down and do what I was supposed to do."[24]

Competitive sports often seduces and disappoints both the talented and the talentless. Boys, eyes glued to their television sets, watch heroes such as Michael Jordan and Joe Montana sell sneakers in the morning, win games in the afternoon, and drive expensive cars to glamorous places in the evening. These media mirages entice male students onto a playing field of broken dreams. Few make the school team, fewer become stars, and fewer still ever play for a college, much less a professional team. It is a system designed to produce a rare Michael Jordan and a multitude of losers.

The Feminine School and the Emasculation of Boys

Through athletics boys are taught that competition, aggression, and endurance build real men, on the playing field and in the workplace. It was precisely because they intensified traditional notions of masculinity that educators found sports so attractive and incorporated them into the official school program. By the early part of the twentieth century, athletics had become an important line of defense, a counterweight against a frightening educational development: the arrival of women teachers.

From the 1870s into the twentieth century, schools experienced a gender revolution. During the Civil War men left their teaching positions to join the army. When schools posted vacancy signs, women lined up. By the early 1900s they had become more than 85 percent of the nation's teachers, more than half the school principals, and in the Midwest, 60 percent of school superintendents, numbers that far exceed today's statistics. Once a world managed by men, schools were being taken over by women.

Not everyone was pleased with these developments. Critics argued that schools had become a battleground between female teachers who were stressing decorum and conformity and free-spirited boys who were struggling to grow into real men. In this battle of the sexes, boys were the victims and losers. Critics had a name for these new instructors: the "woman peril."

By the early part of the twentieth century the public had come to believe that the arrival of female teachers represented a serious threat to the healthy development of boys. These concerns were fanned by critics such as military leader Admiral F. E. Chadwick, who declared that a boy taught by a woman "at his most character-forming age is to render violence to nature [causing] a feminized manhood, emotional, illogical, noncombative." According to the admiral, female teachers represented a threat to healthy male development and endangered the national security.[25] Psychologist G. Stanley Hall agreed, explaining that a time of rough and uncouth development was necessary so boys could forge their masculine identity. Women as teachers or mothers harmed males by feminizing them, taming them, and transforming them into unnatural "little gentlemen." Denied a "wild period" of toughness and independence, these boys would never mature into "real men."

Hall's warnings resonated across the nation. A principal in Louisville, Kentucky, advised his colleagues that American boys were losing their competitive edge and becoming effeminate. The culprit was the female teacher. A University of Wisconsin professor termed the entry of women into teaching an unwanted "invasion."[26] And an educator from England observed that "the boy in America is not being brought up to punch another boy's head or to stand having his own punched in a healthy and proper manner; that there is a strange and indefinable air coming over the man; a tendency toward a common, if I may call it, sexless tone of thought."[27]

To develop tougher males while controlling wild ones, some school administrators experimented with an innovative plan. They co-opted the rough-and-tumble games boys played during recess and in their free time, and made these part of the official curriculum. By sponsoring athletic contests, schools not only developed "manly" boys but also subdued unruly ones, exhausting them into compliance. A New York principal observed in 1909 that when "the most troublesome and backward boys" played basketball for an hour each day, miracles were achieved: "An incorrigible class was brought to the gymnasium; a tired but tractable class left it." The administrator also found that sports created school spirit and helped solve discipline problems. "Many instances have come to my notice where big, strong, incorrigible, and stupid boys have been stimulated by the opportunity to represent their schools."[28]

As part of the educational curriculum, athletics was seen as a panacea, one that would reduce the dropout problem, create a masculine environment, and give unruly males an energy outlet—and schools a public relations bonanza. The community flocked to sporting events, especially football and basketball games; they even paid to attend. School sports were a regular newspaper feature, and high school athletes became local celebrities. But even sports did not stem the tide of the "woman peril." Male teachers continued to feel threatened.

Registering its opposition in 1904, the Male Teachers Association of New York City came forward with its position: Men are "necessary ideals for boys" and are "less mechanical in instruction."[29] Consequently, they are more effective teachers and deserve more money. Woman-bashing reached the highest levels of government when Theodore Roosevelt lamented the arrival of the female teacher and publicly spoke out against her negative impact on boys. But neither presidents nor professors could deter school boards from a good deal. By 1920 a school with forty teachers was typically staffed by thirty-four women and six men, saving thousands of tax dollars since women worked for less pay. As females took the helm of America's classrooms, citizens scrutinized school performance. What they saw only added to their concern.

Less than a century ago, girls' faltering performance on standardized tests, their loss of self-esteem, and their underenrollment in higher education and professional schools were not seen as problems. Back then, girls and schools seemed a match made in heaven. When it came to grades, girls excelled. Sitting on the graduation stage, they sparkled like perfect academic jewels while boys fidgeted. Many males didn't even stay in school long enough to make it to graduation. At the turn of the century, the term for male failure was not "grade repeater"; boys who were left back were called "retarded."

Throughout the first half of the twentieth century, critics continued to blame female teachers for boys' academic problems. As late as 1964, Patricia Sexton wrote in the *Saturday Review*:

> Boys and the schools seem locked in a deadly and ancient conflict that may eventually inflict mortal wounds on both. . . . The problem is not just that teachers are too often women. It is that school is too much a woman's world, governed by women's rules and standards. The school code is that of propriety, obedience, decorum, cleanliness, physical and, too often, mental passivity."[30]

Sexton continued her male distress call in *The Feminized Male*, an influential book published in 1969.[31] Echoing Hall's half-century-old criticism, Sexton argued that schools emasculated boys by imposing feminine norms that demanded docility, neatness, and silence—all the qualities males lacked. Forcing a boy to go to school was like putting a bull in a china shop. Males who submitted to the feminine school environment added new entries to the school vernacular: "mama's boy," "teacher's pet," and "apple polisher." Those who resisted were punished. Because of female teachers, boys were put in an impossible situation—forced to choose between feminization or failure.

In the 1960s and '70s, worry over the "woman peril" was replaced by concern for women in peril as the modern feminist movement took shape. By the time Sexton's *The Feminized Male* arrived in bookstores, Betty Friedan's *The Feminine Mystique* was already there. As women's spheres continued to expand, men's territory shriveled. Like hunting game or fighting intruding tribes, the male role of family protector and breadwinner was becoming a thing of the past.

The early position of the fledgling men's movement was that masculinity had been too long measured by the size of a man's paycheck, by his ability to win, by repressing emotions, toughing it out, and beating other males. In the end this behavior proved self-defeating, and the costs were daunting: alienation from others and early death. Men were advised to allow their "feminine" side to emerge. Caring fathers and sensitive husbands were promoted in movies, books, and talk shows. But a second wave of authors marked a different path, calling upon men not to discover their feminine qualities but instead to reclaim their masculine roots.

In 1991, Robert Bly's *Iron John* sold more copies than any other nonfiction book in America, and a few months later Sam Keen's *Fire in the Belly* became a best-seller. Credited by some with reinventing the modern men's movement and criticized by others as a lunatic fringe leader, Bly asked males to join him on a mythological journey to relive their past through an ancient folktale: Iron John's initiation into manhood. To reach true masculinity Iron John needed to detach himself not only from woman as mother but from all females and return to a legendary past of ancient forests, physical challenge, and male mentors. Bly wrote, "The Industrial Revolution in its need for office and factory workers has pulled boys away from their father[s] and from other men, and placed them in compulsory schools, where the teachers are mostly women."[32] There boys suffocate under female influence that is "not balanced by positive male values."[33] In his resurrection of fears about the "woman peril," Bly's warning is a reminder: When it comes to gender, parents and teachers have spent most of the twentieth century worrying about boys at school—and the kind of men they will become.

Out of Control

The importance of initiation into manhood has been a perennial theme. Bly's *Iron John*, G. Stanley Hall's "wild period," and Teddy Roosevelt's call for "manly" contests with nature all describe the rite of passage from boy to manhood. And all claim that when women are in charge of this passage, males are at risk of feminization. But without the influence of women, the traditional characteristics of masculinity—aggression, toughness, and strength—may become intensified and distorted; sometimes they spin out of control. In all-male groups, females are more likely to be objectified and treated as less than human. Then, as in sports, sexuality is turned into an arena where boys must prove they are real men. Some males take extreme action to "score."

On the television screen he looked clean-cut and handsome, the all-American boy. The Lakewood senior explained to the television audience that school athletes like himself were "the popular men on campus," so popular that they had formed their own group called the Spur Posse. The posse's purpose was to have sex with as many girls as possible, counting each girl as 1 point. The rules were quite clear: Multiple sex encounters with the same girl still counted as only a single point, so different girls were needed for the score to climb high. The star Spur had a score of 67. Other members had much lower scores, having slept with only 40 or 50 girls. "I'm Reggie Jackson," said one, referring to the number 44 worn by the baseball player as the number of points he had accumulated. Expressing no remorse, regret, or second thoughts, posse members viewed themselves as male role models and claimed that "eight out of ten guys would like to have the life we lead." The posse's extreme exploits, covered by national media, gave the Lakewood Secondary School a new nickname: "Rapewood High."

Initially seven girls, ranging in age from eleven to seventeen, brought criminal charges against Spur Posse members, but all but one of the charges were dropped due to lack of evidence. One girl's mother said, "We're living in fear. They're hoodlums." Another girl transferred out of Lakewood to a new high school. But not everyone viewed the posse's behavior as a problem. Some parents saw it as a case of "boys will be boys" and described the girls as willing participants. A father of one of the boys said that the posse was just a group of athletes, an adolescent group like "band, choir, or the PTA." The boys were simply "sowing a few wild seeds" before college.[34]

College life is supposed to be a world apart from the transgressions of groups like the Spur Posse. But stereotypic masculine qualities can become magnified and distorted in higher education, too. Our students at The American University were discussing all-male rites of passage, from Eagle Scout initiation ceremonies to criminal acts required to join street gangs. A week later a young woman stopped by our office with a videotape.

"My friends shot this tape themselves. They go to college in Pennsylvania."

Not knowing what to expect, we loaded our VCR and watched what turned out to be a game called "physical challenge." The first boy on the tape was drinking directly from a hot chili bottle. With his face red and his voice hoarse, he yelled "Challenge!" and then passed the bottle to the next boy. Moaning and screaming, each took a mouthful. Next the boys challenged one another to eat live insects and then to walk down a public street naked. The final scene was called "riding a tree." Each boy crawled onto a second-story ledge and jumped, trying to reach a nearby tree to break the fall. Some caught branches, but others missed and hit the ground hard. The next day we told the student how upsetting we found the tape.

"I know. It's so dangerous," she said. "One boy broke an arm 'riding the tree,' and another didn't get anywhere near it. He plunged to the ground and received a concussion. But they still do it."

"Are they in a fraternity?"

"No. They're just college friends who share an apartment. This is their fun."

In a few colleges, this macho quality permeates campus life. Visitors to Wabash, Morehouse, and Hampden-Sydney, three of America's five remaining all-male colleges, say that a trip to campus is like experiencing a quantum leap back in time. At Wabash in Indiana, freshmen pledges still wear beanies, tip them when they pass a professor, and remind observers of the 1950s when Ivy League schools were all-male worlds.[35] To critics these colleges are historical oddities with little relevance to today's world. To advocates they represent unique and effective academic environments that are worth saving and nourishing. But two all-male colleges, The Citadel and Virginia Military Institute (VMI), both quasi-public and all military, have generated far more intense controversy. The Citadel and VMI argue that when females become students, military toughness and tradition are lost, so women are not welcome. While accepting taxpayer money, these colleges close their doors to half the taxpayers, a policy that has landed them in court.

Although The Citadel and VMI appear to be miniature versions of West Point, they are not. Unlike West Point, where the primary purpose is to prepare army officers, a minority of the students at these two colleges actually enter the military. But a military-style education is regarded as a way of teaching toughness.

At The Citadel, first-year students, called knobs, are closely supervised every waking minute. They must ask permission for each action—eating, leaving, passing, even sneezing or coughing. They salute everyone, talk to no one, serve upperclassmen at mess, and try to swallow a few quick mouthfuls before mealtime is over. This humiliating and grueling system is designed to develop discipline and the ability to function under intense stress and pressure. Many graduates praise their military-style education: "It gives you the feeling that you will confront nothing in life you can't handle. . . . You will not freeze, you will not choke up, you will do what has to be done." Not all students agree.

When Chad was recruited by The Citadel, he looked forward to the experience: "I thought a little responsibility and discipline might be good for me," he said. But when Chad missed crucial field goals and lost a football game, the young man learned firsthand about The Citadel's reputation for "building men." One night he was dragged from his bed, his head was wrapped in a blanket, and he was dunked repeatedly in a utility sink filled with water. Finally he passed out. Another night he was strung up by his fingers and left hanging in a closet with a saber perched between his legs. After three weeks of these lessons in self-discipline, Chad had had enough. He dropped out of school.[36]

Intensified masculinity is not just a situation of "boys will be boys." These rites of initiation and the sexual and physical proving grounds go beyond boyhood. Adult men also push the boundaries of masculinity to the danger point and beyond:

> Anthony Roberts was about to be initiated into a rafting and outdoor group called Mountain Men Anonymous. The Oregon carpenter's rite of passage seemed easy enough: hold a one-gallon fuel can above his head as a friend demonstrated his outdoor skills by shooting an arrow through the elevated vessel. Unfortunately, his friend's aim was low; Roberts lost his eye and almost his life. Recovering in the hospital, he told reporters, "I feel really stupid."[37]

Groups like Mountain Men Anonymous create a cultural time warp, idealizing a time in the past when males battled nature and each other. But today's culture calls for other skills—cooperation in the workplace and parenting at home. When risk-taking, violence, and sexual aggression are out of control and caring and nurturance are repressed, a distorted profile emerges, one that is detrimental to the good of society and to the healthy development of men.

Changing the Script

Boys confront frozen boundaries of the male role at every turn of school life. They grow up learning lines and practicing moves from a time-worn script: Be cool, don't show emotion, repress feelings, be aggressive, compete and win. As the script is internalized, boys learn to look down on girls and to distance themselves from any activity considered feminine. Dutifully they follow the lines of the script, but now changes are being made in the plot. Today's schoolboys are learning lines for a play that is closing. Consider these statistics:

- From elementary school through high school, boys receive lower report card grades. By middle school they are far more likely to be grade repeaters and dropouts.[38]
- Boys experience more difficulty adjusting to school. They are nine times more likely to suffer from hyperactivity and higher levels of academic stress.[39]
- The majority of students identified for special education programs are boys. They represent 58 percent of those in classes for the mentally retarded, 71 percent of the learning disabled, and 80 percent of those in programs for the emotionally disturbed.[40]
- In school, boys' misbehavior results in more frequent penalties, including corporal punishment. Boys comprise 71 percent of all school suspensions.[41]

Beyond academic problems, conforming to a stereotypic role takes a psychological toll:

- Boys are three times more likely to become alcohol dependent and 50 percent more likely to use illicit drugs. Men account for more than 90 percent of alcohol- and drug-related arrests.[42]
- Risk-taking behavior goes beyond drug and alcohol abuse. The leading cause of death among fifteen- to twenty-four-year-old white males is accidents. Teenage boys are more likely to die from gunshot wounds than from all natural causes combined.[43]
- Many boys are encouraged to pursue unrealistically high career goals. When these are not attained, males often feel like failures, and a lifelong sense of frustration may follow.[44]
- Males commit suicide two to three times more frequently than females.[45]

The problems for minority males are more devastating:

- Approximately one in every three black male teenagers is unemployed, and those who are working take home paychecks with 30 percent less salary than white workers.[46] It is estimated that 25 percent of black youths' income results directly from crime and that one in every six African-American males is arrested by age nineteen.[47]
- The odds of a young white woman being a murder victim are one in 369; for a young white man, one in 131; for an African-American woman, one in 104; and for an African-American man, a shocking one in 21. Homicide is the leading cause of death for young black men.[48]

City by city, the statistics are even more alarming. In New York City, about three out of four black males never make it to graduation, and in Milwaukee, 94 percent of all expelled students are African-American boys.[49] Milwaukee, Detroit, and Chicago consider black males an "endangered academic species" and have resorted to some radical solutions.

Milwaukee was one of the first cities to create black male academies, public schools that serve only African-American boys. The idea spread to other metropolitan areas, along with the notion that the best teachers for black boys are black men. At Matthew Henson Elementary School in a poor, drug-infested section of Baltimore, Richard Boynton teaches a class of young black students. Most of them grew up without fathers, so Boynton's responsibilities go beyond the classroom. "There are three things I enforce," he said, "three things I want them to know in that room: responsibility, respect, and self-control. I feel that these three things will not only carry you through school, they'll carry you through life."[50] So Boynton checks to make sure that all the boys have library cards. On weekends he takes them to the Smithsonian or to play ball in the park. "It's almost as if I have twenty-seven sons," he said. Boynton tries to create a school that will turn each of his "sons" on to education. But not everyone is convinced that teaching black males separately is the best approach.

"I read these things, and I can't believe that we're actually regressing like this," said African-American psychologist Kenneth Clark. "Why are we talking about segregating and stigmatizing black males?"[51] Clark's stinging observations are particularly potent since his research paved the way for the 1954 *Brown* decision that desegregated America's schools. Other critics charge that black male academies are little more than a return to the cries of "woman peril," scapegoating female teachers, criticizing black mothers, and ignoring the needs of African-American girls. NOW, the ACLU, and several courts have found separate black male education to be an example of sex discrimination and a violation of the law.

Morningside Elementary School in Prince Georges County, Maryland, is not a black male academy, but its students take special pride in their school team, the Master Knights. Tuesdays and Thursdays are team days, and the members, wearing blue pants and white shirts, devote recess and afternoons to practice. But the Knights, the majority of whom are young black boys, differ from other school teams. Their practices take place in the school library, and the arena in which they compete is chess.

The idea for the team originated in the office of Beulah McManus, the guidance counselor. When children, most often African-American boys, were referred to her as behavior problems, she pulled out a worn chess set. Somehow the game got boys talking, and eventually they found out they enjoyed chess, with its emphasis on tactics and skill, and the chance to compete on a field where size and strength mattered less than brains. As Gregory Bridges, the twelve-year-old president of the Master Knights, said, "When you see someone who is big and bad on the streets, you hardly see anyone who plays chess. . . . You have to have patience and a cool head, and that patience carries outside the chess club."[52] While Morningside emphasizes the importance of getting African-American boys excited about education, girls are not excluded, says principal Elsie Neely. In fact, the school is trying to recruit more female players for next year.

While Morningside stresses extracurricular activities in order to involve boys, some teachers are bringing lessons that challenge the male sex role stereotype directly into the classroom. Often they use the growing number of children's books that show boys expanding their roles. In a fourth-grade class we watched a teacher encouraging boys to push the borders of the male stereotype. As we observed her lesson, we were struck by how much effort it took to stretch outmoded attitudes. She began by writing a letter on the board.

> Dear Adviser:
>   My seven-year-old son wants me to buy him a doll. I don't know what to do. Should I go ahead and get it for him? Is this normal, or is my son sick? Please help!
>   Waiting for your answer,
>   Concerned

"Suppose you were an advice columnist, like Ann Landers," the teacher said to the class, "and you received a letter like this. What would you tell this parent? Write a letter answering 'Concerned,' and then we'll talk about your recommendations."

For the next twenty minutes she walked around the room and gave suggestions about format and spelling. When she invited the students to read their letters, Andy volunteered.

> Dear Concerned:
>   You are in big trouble. Your son is sick, sick, sick! Get him to a psychiatrist fast. And if he keeps asking for a doll, get him bats and balls and guns and other toys boys should play with.
>   Hope this helps,
>   Andy

Several other students also read their letters, and most, like Andy, recommended that the son be denied a doll. Then the teacher read Charlotte Zolotow's *William's Doll*, the story of a boy who is ridiculed by other children when he says he wants a doll. Not until his grandmother visits does he get his wish so that, as the wise woman says, he can learn to be a father one day.

As the teacher was reading, several students began to fidget, laugh, and whisper to one another. When she asked the fourth graders how they liked the book, one group of boys, the most popular clique in the class, acted as if the story was a personal insult. Their reaction was so hostile, the teacher had trouble keeping order. We heard their comments:

"He's a fag."

"He'd better learn how boys are supposed to behave, or he'll never get to be a man."

"If I saw him playing with that baby doll, I'd take it away. Maybe a good kick in the pants would teach him."

"Dolls are dumb. It's a girly thing to do."

Next the teacher played the song "William Wants a Doll" from the *Free to Be You and Me* album. Several boys began to sing along in a mocking tone, dragging out the word *doll* until it became two syllables: "William wants a do-oll, William wants a do-oll." As they chanted, they pointed to Bill, the star athlete of the class. Both boys and girls whispered and laughed as Bill, slumped in his chair, looked ready to explode.

Belatedly the teacher realized the problem of the name coincidence; she assured the class that there was nothing wrong with playing with dolls, that it teaches both girls and boys how to become parents when they grow up. When the students began to settle down, she gave them her next instructions: "I'd like you to reread your letters and make any last-minute corrections. If you want to change your advice, you may, but you don't have to."

Later we read the students' letters. Most of them said a seven-year-old boy should not get a doll. But after listening to William's story, six modified their advice, having reached a similar conclusion: "Oh, all right. Give him a doll if you have to. But no baby dolls or girl dolls. Make sure it's a Turtle or a G.I. Joe."

For some nontraditional programs, reading *William's Doll* is just a first step. At Germantown Friends School in Philadelphia, parenting classes begin in elementary school where children learn to observe, study, and interact with infants. By the sixth grade both boys and girls are in charge of caring for babies at school. Programs that make child-rearing a central and required part of school life find that boys become more nurturant and caring in their relationships with others.

Schools in New York City and other communities are downplaying aggression and encouraging cooperation through programs in conflict resolution. In these courses students learn how to negotiate and compromise while they avoid attitudes and actions that lead to violence. Students learn techniques in how to control anger, to listen carefully to others, and to seek common ground.

These innovative courses are rare. Most schools are locked in a more traditional model, one that promotes competition over cooperation, aggression over nurturing, and sports victories rather than athletic participation. Some boys thrive on this traditional male menu, and most students derive some benefit. But the school program is far from balanced, and the education served to boys is not always healthy despite the extra portions they receive.

From their earliest days at school, boys learn a destructive form of division—how to separate themselves from girls. Once the school world is divided, boys can strive to climb to the top of the male domain, thinking that even if they fall short, they still are ahead of the game because they are not girls. Boys learn in the classroom that they can demean girls at will. Schools that do not permit racist, ethnic, or religious slights still tolerate sexism as a harmless bigotry.

In *American Manhood*, Anthony Rotundo writes that men need to regain "access to stigmatized parts of themselves—tenderness, nurturance, the desire for connection, the skills of cooperation—that are helpful in personal situations and needed for the social good."[53] Studies support Rotundo's contention: Males who can call on a range of qualities, tenderness as well as toughness, are viewed by others as more intelligent, likable, and mentally healthy than rigidly stereotyped men.[54] But boys cannot develop these repressed parts of themselves without abandoning attitudes that degrade girls. Until gender equity becomes a value promoted in every aspect of school, boys, as victims of their own miseducation, will grow up to be troubled men; they will be saddened by unmet expectations, unable to communicate with women as equals, and unprepared for modern life.

9

Different Voices, Different Schools

We were coming to the close of one of our workshops. The participants had learned to look at school life with more perceptive eyes and to recognize the tiny, repetitive incidents of sexism that cut short the potential of girls. Then in the room of almost three hundred people, a woman called out, "These things didn't happen to me. I learned to be assertive, not silent." People turned toward the back of the room where the woman was standing. "I want my daughter to speak up for herself, too, so she's going to get a single-sex education like I did."

The mother's comment sparked controversy and questions. Should we send our daughters to all-girl schools? What about our sons? What are the psychological differences between boys and girls, and how are these differences affected by schools?

What Is Alice?

A philosopher offered a syllogism:

> All men are mortal.
> Socrates is a man.
> Therefore, Socrates is mortal.

That was logical, but then philosopher Elizabeth Minnich asked us to try this one:[1]

> All men are mortal.
> Alice is a _____.

In the case of the second syllogism, the mind boggles and logic derails. We cannot say Alice is a man, but if we insert "woman" in the blank, where are we? Is she immortal? By assuming a male norm, we have left Alice in no-man's-land—literally. She has become a misfit and a conundrum.

In psychology as well as logic, when the male becomes the norm, the female does not fit the theory. "It all goes back, of course," Carol Gilligan writes, "to Adam and Eve, a story which shows, among other things, that if you make a woman out of a man, you are bound to get into trouble. In the life cycle as in the Garden of Eden, the woman has been the deviant."[2] When *In a Different Voice* was published in 1982, Gilligan took close aim at Lawrence Kohlberg's model of moral development, one that had gained preeminence during the previous decade. In so doing she turned the field of psychology upside down.

In Kohlberg's hierarchy of moral development, the lowest stages show human behavior driven by fear of punishment and by self-interest. People at stage three act responsibly by caring about others, while those at stage four behave in accordance with rules and laws that maintain the social order. The most advanced levels of the hierarchy reflect commitment to abstract principles of justice and individual rights.

Women, Kohlberg discovered, were less moral than men; typically they scored at stage three while males, reasoning more morally, made it to higher levels, those closer to principles of rights and justice. His theory was widely publicized and became required reading in colleges across the country. One woman who was studying for a graduate degree in education during the 1970s recalled how shocked she had been to learn of her lesser moral status: "I remember the professor putting those Kohlberg stages on the board. He put a line next to stage three and wrote *Women* and a line next to stage four and wrote *Men*. Then he gave a lecture on how men reasoned at a higher moral level. I couldn't believe it. I had always worked hard to be a principled person—if anything more moral than most men I knew. The drawing of that male-superior hierarchy was burned into my brain."

When Gilligan's *In a Different Voice* pointed out that Kohlberg had constructed his moral theory from an all-male research sample, the book opened eyes; and it called into question not only Kohlberg's research but that of other psychologists who had used only male subjects to construct generic theories of human behavior. "It was like a first-year graduate student had conducted all those studies—and left out half the sample," Gilligan said.[3]

A decade later, when reading *In a Different Voice*, the female graduate student who had once been astounded to learn of women's moral inferiority recalled her sense of vindication: "When I learned that

Kohlberg had done his major research on an all-male sample, I felt so relieved. The model was already made by the time women were included. No wonder females didn't fit! Now I don't think I'm less moral. I think we need a new model."

Gilligan felt a new model was needed as well, and she attempted to develop one. From three studies, all based on small samples of individuals who were interviewed about moral conflict and choices, Gilligan derived her own theory: Men reason morally through a voice of individual rights and justice, but there is also a different voice, one of connection and caring, that belongs primarily to women.

To prove her argument, Gilligan quoted extensively from interviews. In one study, two sixth graders, Jake and Amy, attempted to solve a moral problem. In deciding whether a man named Heinz should steal a drug he could not afford in order to save the life of his spouse, Jake, representing the male voice, set up the dilemma "like a math problem with humans." In making a choice between the value of property and the worth of life, the boy opted for life and gave Heinz the right to steal. But Amy, who was speaking in the female voice, was unsure; if the man stole the money, he might go to jail, and this, too, could destroy his wife. Casting about for other solutions, the girl gave Heinz permission to beg or borrow but not steal. According to Gilligan, Amy saw the dilemma not as an exercise in math or as a matter of rights but instead as "a narrative of relationships that extends over time." By the book's end Gilligan's conclusion was clear: "In the different voice of women lies the truth of an ethic of care."[4] So, even as she was challenging a sexist system of psychology, she fell into the very stereotypes that have historically relegated women to a separate sphere.

During the 1980s, *In a Different Voice* became a cult symbol, turning female difference into superiority. As a reviewer in *Vogue* enthused, "It is impossible to consider Gilligan's ideas without having your estimation of women rise."[5] The problem was no longer the overly emotional, defective female who failed to reason with sufficient moral abstraction. There was now a new problem: the disconnected male who did not care or love enough.

Through the decade, this different-and-better theory of female development captured public attention. As Susan Faludi commented in *Backlash*, "Authors wrote, sometimes in starry-eyed terms, of women's inordinate capacity for kindness, service to others, and cooperation. Soon 'feminine caring' became the all-purpose tag to sum up the female psyche."[6] And in the 1990s, books like *Men Are from Mars, Women Are from Venus* reinforced the popular notion of starkly drawn sex differences.

While catchy titles put men and women on different planets, scientific studies kept showing more psychological similarity than such broad stereotypes allow. "Overlap of scores by males and females is always greater than the differences in those scores, particularly on psychological measures," Tufts psychologist Zella Luria wrote. "We are not two species. We are two sexes."[7] And Stanford professor Eleanor Maccoby, coauthor of the landmark book *The Psychology of Sex Differences*, also called for balance, emphasizing that there is more similarity than difference between men and women.[8] Even in the controversial domain of moral development, recent research shows that women and men score at similar levels on Kohlberg's taxonomy.[9] Although there is evidence that women tend to emphasize compassion and responsibility slightly more, fortunately for the well-being of humanity, the voice of care belongs to both males and females.

The quality on which women and men differ most is aggression. But even here, the extent of difference depends on the situation and the interpretation.[10] For example, in studies of young children, girls behave assertively when they play with other girls but become more passive when paired with boys; they are more likely to stand on the sidelines and let the males take over.[11] Linda Carli studied college students and reached a similar conclusion: Women spoke more assertively with one another but became tentative when men were around.[12] So the size of the sex difference in aggression changes with the situation and increases in mixed gender groups.

Other sex differences, while less significant and consistent than aggression, have been proven. Many revolve around interpersonal communication. Women are more expressive, communicating with their faces and bodies, are more likely to disclose personal information, and are better able to interpret nonverbal behavior and to facilitate positive interpersonal dynamics in groups.[13]

The interpretation of these differences seems to be in the eye of the researcher. Some think they prove women are more caring about relationships, but others point out that these behaviors are the same ones used by people, both male and female, who are powerless.[14] And, most important of all, the magnitude of any sex difference can be altered by education. Because sex differences are malleable, they can be decreased or intensified. Therefore, since schools play such a powerful role, it is important to reconsider the history of single-sex versus coeducation.

The Coeducation Question

Although coeducation is taken for granted today, over the course of history it has been at the center of controversy.[15] America usually reconsiders the coeducation question in times of transition, when gender roles are shifting. Should boys and girls learn together or in single-sex schools? Which better prepares them to meet the nation's needs?

As we showed in Chapter Two, in their early struggle for education, girls attended school in the evenings or summers, whenever boys were not there. By the middle of the nineteenth century, the free or common school system, pioneered by Horace Mann, was seen as the nation's "great equalizer." Few records still exist to show whether controversy accompanied girls as they entered the door of this common elementary school to integrate classrooms that had been all male. But as historians David Tyack and Elisabeth Hansot point out, their admission "was arguably the most important event in the gender history of American public education."[16]

Mixed instruction in elementary school was one thing, coeducation for adolescents quite another. As Chapter Two showed, the public high school was a male-only system. Unless a girl was lucky enough to live in one of the few cities or large towns with an all-female secondary school, her education was over after completing elementary school. By the latter decades of the nineteenth century, however, coeducation was becoming the trend at every level of schooling. As girls attended in increasing numbers, this open-door policy created a public uproar. Many considered coeducation "the question of the day."[17] As one educator wrote in the *New York Teacher*, "The whole human race, and true civilization, progress, and religion, depended upon the settlement."[18]

Advocates of single-sex schools invoked God, morality, and family to bolster their position. They feared coeducation would shatter the family because it would erase the differences between male and female. Could a man, they asked, "love and esteem a wife that was in her mind, feeling, and disposition the exact replica of himself. . . ?"[19]

Coeducation supporters also laid claim to God, goodness, and family. They described boys in all-male schools as "sailors and soldiers in foreign lands" who felt free to "engage in all kinds of immorality," including obscenity, drinking, and midnight debauchery.[20] These advocates said coeducation was like life. As one writer to the *Common School Journal* urged: "Let boys and girls be trained together in the schoolroom as they are in families. This is Nature's way, God's way, and the more closely we follow it, the better."[21] The advocates asked, "If the sexes must be segregated at school, why not be uniform and carry the separation into the very streets themselves?"[22]

The question was not easily brushed aside. And proponents of single-sex schools had another foe even more powerful—the force of economics. It was difficult to persuade taxpayers to pay for two high schools, one for boys and the other for girls, when a single high school with mixed instruction seemed to do the job very well. In some communities the choice for girls boiled down to coeducation or no education.

Even the 1873 publication of Dr. Edward Clarke's notorious book, *Sex and Education*, could not sway public opinion. Clarke argued that coeducation was at odds with the physical needs of females, that it diverted to the brain the blood needed for menstruation. Any girl who tried to attend school with boys and compete on an academic par was doing herself irreparable harm.[23] The popular press engaged in a fierce debate over *Sex and Education*, but most girls were not frightened away by coeducation's alleged health hazards; they continued to enroll in high schools in record numbers. But Clarke's ideas did not die. Instead they went underground, resurfacing in 1905 in G. Stanley Hall's book *Adolescence*.

At the turn of the century, the child study movement, spearheaded by psychologist G. Stanley Hall, focused on sex differences, which Hall claimed were large and crucial.[24] Evidently Hall considered them malleable as well because it was the purpose of education to accentuate them; this intensification could be best accomplished by separate schools, especially during adolescence, with male teachers for boys and female teachers for girls. In these single-sex schools, a botany course for boys could stress scientific aspects while one for girls could emphasize aesthetics. According to Hall, education for girls should "keep the purely mental back and by every method . . . bring the intuitions to the front."[25]

Other educators found Hall's ideas outrageous. Writing in the *Ladies' Home Journal* in 1911, John Dewey scoffed at "'female botany,' 'female algebra,' and for all I know a female multiplication table" adapted to the "female mind." He went on to say, "Upon no subject has there been so much dogmatic assertion based on so little scientific evidence, as upon male and female types of mind."[26] And as late as 1923, Columbia University professor Willystine Goodsell, still fighting Hall's influence, charged that his approach "could thrust girls with eager minds and widening vision back into the exclusively domestic circle from which they have but recently emerged."[27]

Ironically, the twentieth-century trend toward a more practical curriculum did more to resegregate girls than all the books and speeches by Clarke and Hall. As girls studied home economics, typing, and shorthand, and boys took manual training and courses in the trades, sex differentiation within coeducation emerged.

By the 1960s and '70s, sex segregation had sliced the curriculum. In secondary schools across the country, girls were barred from shop and boys from home economics. And in segregated physical education, where males received better training and equipment, separate clearly was not equal. At a time when psychologists were heralding the absence of sex differences, feminists saw single-sex programs as creating them. For example, a 1966 article in *The National Elementary Principal* lauded sex segregation. The author enthusiastically described how teachers used more science materials and experiments with boys' classes. "Mold," he suggested, "can be studied from a medical standpoint by boys and in terms of cooking by girls." There were different play activities, too. In the girls' classes teachers played games that "emphasize activities such as sewing and housekeeping." In the boys' classes the games involved "noise and muscle movement and are based on a transportation theme."[28]

During the 1970s and early '80s, Title IX of the 1972 Education Amendments, the law designed to abolish sex discrimination in public schools, helped to desegregate courses and programs. Because enforcement was lax, Title IX was often ignored, but gradually, with this law as a lever, single-sex education in the public schools began to disappear. History has a funny way of playing tricks, however. Single-sex schools, once dismissed as an anachronism, are now seen by many as a model for educating girls.

A School for Girls

Today, single-sex schools are an endangered species; they are illegal in the public system and vanishing rapidly from the private sector. In the 1960s approximately 62 percent of the nonreligious independent schools were single-sex. That figure is now 19 percent; 11 percent are schools for girls, and 8 percent are for boys. Originally 100 percent of

Catholic schools were single-sex, but now almost 60 percent are coeducational. In the 1960s there were almost three hundred single-sex colleges and universities, but now there remain only eighty-four for women and five for men. And even as single-sex schools fight to survive, new studies offer a stunning message: Schools without boys seem to be good for girls.[29]

Although critics point to flaws in the research methods, the evidence is persuasive. Girls in single-sex schools have higher self-esteem, are more interested in nontraditional subjects such as science and math, and are less likely to stereotype jobs and careers. They are intellectually curious, serious about their studies, and achieve more. Robert Johnson, a male English teacher in a girls' school, says all-female education provides "an atmosphere these girls may well never find again in their lives: an island in our culture that is about women . . . one where their major responsibility is to learn and to be themselves."[30] In a nationwide survey commissioned by the Coalition of Girls' Schools, alumnae from schools across the nation supported his perception. They reported that single-sex schools helped them develop self-confidence, assertiveness, and a strong sense of identity. And most surprising to the pollsters, the younger group of women, those who graduated between 1975 and 1980, were more positive about the benefits of girls' schools than those who had graduated during the 1950s.[31]

Women from single-sex colleges benefit, too, exhibiting positive self-esteem and high academic and career achievement.[32] According to Yadwega Sebrechts, executive director of the Women's College Coalition, "Single-sex schools are a unique place where women are valued and supported; they offer the kind of environment available to men at coed schools and in society. The single-sex high school can help girls make it through low self-esteem during adolescence. And the single-sex college develops women professionally, helping them realize they can be experts and authorities." In fact, graduates from women's colleges attain more degrees in nontraditional fields such as economics, life science, physical science, and mathematics. They are two to three times more likely than their coeducational peers to enter medical school; and, as advocates of women's colleges are quick to point out, their graduates are well represented in Fortune 500 companies and at the highest levels of government.[33]

The success of single-sex schools and the women's colleges is often attributed to role models and mentors. For example, almost 50 percent of science and math faculty at women's colleges are female, compared with less than 12 percent at coed institutions. Writer Mary Conroy remembers female role models and leaders in the Catholic girls school she attended in Chicago:

> Almost by osmosis we learned one very basic assumption: that girls could achieve, that there was nothing unusual about girls being leaders. Everywhere we looked we saw girls as star athletes, class officers, and editors of the school publications. We also saw role models among the faculty: Since there were only two male teachers at our school, we learned that women could run the business office, enforce school rules, and take the lead as a school principal. After four years of this environment, it never occurred to us that women couldn't lead.[34]

Many claim the single-sex advantage is also due to classrooms where girls are educational players rather than spectators. To learn more about the single-sex classroom, we visited a highly selective girls' school.

Speaking Their Minds

Thirteen girls in uniform, gray sweatshirts and plaid skirts, sat in a semicircle and talked quietly. The teacher walked over to the side of the room where we were watching and handed us the book the class was using. "It's officially called *Essays Old and New*," she said with a smile, "but the students call it *Essays Old and Older*." She began the class with a series of questions: "Why are the lower classes more willing to be passionate?" "Do you agree with Thoreau that 'a foolish consistency is the hobgoblin of little minds'?" "Thoreau says that to be great is to be misunderstood. Do you agree?" After she offered each question, there was a short silence, and then several girls responded at once, their answers overlapping. There was no wild hand-waving or grandstanding, but the girls spoke freely as though in a conversation. This was a startling difference from the coeducational classroom where boys called out and girls waited to be recognized. When some of the quieter girls apologized for answers they felt were inadequate, the teacher did not let them. "No, no, it's fine," she urged. "Say it again."

The more outspoken girls didn't just call out answers, they pushed the teacher with questions of their own. "Thoreau says you should follow what you believe. What if you're a racist? Is it okay to follow what you believe then?" The teacher offered an explanation, but the students were not convinced; they pressed on with more questions. "Doesn't this justify bad things and evil people, like Hitler?" The girls in this class demanded answers that satisfied them. If they didn't get them, they persisted, asking again and again in a display of female assertiveness we had rarely seen in coeducational settings.

Eighth-grade algebra, the next class we visited, made the English class seem subdued. As math problems were put on the board, the students bombarded the teacher with questions: "I have a question about that." "Wait, go back and do that again. It doesn't make sense." "I don't get it. Can you explain it again?"

We had rarely seen girls admit their confusion so openly, not with any sense of defeat or self-put-down but with a tenacity to understand. Sometimes the teacher answered the questions, and sometimes she threw them back at the class, encouraging the girls to help one another. At the end of the period we asked a group of students who had formerly attended a coeducational school if they acted differently there.

"I don't think it matters whether it's single-sex or coed," said one of the girls who talked most often in class. "I'm not afraid to talk wherever I am."

But another girl, one who had been much quieter in class, had a different opinion: "I was a lot more nervous when I went to a coeducational school. I was afraid I would be made fun of, so I just got quiet."

"Did boys make fun of you?" we asked.

"Only sometimes, but once it happened, I was afraid it would happen again, so I stopped talking."

"Won't girls here make fun of you?"

"No, they won't." She spoke softly. "They take me seriously here." In advanced-placement biology, the next class on our schedule, the barrage of student questions began again, even heavier than in the math class we had just left. We began to wonder if the girls were trying to give the science teacher a hard time, literally burying her under an avalanche of interrogation, but as we watched, we become convinced they were driven by genuine curiosity and a desire to understand. As the teacher chose one question to answer, side conversations broke out with girls helping one another. After class we caught up with one of the students.

"Do the students in your class always ask so many questions?" we asked.

"Of course," she said. "This stuff is hard to understand, so when we don't get it, we ask questions. What else would you do? How else could you run a class anyway?" The girl began to question us.

"We've seen lots of classes where students didn't ask many questions. For example, the teacher gave a lecture and then asked the students questions."

The girl looked thoughtful. "I guess it could be done that way," she said. "Our English and history classes are a little more like that. But math and science are really hard, so the way we learn here is, we ask."

In twelfth-grade history we saw what she meant. The class was discussing *From Beirut to Jerusalem*, ten students with a male teacher. The dynamic here was more traditional: The teacher asked and the students answered. Sometimes raising their hands and sometimes calling out, they handled a very sophisticated level of discussion, and the tone, as in the morning English class, was that of a quiet and serious conversation. But occasionally questions broke out here, too. When one girl asked a question, a "tipping" effect occurred, with several students questioning in quick succession. Then the pattern reversed, and the teacher once again became the authority figure, the one questioning.

When we interviewed teachers in this school, they expressed a sense of mission about educating girls. A math teacher talked about how male students diverted attention from females: "When I taught in a coed school," she said, "I found the boys were so much more demanding of my attention. In my classes here, if I forget a paper, I can leave the class, walk to the office, and copy something, and the girls would just chat among themselves. If I did that with boys, I'd come back to find them running around the room and hitting one another over the head."

A science teacher said, "I used to teach in a coed school, too. I had to be constantly vigilant. The boys were so verbally aggressive, they demanded that you focus in on them. I found I had to establish a personal relationship with girls before they would talk or take risks. Now I'm the parent of a daughter who's in a coed school. I watch as her aggressiveness, her spirit, diminishes with age. It's as if she's learning by osmosis not to speak out. I can't wait until she's old enough to come here."

The history teacher had taught in several cross-registration classes, those admitting male students from the coordinate boys' school. He said, "When it's all female, the girls take chances. But when guys are in the class, the girls stop asking questions the way they do now. They begin to say things like, 'I'm not sure if this is the right answer, but . . .'"

"How do the boys act?"

"They take wild risks. They make comments even when they haven't read the material. They're right out there with a nerve, a spontaneity, a courageousness that's almost athletic. And there's a one-upmanship that I rarely see among the girls."

When we talked with students, their comments echoed the perceptions of their teachers. Most liked going to school without being distracted or intimidated by boys. An all-girl school "lets you be yourself without worrying about how you look or being pressured and embarrassed by guys," one girl said. Another added, "It's a place where you can concentrate on academics rather than that 'social popularity thing.'"

While most girls offered endorsements, others had their doubts. One flatly admitted, "After being here for ten years, I just don't know how to deal with boys." Another told us, "I have trouble thinking of boys as actual people with ideas. I get intimidated by them easily and don't know how to be myself around them. I think a single-sex school prepares students poorly for a double-sex world."

Nerds and Roses

Several girls had pointed to the eleventh- and twelfth-grade cross-registration program as one way to get used to boys, so we organized a group interview.

"What's it like attending classes at the boys' school?" we asked.

"The guys fool around more," a dark-haired girl said, smiling at the others as if remembering a private joke. Then several chimed in:

"They throw erasers and pencils in class."

"They call one another names and make fun of one another. That would never happen in our school."

"It's not that they're stupid, they're witty and smart and all, but they just joke around."

"Do you enjoy that?" we asked. There was a pause. The girls looked at one another and then started talking at once, at first all positively: "Yeah, I think it's fun." "It makes going to class more interesting." "One guy used to come to class with his telephone number written on his jacket, and he kept flashing it at us. I thought he was funny."

But then came the negatives: "Sometimes the jokes made me feel uncomfortable. I felt different, like I was there but never really accepted." Another girl, one who looked as if she were remembering something painful, agreed and added, "It was worse than that. I was the only girl in an English class. It took me two weeks before I said anything. I felt really intimidated. Every time I said something, they all turned around and looked at me. And if you said something, they began to talk, and you wondered what they were saying about you."

"I didn't feel that way in my Spanish class," said another, joining in. "But there were four of us. The teacher loved having girls. The first day we walked in he said, 'It's so nice having roses among the thorns.'" The girls laughed.

"Did you like being treated like roses?"

"It wasn't always like that. Just sometimes—like when it was cold and the teacher turned the heat up. He said the boys could take it, but he was making it warmer for the girls."

Another girl shook her head. "Our French class was completely different. I thought it was sexist."

"What do you mean, sexist?" We prompted her to be specific.

"We had this vocabulary contest. The teacher gave us a word, and if you knew the synonym in French, you banged your hand down on the table. Well, the girls were the only ones who had studied, so we were way ahead. And the teacher kept saying to the boys, 'C'mon! You can't let girls get ahead of you.'"

Another girl added to the story: "And Natalie"—she pointed to the girl who had described the contest—"had the most points of all. When the teacher couldn't get the boys to do better, he drew a funny little face with glasses on the board, wrote Natalie's name by it, and said, 'Here we call people like this nerds.'"

"How did you feel when that happened?"

"That wasn't so bad," Natalie said. "The play was worse. It was so sexist, about the Trojan War. The girls had to read the part of Helen. We wanted to read the guys' parts because there were more of them. Over here in the girls' school you get to read all the parts, and a lot of the time the men's roles are better."

Other girls from the French class joined in. "There was this woman standing naked in water."

"I guess it was Helen. And these guys came along and captured her."

"And her big line throughout the play was, 'I live to obey you.'"

Several of the girls were laughing now, repeating the line in a parody that almost became a chant: 'I live to obey you. I live to obey you.'" Then Natalie stopped laughing. "I hated that play," she said.

"It really bothered you to read that line."

She turned beet red. "I refused. I wouldn't do it. I would rather not have a part than read a line like that."

Jeanna, a vivacious girl who had been laughing through much of the discussion, now also looked thoughtful and serious. "There was something else that bothered me at the boys' school. It was the stuff they had on the wall."

"You mean the pictures?"

"In our class there were two big pictures. One was really a poster and the other a picture of the poster. They were both of the same woman, just her torso. She was blond, of course, and tan. She had the tiniest waist." Jeanna gestured with her hands as if pushing her own waist in eight inches. "And she had Perrier bottle caps over her." The girl gestured again, this time covering her breasts. "And there was this corkscrew right next to her, pointing right at her. And it was so suggestive, even of violence. The guys really liked it, but a few of them said it was disgusting. I talked to the teacher and told her I didn't like it, that it made me feel uncomfortable. She said I could take it down if I wanted to."

"Did you?"

"Well, no."

"Why not?"

"It's not my school. Everyone would have been mad at me. I wanted the teacher to take it down. I thought it was her place to do it. I still can't believe a teacher—a woman teacher—would have a picture like that in her room."

"But eventually the picture did come down." Natalie said. "One day when we went to class it was gone. We don't know how it happened, but it just wasn't there anymore."

The Jury Is Still Out

Teachers at boys' schools expressed a wide spectrum of opinions about the value of all-male education. Some said males were better off in single-sex schools with men as teachers and role models. They thought boys concentrated more on their studies and were freer to express themselves honestly when girls were not in the room. But others con-

sidered coeducation a healthier environment, one where boys benefited from interaction with girls.

Research findings echo the mixed opinions of these teachers. Some
studies show that boys in single-sex schools achieve more, but others
say the academic advantage goes to males in the coeducational classroom. And yet others have found no difference at all. Given such ambiguous results, the jury is still out when it comes to all-male
education.[35]

Amid the contradictory findings, one positive pattern has emerged:
Boys in single-sex schools seem to value and enjoy nontraditional subjects such as literature and art.[36] But another recent investigation
sounds a warning bell: Boys' schools may harbor some shocking forms
of sexism.[37]

University of Michigan researcher Valerie Lee, with her colleagues
Helen Marks and Tina Byrd, conducted site visits in a random sample
of twenty-one nonreligious independent schools, seven male, seven female, and seven coeducational. In coed schools they found boys dominating discussions, and sexist incidents were particularly prevalent in
chemistry classes. In intellectually rigorous girls' schools, few incidents of sexism were uncovered, but in less academically demanding
schools, the researchers found female adolescents were often treated
like little girls. In these schools the students responded in overly dependent ways: asking for help, showing little initiative, and taking few
risks.

But the most clearly disturbing forms of sexism occurred in boys'
schools. In all-male classrooms teachers encouraged boys to be aggressive, to "give 'em hell"; one even addressed his students as "studs."
The worst culprits were English classes where discussions of sexual
scenes in literature sometimes degenerated into the treatment of girls
as sex objects. In one English class, a male teacher encouraged boys to
use specific examples in their writing. Then he gave an example of his
own, suggesting body measurements as a relevant detail in describing
female characters. In a unit on Shakespeare, another male teacher analyzed the meaning of a sonnet as "lust, animal lust, nothing but pure
mechanistic lovemaking." One student offered the class his own interpretation: "He wanted sex with this chick, this 'shanky' chick, and he
didn't even like her." The observer noticed a cartoon on the wall of this
room: a woman naked from the waist up. In fact, sexual depictions of
women decorated the walls in several all-boy schools. In a room where
boys were studying French, there was a large picture of a woman's lips
without her face, and a bikini-clad woman with her arms raised was
displayed in a calculus classroom.

When we talked with Valerie Lee, one of the most influential researchers on single-sex schools, we asked if she had reached a decision about the merits of single-sex education. She said:

> Right now I'm equivocal [the word most repeated throughout the interview]. I can't conclude that all you need to do is send your girls to an all-female school and your problems will be solved. It really depends on the school. You have to sit in on the classes and find out what's going on there. Even in the best girls' schools we saw sexism. For example, we saw a history teacher give a research paper to a class of very capable girls. She said, "This is a difficult assignment, so there will be major hand-holding available." I think that's overly supportive. I can't imagine a teacher offering "major hand-holding"' to boys.
>
> I'm also equivocal because when we saw really outlandish behavior, it was most likely to happen in single-sex schools. In a few girls' schools we saw male bashing, which I think is entirely inappropriate. And in boys' schools we saw incidents that went beyond the pale. When I see a class of boys talking about women as a collection of body parts hooked together, I think it's a scandal.

It's clear that each boys' school must be considered separately to see if it is expanding options or solidifying old stereotypes. To learn more, we visited two boys' schools, observed classes, and talked with students and teachers.

Lost in the Past

Wearing jackets and ties, boys who have second period free sprawl over chairs, their books open but mainly unread while they talk to one another. We are introduced to the group by the assistant headmaster and then left on our own.

"We're trying to find out how coeducation compares with single-sex schools," we say. The students regard us with curiosity and caution. "Has anyone here been in coed classrooms or those that have coregistration with girls?"

Several boys laugh and point to others as potential subjects for interview. "Go talk to Jerry, he's a woman. He's been in classes in the girls' school." "Talk to Ed. He can tell you all about going to school with girls." Finally Tony is identified as one who is taking advanced-placement biology at the girls' school. As we approach him, he sits up and looks serious.

"It's pretty much the same whether there are girls in the class or it's all boys" is Tony's response to our question.

"Do you think boys and girls behave the same in class, or do they act differently?"

"Pretty much the same." He pauses. "Well, I guess the girls aren't as rowdy."

"What happens here that's rowdy?" The question generates interest from the others who have been bystanders. They join the conversation and describe rowdy behavior with obvious relish.

"We kick balls around."

"We have snowball fights."

We try to clarify their remarks: "You mean outside?"

"No, we do it inside. In the hallways." Several boys laugh and playfully punch one another. Then they continue with more examples:

"Boys give teachers more of a hard time."

"We throw spitballs. And we play dumb jokes in class."

"What kind of dumb jokes?" A circle of boys has now officially joined the interview.

"If someone says something dumb in class, we make cracks."

"We're sarcastic."

"We tear him apart."

"When someone does something stupid, we laugh."

"When guys make jokes and laugh, does that make you feel bad or keep you from answering questions?" The circle widens as more boys try to help us understand how one-upmanship works in their classes.

"No, we all know one another, and we expect it."

"We wouldn't do it as much to strangers."

"Yeah, and if someone was really in trouble in class, we wouldn't do it. We only go for someone when he makes a *humorous* mistake."

"When girls are in your classes, how do they feel when you make cracks and jokes and put each other down?"

The boys look puzzled, and then one says, "You've got to talk to Ed. He's in this calculus class, and there's one girl in it from another school. He gave her a rose on Valentine's Day." Several boys are now pointing to the other side of the room. "He's over there."

When we arrive at the table, Ed is staring intently at his book as though we would go away if he doesn't look up. "We hear you're in a cross-registered calculus class. Can you tell us what it's like?"

Flushing, he points to other boys at the table. "Ask them, too," he says. "They're in the class." We open the question up to involve the other boys. Karen, the lone girl in the class, has obviously been the subject of prior discussion.

"She's a ditz!" one boy says vehemently. "She's a Valley Girl, but she's got the highest average in the class." He shakes his head as if in disbelief.

"Yeah," another boy agrees. "I can't figure out how she does it."

Others around the table offer their opinions:

"She's book smart, but she has no common sense."

"She can't find her way around the school. She's been here for months now, and she still can't get around the building."

"She can't even drive right. She keeps getting into accidents."

"I bet she studies nonstop. There's no other way she could get those grades."

"Come to our class. Fourth period."

Fourteen students, thirteen boys and one girl, are sitting in rows. The room is immaculate, except for graffiti on the desks: "Henderson's face looks like a Pap smear." "Henderson needs a penal prosthesis." Posters of famous sports figures and all-male teams are on the walls. The class proceeds at a brisk businesslike pace as the teacher puts examples on the board and asks questions. Occasionally students request clarification, but mostly the teacher directs, a pattern similar to the coeducational classes we have spent a decade observing.

But one dynamic is clearly different—the level of showmanship. If observing classes in the girls' school is like listening in on a conversation, watching the classes in this boys' school is like sitting in on a performance, one with very public peer evaluation. For example, a boy in the front of the room answers a tough question correctly, and the class groans. The boy turns around to his classmates, holds his arms up in a mock shrug, and smiles. "What can I say? I'm just on today." This pattern of showmanship continues throughout the period, and the teacher eventually turns to us and says with a smile, "They're showing off for you." Then his gaze turns back to the class. "I'll get them tomorrow," he says, but his tone is friendly rather than threatening.

"What's it like to teach an advanced math class of all boys and only one girl?" we ask the teacher after the students have left.

"This class is not a problem," he says. "One reason it works is that Karen is the top student. She has the highest grades in the class. The boys here respect academic achievement, so no matter how much they might like to, they can't put her down."

Next on our schedule is eleventh-grade English. We arrive early to watch the eleven boys enter the room, and they cause a commotion. The teacher enters and surveys the class seriously. "I want to make sure you know how to do the footnotes for your research paper." He speaks softly, but the class quiets down. "Tune in, Josh"—the tone is calm but firm. As the teacher explains how he wants the footnotes, it is as if there has been a magical change: Boys who were loud and boisterous are now intent, earnest, and serious. And then the showmanship begins. One boy makes a clever comment; the teacher responds with a quiet, appraising look. "Wow, are you sharp," he says softly. "Whooo!" the other boys chorus. "I'm all fired up today," the boy acknowledges.

After class we talk with the teacher about the pattern of putting each other down. "The boys do a lot of hazing," he says, "jockeying for place, trying to establish where they are in the pack. I think it goes along with sports. It's how they behave on the athletic field."

"What happens to the class atmosphere when there are girls?"

"It depends on who they are. One year I had a group of girls who were strong both academically and personally. They just gave the boys a look or even hazed back. That group of strong girls really helped the class. They were so smart and focused, and the boys were determined not to be shown up. There were some crude jocks in that class, and I think the girls had a healing influence. But another year I had six girls who were very weak academically. Those girls had a terrible time."

Linguist Deborah Tannen said that a source of inspiration for her book, *You Just Don't Understand*, was a research project in which she observed videotapes of pairs of friends on different age levels as they communicated with each other.[38] Instructed to "find something serious to talk about," elementary and secondary school girls on the videotapes faced each other directly and quietly discussed personal events. But the boys behaved differently. More accustomed to playing games and doing things, elementary school boys on the videotapes had trouble complying with the instructions. Restless, they pretended to fight, teased each other, and told jokes. While topics of conversation differed by age, the communication behavior Tannen saw parallels the interaction we observed in the boys' school: joking and teasing, sometimes offensively, performing, defying authority, putting each other down, and jockeying for place within the pack.

But among the videotaped conversations of male friends, Tannen listened to one that was very different, one where the discussion was intensely personal. In this dialogue one boy, Todd, revealed how alienated he felt, how he was left out at parties and was ill at ease with girls and even his own close friends. He spoke haltingly and wistfully of a time when he could really communicate with others. The conversation, Tannen said, was the most "intimate talk" she heard on all the research videotapes.

Amid all the joking and performing and putting down we observed at the boys' school, we also heard this kind of intimate and personal discussion. A psychology class with eleven boys and a female teacher (the only one we saw in the school) talked about gender roles.

"Those of you who have been reading your book have come across the terms 'animus' and 'anima,' a male side and a female side," the teacher says to begin the class.

"You mean enema!" a boy calls out. Others laugh, but the teacher ignores the outburst. "This could show up in a lot of simple things like colors. Look at the suits you're wearing. You're all in dark blue and brown and gray, but I'm allowed to express myself through colors. I can wear pink—"

"Excuse me," a boy says, interrupting. "I'm in pink. I wear pink boxers."

"But they're not showing." The teacher grins. "I guess that side of you is repressed." The students laugh, but the teacher persists with her point. "Now I want you to be serious. Do you think men can be gentle and nurturing? Or do they have to be macho?"

Almost magically the class becomes serious. "I think we act macho now," a tall, thin boy says, "and it feels awkward to be gentle. But I think gentleness develops with age. Once you have resolved your own personality, then artificial walls break down. It's society that limits you."

"Actually," says the teacher, "we have some experts on this very subject." She introduces us. Pulled into the discussion, we ask the boys how all-boy classes compare to coeducation.

"We're much more open here," a redhead called Danny says. "When I was fourteen, I hated going to school with girls. I felt awkward. So I came here. I think you get a much better education when you're with guys. We feel comfortable with each other. If I were trying to get a date with some girl in the class, I wouldn't feel free to say whatever I wanted. In a coed class you look at the girl and then you gauge your answers and say what you think the girl wants to hear."

"But what if the girl isn't sexually attractive to you?" another boy asks. "Couldn't you say what you wanted to then? It's just that girls are different. Like if there were black students in this class, there would be a difference."

"No," Danny says vehemently. "I don't think girls can be just friends. The issue isn't difference. It's *sex*."

"Do you think women reinforce your macho qualities?" the teacher asks, joining the conversation.

"Some do and some don't. From my experience, which is admittedly limited"—the tall, thin boy shrugs and smiles—"some women want you to be a hunter, and some women want you to wear a tutu and cry."

"Which kind of girl do you like better?" the teacher asks.

"I like the one who lets me wear a tutu and cry."

"How many of you would like the other kind of girl?" the teacher asks.

Several boys, including Danny, raise their hands. "I like it when a girl makes me feel like a man," Danny says.

"I like the kind of girl who lets me be myself," another boy says. "I like it when I can be comfortable and I don't have to pretend."

Throughout the latter part of this discussion there has been no teasing, insulting, or putting down. These boys have been remarkably open and very vulnerable, but nobody has taken advantage. After class the teacher talks about "her boys": "The joking around is a veneer they have. In a way they've just learned to mask their feelings, but they have such intense feelings. Go look in the art room. They do such beautiful, expressive work."

"What happens when there are girls in your class?" we ask.

"I have to work harder at involving them, getting them to talk. And when girls are there, boys don't share their feelings as much. The males make the analytical comments while the girls do the expressive work."

"Do you think an all-male environment is good for these boys?"

The teacher pauses and then says thoughtfully, "Not really. Maybe during junior high school. Otherwise, I don't. I think interaction with girls is healthy. Girls today are testing every frontier of their psyche, but these boys are feeling left out and left behind. They're lost in the past, and someone needs to bring them out."

Keeping Our Options Open

Today, as in the final quarter of the 1800s, debate rages about the benefits of coeducation versus single-sex schools. Some arguments echo those used a century ago, but others have taken a 180-degree turn.

In 1905, G. Stanley Hall extolled the single-sex school as a place where females could "metaphorically be turned out to grass and lie fallow so far as strenuous intellectual effort goes."[39] His ideal girls' school was set in the middle of hills where students could rest during menstrual periods, acquire domestic skills, and learn to please by studying good manners, religion, and the arts. Good girls' schools today focus on entirely different goals: the development of intellectual growth, academic curiosity, independence, and self-esteem.

Advocates are struggling to keep the doors of these schools open, and passions run high as their survival is threatened. When two independent schools, all-female Westlake and all-male Harvard in Los Angeles, planned to merge, opposition at Westlake was vociferous. A group of parents filed a lawsuit (which was ultimately unsuccessful), and girls showed up on campus with yellow buttons that pleaded BREAK THE ENGAGEMENT. When Wheaton College announced plans to go coeducational, women picketed with placards that read BETTER DEAD THAN COED, and Mills College reversed its decision to admit men after the campus exploded with protest.

Although research is ambiguous when it comes to the effectiveness of boys' schools, those who defend them believe fervently in their value. Richard Hawley, the head of a boys' school, remembers his first encounter with all-male education, an impression that has remained unchanged for two decades: "In each class, at each baseball practice, at the luncheon table . . . I was aware of something altogether new to me. There was an unaffected directness, an authenticity I had not experienced before in a school. . . . There was a special edge to boys' life, a positive edge."[40] Those who want to establish African-American male academies also see this approach as a way of offering a special edge. Advocates with the toughest challenges are the ones who support Virginia Military Institute and The Citadel, two all-male colleges that use military strategies, hazing, and intense physical and mental stress, to prepare men to take their place in society. Both of these colleges have gone to court to deny access to female students.[41]

Promoters of coeducation use the century-old argument that boys and girls learning together is the more realistic system, the "natural" ideal, and the best preparation for a democratic society. These advocates have the support of most of today's students who see coeducation as the way the world is. And even some staunch feminists do not consider single-sex schools the best route to educational equality. It blames the victim, they say, aiding females but leaving boys and the nation's coeducational system unchanged. While recognizing that good single-sex schools benefit girls, they view the approach as defeatist, giving up on the possibility that females and males can learn as equals side by side. And the gains made by the girls, they say, are temporary and are not able to survive the transition to a male-dominated world.

Girls' school advocates retort that the advantages are more than a short-lived inoculation. After years spent as first-class educational citizens, girls develop assertiveness, self-confidence, and leadership, skills that are typically acquired by the higher status gender. And this training, they say, endures. When Kathleen Welch compared verbal assertiveness in discussions in classrooms at Wellesley, Smith, Brown, and Yale, she found that the women from single-sex schools were not only more assertive than women from coed institutions but they were more assertive than the men as well.[42] And one student who graduated from Westlake when it was still all female claims that the confidence she developed carried over to college: "In my eighty-person English class at UCLA, there were seventy-five women and five men. . . . The class was dominated by four men and one woman—that one woman being me. I don't know that I would have done that if I hadn't been trained that way."[43]

Some single-sex advocates say the experience should be open to all students, not just those who are able or willing to pay for private school. To be more inclusive, they urge a revision of Title IX, the law that prohibits public school sex segregation except in contact sports and sex education. If there is persuasive research that a single-sex experience works for females, these advocates state, why should the overwhelming majority of America's schoolgirls be denied this advantage? But others are more cautious about revamping Title IX. Remembering times not that long ago when mold was studied scientifically by boys and from a cooking perspective by girls, they view Title IX, unrevised, as powerful protection against unpredictable political times.

Even as controversy swirls around them, independent schools are experimenting. For example, some leave lower and upper schools coeducational but offer single-sex middle schools since this is the time when female achievement and confidence decline. Other coeducational schools are trying out single-sex classes in courses like physics, where females have traditionally fallen behind. Some girls' schools now emphasize single-sex academics and coed extracurricular activities.[44] As they try out new strategies based on gender, these schools become a testing ground for new information, and there is so much more we need to know. Is single-sex education more helpful at certain age levels? In certain kinds of classes? For certain types of children? For example, are shy or quiet girls better off when the environment is all female? And under what circumstances is coeducation more beneficial?

Valerie Lee has repeatedly emphasized that "so much depends on the school. Some girls' schools we saw looked like throwbacks, nineteenth-century finishing schools to prepare little ladies. But other girls' schools really are paying attention to gender—what is in the books and on the walls, as well as the interaction. They encourage assertiveness, curiosity, and questions. Visiting these schools makes your heart sing."

As the University of Michigan researchers found out, there is a wide range of quality and equality in single-sex schools, but given research results, the good ones—those that are academically rigorous and work hard at developing self-esteem—should not be allowed to become extinct. Although Lee is equivocal on the subject of single-sex schools as a whole, on one point she is clear: "You can make an affirmative action case for girls' schools. Maybe we won't always need them, but we need them now. The world would be a worse place if they were to close their doors."

For both economic and philosophic reasons America will continue to be a nation that relies on coeducation, but even as we continue to keep our educational options open, our national system requires an action agenda for change.

Some solutions are already at hand. For the past two decades teachers, parents, and students across the country have taken steps to confront gender bias head-on in the coed school. And even these piecemeal, part-time efforts have reaped benefits. While a gender gap in achievement endures, during the past two decades it has been slashed so dramatically that arguments based on biology must be dismissed. Change is happening, in the words of researchers Robert Rosenthal and Donald Rubin, "faster than the gene can travel."[45]

And what would happen if the efforts were more than halfhearted? What if people across the nation focused on eradicating sexism in schools? We can only imagine the stunning gains that girls could then achieve.

10

The Edge of Change

In 1973, after the publication of Myra's *Sexism in School and Society*, the first textbook for teachers on gender bias in education, the National Association of Elementary School Principals asked her to speak at their convention. More than one hundred mostly male school administrators crowded into the hotel meeting room for her "Meet the Authors" session on sexism in school. She was excited as she began the presentation; if these principals from schools all across the country would get involved, a solution might be at hand. But within a few minutes an undercurrent of whispering became so distracting, it was difficult to continue.

"What is she talking about?"

"I don't get it."

"This isn't what I expected. I thought this was supposed to be about sex education."

A group of principals got up, pushed their way through the crowd, and walked out of the room. Others followed. Myra wondered what was wrong as she raised her voice to be heard above the noise.[1]

Playing the Whole Court

This conflict with the principals at the NAESP convention became a personal landmark, one that we use to gauge the pace of change. Two decades after the roomful of administrators misunderstood the meaning of "sexism," the American Association of University Women's report *How Schools Shortchange Girls* made national headlines. In 1973 people walked out on the issue of gender equity, but by 1993 both parents and teachers had been jolted into concern. Mothers who remember sexist barriers at school are especially concerned about providing clearer pathways for their daughters. A woman from Illinois recalled her own personal landmark:

> When I went to high school during the late 1950s, girls were allowed to be cheerleaders or members of the Pep Squad, but never members of a competitive team; that was unheard of. . . . According to the girls' rules of basketball, females could not play the full court. Instead, we were divided into two teams, forwards and guards, each team occupying half the court and forbidden to cross the center line, even by a toe. The guards would thunder up to the blue line, skid to a halt, and pass the ball to the forwards on the other side of the line. While action was on one end of the court, the players on the other end could only stand and watch. Sound absurd? It was, but perhaps even more ridiculous was the reasoning behind the girls' rules of basketball. Females were forbidden from running the full length of the basketball court because it was too strenuous for our "fragile internal organs."

Today, the girl forbidden to play the full court is a teacher and a mother who makes sure her daughter does not encounter similar barriers:

> It has been my pleasure to watch my teenage daughter swim competitively, water ski, bowl, play basketball and baseball, ride bikes, run, and bench press. And it has been my quiet revenge that five-foot-two-inch Holly, petite and pretty, has not only done these things without ever damaging her "fragile internal organs" or losing her femininity, but she has done them better than most of the boys.

A New England woman recalled the career counseling she received in the 1960s. Now she vows that the limits imposed on her will not restrict her daughter:

> When I was a teenager, my parents said I could be a nurse, a secretary, or a teacher. They suggested teaching would be best because it was prestigious for a girl, and I would have lots of free time to spend with my family. Now I love teaching—although it's harder and more time-consuming than my parents ever dreamed—but I have always wanted to be

a lawyer. The problem was that I didn't have any real options. Nurse, secretary, or teacher—that's the way it was in 1962. I promise it will be different for my daughter.

Parent Power

As their children's first and most enduring teachers, parents play a powerful role. But ensuring equity for their daughters is still a long struggle. Although discrimination is not as blatant as it used to be, subtle bias can be treacherous. Even the most well-meaning adults can inadvertently let sexist expectations slip into their own behavior. An influential study, *Pygmalion in the Classroom*, has documented the impact of these expectations.

Children in an elementary school were given a special assessment, one designed to identify "intellectual bloomers," those pupils most likely to show remarkable academic gains during the school year. Researchers told the teacher the names of the students who were ready to spurt ahead. Eight months later the accuracy of the special assessment was confirmed. When the "intellectual bloomers" were given an IQ test, they scored much higher than they had on previous exams. Apparently the new test was an educational breakthrough because it could predict students poised for academic acceleration.

But Robert Rosenthal and Lenore Jacobson, the researchers conducting the study, had tricked the teachers. The special assessment was phony; it was not really a harbinger of intellectual readiness but rather a standard intelligence test. And the student names given to the teachers were not carefully selected from test scores but simply picked at random. According to the researchers, teacher expectations caused the students to make exceptional gains. When the teacher thought children were ready to spurt ahead intellectually, she did little things to encourage them—a smile, perhaps, or an extra question or a few minutes of additional attention or praise. Through these nuances, the teacher conveyed the message "You are talented and capable. I have faith in you." Several other studies confirmed these results: Students live up to what their teachers expect.[2]

Every day in unnoticed ways parents' expectations, slipping inadvertently into conversation and behavior, also affect their children's development. For example, with girls, both mothers and fathers express more warmth, use more emotional words, and are more likely to talk about sad events and feelings.[3] But in their interactions with boys, they encourage activity and aggression. One mother of twins, a girl and a boy, described how startled she was to discover these different assumptions in her own interaction:

> My daughter and son were riding their bikes, training wheels recently removed, around our cul-de-sac when they collided and fell. I rushed over and checked to make sure they were not hurt. Then I said to my son, "Up and at 'em, Tiger," and instructed him to get back on his bike. But to my daughter I said, "Honey, are you sure you're all right? Come and sit with me a minute." So my daughter and I sat on the steps, her bike lying on the lawn, and we watched her brother race around the circle.

Through tiny incidents like this one—hardly noticeable during the hectic course of a day's events—parents who consciously do not want their children trapped in stereotypes may unconsciously convey the opposite message. Like teachers, they need to halt the micro-inequities, catch them before or as they happen. When the woman who taught her twins to ride two-wheel bikes realized she was conveying different messages about courage and perseverance to her daughter and son, she revised the outcome:

> As my daughter sat there watching her brother ride, I was horrified to see what I had done. So I told her that it was important to get back on a bike after you fall down, and soon she was riding along with her brother. But what if I hadn't caught myself? And what about all the times when I expect different things and don't even know I'm doing it?

Fathers are even more likely to fall into the trap of stereotyped expectations, and the effect on daughters can be devastating. A woman from Connecticut remembered:

> It was evident in my own family whose sports were taken seriously. In the four years my brothers played sports, my dad missed only a few games. In the four years I played, my dad came to a grand total of *one* of my games. It really hurt then, and even looking back as a wife, mother, teacher, and thirty-five-year-old person, it still hurts. I feel my dad didn't

think my interests and efforts were as important as my brothers, that I wasn't as good.

This woman never told her father how she felt. But another parent described how his children react directly when they see gender bias in his behavior:

> My kids say I reprimand them differently. They tell me that when I'm working at home and my son comes into the study and pesters me, I shout, "Get out of here!" When my daughter does the same thing, I say, "Young lady, would you please leave." When we talked it over, my two alert kids told me about other differences. My daughter claims I compliment her for wearing a new dress or looking pretty, but I praise my son for achievement, especially in sports. We're still talking, and I'm still trying.

The mirror held up to this father by his own children is echoed in studies of parenting behaviors. More likely to encourage sex-typed behavior, males protect their daughters, compliment them on appearance, and show them affection. Meanwhile, they roughhouse with sons, encourage athletic participation, and punish them more harshly. Many fathers come down particularly hard on boys for playing with dolls or other cuddly toys.[4]

Parents who pay close attention to children's playthings understand that toys shape personality traits, interests, and even physical and academic skills. In 1990 a team of Canadian researchers visited young children's homes. They found boys' rooms filled with sports equipment, toy vehicles, tools, and building kits. The girls' rooms contained children's furniture, kitchen utensils, and lots of dolls. Girls slept in multicolored beds with sheets of pink and yellow. For boys the bedding was mostly blue. The research team concluded that parents are still raising girls and boys in environments that are "globally different"; they are still encouraging "sex-typed play by selecting different toys for female and male children, even before the child can express her or his own preferences."[5]

Playing with building blocks and transportation toys increases spatial skills, an area where boys later excel. Meanwhile, doll play encourages nurturance, interpersonal skills, and caring for babies—traditionally female domains. And when children grow old enough to choose toys for themselves, many select more sophisticated versions of the playthings they already know, setting in place a gender gap in interests and abilities later solidified at school.

Since toy companies continue to promote the purchase of strongly stereotyped playthings, parents must consciously swim against the tide to avoid rigidly channeling children's play.[6] But choosing toys is only the beginning. One father described how he learned there was more to be done:

> After attending your workshop, I went home to check my daughters' toy box. There was one Barbie after another, most of them without heads. I couldn't believe it. I know I bought chemistry sets and science kits, but they were nowhere to be found. I couldn't understand how they had disappeared until I asked the kids.
> "We swapped them," the girls explained.
> "Swapped them?" I was flabbergasted.
> "We didn't know why you bought us those things. We didn't like some of them, and we didn't know how to work the science things. So we gave them away and got Barbies instead. We never told you because we didn't want to hurt your feelings."

This father had taken the first step—he had provided a range of toys—and thought the job was done, but he had not made the extra effort to introduce the chemistry and science kits to his daughters or to join them in experiments. By actually playing with their daughters, throwing balls, and sitting with them while constructing with logs and Legos, fathers send an important message: Building, playing basketball, and doing science and math are all appropriate for girls and are fun as well. And mothers who set up trains or look at slides through a microscope become role models, demonstrating for their daughters the wide range of behavior that is possible. Without adults showing the way, the science kits or sports equipment may be unused, discarded, swapped, or given away.

Expectations go beyond child's play. They are at the heart of academic achievement. A 1992 survey showed that when adults are asked to picture an intelligent child, 57 percent of women and a whopping 71 percent of men visualize male children.[7] In math and science especially, parents attribute more brain power to boys. These different academic expectations begin as early as first grade and continue throughout school. If girls bring home low grades in math and science, parents say their daughters are not as smart in these subjects. If boys bring home similar grades, parents say their sons are lazy and push them to work harder.[8]

When stereotypes about math and science are discarded, when adults expect girls to do well, when they help them with schoolwork at home and insist that they persevere in difficult advanced courses, girls succeed.[9] Looking back on their childhood, women who have achieved in nontraditional careers point to the expectations and encouragement of parents as key to their success.[10] A New England woman remembered the power of her father's unwavering belief:

> I was accepted into the school of engineering in our state university. I enrolled and began what I thought was an ordinary journey. On the first day the whole class met, out of 309 students, only 4 of us were female. Two of us finished our degrees in chemistry in the school of engineering. The other two dropped out.
>
> Sometimes I look back and wonder how I got through it. But really, I know how. I did it because my father believed I could. He never saw failure in anything I tried. And he continuously encouraged me to try anything and everything. He recognized my math and science ability, and *he* signed me up for engineering. And even when I only made C's, he said he was proud of me for tackling such tough courses. If my guidance counselor had had *his* way, I would have been a liberal arts major because women just didn't go into engineering.

Show and Tell

Expectations matter, and so do role models. By watching adults, children learn about life's options. Sometimes their astute observations take parents by surprise, as a woman at a California workshop told us:

> I walked by the room of our two sons, ages ten and five. Noticing the late hour, I asked them to turn out their light and go to sleep.
>
> "Dad said we could have the lights on for five minutes," my older son answered.
>
> "I'd like the lights off now."

"Well, Dad's the boss," said my son. "You're just the assistant."

If children see business offices where men, for the most part, are managers and women are secretaries; if they see hospitals where males are mainly doctors and females are nurses; if in their schools they watch male principals giving directions to mostly female teachers, they reach an inescapable conclusion: Men are bosses and women work for them. Once crystallized, these assumptions may seem unshakable. Children's early contact with the world of medicine creates some of the staunchest stereotypes. A kindergarten teacher told this story:

> Six-year-old Sarah initiated a heated class discussion by announcing that only boys could be doctors and only girls could be nurses. Surprised by the girl's adamant conclusion, I arranged for a field trip to the local hospital. There my class met both male and female nurses and doctors. I was proud of nipping sexism in the bud—until I asked the students their reaction to the man who was a nurse and the woman who was a doctor. Sarah had only one question: "Why did they lie?"

Even parents who work in nontraditional roles cannot assume their children see them as role models. They, too, need to make extra efforts to stop stereotypes from forming. One mother, a pediatrician, told how baffled she was when her three-year-old daughter looked straight at her and made the following announcement: "Girls can't be doctors. That's a boy's job." The woman said, "I couldn't believe my daughter was saying this to me, a physician! But then I realized she knew nothing about my work. She had never seen me in my role as a doctor but knew me only as her mom at home. Ever since then, I often take her with me to my office and explain to her the work I do."

The Ms. Foundation wanted to alert all parents that girls need to see firsthand the range of work that women do, so April 28, 1993, became "Take Our Daughters to Work Day." In this national initiative, almost a million girls ages nine to fifteen went to work with parents, relatives, and friends to see women in every imaginable place of employment: hospitals, police and fire stations, business offices, media studios, courts, and Congress. By taking our daughters into the workplace, we present them with important role models and introduce them to potential careers. For example, studies have shown that girls who meet scientists and watch them at work are more likely to consider becoming scientists, too. But girls need to see role models even before they turn nine. A Girl Scout leader from the Midwest learned how early these influences take effect:

> My young granddaughter is very interested in religion. She decided she wanted to be a saint when she grew up and asked if girls could become saints. Her parents said they could, but since she wasn't a Catholic, it might not be the best career path. Her problem was solved when she went to a church with a female minister. That, she decided, was the job for her!

The power of providing female role models for young children as an everyday part of their lives is evident in this incident described to us by a woman at a workshop in New Jersey:

> Our female dentist and her female partner both recommended that my eight-year-old daughter see an orthodontist about her overbite. Just before we left for our appointment, I tried to explain what the new doctor would do. "He'll look in your mouth and ask you to bite down," I said.
> "*He?*" my daughter exclaimed, shocked. "You mean *men* can be dentists?"

While real-life role models influence children, so do characters in books. "Read it again," children plead. At a young and impressionable age girls listen repeatedly to classic sexist themes: Cinderella finds success in beauty and marriage to the prince. Snow White and Sleeping Beauty are so passive, they literally sleep until a man saves them. Although there are folktale females who rely on brains to save themselves, most parents and teachers don't know these stories exist.

One mother, a former teacher, told us how she conscientiously collected the best literature, the Caldecott winners and Honor books decorated by the American Library Association with gold and silver medals as the finest picture books of the year. The night after attending one of our workshops, she looked through her daughter's bookshelf to count the number of stories about active, resourceful girls and was amazed to find only one book with a female main character:

> There was Max and the Wild Things and Sylvester, the donkey, with his magic pebble. And all those Doctor Seuss books—so many imaginative characters and so few females. Did you ever read *And to Think That I Saw It on Mulberry Street*? This boy comes home from school and imagines meeting hundreds of zany characters. But there's not a sin-

gle girl on Mulberry Street. My daughter loves that book. We read it over and over and over. I hate to think how I've been programming her for invisibility.

Thank heavens for *Madeline*! Without her there would have been no girls at all in my daughter's book collection.

Studies of children's literature explain why half of the human race was missing from this young child's reading material. Between 1967 and 1971, for every girl drawn in a Caldecott winner, eleven boys were pictured. When female characters were included, they were inconspicuous: a girl playing quietly in the corner, a silent woman carrying wood, a princess whose hand is given in marriage, a mother who packs lunch and waves good-bye. Jobs for adult women were limited to mother, mermaid, and fairy. In contrast, men were main characters and were shown as house builders, storekeepers, kings, farmers, judges, preachers, fathers, adventurers, soldiers, policemen, fishermen, monks, fighters, gods, and storytellers.[11]

Newer studies have shown improvement in children's books—but not enough. While more females are included, representation is far from equal, and starkly drawn stereotypes remain: competitive, creative, and active boys; dependent, submissive, and passive girls.[12] As parents become aware of these demeaning images, more and more are determined to fight their influence. A Connecticut mother told us how she analyzed the picture books and television, too.

> Your topic lurched into my consciousness with the Anita Hill hearings. I looked at my daughter, then two, and wondered how early women start mistrusting their own (and other women's) voices. I began my own informal research, counting protagonists in one thousand picture books in a library listing. My figures ran seven to one, male to female. . . . Then I looked at "Sesame Street." Surely in 1991 this benchmark program would do better. Wrong. Male characters, male voice-overs, even images of male children in the street dominated eight to one. . . . What to do?

So many stories still have males as main characters that some parents have begun to change the names, substituting females for males when they read to their children so girls can see themselves in their fair share of action and adventure. But changing names is not enough. Research shows that a direct approach works best. From movies to magazines, from picture books to real life, parents need to point out sexism when they see it and directly explain to their children the roles now open to women. They should be frank about obstacles, too, and discuss openly and honestly specific steps that girls can take to surmount them.

Reaching the Stars

As children grow older, all work done at home can be undone, especially at school. Some parents have therefore begun to educate the educators, helping them discover books about wise and resourceful women and girls to use in the classroom.

For her senior thesis at Harvard, Lisa Stulberg studied the early grades in three Massachusetts elementary schools and found teachers working hard to develop a multicultural curriculum. The classes she observed studied units on African-Americans for Black History Month, but all the reading material displayed in class was about men, with the single exception of a book on Harriet Tubman. Little effort was made to include females until a parent volunteered to come in and read a story. When a boy asked why the book the father had selected was not about Martin Luther King, the parent explained, "There are lots of other important people in the movement. There were lots of important women." And then he referred to another event, one not celebrated in the school. "February is Black History Month," he said, "and March is Women's History Month, and now we're going to study someone who is both: Fannie Lou Hamer."[13]

Parents at our workshops have described different strategies they used to bring positive books about girls into the classroom. A mother from the Midwest said nothing was more important than vigilance and persistence. When she complained about sexist reading materials, the school's response was hostile, but she refused to be intimidated. She continued to insist on a curriculum that did not demean her daughter:

> When my daughter was in kindergarten, she brought home *I'm Glad I'm a Boy! I'm Glad I'm a Girl!* from the school library. I thought it was terrible. I wrote to the school and suggested they could find better things to spend their money on, and I said I didn't want my daughter ever again to bring home anything that portrayed such poor role models for girls. I received a reply about a month later. The school

chastised me for trying to censor the school library. However, my daughter never brought home anything like that again—and every teacher in that school knew my opinion on sexist materials.

A parent active in the New Jersey chapter of the American Association of University Women said she also refused to let her daughter get short-changed at school, especially when it came to role models in literature. She found that working with teachers got results.

> In spring 1992, Heather, an avid reader, came home and threw her book across the room. "I don't want this," she shouted. Concerned, I noticed the book was *Maniac McGee*, a Newbery Award winner. I told Heather I had heard it was a good book and asked her why she didn't want to read it. Her response: "It's the fourth book we've read this year that doesn't have a girl as the main character." The teacher had unintentionally selected all books in the fourth grade with male protagonists. I had a reading list for elementary school students that had books with strong female characters, so I shared it with the teacher and librarian. This year in fifth grade, Heather is reading four books—two with male and two with female protagonists.

In this case the problem was unintentional and the solution an offer of assistance—sharing a list of good books about girls. In fact, children's literature now includes sparkling exceptions to a sexist past, books with smart and resourceful females in leading roles. Some of the best of these are included in the Recommended Reading list at the end of this book, and they provide an important resource; when parents and teachers do not know about the better books, they continue to select stories they read as children, the ones with females who are subservient, uninteresting, or inactive.

Heather's mother went beyond providing alternatives to an all-male reading list. She took on a tougher task—defying the classics:

> When my daughter's class was selected to present the holiday play, *A Christmas Carol*, Heather wanted to try out for the role of Scrooge, but she was told by her music teacher that it was impossible for a girl to audition for that role. "Why can't Scrooge be a girl?" she asked. The answer: "Because it's not traditional." Heather talked with me about it, and I suggested she speak with her teacher again and explain that the play had no good parts for girls.

This story has a kind of happy ending: Two traditionally male roles were redesigned for females. Scrooge was still a male, but Uncle Freddy became Aunt Frieda and ghost Marley was a girl.

The change of two minor characters in the play was an improvement but not a real solution. Challenging the classics of the curriculum is a tough battle, and it is likely to meet with stiff resistance from schools. The conflict can even put teachers' jobs on the line. One woman, frustrated by her school's refusal to treat sexism in the curriculum as a serious matter, attended a workshop in New Jersey and wrote us this note:

> In my district, the students read several trade books each year. There were five books selected for my fifth grade. In one book the only female character makes a poor decision and dies in the first chapter. In the second, a mother is unable to travel because she is expecting a baby. The story is about her husband and son who travel into the wilderness to establish a new home. The third book was the story of relationships between generations, grandson and grandfather. In the fourth book the only female character is a flower. The fifth book includes a neat female character, but she dies.
>
> When I expressed concern about this, I was told it was my emotional baggage. I was told not to cause a problem, not to criticize the reading program.
>
> What next?
>
> I'm not tenured. I was removed from the fifth-grade level. The curriculum was not changed. *I* was.

Other teachers are classroom revolutionaries, each day making small changes in instruction and curriculum. Even pronouns can have a powerful impact, as one of our student teachers, Paul, discovered. His class had been reading books about boys, and the new story he was about to introduce, a Celtic legend, also featured male main characters. He was considering making one of the boys in the story a girl, but he felt uncomfortable about changing literature. We suggested that he talk the problem over with his students and then decide what to do.

We are sitting in the back of Paul's fifth-grade class to observe his lesson. He enters the room carrying a mysterious box with the words BEWARE: BRITTLE PAPER written prominently on the cover. Puzzled, the students look at one another. Without saying a word, the teacher holds the box in front of him and tips it slightly. Sand slides from the crevices and falls to the classroom floor. He has the students' attention; their curiosity is obvious: What could be inside? Slowly the teacher opens the box, removes an ancient-looking book, and carefully holds it up to show the class. As he blows dust off the jacket, the title becomes clear: *The Celtic Dragon Myth*. All eyes are on the teacher as he introduces the array of characters in the story—giants, lions, blacksmiths, falcons, magic fish, kings, fishermen, dragons, and princesses.

"Would you like to read this book?" the teacher asks the class. The students are united in enthusiasm, their excitement almost palpable. "First, I have something to ask you," Paul continues. "The three main characters in this book are boys. Do you think it's fair to read and listen to books in which all the main characters are male?"

The students are clearly taken aback. This is a question no teacher has ever asked them before. Boys respond first.

"I think it's fair to read a myth about boys. What's wrong with that?"

"I don't care if it's a book about girls or boys or half and half. I just want it to be a good story."

"What's the big deal? You said there are princesses, so there's some girls in it."

"Let's get the female point of view," the teacher intervenes.

"I agree with Mark," one girl says matter-of-factly. "I don't care if it's about boys or girls as long as it's a good story. That's what matters."

But a girl sitting on the other side of the room objects:

"Why should we have to listen to it if there are no girls? Why does it always have to be about boys?"

"It doesn't really bother me, but I think the author must be a little sexist," a girl in the front says. "Who wrote it anyway?"

As the students try to figure out if a legend has an author, a girl raises her hand and asks, "It says it's Celtic, so could the Celtic people have been sexist?"

"I don't think you can say that a whole group of people are sexist," another girl from the front says thoughtfully. "Maybe it's because the story was written so long ago. All women did then was stay home and clean the house."

"Why are you getting upset about this?" One of the boys is back in the discussion. "It's no big deal, just a few characters in a story."

"Well, I think it is important." The girl speaking now is angry. "I get really bored when I read only about boys. I'm tired of hearing 'he, he, he' all the time! Why can't it be 'he, he, *she*' once in a while? Didn't those brothers have any sisters?"

Based on the discussion, the teacher reaches a decision. "I didn't understand that some of you felt so strongly about this," he says. "I'm beginning to think these brothers do need a sister, so I'm going to make one of the characters a girl."

In reading and language arts classes, teachers can find books about resourceful girls or they can change the names, but in history they have an additional burden: relearning the past and finding out about the women they never studied in school. More and more teachers are making that effort, and they are also discovering the books and posters developed by the National Women's History Project. Since the 1970s, the mission of this California-based group has been to create awareness of multicultural women's history in every school system in America. Their efforts have already been far-reaching, providing the impetus for National Women's History week, which was later expanded from seven days to the month of March.

"Students who read our books and see our displays say they can't believe how badly they've been cheated out of their own history," said Molly MacGregor, one of the project's founders. And historian Sara Evans wrote, "Having a history is a prerequisite to claiming a right to shape the future."

Girls empowered with knowledge about women in history do lay claim to the future, as this essay by a sixth-grade girl in Maryland shows:

An old soothsayer sat down, discouraged. "Women can't go very far—just to a point." With trepidation she picked up her crystal ball, rubbed it, and looked into the future. Her eyes opened wide. "A woman leader!" she cried. "A woman general, too! How did this happen? Perhaps the roots of this miracle are in the past."

Again she looked into the crystal ball, this time toward the past, searching for more brave women. Suddenly the globe radiated with the courage of pioneer women riding covered wagons. Then Molly Pitcher came into view, firing the cannon for her sick husband. Then Harriet Tubman emerged, boldly leading her people from slavery. Next came Elizabeth Cady Stanton, shaper of the suffrage movement. Finally Elizabeth Blackwell appeared, the first woman doctor in the United States.

"Many intrepid women of the past have shaped our future, but what about today?" the old woman wondered. Again the answer was in the crystal ball. A silver space shuttle loomed over the darkness, and Christa McAuliffe spoke, "I hope girls in the future reach the stars." The old woman smiled. She knew they would.[14]

The eleven-year-old who wrote the essay said that when she learned about remarkable women from the past, it made her feel more confident about what she could accomplish herself. Research echoes this girl's insight. When children read books that portray women in traditional jobs, their perceptions become more stereotyped. But when they read about females who accomplish outstanding deeds, both girls and boys believe that women are capable of great achievement.[15]

Believing Is Seeing

Anthropologist Margaret Mead once said that if a fish were an anthropologist, the last thing it would discover would be water. Most of us have grown up taking for granted a sea of gender bias so encompassing that, like Mead's fish, we don't even notice it. We must be jolted into seeing the water. And this clear perception demands vigilant and systematic observation, not subjective impressions. Only then will the tiny repetitive inequities of the classroom come into sharp focus.

We gave a workshop on gender equity at a school in New York. Most of the seventy-five teachers, parents, and administrators had heard something about gender bias in education, but they were not convinced it existed. And certainly not in *their* schools.

"We're going to show you a short video," we said to them, "a middle school science lesson. Your assignment is to decide whether you are observing a fair teacher or one with bias."

The educators and parents sat back and watched as a young science teacher worked with a small group of four middle school students. As the tape ended and the lights went on, the audience was ready to react.

"I don't want her in our school system," a teacher said. "She talked more to the boys. And when she called on the girls, she asked them easier questions."

"I didn't see anything like that," another teacher objected. "I was impressed with the way she called on every student. Each child spoke at least once."

"But she praised the boys more." The parent sitting in front was adamant. "She didn't praise the girls at all."

"You know, you can nitpick anything to death," the principal interjected. "Give or take a little here or there, I think she was pretty fair."

We asked the audience to vote. Most said the teacher was "pretty fair." A few said there was "some bias." Only two voted for the third choice, "significant bias."

With the vote completed, we taught the teachers and parents how to analyze classrooms with an objective observation system. An hour later they watched the same science lesson, but they observed completely differently now. They no longer casually viewed the class, they coded interaction and recorded the race and gender of every student who spoke, as well as the teacher's reactions. When the scene was over and the marks were tallied, most of the group was surprised to find that the teacher had called on boys more than twice as often as she had called on girls, and she had praised the boys four times as often. When casually watching, almost no one saw the hidden sexist lessons; when objectively coding, no one could miss them.

Techniques for Change

Given the hectic pace of classroom life, clocked at several hundred to a thousand interactions daily, most teachers cannot monitor accurately who receives their attention. An outside observer—a colleague, parent, or even a student—must help. In our research studies, we spent weeks preparing graduate students and former teachers to code classrooms using a formal observation system. While rigorous training is necessary for research, less complex techniques can still uncover a wealth of practical information and show teachers unintentional patterns in their own instruction.

Tallying how many times teachers call on or respond to boys versus girls provides a baseline of bias. To achieve equity, the distribution of attention should represent the proportion of each gender in the classroom. A seventh-grade teacher told what happened the first time she asked a colleague to come in and count the questions going to each gender.

> "Girls definitely talked half the time in your class," the colleague reported when the class was over and the check marks had been tallied.
>
> "That's great," the conscientious teacher said with relief. "Thanks for letting me know it was fair."
>
> "Well," the observer said with a smile, "I didn't say it was fair. I just said girls talked half the time. More than three-quarters of your students are female, but they're only talking half the time. In terms of their representation in the class, boys, who are 25 percent of the students, are getting 50 percent of your time."

An observer can offer even more specific information by drawing a class seating plan that indicates where each boy or girl is located in the room. Every time a teacher speaks to a student, the observer makes a check on the chart, tracking each individual's participation. Then a teacher who studies the chart has a visible record of otherwise elusive patterns: Is one gender receiving more attention? Who dominates and who is left out? Which areas of the room are attention rich, and where are the dead zones, those places students can hide unnoticed? The observer can even record who is praised or criticized and who gets instruction on how to improve.

Holding up this mirror, an objective record, helps instructors recognize their own patterns, but looking at the reflection is only the first step on a long journey. The pattern of female invisibility is stubborn and resists change, but when teachers participate in effective training, they can eradicate gender bias from their instruction.

In our research studies during the past decade we have analyzed the classrooms of elementary, secondary, and college teachers who participated in faculty development workshops. When college professors who received training were compared with a control group who had not, striking differences emerged. In the control group, typically half the class did not speak, and most of the silent students were women. But in the classrooms of professors who had been trained for gender equity, only 7 percent of students were silent, and females and males were equally active in discussion.

We discovered a particularly surprising shift in elementary and secondary schools. When teachers went about instruction as usual, boys dominated discussions and called out questions and comments eight times more than girls. But an eye-opening change occurred in the classrooms of trained teachers: Girls no longer waited to be selected by the teacher; they became much more assertive, and the gender gap in calling out almost disappeared. The ratio of males to females calling out, which had been eight to one, shrank to eight to seven. When the classroom climate was warm and accepting, girls left the spectator role and joined the boys in the interaction.[16]

Teachers from around the country have told us their own creative strategies to equalize the gender gap in classroom attention, such as the one devised by a Wisconsin teacher who attended a workshop:

"I read about your research before I came," she said, "and I tried an idea in my own classroom that really got quiet girls involved. I discovered poker chips. Several times a week at the beginning of my class, I gave each student two chips. Whenever they wanted to ask or answer a question, they had to spend a chip. And everybody had to spend their chips before the class was over."

We congratulated the teacher on her innovative technique to involve silent students, who were more likely to be girls.

"But it's better than that," she said. "The students who usually dominate the classroom receive a wonderful lesson, too. Because they can talk only twice, they must choose which comments to say. Now noisy students are doing something they never did before: They think before they speak."

Almost all teachers we have talked with made it clear that relying on noisy students, the ones who volunteer, is a direct path to a classroom controlled by boys. Girls who know the answer are more likely to wait to be called on, while males are more apt to shout out.

Many teachers have also said that using wait time works well. In classrooms where discussion moves rapidly and less than one second goes by between the teacher's question and a student's answer, girls may be left out. This breakneck pace, usually set by boys, blocks the participation of shy students who need more time to think or muster their confidence. When teachers consciously extend their wait time to three to five seconds, especially where a thoughtful response is warranted, more girls—and quiet boys—are pulled into the discussion.

Other teachers are experimenting with cooperative learning. In this innovation, popular in elementary and secondary schools, groups of students, mixed in terms of race, gender, and ability, coach and teach one another and earn group rewards for good academic performance. The approach leads to achievement, and it promotes friendships among students from different racial groups. Many teachers initially thought it would encourage gender equity, too, but when they watched groups at work, they saw disturbing patterns: Aggressive students, who are more likely to be male, were taking the speaking parts and the leadership roles.

Research has supported these teachers' observations. In a study of junior high school math groups, observers found that females were generally helpful to all other group members, but males were more likely to help other males. Even in groups with more girls, boys became the focus of attention.[17] Another researcher evaluated the opinions of fourth and fifth graders who had spent several weeks in mixed gender groups. She found that these groups encouraged boys and girls to communicate more with each other, and the boys were more positive about working with girls after the experience. For girls the group work was evidently not as enjoyable; they expressed no increased preference for working with boys.[18]

When teachers are aware that girls and quiet boys may be left on the sidelines, they can set up rules to make cooperative groups work. "You need to talk frankly with the kids," a Maryland teacher advised. "You have to explain that boys can't take over, that girls and quiet students in general need to lead, too. And rotating roles have to be set up that each student must fill. One day a girl may be designated as a group leader, and a boy is the recorder and takes notes. The next day they switch roles so each has a chance to lead and each has a chance to follow. And you need to keep monitoring the groups carefully so that old 'take over' moves don't reemerge."

Leveling with students is one of our favorite strategies. Since gender equity should not be a secret goal but one shared with students, we give a handout to classes. Called "Education Is Not a Spectator Sport," it describes research on gender differences in classroom discussion and asks students to consider whether girls or boys talk more in their own classrooms. And when we encounter situations where boys are dominating and demanding more of our attention, we point this out and talk it over with the students.

We were in an auditorium in a high school in the Midwest. More than a hundred school newspaper reporters were gathered for a "press conference" to ask us, the visiting researchers, about our studies. At first the students seemed reluctant to interview us, but then the comments came quickly, an avalanche of questions.

"Hold it a minute," we said, halting the rapid-fire pace of the press conference. "Do you notice anything ironic going on here?" The room of reporters looked at us blankly until a girl from the back, where most of the females were clustered, said, "The boys are asking all the questions." There was an audible gasp as the students realized they had become living proof of the story they were supposed to report.

"Here we are, talking about boys dominating discussions, and it's happening right in front of us. How can we change this?"

The students looked at one another uncomfortably, and then the girls began asking questions, some even more assertively than the boys. But after ten minutes the burst was over, and the original pattern reemerged with the boys dominating the discussion. Again we stopped to call the students' attention to the imbalance, but this time we gave specific suggestions to change the pattern. We recommended that students write down good questions instead of shouting out anything that came to mind, and we integrated the seating so that the girls were no longer clustered in the back. We also asked the boys to do something they were rarely asked to do—share time.

A private school teacher in Chicago has also found that she must be doggedly persistent and continually vigilant to keep girls from being left on the sidelines. She said, "One day I noticed how inevitably a girl's head turned toward a boy as he approached, even if she and I were discussing her current piece of writing. Next I realized with a jolt that my head invariably turned toward him, too."

Learning not to hear boys more than girls became a daily act of personal resistance for this teacher, one that played out like this:

TEACHER: Well, Patricia, how do you think you can convince your reader that— (Steven approaches, waving his paper. Patricia turns toward him.) No, Patricia. I'm talking with *you*. Keep watching me. (The teacher takes Patricia's chin in

her hand and forces eye contact.) Don't look at Steven. You
are the important one right now.

This teacher also needed to keep her own attention focused, using her
hand "like a horse's blinder" to keep Steven and other boys from
pulling her attention away from Patricia. She said: "As my focus on the
girls has grown sharper, I find it easier to attend to their concerns and
not set them aside when a boy fills the horizon. It's a daily challenge
because most boys haven't set aside their feeling that they come first. I
still haven't trained my ears not to turn toward Steven's insistent questions from halfway across the room."[19]

This need for watchful intentionality is echoed in research findings. A
study of a university-based preschool class showed again how male
students take over and teachers unintentionally let it happen. During
snack time two girls, two boys, and one teacher sat at each table, and
researchers analyzed their conversations. The teachers were scrupu-
lously fair in how food was given out, but they never considered how
they distributed the invisible staples of time and attention. During their
conversations, the teachers frequently interrupted female students.
And the boys, secure in their right to be heard, freely interrupted their
female teachers. The lessons were insidious but devastating: If you are
a young male, you are entitled to talk; and if you are female, no matter
your age, your words are worth less and can be cut short. This
preschool study is similar to research on interaction in families that
show fathers talk more with male children and both parents interrupt
daughters more than sons.[20]

After describing this preschool study at a workshop in Missouri, we
received a note from a teacher who was also a parent of young children:

We have two daughters and two sons, and when you talked
about that study, our family dinner table at home flashed
into my mind. As I began to think about it, it seemed as
though our sons were usually talking and our daughters
were waiting to speak. So I counted the interruptions. Our
house is like the preschool, with the boys talking, laughing,
interrupting their sisters, and vying for their father's attention, and the girls trying to get a word in edgewise. Last
night my sons had a lesson on letting girls talk, too.

While some parents are teaching their sons not to interrupt, others are
working with their daughters and developing strategies to help them

speak up. A lawyer from Indiana, who is also the parent of two children, wrote us this letter:

> When I returned home after your symposium, I asked my daughter who got called on the most in class. I did not specify whether I wanted a name or a group. She said, "The boys." I then asked her if she ever gave an answer before the teacher called on her. She said, "No, the teacher wouldn't like that." I asked if anyone gave answers before being called on, and she said, "Sure. The boys do all the time."
>
> Elementary teachings, perhaps, but I had no idea. I may not be able to change the schools, but I can change how I help my daughter, and I can help my son and husband understand.

A woman from Illinois, one with an unusually sophisticated awareness of gender bias, told us about the successful strategies she and her husband used to help their gifted daughter shatter the barrier of silence and speak her mind at school:

> When our daughter Lara was in high school, she was extremely reluctant to speak out in class. In fact, she refused to wear red (a color that accentuates her dark hair and coloring) to school because it made her too noticeable. . . . One history teacher notified the students that they could not receive a grade of A if they did not participate in class. This teacher was also notorious for "pushing" students when they gave an answer. Many students were not used to this type of give-and-take and would not answer in class. Our daughter, with her reticent nature, would have been quite content to sit back and listen. . . .
>
> She was in tears at home. "I can't talk in there. All those debaters know everything. [All those debaters were boys.] I'll feel like an idiot if I'm wrong." We asked her if she would rather get a B even though she knew the material perfectly. She decided she wanted to try to participate. We helped her set goals. At first she had to volunteer a certain number of times per week. Then it was a set number of times per day. We told her we didn't care if she got wrong answers, all she had to do was talk, and we would pay her the magnificent sum of five cents for each interaction. She laughed at our cheap reward but was sufficiently motivated to try the scheme.
>
> There were many days when she came home in tears be-

cause she just couldn't make herself raise her hand. Finally she forced herself to take the plunge on a regular basis, and by the end of the semester she was participating freely and even received a comment on her report card that she "participates well in class"; this was next to her grade—an A.

Lara's academic career was one of extraordinary accomplishment. After graduating as valedictorian of her high school class, she attended Harvard/Radcliffe, was a member of Phi Beta Kappa, graduated magna cum laude as a physics major, and won a fellowship for graduate work in biophysics at Berkeley. But without vigilance and the willingness to intervene, her mother suspects that Lara's story might not have had such a happy ending.

Like this girl's mother and father, parents need to keep an eye on the curriculum and protest sexism when they see it. And they must offer support from the home, refusing to let their daughters vanish into the classroom woodwork and helping them develop the courage to speak their minds.[21]

Tomorrow's Women

In 1993, Curtis Sittenfeld graduated from Groton, a formerly all-male private school and "the alma mater of Franklin Roosevelt, Dean Acheson, and several other famous men." While there, she found misogyny prevalent and eating disorders rampant, so she and a few other girls attempted to form the Group for Female Awareness (they had been told that using the term "feminism" would put people off); and she tried to speak out against sexism, despite warnings that she would offend all the boys at the school.

Gender bias was a daily part of school culture at Groton. Some boys addressed girls by calling out "Bitch!" or "Wench!" but these seemed to be terms of affection because males used them only with females they knew well. Boys found it "cute" to tell sexist jokes: "What's long and skinny and goes from the bedroom to the kitchen?" Answer: "A woman's leash." During spring fling, a day of inter-dorm competition, boys wore sexually degrading T-shirts; for example, one that pictured a cat (a reference to a vagina) read, DON'T KILL THE CAT, JUST THROW IT AROUND.

Writing about these experiences in a *Washington Post* article subtitled "Why I Gave Up the Good Fight for Feminism at Groton," Curtis regretted that she let the relentless, daily gender bias wear her down. She related how sometimes she felt sad rather than angry and failed to fight back. When she went into a male dorm to study with a friend, a senior referred to a male athlete as "so bad he 'played like a girl.'" Curtis could not make herself challenge the comment, so she left the room. When she went into the hallway, she heard this exchange:

> SENIOR: What were those ten commandments your group made up?
>
> SOPHOMORE: One was "Anything for play" [that is, a sexual encounter].
>
> SENIOR: No, I mean what was the commandment about bitches?
>
> SOPHOMORE: "It's always the bitch's fault."

Then the male students began to talk about inferior girls' sports such as field hockey, which they said "sucks except that they wear skirts." The boys went on to approve of cheerleading as "a real girls' sport [because] they cheer on their superiors." Curtis thought the boys were deliberately trying to provoke her, but she never determined this or objected to the conversation. "I bet Curtis is loving this," the senior said as she left the room.

"I still believe there are problems at Groton, not just in terms of sexism but also in terms of the fact that most girls at the school feel terrible about themselves," Curtis wrote. "But I don't know what that 'ism' is called. And although I sometimes get momentarily fired up by reading *Ms.* magazine, I have learned during the last year and a half that I am not the one who will be able to resolve it."[22]

Curtis thinks she has failed, but it is our schools that are failing. At adolescence, when being pretty and popular is paramount and so many girls grow silent, Curtis continues to speak out. Every time she writes an article, she resists. But she needs help. Leslie Wolfe, director of the Center on Women's Policy Studies, recommends that everyone who cares about girls, their intellectual, psychological, and financial well-being, must see themselves as advocates for educational equity. "Whether we're plumbers or lawyers or bankers or teachers," she says, "we must do community service for girls, make the extra effort, and train ourselves to take time for our daughters."

As we visit schools in small towns and large cities across America, we are struck by the growing number of people who are taking the time, making the effort, and working conscientiously so that schools will stop cheating tomorrow's women and start giving them the support they deserve. The examples below are just a few of the actions we have observed:

> The students were seated in a circle in a high school sociology class, one with an imaginary line intersecting it at the center, leaving boys on one side and girls on the other. Instead of ignoring the segregation, the teacher offered a real-life sociology lesson. She called the students' attention to the gender divide and explained the need for women and men to communicate at home and in the workplace. She asked the students to rearrange the seating pattern to eliminate the sex separation.
>
> The students shifted in their seats and looked around at one another. Then a girl grabbed her books, walked over to the male side of the circle, and sat down. Following her lead, the other students also exchanged places. Once the circle was integrated, the teacher found she was no longer pulled toward the male semicircle, and her attention was distributed more fairly.
>
> A science teacher analyzed the walls of his rooms and saw a dozen posters of male sports teams but none of females. Searching for posters of girls in sports, he found few he liked, so he took pictures of girls playing field hockey, basketball, and soccer for the school. Selecting images of energy and achievement, he had the photos blown up to poster size, and mounted them all over the room. Girls, even those who were not taking science, stopped by the class to see the exhibit.
>
> A suburban school system instituted a self-study on gender equity in athletics. Everything from finances to game attendance was reviewed. Two softball players testified in an open hearing that compared resources given to the baseball and softball teams. They told the task force that baseball had bleachers, a scoreboard, and a batting cage, and the team had jackets. Softball had none of these. "Baseball has the school's support," they said. The testimony ended with a question: The girls asked, "Do we?" As a result of the self-study, the school system worked on equalizing money and resources for male and female athletes.

A recently hired English teacher was explaining the term "oxymoron," and he put these examples on the board:

cold fire
hot ice
intelligent woman

A supervisor who was observing the lesson pointed out that "intelligent woman" was an offensive example. The teacher said he was just joking. The supervisor was not appeased. Instead, she made it clear that the gender slur was as harmful as racial, ethnic, or religious bigotry.

A young woman in a college classroom prefaced her answers to the professor's questions with comments such as "This probably isn't what you're after," and then proceeded to give excellent responses. The professor decided to let the student know the disservice she was doing herself. At the end of the class he called the woman up to his desk. "You're such a bright student," he said. "Don't discredit your answer before you even give it. You're too good to put yourself down like that."

A group of vocational educators videotaped one another's classrooms and then analyzed the tapes for gender bias. One teacher wrote: "I was amazed to see myself on videotape responding more to the male students than to the females. It made me realize that such inequitable treatment can be extremely subtle and so deeply ingrained that those with the best of intentions can be oblivious to their own weaknesses." The teachers kept visiting and helping one another, suggesting strategies to make their classrooms fairer.

A sixth-grade teacher let students choose whether they wanted to use computers during recess. As a result the computer room was filled with males, and few girls tried to enter what had become a boys' room. When a girl did go in, the males made rude comments, and other girls looked at her askance. The teacher decided to require fifteen minutes a week of computer time rather than leave it to choice. The computer room then became integrated and was eventually used during recess and other free periods by almost equal numbers of girls and boys.

A high school announced its new policy on sexual harassment. The guidelines urged girls to dress carefully so as not to excite male students and to rebuff their advances tactfully in order not to offend them. The boys received no instructions on appropriate attire or behavior. A group of students protested and held a press conference. Several students researched the topic of sexual harassment. Several hundred signed a petition demanding that the policy and the training materials be changed.

The teacher brought a scientist into the class to talk to the students. The woman told the seventh graders that when she was younger, she didn't think science was a good field for girls because all the scientists she ever saw were men. She described a typical day at work and discussed salaries in the sciences compared to other jobs. When a girl asked if she had any children, she talked frankly about the difficulties and rewards of combining the roles of scientist and mother. After she left, several girls asked to do their biography reports on Rosalyn Yalow and Barbara McClintock.

A high school girl often brought her friends home, where they "hung out." Her father was upset with the way both boys and girls who never used racial or religious slurs casually referred to girls as chicks and bitches. He talked to them about it and explained why it concerned him. His daughter told him, "I was so embarrassed at first, but now I'm glad you said something."

More and more parents, teachers, and students are making individual efforts that, taken together, presage a unified movement for gender equity in schools. And they are discovering the resources available for national use, materials that have been developed over the past two decades by educators who refused to give up when backlash discredited their programs. For example, EQUALS, based in Berkeley, California, offers seminars to encourage girls and minorities in math. The American Association for the Advancement of Sciences in Washington, D.C., works to eradicate the gender gap in science. Horizons 2000 in Virginia offers programs to enhance girls' knowledge of careers as well as their self-esteem. And at the Women's Educational Equity Act Publishing Center in Massachusetts, staff members say that requests for materials have surged, especially in math and science.

Traditionally all-female groups are also becoming involved. The Girl

Scouts now scrutinizes its materials for subtle sexism. It also highlights badges related to science and math, and pilots gender equity training for troop leaders. Operation SMART, developed by Girls Incorporated (formerly Girls Clubs of America), emphasizes hands-on participation to build confidence in math, science, and technology. The American Association of University Women, a century-old organization that had been losing members and lacked clear goals, has responded to the failure of a decade of educational reform to target gender equity, from the 1983 report *A Nation at Risk* to the 1991 initiative *America 2000*. Since Anne Bryant became their executive director, addressing the educational needs of girls has become the association's major goal.

In 1992, when the AAUW published *How Schools Shortchange Girls*, a synthesis of studies prepared by the Wellesley Center for Research on Women, Bryant was worried about defensiveness from the educational establishment. She remembered her meeting with Keith Geiger, president of the National Education Association: "When I walked into the office, the report was on his desk, heavily marked and underlined. He picked it up, slammed it down, and said, 'This is dynamite!' I remember wondering, 'Dynamite good or dynamite bad?' But then he said, 'As I read it I kept thinking to myself, "When I was a math teacher, did I do these things?"' Then I knew we were going to be able to work together."

The report made national headlines, salvaged gender equity from the backwaters of backlash, and put it squarely on the American agenda. Anne said, "I remember going to bed the night our report was issued, totally exhilarated. When I woke up the next morning, the first thought in my mind was, 'Oh my God, what do we do next?'"

The AAUW has kept the momentum going with national, state, and local roundtables. There are also new research projects, and along with other groups the association has worked to pass new legislation. The Gender Equity in Education Act, a group of nine separate bills sponsored by Pat Schroeder, Patsy Mink, Olympia Snowe, and others, proposes to revitalize the decimated Women's Educational Equity Act, establish an Office of Gender Equity at the Department of Education, build programs to help pregnant teenagers, combat sexual harassment in schools, and train a new generation of nonsexist teachers.

Bryant said she was pleased with the AAUW's efforts. "Although the issue is controversial in some chapters, most of our members are proud of what they have accomplished. Even in retirement communities, the members are making a difference. One chapter has a grandmother storytellers program, and these women are now combing libraries looking for good nonsexist books to read to kids."

In the past the isolated efforts of courageous individuals kept the quest for gender equity alive, even in difficult times. Back in the 1960s and early '70s when sexism was a word few people understood, pioneers defined the cause and brought it to national attention. During the Reagan and Bush administrations, promising programs were wiped out and research funds were eliminated, but a small number of dedicated educators stood up to the conservative backlash and continued their work. Today, as the political tide is shifting once again, a new generation of teachers and parents are swelling the ranks of these veterans, and the nation stands poised on the edge of change.

An African proverb says it takes the whole village to educate a child: grandparents and parents, teachers and school administrators, lawmakers and civic leaders. When all these citizens from our American village join forces, they can transform our educational institutions into the most powerful levers for equity, places where girls are valued as much as boys, daughters are cherished as fully as sons, and tomorrow's women are prepared to be full partners in all activities of the next century and beyond.

Notes

Preface

1. Frazier, Nancy, and Myra Sadker. *Sexism in School and Society.* New York: Harper & Row, 1973.

1. Hidden Lessons

1. Faludi, Susan. *Backlash: The Undeclared War Against American Women.* New York: Crown, 1991, p. xxii.
2. Our first study, which analyzed gender bias in elementary and secondary classrooms, lasted more than three years and was funded by the National Institute of Education. The report submitted to the government was Sadker, Myra, and David Sadker, *Year 3: Final Report: Promoting Effectiveness in Classroom Instruction.* Washington, DC: National Institute of Education, 1984.

   Sadker, Myra, and David Sadker. "Sexism in the Schoolroom of the Eighties," *Psychology Today* (March 1985), pp. 54–57.

   Sadker, Myra, and David Sadker. "Sexism in the Classroom: From Grade School to Graduate School," *Phi Delta Kappan* 67:7 (March 1986), pp. 512–15.

   We also reported this study as one of the contributing authors to Wellesley College Center for Research on Women. *How Schools Shortchange Girls: The AAUW Report.* Washington, DC: American Association of University Women Educational Foundation, 1992.
3. Kidder, Tracy. *Among Schoolchildren.* Boston: Houghton Mifflin, 1989, p. 3.
4. Kidder, *Among Schoolchildren*, p. 262.
5. These episodes are drawn primarily from our three-year study of sex bias in elementary and secondary classrooms. They are also taken from classroom observations conducted as we supervised

student teachers at The American University and as we consulted with schools around the country and assessed their classrooms for gender bias.

6. Trecker, Janice Law. "Women in U.S. History High School Textbooks," *Social Education* 35 (1971), pp. 249–60.

7. Weitzman, Lenore, and Diane Rizzo. *Biased Textbooks: Images of Males and Females in Elementary School Textbooks*. Washington, DC: Resource Center on Sex Roles in Education, 1976.

   Saario, Terry, Carol Jacklin, and Carol Tittle. "Sex Role Stereotyping in the Public Schools," *Harvard Educational Review* 43, pp. 386–416.

   Women on Words and Images. *Dick and Jane as Victims: Sex Stereotyping in Children's Readers*. Princeton, NJ: Carolingian Press, 1972.

8. For more than a decade we have offered workshops on gender bias for educators and parents around the country. At these workshops we have collected anecdotes and stories from students, teachers, and parents about sex bias that they faced at school.

9. "This Is What You Thought: Were Any of Your Teachers Biased Against Females?" *Glamour* (August 1992), p. 157.

10. Following our three-year study of elementary and secondary classrooms, we conducted a two-year study of college classrooms and were sponsored by the Fund for the Improvement of Postsecondary Education. The project report submitted to the government was Sadker, Myra, and David Sadker, *Final Report: Project Effect (Effectiveness and Equity in College Teaching)*. Washington, DC: Fund for the Improvement of Postsecondary Education, 1986.

    Sadker, Myra, and David Sadker. "Confronting Sexism in the College Classroom." In Gabriel, Susan, and Isaiah Smithson (eds.), *Gender in the Classroom: Power and Pedagogy*. Urbana: University of Illinois Press, 1990, pp. 176–87.

11. Sadker, Myra, David Sadker, and Susan Klein. "The Issue of Gender in Elementary and Secondary Education." In Grant, Gerald (ed.), *Review of Research in Education*, vol. 17. Washington, DC: American Educational Research Association, 1991.

    Wellesley College Center for Research on Women, *How Schools Shortchange Girls: The AAUW Report*.

12. Data documenting the loss of academic achievement were obtained from reports, tables, news releases, and studies issued by test publishers. The Educational Testing Service in Princeton, New Jersey, provided several reports and statistics related to the Preliminary Scholastic Aptitude Test, the Scholastic Aptitude Test, the

Achievement tests, the Graduate Record Exam, and the Graduate Management Admissions Test. While the Graduate Record Exam data were from 1987–1988 (the most recently published), all other data reflected 1991 and 1992 test administrations. The American College Testing Program data were derived from a variety of profile and normative reports for 1990 and 1991 issued by American College Testing in Iowa City, Iowa.

Professional organizations and schools often contract with testing services to develop and administer their admissions tests. For example, the Medical College Admission Test (MCAT) is developed by ACT in Iowa City. For each of these admission tests the professional association responsible was contacted first, and it provided the requisite information. These organizations included the Association of American Medical Colleges, the Graduate Management Admissions Council, and the Law School Data Assembly Service.

13. Sadker and Sadker, *Year 3: Final Report.*
    Sadker and Sadker, *Final Report: Project Effect.*
14. Nagel, K. L., and Karen H. Jones. "Sociological Factors in the Development of Eating Disorders," *Adolescence* 27 (Spring 1992), pp. 107–13.
    Wiseman, Claire, James Gray, James Mosimann, and Anthony Ahrens. "Cultural Expectations of Thinness in Women: An Update," *International Journal of Eating Disorders* 11:1 (1992), pp. 85–89.
    Button, Eric. "Self-Esteem in Girls Aged 11–12: Baseline Findings from a Planned Prospective Study of Vulnerability to Eating Disorders," *Journal of Adolescence* 13 (December 7, 1990), pp. 407–13.
15. Hughes, Jean O'Gorman, and Bernice Sandler. *Peer Harassment: Hassles for Women on Campus.* Washington, DC: Project on the Status and Education of Women, Association of American Colleges, 1988.
    Stein, Nan. "Sexual Harassment in Schools," *The School Administrator* (January 1993), pp. 14–21.
16. Earle, Janice. *Counselor/Advocates: Keeping Pregnant and Parenting Teens in School.* Alexandria, VA: National Association of State Boards of Education, 1990.
17. A vast body of research documents girls' declining self-esteem at adolescence:
    Allgood-Merten, Betty, Peter Lewinsohn, and Hyman Hops. "Sex Differences and Adolescent Depression," *Journal of Abnormal Psychology* 99:1 (February 1990), pp. 55–63.

Brutsaert, Herman. "Changing Sources of Self-Esteem Among Girls and Boys in Secondary Schools," *Urban Education* 24:4 (January 1990), pp. 432–39.

Kelly, Kevin, and LaVerne Jordan. "Effects of Academic Achievement and Gender on Academic and Social Self-Concept: A Replication Study," *Journal of Counseling and Development* 69 (November-December 1990), pp. 173–77.

Widaman, Keith, et al. "Differences in Adolescents' Self-Concept as a Function of Academic Level, Ethnicity, and Gender," *American Journal of Mental Retardation* 96:4 (1992), pp. 387–404.

Williams, Sheila, and Rob McGee. "Adolescents' Self-Perceptions of Their Strengths," *Journal of Youth and Adolescence* 20:3 (June 1991), pp. 325–37.

2. Through the Back Door: The History of Women's Education

1. Woody, Thomas. *A History of Women's Education in the United States*, vols. I and II. New York: Octagon Books, 1966, p. 273.
2. Greene, Maxine. *Landscapes of Learning*. New York: Teachers College Press, 1978, pp. 225–43.

Tannenbaum Deutsch, David. "The Polite Lady: Portraits of American Schoolgirls and Their Accomplishments, 1725–1830," *Antiques* 135 (March 1980), pp. 742–53.
3. Earle, Alice Morse. *Child Life in Colonial Days*. New York: Macmillan, 1899, p. 96.
4. Tyack, David, and Elisabeth Hansot. *Learning Together: A History of Coeducation in American Schools*. New Haven, CT: Yale University Press, 1990, pp. 13–27.

Bailyn, Bernard. *Education in the Forming of American Society*. Chapel Hill: University of North Carolina Press, 1960.

Cremin, Lawrence. *American Education: The Colonial Experience, 1607–1783*. New York: Harper & Row, 1970.
5. Axtell, James. *The School Upon a Hill: Education and Society in Colonial New England*. New Haven, CT: Yale University Press, 1974.
6. Higginson, J. *Common Sense About Women*. Quoted in Woody, *A History of Women's Education*, vol. 2, pp. 200–1.

Krug, Edward A. *The Shaping of the American High School*. New York: Harper & Row, 1964.

Cremin, Lawrence A. *The Transformation of the School: Progressivism in American Education, 1876–1957*. New York: Knopf, 1961.

7. A comprehensive discussion of coeducation is provided in Keller, Arnold Jack, *A Historical Analysis of the Arguments for and Against Coeducational Public High Schools in the United States.* Unpublished doctoral dissertation, Columbia University, New York, 1971.

8. Curti, Merle. *The Social Ideas of American Educators.* Totowa, NJ: Littlefield, 1959, p. 185.

9. Clark, Alice. *Working Life of Women in the Seventeenth Century.* London: Routledge and Kegan Paul, 1982 (1919), pp. 259–63.

10. Pearson, Carol, Judith Touchton, and Donna Shavlik,. *Educating the Majority: Women Challenge Tradition in Higher Education.* New York: Macmillan, 1989, pp. 48–49.

    Solomon, Barbara. *In the Company of Educated Women.* New Haven, CT: Yale University Press, 1985, p. 152.

11. Mann, Horace. *A Few Thoughts on the Powers and Duties of Women.* Syracuse, NY: Hall, Mills, 1853, p. 82.

12. Griffin, Gail. "Women's Education and the American Midwest," *Change* (January-February 1984), p. 36.

13. "A Satire on a College for Women in Kentucky," *Springfield [Massachusetts] Republican and Journal,* March 14, 1835.

14. Gordon, Lynn Dorothy. *Gender and Higher Education in the Progressive Era.* New Haven, CT: Yale University Press, 1990, pp. 22–23.

15. Griffin, "Women's Education and the American Midwest," p. 37.

16. Gordon, J. E. H. "The After Careers of University-Educated Women," *Nineteenth Century* 37 (June 1895), pp. 955–60. Quoted in Woody, *A History of Women's Education,* vol. 2, p. 206.

17. Woody, *A History of Women's Education,* vol. 2, p. 319.

18. Lucy Downing, quoted in Woody, *A History of Women's Education,* vol. 2, p. 137.

19. Jewett, Milo. "Origin of Vassar College," March 1879, typed copy, p. 5, Vassar College Library, Poughkeepsie, NY. Quoted in Horowitz, Helen Lefkowitz, *Alma Mater.* New York: Alfred A. Knopf, 1984, p. 29.

20. Quoted in Horowitz, *Alma Mater,* pp. 74–75.

21. Howe, Julia Ward. "Introduction." In Meyer, Annie Nathan, *Woman's Work in America.* New York: Henry Holt, 1891.

22. Quoted in Butcher, Patricia Smith, *Education for Equality: Women's Rights Periodicals and Women's Higher Education, 1849–1920.* New York: Greenwood Press, 1989, p. 89.

23. Clarke, Edward H. *Sex in Education: Or, A Fair Chance for Girls.* Boston: Houghton Mifflin, 1873, pp. 120–28.

24. A good discussion of Edward Clarke's beliefs and impact is provided in Tyack and Hansot, *Learning Together*, pp. 146–54.
25. Thomas, M. Carey. "Present Tendencies in Women's Education," *Education Review* 25 (1908), pp. 64–85. Quoted in Tyack and Hansot, *Learning Together*, p. 68.
26. Faludi, Susan. *Backlash: The Undeclared War Against American Women*. New York: Crown, 1991, pp. 259–63.
27. Faludi, *Backlash*, xix.

3. Missing in Interaction

1. Sadker, Myra, and David Sadker. *Year 3: Final Report: Promoting Effectiveness in Classroom Instruction*. Washington, DC: National Institute of Education, 1984.

Sadker, Myra, and David Sadker. "Sexism in the Classroom: From Grade School to Graduate School," *Phi Delta Kappan* 67:7 (March 1986), pp. 512–15.

Leinhardt, Gaea, Andrea Seewald, and Mary Engel. "Learning What's Taught: Sex Differences in Instruction," *Journal of Educational Psychology* 71:4 (1979), pp. 432–39.

Jones, M. Gail. "Gender Issues in Teacher Education," *Journal of Teacher Education* (January-February 1989), pp. 33–38.

Wellesley College Center for Research on Women. *How Schools Shortchange Girls: The AAUW Report*. Washington, DC: American Association of University Women Educational Foundation, 1992.

Sadker, Myra, David Sadker, and Lisa Stulberg. "Fair and Square? Creating a Nonsexist Classroom," *Instructor* 102:7 (March 1993), pp. 45–46, 67.
2. Gore, Dolores. *Sex-Related Differences in Relation to Teacher Behavior as Wait-Time During Fourth-Grade Mathematics Instruction*. Unpublished doctoral dissertation, University of Arkansas, 1981.
3. Wilkinson, Louise Cherry, and Cora Marrett (eds.). *Gender Influences in Classroom Interaction*. Orlando, FL: Academic Press, 1985.
4. Irvine, Jacqueline Jordan. "Teacher-Student Interactions: Effects of Student Race, Sex, and Grade Level," *Journal of Educational Psychology* 78:1 (1986), pp. 14–21.
5. Dweck, Carol, William Davidson, Sharon Nelson, and Bradley Enna. "Sex Differences in Learned Helplessness: II. The Contingencies of Evaluative Feedback in the Classroom, III. An Experimental Analysis," *Developmental Psychology* 14:3 (1978), pp. 268–76.

6. Rowe, Mary Budd. "Wait-Time and Rewards as Instructional Variables: Their Influence on Language, Logic, and Fate Control." Paper presented at the National Association for Research in Science Teaching, Chicago, Illinois, April 1972.

7. Gore, Dolores, and Daniel Roumagoux. "Wait-Time as a Variable in Sex-Related Differences During Fourth-Grade Mathematics Instruction," *Journal of Educational Research* 76:5 (1983), pp. 273–75.

8. Best, Raphaela. *We've All Got Scars: What Boys and Girls Learn in Elementary School.* Bloomington, IN: Indiana University Press, 1983.

9. Thorne, Barrie. "Girls and Boys Together . . . but Mostly Apart: Gender Arrangements in Elementary Schools." In Wrigley, Julia (ed.), *Education and Gender Equality.* London: The Falmer Press, 1992.

10. Mahaffey, Foyne. "An Elementary School Teacher Reflects on Harassment: Are We Accepting Too Much?" *Rethinking Schools* (May-June 1992), p. 6.

11. Darrow, Whitney, Jr., *I'm Glad I'm a Boy! I'm Glad I'm a Girl!* New York: Simon and Schuster, 1970.

12. Vare, Ethlie Ann, and Greg Ptacek. *Mothers of Invention.* New York: William Morrow, 1988.

13. Women on Words and Images. *Dick and Jane as Victims: Sex Stereotyping in Children's Readers.* Princeton, NJ: Women on Words and Images, 1975.

14. Weitzman, Lenore, and Diane Rizzo. *Biased Textbooks: A Research Perspective.* Washington, DC: The Research Center on Sex Roles in Education, 1974.

15. Weitzman, Lenore, et al. "Sex Role Socialization in Picture Books for Preschool Children," *American Journal of Sociology* 77:6 (1972), pp. 1125–50.

16. Feminists on Children's Literature. "A Feminist Look at Children's Books," *School Library Journal* 17:5 (January 1971), pp. 19–24.
    Graebner, Diane Bennett. "A Decade of Sexism in Readers," *Reading Teacher* 16:1 (October 1972), pp. 52–58.

17. McCracken, Glenn, and Charles Walcutt, eds. Lippincott Basic Reading Series, Book H, 1970.
    O'Donnell, M., and Van Roekel, eds. *Around the Corner,* Harper & Row, 1966.
    Robinson, Helen et al., eds. *Ventures,* Book 4, Scott Foresman, 1965.
    Handforth, Thomas. *Mei Li.* New York: Doubleday, 1938.

18. During the 1970s publishers developed and disseminated the fol-

lowing guidelines for the preparation of nonsexist materials:

Avoiding Stereotypes. College Division, Houghton Mifflin Co., Boston, MA.

Guidelines for Creating Positive Sexual and Racial Images in Educational Materials. Macmillan Publishing Co., New York, NY.

Guidelines for the Development of Elementary and Secondary Instructional Materials. Holt, Rinehart and Winston, New York, NY.

Guidelines for Eliminating Stereotypes from Instructional Materials, Grades K–12. School Department, Harper & Row, New York, NY.

Guidelines for Equal Treatment of the Sexes in McGraw-Hill Book Company Publications. McGraw-Hill, New York, NY.

Guidelines for Improving the Image of Women in Textbooks. Scott, Foresman & Co., Glenview, IL.

Statement on Bias-Free Materials. School Division, Association of American Publishers, New York, NY.

Suggestions for Developing Materials That Are Free of Racial, Sexual, Cultural and Social Bias. Science Research Associates, Chicago, IL.

19. Gritzner, Charles. *Exploring Our World, Past and Present*. Lexington, MA: D.C. Heath, 1991.

20. Alton-Lee, Adrienne, P. A. Densem, and G. A. Nuthall. "Imperatives of Classroom Research: Understanding What Children Learn About Gender and Race." In Morss, J., and T. Linzey (eds.), *Growing Up: The Politics of Human Learning*. Auckland, New Zealand: Longman Paul, 1991.

4. The Self-Esteem Slide

1. Kerr, Barbara. *Smart Girls, Gifted Women*. Columbus, OH: Ohio Psychology Publishing Co., 1985, p. 87.

2. Hancock, Emily. *The Girl Within*. New York: E. P. Dutton, pp. 13–14.

3. Researched by the Analysis Group, Greenberg-Lake. *Shortchanging Girls, Shortchanging America*. Commissioned by the American Association of University Women, Washington, DC, 1990. A vast body of research documents girls' declining self-esteem at adolescence:

    Allgood-Merten, Betty, Peter Lewinsohn, and Hyman Hops. "Sex Differences and Adolescent Depression," *Journal of Abnormal Psychology* 99:1 (1990), pp. 55–63.

Brutsaert, Herman. "Changing Sources of Self-Esteem Among Girls and Boys in Secondary Schools," *Urban Education* 24:4 (January 1990), pp. 432–39.

Kelly, Kevin, and LaVerne Jordan. "Effects of Academic Achievement and Gender on Academic and Social Self-Concept: A Replication Study," *Journal of Counseling and Development* 69 (November-December 1990), pp. 173–77.

Widaman, Keith, et al. "Differences in Adolescents' Self-Concept as a Function of Academic Level, Ethnicity, and Gender," *American Journal of Mental Retardation* 96:4 (1992), pp. 387–404.

Williams, Sheila, and Rob McGee. "Adolescents' Self-Perceptions of Their Strengths," *Journal of Youth and Adolescence* 20:3 (1991), pp. 325–37.

4. Petersen, Anne, Pamela Sarigiani, and Robert Kennedy. "Adolescent Depression: Why More Girls?" *Journal of Youth and Adolescence* 20:2 (1991), pp. 247–71.

5. Researched by the Analysis Group, Greenberg-Lake. *Shortchanging Girls, Shortchanging America.* Commissioned by the American Association of University Women.

6. Serbin, Lisa, and Daniel O'Leary. "How Nursery Schools Teach Girls to Shut Up," *Psychology Today* (July 1975), pp. 56–58, 102–3.

7. Janzen, Marta Cruz. "A Case Study of Gender Interactions in a Bilingual Early Childhood Education Classroom." Paper presented at the American Educational Research Association, San Francisco, California, 1992.

8. These examples are drawn from field notes in our three-year study of classroom interaction, *Year 3: Final Report: Promoting Effectiveness in Classroom Instruction.* Washington, DC: National Institute of Education, 1984.

9. Kramer, Linda. *Gifted Adolescent Girls: Self-Perceptions of Ability Within One Middle School Setting.* Unpublished doctoral dissertation, University of Florida, 1985, pp. 127–28.

10. As we consult with schools around the country to help them eliminate sex bias, we often visit classrooms to talk with students. We have found one of the best ways to elicit reactions about gender quickly is to ask them to write essays about waking up as a member of the other sex. The quotes in this chapter were drawn from essays written by upper-elementary and middle school students from twenty-four classrooms in Maryland, Virginia, and Washington, DC.

11. Office for Sex Equity in Education, Michigan Department of Edu-

cation. "The Influence of Gender-Role Socialization on Student Perceptions: A Report Based on Data Collected from Michigan Public School Students" (revised June 1990).

12. Researched by the Analysis Group, Greenberg-Lake. *Shortchanging Girls, Shortchanging America*. Commissioned by the American Association of University Women.

13. Researched by the Analysis Group, Greenberg-Lake. *Shortchanging Girls, Shortchanging America*. Commissioned by the American Association of University Women.

14. Brown, Lyn Mikel, and Carol Gilligan. *Meeting at the Crossroads: Women's Psychology and Girls' Development*. Cambridge, MA: Harvard University Press, 1992.

    See also: "Hidden Girls," *Middle Years* (April 1993), pp. 10–13.

15. Brown and Gilligan, *Meeting at the Crossroads*, p. 56.

16. Brown and Gilligan, *Meeting at the Crossroads*, p. 126.

17. Brown and Gilligan, *Meeting at the Crossroads*, p. 135.

18. Brown and Gilligan, *Meeting at the Crossroads*, p. 40.

19. Kramer, *Gifted Adolescent Girls*, p. 126.

20. Brown and Gilligan, *Meeting at the Crossroads*, p. 100.

21. Eder, Donna, and Stephen Parker. "The Cultural Production and Reproduction of Gender: The Effect of Extracurricular Activities on Peer Group Culture," *Sociology of Education* 60 (July 1987), pp. 200–13.

22. Eder, Donna. "The Cycle of Popularity: Interpersonal Relations Among Female Adolescents," *Sociology of Education* 58 (July 1985), pp. 154–65; quote from p. 159.

23. Kramer, *Gifted Adolescent Girls*, p. 113.

24. Kramer, *Gifted Adolescent Girls*, p. 127.

25. Kramer, *Gifted Adolescent Girls*, p. 109.

26. Shepardson, Daniel, and Edward Pizzini. "Gender Bias in Female Elementary Teachers' Perceptions of the Scientific Ability of Students," *Science Education* 76:2 (1992), pp. 147–53.

    Kimball, Meredith. "A New Perspective on Women's Math Achievement," *Psychological Bulletin* 105:2 (1989), pp. 198–214.

27. Dweck, Carol, and Diane Gilliard. "Expectancy Statements as Determinants of Reactions to Failure: Sex Differences in Persistence and Expectancy Change," *Journal of Personality and Social Psychology* 32:6, pp. 1077–84.

    Dweck, Carol, William Davidson, Sharon Nelson, and Bradley Enna. "Sex Differences in Learned Helplessness: II. The Contingencies of Evaluative Feedback in the Classroom, III. An Experimental Analysis," *Developmental Psychology* 14:3 (1978), pp. 268–76.

Ryckman, David, and Percy Peckham. "Gender Differences in Attributions for Success and Failure Situations Across Subject Areas," *Journal of Educational Research* 81 (November-December 1987), pp. 120–25.

Elliott, Elaine, and Carol Dweck. "Goals: An Approach to Motivation and Achievement," *Journal of Personality and Social Psychology* 54:1 (1988), pp. 5–12.

Levine, Gavrielle. "Grade Level Differences Between Females and Males in Mathematics Computation and Motivation Factors." Paper presented at the American Educational Research Association, Chicago, Illinois, 1991.

28. Researched by the Analysis Group, Greenberg-Lake. *Shortchanging Girls, Shortchanging America*. Commissioned by the American Association of University Women.

29. Sadker, Myra, David Sadker, and Susan Klein. "The Issue of Gender in Elementary and Secondary Education." In Grant, Gerald (ed.), *Review of Research in Education*, vol. 17. Washington, DC: American Educational Research Association, 1991.

Mullis, Ina, et al. *Trends in Academic Progress*. Washington, DC: U.S. Department of Education, 1991. Prepared by Educational Testing Service under contract with the National Center for Education Statistics.

Terman, L., and M. Oden. "The Promise of Youth." In Terman, L. (ed.), *Genetic Studies of Genius*, vol. 3. Stanford, CA: Stanford University Press, 1935.

30. Kline, Bruce, and Elizabeth Short. "Changes in Emotional Resilience: Gifted Adolescent Females," *Roeper Review* 13:3 (1991), pp. 118–21.

31. Quoted in Kerr, *Smart Girls, Gifted Women*, p. 106.

5. High School: In Search of Herself

1. Keyes, Ralph. *Is There Life After High School?* Boston: Little, Brown, 1976.

2. Friedenberg, Edgar Z. *Coming of Age in America*. New York: Vintage Books, Random House, 1965, p. 33.

3. Vonnegut, Kurt, in John Birmingham (ed.), *Our Time Is Now*. New York: Praeger, 1970, introduction, p. x.

4. Harter, Susan, "Self and Identity Development." In Feldman,

Shirley, and Glen Eliott (eds.), *At the Threshold*. Cambridge, MA: Harvard University Press, 1990, p. 356.

5. Cooley, Charles Horton. *Human Nature and the Social Order*. New York: Charles Scribner and Sons, 1902.
6. Coleman, James. *The Adolescent Society*. New York: The Free Press, 1961.
7. Coleman, *The Adolescent Society*, p. 37.
8. Keyes, *Is There Life After High School?*, p. 194.
9. Ephron quoted in Keyes, *Is There Life After High School?*, p. 106.
10. Ephron quoted in Keyes, *Is There Life After High School?*, p. 107.
11. Downs, A. C., and G. R. Abshier. "Conceptions of Physical Appearance Among Young Adolescents: The Interrelationships Among Self-Judged Appearance, Attractiveness, Stereotyping, and Sex-Typed Characteristics," *Journal of Early Adolescence* 2 (1982), pp. 255–65.
12. Attie, Ilana, and J. Brooks-Gunn. "Weight Concerns as Chronic Stressors in Women." In Barnett, Rosalind, Lois Beiner, and Grace Baruch (eds.), *Gender and Stress*. New York: The Free Press, 1987.
13. Davis, Jennifer, and Robert Oswald. "Societal Influences on a Thinner Body Size in Children," *Perceptual and Motor Skills* 74:3 (1992), pp. 697–98.
14. Wiseman, Claire, James Gray, James Mosimann, and Anthony Ahrens. "Cultural Expectations of Thinness in Women: An Update," *International Journal of Eating Disorders* 11:1 (1992), pp. 85–89.
15. Rosen, James, Janet Gross, and Linda Vara. "Psychological Adjustment of Adolescents Attempting to Lose or Gain Weight," *Journal of Consulting and Clinical Psychology* 55:5 (1987), pp. 742–47.
16. Keys, Ancel, et al. *The Biology of Human Starvation*. Minneapolis, MN: University of Minnesota Press, 1950.
17. Wolf, Naomi. *The Beauty Myth*. New York: William Morrow, 1991.
18. Nagel-Murray, K. *A Study Investigating How Concepts Associated with Eating Disorders Are Addressed in a Preventative Context in the Home Economics Classroom*. Unpublished doctoral dissertation, University of Georgia, 1989.
19. Golden is quoted in Perry, Nancy, "Why It's So Tough to Be a Girl," *Fortune* (August 10, 1992), p. 82.
20. Wolf, *The Beauty Myth*, p. 202 of Anchor Books edition.
21. The prevalence of eating disorders among adolescent females and the connection to self-esteem have been documented in the following sources:

Button, Eric. "Self-Esteem in Girls Aged 11–12: Baseline Findings from a Planned Prospective Study of Vulnerability to Eating Disorders," *Journal of Adolescence* 13:4 (1990), pp. 407–13.

Fisher, Martin, Marcie Schneider, Cynthia Pegler, and Barbara Napolitano. "Eating Attitudes, Health-Risk Behaviors, Self-Esteem, and Anxiety Among Adolescent Females in a Suburban High School," *Journal of Adolescent Health* 12 (1991), pp. 377–84.

Nagel-Murray, K. L., and Karen Jones. "Sociological Factors in the Development of Eating Disorders," *Adolescence* 27:105 (Spring 1992), pp. 107–13.

Nassar, Carine Mokhel, Patricia Hodges, and Tom Ollendick. "Self-Concept, Eating Attitudes, and Dietary Patterns in Young Adolescent Girls," *The School Counselor* 39:5 (May 1992), pp. 338–43.

The prevalence of adolescent female depression and the connection to self-esteem and eating disorders have been documented in the following sources:

Avison, William, and Donna McAlpine. "Gender Differences in Symptoms of Depression Among Adolescents," *Journal of Health and Social Behavior* 33:2 (June 1992), pp. 77–96.

Ehrenberg, Marion, David Cox, and Raymond Koopman. "The Prevalence of Depression in High School Students," *Adolescence* 25:100 (Winter 1990), pp. 905–12.

Nolen-Hoeksema, Susan, Joan Girgus, and Martin Seligman. "Sex Differences in Depression and Explanatory Style in Children," *Journal of Youth and Adolescence* 20:2 (April 1991), pp. 233–45.

Petersen, Anne, Pamela Sarigiani, and Robert Kennedy. "Adolescent Depression: Why More Girls?" *Journal of Youth and Adolescence* 20:2 (1991), pp. 247–61.

For the Oregon High School study see Allgood-Merten, Betty, Peter Lewinsohn, and Hyman Hops, "Sex Differences and Adolescent Depression," *Journal of Abnormal Psychology* 99:1 (1990), pp. 55–63, especially "Helpless, Hopeless and Stressed Phase," p. 61.
22. The classroom scenes in this chapter are based on our discussions with classes of high school students; however, the names of individual students have been changed.
23. Stein, Nan. "It Happens Here, Too: Sexual Harassment in the Schools," *Education Week* (November 27, 1991), p. 37.
24. Conversations with California students reported in Gross, Jane, "Schools, the Newest Arena for Sex-Harassment Cases," *The New York Times* (March 11, 1992), p. B8.
25. LeBlanc, Adrian Nicole. "Harassment in the Hall," *Seventeen* (September 1992), pp. 163–65, 170; quote from p. 163.

26. Researched by Louis Harris and Associates. *Hostile Hallways: The AAUW Survey on Sexual Harassment in America's Schools.* Washington, DC: American Association of University Women, 1993.
27. "What's Happening to You?" *Seventeen,* quote on p. 163.
28. Blumberg, Michelle, and David Lester. "High School and College Students' Attitudes Toward Rape," *Adolescence* 26:103 (Fall 1991), pp. 727–29.

    Feltey, Kathryn, Julie Ainslie, and Aleta Geib. "Sexual Coercion Attitudes Among High School Students," *Youth and Society* 23:2 (December 1991), pp. 229–50.
29. These incidents have been told to us by teachers and administrators at our workshops. Others were reported in Stein, Nan, "Sexual Harassment in Schools," *School Administrator* (January 1993), pp. 14–21.
30. Le Draoulec, Pascale. "Student Seduction: When Teachers Betray Trust," *The San Diego Union Tribune* (October 25, 1992), pp. A1, A6.
31. Zirkel, Perry. "Damages for Sexual Harassment," *Phi Delta Kappan* 73:10 (June 1992), pp. 812–13.
32. Guttmacher statistics cited in Perry, Nancy, "Why It's So Tough to Be a Girl," *Fortune* (August 10, 1992), pp. 82–84.
33. Children's Defense Fund. *The State of America's Children, 1992.* Washington, DC: Children's Defense Fund, 1992.
34. Nath, Pamela, John Borkowski, Thomas Whitman, and Cynthia Schellenback. "Understanding Adolescent Parenting: The Dimensions and Functions of Social Support," *Family Relations* 40:4 (October 1991), pp. 411–20.
35. Children's Defense Fund, *The State of America's Children, 1992.*
36. Dash, Leon. "Black Teen-age Pregnancy in Washington, D.C.," *International Social Science Review* 61:4 (1986), pp. 169–76.
37. Williams, Constance Willard. *Black Teenage Mothers.* Lexington, MA: Lexington Books, D.C. Heath, 1991.
38. Williams, *Black Teenage Mothers,* p. 107.
39. Williams, *Black Teenage Mothers,* p. 95.
40. Rauch-Elnekave, Helen. "Teenage Motherhood: Its Relationship to Undetected Learning Problems," *Adolescence,* in press.
41. Rauch-Elnekave, Helen. Personal correspondence, October 19, 1992.
42. Shaywitz, Sally, Bennett Shaywitz, Jack Fletcher, and Michael Escobar. "Prevalence of Reading Disability in Boys and Girls," *Journal of the American Medical Association* 264:8 (1990), pp. 998–1002.

43. Vogel, Susan. "Gender Differences in Intelligence, Language, Visual-Motor Abilities, and Academic Achievement in Students with Learning Disabilities: A Review of the Literature," *Journal of Learning Disabilities* 23:1 (January 1990), pp. 44–52.

44. Fine, Michelle. "Sexuality, Schooling, and Adolescent Females: The Missing Discourse of Desire," *Harvard Educational Review* 58:1 (February 1988), pp. 29–53.

45. Fine, "Sexuality, Schooling, and Adolescent Females," p. 49.

46. Fine, Michelle. "Silencing in Public Schools," *Language Arts* 64:2 (February 1987), p. 172.

47. U.S. Bureau of the Census, Current Population Reports, Series P-20, No. 462: *Educational Attainment in the United States: March 1990 and 1991.* Washington, DC: U.S. Government Printing Office, 1992.

48. Earle, Janice, Virginia Roach, and Katherine Fraser. *Female Dropouts: A New Perspective.* Alexandria, VA: National Association of State Boards of Education, 1987.

49. Children's Defense Fund, *The State of America's Children, 1992.*

    Simons, Janet, Belva Finlay, and Alice Yang. *The Adolescent Young Adult Fact Book.* Washington, DC: Children's Defense Fund, 1991.

    Schellenbach, Cynthia, Thomas Whitman, and John Borkowski. "Toward an Integrative Model of Adolescent Parenting," *Human Development* 35:2 (March-April 1992), pp. 81–89.

50. Furstenberg, Frank. "As the Pendulum Swings: Teenage Childbearing and Social Concern," *Family Life Education* 40:2 (April 1991), pp. 127–38.

    Kinard, E. Milling. "Children of Adolescents: Behavioral and Emotional Functioning," *Advances in Adolescent Mental Health* 4 (1990), pp. 239–62.

    Brooks-Gunn, J., and Frank Furstenberg. "The Children of Adolescent Mothers: Physical, Academic, and Psychological Outcomes," *Developmental Review* 6 (1986), pp. 224–51.

51. Sullivan, Kevin. "Foot-in-Mouth Barbie," *The Washington Post* (September 30, 1992), p. A1.

52. The discussion of girls and mathematics is based on the following sources:

    Hanson, Katherine. "Teaching Mathematics Effectively and Equitably to Females," *Trends and Issues* 17 (1992). ERIC Clearinghouse on Urban Education, Teachers College, Columbia University, New York.

Tocci, Cynthia, and George Engelhard. "Achievement, Parental Support, and Gender Differences in Attitudes Toward Mathematics," *Journal of Educational Research* 84:5 (May-June 1991), pp. 280–86.

Olszewski-Kubilius, Paula, et al. "Predictors in Achievement in Mathematics for Gifted Males and Females," *Gifted Child Quarterly* 34:2 (Spring 1990), pp. 64–71.

53. The discussion of girls and computers is based on the following sources:

Fish, Marian, Alan Gross, and Jo Sanders. "The Effect of Equity Strategies on Girls' Computer Usage in School," *Computers in Human Behavior* 2:2 (1986), pp. 127–84.

Kramer, Pamela, and Sheila Lehman. "Mismeasuring Women: A Critique of Research on Computer Ability and Avoidance," *Signs: Journal of Women in Culture and Society* 16:1 (1990), pp. 158–72.

Mark, June. "Beyond Equal Access: Gender Equity in Learning with Computers." Women's Educational Equity Act Publishing Center, June 1992, pp. 1–8.

McCormick, Theresa. "A Critique of Computer-Assisted Instruction for Race, Ethnic, Age, and Gender Equity." Paper presented at the American Educational Research Association, San Francisco, California, April 1992.

Nelson, Carole, and J. Allen Watson. "The Computer Gender Gap: Children's Attitudes, Performance, and Socialization," *Journal of Educational Technology Systems* 19:4 (1990–1991), pp. 345–53.

54. The discussion of girls and science is based on the following sources:

Blank, R., and M. Dalkilis. *State Indicators of Science and Math Education, 1990.* Washington, DC: Council of Chief State School Officers, State Education Assessment Center, 1991.

Klein, Carol. ". . .About Girls and Science," *Science and Children* 27:2 (October 1989), pp. 28–31.

Levin, Tamar, Naama Sabar, and Zipora Libman. "Achievements and Attitudinal Patterns of Boys and Girls in Science," *Journal of Research in Science Teaching* 28:4 (1991), pp. 315–28.

Mason, Cheryl, Jane Butler Kahle, and April Gardner. "Draw-a-Scientist Test: Future Implications," *School Science and Mathematics* 91:5 (May-June 1991), pp. 193–98.

Peltz, William. "Can Girls + Science – Stereotypes = Success?" *The Science Teacher* 57:9 (December 1990), pp. 44–49.

55. The discussion of successful strategies for teaching science was drawn from the following sources:

Martinez, Michael. "Interest Enhancements to Science Experiments: Interactions with Student Gender," *Journal of Research in Science Teaching* 29:2 (1992), pp. 167–77.

Mason, Cheryl, and Jane Butler Kahle. "Student Attitudes Toward Science and Science-Related Careers: A Program Designed to Promote a Stimulating Gender-Free Learning Environment," *Journal of Research in Science Teaching* 26:1 (1988), pp. 25–39.

Smith, Walter, and Thomas Owen Erb. "Effect of Women Science Career Role Models on Early Adolescents' Attitudes Toward Scientists and Women in Science," *Journal of Research in Science Teaching* 23:8 (1986), pp. 664–76.

56. Jones, M. Gail, and Jack Wheatley. "Gender Differences in Teacher-Student Interactions in Science Classrooms," *Journal of Research in Science Teaching* 27:9 (1990), pp. 861–74.

Jones, M. Gail. "Action Zone Theory, Target Students and Science Classroom Interactions," *Journal of Research in Science Teaching* 27:7 (1990), pp. 651–60.

Lee, Valerie, Helen Marks, and Tina Byrd. "Sexism in Single-Sex and Coeducational Secondary School Classrooms," *Sociology of Education*, 1993, in press.

57. National Science Foundation. *Women and Minorities in Science and Engineering*. Washington, DC: National Science Foundation, 1990.

58. The discussion of women and sports was drawn from the following sources:

Buckley, Stephen. "Montgomery's Girl Athletes Face Inequities, Panel Finds," *The Washington Post* (January 15, 1992), p. A1:1.

Isaac, Teresa, and Susan Shafer. *Sex Equity in Sports Leadership: Implementing the Game Plan*. Lexington, KY: Eastern Kentucky University, 1989.

Lirgg, Cathy. "Girls and Women, Sport, and Self-Confidence," *Quest* 44:2 (August 1992), pp. 158–78.

Sanger Keys, Eleanor. "Fair Play: Girls, Women and Sports," *AAUW Outlook* 86:2 (Summer 1992), pp. 18–22.

Wellesley College Center for Research on Women, *How Schools Shortchange Girls: The AAUW Report*. Washington, DC: American Association of University Women Educational Foundation, 1992.

59. National Center for Education Statistics. *Digest of Education Sta-*

tistics 1991. Washington, DC: Office of Educational Research and Improvement, U.S. Department of Education, 1991.

Wellesley College Center for Research on Women, *How Schools Shortchange Girls.*

Smith, Douglas. "Classroom Interaction and Gender Disparity in Secondary Vocational Instruction," *Journal of Vocational Education Research* 16:3 (1991), pp. 35–58.

60. Heilbrun, Carolyn. *Writing a Woman's Life.* New York: W. W. Norton, 1988, p. 37.

61. Fouts, Jeffrey. "Female Students, Female Teachers, and Perceptions of the Social Studies Classroom," *Social Education* 54:7 (November-December 1990), pp. 418–20.

62. Boorstin, Daniel, and Brooks Mather Kelley. *A History of the United States.* Englewood Cliffs, NJ: Prentice-Hall, 1992.

63. *World History: Traditions and New Directions, 1991.* Menlo Park, CA: Addison-Wesley, p. 524.

64. Koza, Julia Eklund. "The Boys in the Band: Sexism and the Construction of Gender in Middle School Textbook Illustrations," *Educational Foundations* 6:3 (Summer 1992), pp. 85–105.

65. Bazler, Judith, and Doris Simonis. "Are Women Out of the Picture?" *Science Teacher* 57:9 (December 1990), pp. 24–26.

Potter, Ellen, and Sue Rosser. "Factors in Life Science Textbooks That May Deter Girls' Interest in Science," *Journal of Research in Science Teaching* 29:7 (1992), pp. 669–86.

66. Alton-Lee, Adrienne, and Prue Densem. "Towards a Gender-Inclusive School Curriculum: Changing Educational Practice." In Middleton, S., and A. Jones (eds.), *Women and Education in Aotearoa,* vol. 2. Wellington, New Zealand: Bridget Williams, 1992.

6. Test Dive

1. Mullis, Ina V. S., et al. *Trends in Academic Progress.* Prepared by the Educational Testing Service for the National Center for Educational Statistics, Office of Educational Research and Improvement, U.S. Department of Education, Washington, DC, November 1991.

Hafner, Anne, et al. *National Education Longitudinal Study of 1988: A Profile of the American Eighth Grader.* Washington, DC: National Center for Educational Statistics, Office of Educational Research and Improvement, U.S. Department of Education, June 1990.

Mullis, Ina V. S., John A. Dossey, Eugene H. Owen, and Gary Phillips. *The State of Mathematics Achievement: Executive Summary*. Washington, DC: National Center for Educational Statistics, Office of Educational Research and Improvement, U.S. Department of Education, June 1991.

Jones, Lee R., et al. *The 1990 Science Report Card: NAEP's Assessment of Fourth, Eighth and Twelfth Graders*. Prepared by the Educational Testing Service for the National Center for Educational Statistics, Office of Educational Research and Improvement, U.S. Department of Education, Washington, DC, March 1992.

2. Zoller, Uri, and David Ben-Chaim. "Gender Differences in Examination-Type Preferences, Test Anxiety and Academic Achievement in College Science Education—A Case Study," *Science Education* 74:6 (April 1990), pp. 597–608.

Hueftle, S. J., Steven Rakow, and W. W. Welch. *Images of Science*. Minneapolis: Science Assessment and Research Project, University of Minnesota, 1983.

Zimmerer, L. K., and S. M. Bennett. "Gender Differences in the California Statewide Assessment of Attitudes and Achievement in Science." Paper presented at the American Educational Research Association, Washington, DC, April 1987.

Linn, Marcia C., and J. S. Hyde. "Gender, Mathematics and Science," *Educational Researcher* 18:8 (1989), pp. 17–19, 21–22.

Howe, A. C., and W. Doody. "Spatial Visualization and Sex-Related Differences in Science Achievement," *Science Education* 73:6 (1989), pp. 703–9.

3. Wilt, Elizabeth A., Stephen B. Dunbar, and H. D. Hoover. "A Multivariate Perspective on Sex Differences in Achievement and Later Performance Among Adolescents." Paper presented at the American Educational Research Association, Chicago, Illinois, March 20, 1991.

Kimball, Meredith M. "A New Perspective on Women's Math Achievement," *Psychological Bulletin* 105:2 (1989), pp. 198–214.

4. Test data used in this chapter were obtained from reports, tables, news releases, and studies issued by the test publishers. The Educational Testing Service in Princeton, NJ, provided numerous reports and statistics related to the PSAT, SAT, Achievement tests, GRE, and GMAT. While the GRE data provided were from 1987–88, all other data reflected 1991 and 1992 test administrations. The ACT data were derived from a variety of profile and nor-

mative reports for 1990 and 1991 issued by American College Testing in Iowa City, Iowa.

Professional organizations and schools often contract with testing services to develop and administer their admissions tests. For example, the Medical College Admission Test (MCAT) is developed by ACT in Iowa City. For each of these admissions tests, the professional association responsible was contacted first and usually provided the information and statistics for this chapter. These organizations included but were not limited to the Association of American Medical Colleges, Dental Admissions Testing Program, Optometry Admissions Testing Program, Graduate Management Admission Council, and the Law School Data Assembly Service.

The Psychological Corporation in San Antonio, Texas, was asked to provide data on numerous tests they administer. They provided data only on the Miller Analogies Test. It should be noted that on this test, women had a higher mean score than men. However, none of the data concerning other tests distributed by the Psychological Corporation was provided. Since all of their tests cannot be evaluated equally, none of the tests, including the Miller Analogies Test, was included in this chapter.

A good summary of test data and legal rights is provided in Connor, Katherine, and Ellen J. Vargyas, "The Legal Implications of Gender Bias in Standardized Testing," *Berkeley Women's Law Journal* 7 (1992), pp. 13–89.

5. Rosser, Phyllis, and the National Center for Fair and Open Testing. *Sex Bias in College Admissions Tests: Why Women Lose Out.* Cambridge, MA: FairTest, 1989.

Personal correspondence from William C. Gustin, coordinator, Center for Talented Youth (CTY), The Johns Hopkins University, October 27, 1992.

6. Telephone conversation with Bob Schaffer at FairTest, September 30, 1992.

7. Rosser, Phyllis. *The SAT Gender Gap: Identifying the Causes.* Washington, DC: Center for Women Policy Studies, 1989.

8. Quoted in Glaberson, William, "U.S. Court Says Awards Based on S.A.T.s Are Unfair to Girls," *The New York Times* (February 4, 1989), pp. 1, 50.

9. Dorsher, Mike. "Are Biased Tests Hurting Girls?" *The Wall Street Journal* (September 17, 1992).

Davidoff, Judith. "Are Girls Getting Cheated?" *Isthmus* (September 3, 1992), p. 6.

Reid, Alexander. "Ruling Seen Changing How Scholarships Are Won," *The Boston Globe* 35:1 (February 10, 1989).

10. Rosser, Phyllis. "Gender and Testing." Paper commissioned by the National Commission on Testing and Public Policy, Graduate School of Education, University of California at Berkeley, 1989.

11. "College Board Reports Rise in SAT Scores for Class of 1992, but Many Urban, Rural and Minority Students Being Left Behind," College Board News Release (August 27, 1992).

12. Owen, David. *None of the Above: Behind the Myth of Scholastic Aptitude.* Boston: Houghton Mifflin, 1985, pp. 181, 183.

Hoffman, Banesh. *The Tyranny of Testing.* New York: Crowell-Collier, 1962.

13. Crouse, James, and Dale Trusheim. *The Case Against the SAT.* Chicago: University of Chicago Press, 1988, pp. 19, 23.

14. Bridgeman, Brent, and Cathy Wendler. *Prediction of Grades in College Mathematical Courses as a Component of SAT-M Placement Validity.* New York: College Entrance Examination Board (February 1990).

McCornack, R., and M. McLeod. "Gender Bias in the Prediction of College Course Performance," *Journal of Educational Measurement* 25:4 (1988), pp. 321–32.

Wainer, Howard, and Linda Steinberg. "Sex Differences in Performance on the Mathematics Section of the Scholastic Aptitude Test: A Bidirectional Validity Study." Princeton, NJ: Educational Testing Service, 1990.

Horner, Blair, and Joe Sammons with FairTest staff. *Rolling Loaded Dice: Use of the Scholastic Aptitude Test (SAT) for Higher Education Admissions in New York State.* New York: Public Interest Research Group, 1989.

15. Items from the PSAT and SAT are taken from Rosser, *The SAT Gender Gap: Identifying the Causes*, pp. 141–42.

16. Telephone interview with Phyllis Rosser, September 1992.

17. Eckstrom, Ruth B., Marlaine E. Lockheed, and Thomas F. Donlon. "Sex Differences and Sex Bias in Test Content," *Educational Horizons* 58:1 (Fall 1979), pp. 47–52.

Becker, Betsy Jane. "Item Characteristics and Gender Differences on the SAT-M for Mathematically Able Youths," *American Educational Research Journal* 27:1 (Spring 1990), pp. 65–87.

Loewen, James, Phyllis Rosser, and J. Katzman. "Gender Bias in SAT Items." Paper presented at the Annual Meeting of the American Educational Research Association, New Orleans, Louisiana, April 5–9, 1988.

Chipman, Susan. "Word Problems Where Test Bias Creeps In." Paper presented at the Annual Meeting of the American Educational Research Association, New Orleans, Louisiana, April 5–9, 1988.

Pearlman, M. "Trends in Women's Total Score and Item Performance on Verbal Measures." Paper presented at the Annual Meeting of the American Educational Research Association, Washington, DC, April 1987.

Zwick, Rebecca, and Erickan Kadriye. "Analysis of Differential Item Functioning in the NAEP History Assessment," *Journal of Educational Measurement* 26:1 (Spring 1989), pp. 55–66.

Wendler, Cathy L. W., and Sydell T. Carlton. "An Examination of SAT Verbal Items for Differential Performance by Women and Men: An Exploratory Study." Paper presented at the American Educational Research Association, Washington, DC, April 1987.

Sappington, John, Chris Larsen, James Martin, and Kari Murphy. "Sex Differences in Math Problem Solving as a Function of Gender-Specific Item Content," *Educational and Psychological Measurement* 51 (1991), pp. 1041-48.

Murphy, Laura, and Steven Ross. "Protagonist Gender as a Design Variable in Adapting Mathematics Story Problems to Learner Interests," *Educational Technology Research and Development* 38:3 (1990), pp. 27–37.

18. Linn, Marcia C. "Gender Differences in Educational Achievement." Unpublished paper based on research funded by the National Science Foundation, grant MDR-88-50552 and grant MDR-89-54753.

19. Mazzeo, John, Alicia P. Schmitt, and Carole A. Bleistein. "Do Women Perform Better, Relative to Men, on Constructed-Response Tests or Multiple-Choice Tests? Evidence from the Advanced Placement Examinations." Paper presented at the Annual Meeting of the National Council of Measurement in Education, Chicago, Illinois, April 1991.

Gallagher, Shelagh, and Edward S. Johnson. "The Effect of Time Limits on Performance of Mental Rotations by Gifted Adolescents," *Gifted Child Quarterly* 36:1 (Winter 1992), pp. 19–22.

20. "Trivial Changes Highlight 'New SAT,'" *FairTest Examiner* 7:1 (Winter 92–93), pp. 1, 4–5.

Jordan, Mary. "SAT Changes Name, but It Won't Score 1,600 with Critics," *The Washington Post* (March 27, 1993), p. A7.

21. Kubota, Mel, and Anne Connell. "On Diversity and the SAT," *The College Board Review* 162 (Winter 1991–92), pp. 6–17.

College Entrance Examination Board. *College-Bound Seniors: 1989 Profile of SAT and Achievement Test Takers.* New York: College Entrance Examination Board, 1989.

College Entrance Examination Board. *Guidelines on the Uses of College Board Test Scores and Related Data.* New York: College Entrance Examination Board, March 1988.

Cameron, Robert G. "Issues in Testing Bias," *College and University* 64:3 (Spring 1989), pp 269–79.

College Entrance Examination Board. *1988–89 ATP Guide for High Schools and Colleges.* New York: College Entrance Examination Board, 1988.

22. Gold, Dolores, Gail Crombie, and Sally Noble. "Relations Between Teachers' Judgments of Girls' and Boys' Compliance and Intellectual Competence," *Sex Roles* 16:7–8 (April 1987), pp. 351–58.

Kornblau, B. "The Teachable Pupil Survey: A Technique for Assessing Teacher's Perceptions of Pupil Attributes," *Psychology in the Schools* 19 (1982), pp. 170–74.

23. Grant, Linda. "Race and the Schooling of Young Girls." In Wrigley, Julia (ed.), *Education and Gender Equality.* London: Falmer Press, 1992, pp. 91–114.

24. Best, Raphaela. *We've All Got Scars: What Boys and Girls Learn in Elementary School.* Bloomington, IN: Indiana University Press, 1983, p. 90.

25. Arnold, Karen D. "The Illinois Valedictorian Project: Academically Talented Women Ten Years After High School Graduation." Paper presented at the Annual Meeting of the American Educational Research Association, San Francisco, California, April 24, 1992.

Arnold, Karen. "Values and Vocations: The Career Aspirations of Academically Gifted Females in the First Five Years After High School." Paper presented at the Annual Meeting of the American Educational Research Association, Washington, DC, April 24, 1987.

Arnold, Karen, and Terry Denny. "The Lives of Academic Achievers: The Career Aspirations of Male and Female High School Valedictorians and Salutatorians." Paper presented at the Annual Meeting of the American Educational Research Association, Chicago, Illinois, April 1985.

26. Brown, Lyn Mikel, and Carol Gilligan. *Meeting at the Crossroads.* Cambridge, MA: Harvard University Press, 1992.

27. Linn, Marcia, et al. "Gender Differences in National Assessment of Educational Progress Science Items: What Does 'I Don't Know'

Really Mean?" *Journal of Research in Science Teaching* 24:3 (1987), pp. 267–78.

7. Higher Education: Colder by Degrees

1. An interesting and lively discussion of this period is provided in Horowitz, Helen Lefkowitz, *Campus Life: Undergraduate Cultures from the End of the Eighteenth Century to the Present*. New York: Alfred A. Knopf, 1987.
2. Chamberlain, Miriam K. (ed.) *Women in Academe: Progress and Prospects*. New York: Russell Sage Foundation, 1988, p. 4.
3. Solomon, Barbara Miller. *In the Company of Educated Women: A History of Women and Higher Education in America*. New Haven, CT: Yale University Press, 1985, pp. 78–93.
4. Blake, Patricia. "Why College Girls Dress That Way," *The New York Times Magazine* (April 7, 1946), p. 23. Quoted in Horowitz, *Campus Life*, p. 212.
5. Quoted in Horowitz, *Campus Life*, p. 92.
6. Snyder, Thomas, and Charlene Hoffman. *Digest of Education Statistics 1992*. Washington, DC: U.S. Department of Education, 1992, pp. 275, 277, 295, 296.

    Ransom, Michael R. "Gender Segregation by Field in Higher Education," *Research in Higher Education* 31:5 (October 5, 1990), pp. 477–94.

    Touchton, Judith G., and Lynne Davis, with the assistance of Vivian Parker Makosky. *Fact Book on Women in Higher Education*. New York: Macmillan, 1991.
7. Even in the social sciences and humanities, women earn only 46 percent of the doctoral degrees. In the life sciences, as in biology, women earn 37 percent of all doctorates. Although women acquire close to half of the bachelor's degrees in mathematics, their share drops to 40 percent at the master's level and less than 18 percent at the doctoral level.
8. DePalma, Anthony. "Rare in Ivy League: Women Who Work as Full Professors," *The New York Times* (January 24, 1993), pp. 1, 23.
9. Snyder and Hoffman, *Digest of Education Statistics, 1992*, p. 296.
10. Klein, Susan, and Karen Bogart. "Achieving Sex Equity in Education: A Comparison of Pre- and Post-Secondary Levels," *Equity and Excellence* 23:1–2 (Spring 1987), pp. 114–22.
11. *The Insider's Guide to Colleges*, compiled and edited by the staff of the *Yale Daily News*. New York: St. Martin's Press, 1993.

12. Persell, Caroline Hodges, Sophia Catsambis, and Peter W. Cookson, Jr. "Differential Asset Conversion: Class and Gendered Pathways to Selective Colleges," *Sociology of Education* 65:3 (July 1992), pp. 208–25.

13. Krupnick, Catherine. "Unlearning Gender Roles." In Winston, Kenneth and Mary Jo Bane (eds.), *Gender and Public Policy: Cases and Comments*. Boulder, CO: Westview Press, 1992.

    Krupnick, Catherine. "Women and Men in the Classroom: Inequality and Its Remedies," *Teaching and Learning: Journal of the Harvard Danforth Center* 1:1 (May 1985), pp. 18–25.

14. Hall, Roberta, and Bernice Sandler. *The Classroom Climate: A Chilly One for Women?* Washington, DC: Project on the Status and Education of Women, Association of American Colleges, 1982.

    For a summary of differences in women's and men's views of Harvard, see Light, Richard, *The Harvard Assessment Seminars, First Report*. Cambridge, MA: Harvard University Press, 1990.

15. For a discussion of how classroom communication is more compatible with male communication training, see Tannen, Deborah, "Teachers' Classroom Strategies Should Recognize That Men and Women Use Language Differently," *Chronicle of Higher Education* 37 (June 19, 1991), pp. B1–B3.

16. Glaser, Robert D., and Joseph S. Thorpe. "Unethical Intimacy: A Survey of Sexual Contact and Advances Between Psychology Educators and Female Graduate Students," *American Psychologist* 40 (January 1986), pp. 43–51.

    Dziech, Billie Wright, and Linda Weiner. *The Lecherous Professor: Sexual Harassment on Campus*. Boston: Beacon Press, 1984, pp. 13, 115–16.

    Dreifus, Claudia. "Sex with Professors," *Glamour* (August 1986), pp. 264–65, 308–9, 311.

17. Bask, Patricia L., Joanne L. Jensen, and Jami Price. "Women's Graduate School Experiences, Professional Career Expectations and Their Relationship." Paper presented at the American Educational Research Association, Chicago, Illinois, April 1991.

    Jenkins, S. Y. *Gender Differences in Graduate Student Relationships with Their Major Faculty Advisor*. Unpublished doctoral dissertation, University of Oregon, 1985.

    Pope, Kenneth S., Hanna Levinson, and L. R. Schover. "Sexual Relationships in Psychology Training: Results and Implications of a National Survey," *American Psychologist* 34 (1979), pp. 682–89.

    Ethington, Corinna A., and Rita Bode. "Differences in the Graduate Experience for Males and Females." Paper presented at the American Educational Research Association, San Francisco, California, April 1991.

18. Sadker, Myra, and David Sadker. *Beyond Pictures and Pronouns: Sexism in Teacher Education Textbooks*. Washington, DC: Office of Education, 1980, pp. 8, 38.

19. Sadker and Sadker, *Beyond Pictures and Pronouns*, pp. 38, 39.

20. Sullivan, William. "The *Norton Anthology* and the Canon of English Literature." Paper presented at the Annual Meeting of the College English Association, San Antonio, Texas, 1991.

   Titus, Jordan J. "Gender Messages in Education Foundations Textbooks," *Journal of Teacher Education* 44:1 (January-February 1993), pp. 38–44.

21. Lewis, Magda. "Interrupting Patriarchy: Politics, Resistance, and Transformation in the Feminist Classroom," *Harvard Educational Review* 60:4 (November 1990), pp. 467–88.

22. Welch, Susan, et al. *Understanding American Government*. St. Paul, MN: West Publishing Co., 1991, p. 24.

23. Eakins, Barbara Westbrook, and R. Gene Eakins. *Sex Differences in Human Communication*. Boston: Houghton Mifflin, 1978.

   Schneider, Joseph, and Sally Hacker. "Sex Role Imagery and the Use of Generic 'Man' in Introductory Texts: A Case in the Sociology of Sociology," *American Sociologist* 8 (February 1973), pp. 12-18.

   Kramer, Cheris, Barrie Thorne, and Nancy Henley. "Perspectives on Language and Communication," *Signs: Journal of Women in Culture and Society* 3:3 (1978), pp. 638–51.

   Brannon, Robert. "The Consequences of Sexist Language." Paper presented at the American Psychological Association, August 1978.

24. Gold, Martin, and David Mann. *Expelled to a Friendlier Place: A Study of Effective Alternative Schools*. Ann Arbor, MI: University of Michigan Press, 1984, p. 6.

25. Klein, Richard. *Everyone Wins! A Citizen's Guide to Development*. Chicago: Planners Press, 1990.

26. Corbett, Judith, and Robert Sommer. "Anatomy of a Coed Residence Hall," *Journal of College Student Personnel* 13:3 (May 1972), pp. 215–17.

   Moos, Rudolf H., and Jean Otto. "The Impact of Coed Living on Males and Females," *Journal of College Student Personnel* 16:6 (November 1975), pp 459–67.

   Brown, Robert, John Winkworth, and Larry Brakskamp. "Student Development in a Coed Residence Hall: Promiscuity, Prophylactic, or Panacea?" *Journal of College Student Personnel* 14:2 (March 1973), pp. 98–104.

Schroeder, Charles C., and Morris LeMay. "The Impact of Coed Residence Halls on Self-Actualization," *Journal of College Student Personnel* 14:2 (March 1973), pp. 105–10.

27. "Harassing Women Becomes a Sick College Sport," *Utne Reader* (May-June 1990), pp. 70–71.

Rubin, Linda J., and Sherry B. Borgers. "Sexual Harassment in Universities During the 1980s," *Sex Roles* 23:7–8 (1990), pp. 397–411.

28. Merton, Andrew. "Return to Brotherhood," *Ms* (September 1985), pp. 60–62.

29. Krier, Beth Ann. "Frat Row," *The Los Angeles Times* (February 9, 1990), pp. E1, E7–9.

30. For additional examples and analyses of these activities, see Hughes, Jean O'Gorman, and Bernice Sandler, *Peer Harassment: Hassles for Women on Campus*. Washington, DC: Project on the Status and Education of Women, Association of American Colleges, 1988.

31. McMillen, Lis. "An Anthropologist's Disturbing Picture of Gang Rape on Campus," *Chronicle of Higher Education* 37 (September 19, 1990), p. A3.

Sanday, Peggy Reeves. *Fraternity Gang Rape: Sex, Brotherhood, and Privilege on Campus*. New York: New York University Press, 1990.

32. Hirschorn, Michael. "Two Colleges Drop Recognition of Fraternities, Sororities Amid Continuing Concern Over Groups' Behavior," *Chronicle of Higher Education* (May 11, 1988), pp. A27–28.

33. Koss, Mary P., Christine A. Gidycz, and Nadine Wisniewski. "The Scope of Rape: Incidence and Prevalence of Sexual Aggression and Victimization in a National Sample of Higher Education Students," *Journal Consulting and Clinical Psychology* 55:2 (1987), pp. 162–70.

34. Adams, Aileen, and Gail Abarbanel. *Sexual Assault on Campus: What Colleges Can Do*. Santa Monica, CA: Rape Treatment Center, 1988.

Russell, Diana E. H. *Sexual Exploitation: Rape, Child Sexual Assault, and Workplace Harassment*. Beverly Hills, CA: Sage, 1984.

35. Berkowitz, Alan. "College Men as Perpetrators of Acquaintance Rape and Sexual Assault: A Review of Recent Research," *College Health* 40 (January 1992), pp. 175–81.

Koss, Mary, Thomas E. Dinero, Cynthia Seibel, and Susan Cox. "Stranger and Acquaintance Rape: Are There Differences in the Victim's Experience?" *Psychology of Women Quarterly* 12 (March 1988), pp. 1–24.

36. Muehlenhard, Charlene, and Melaney Linton. "Date Rape and Sexual Aggression in Dating Situations: Incidence and Risk Factors," *Journal of Counseling Psychology* 34:2 (1987), pp. 186–96.

Naylor, Kelly Elizabeth. *Gender Role Strain: A Contributing Factor to Acquaintance Rape in a College Population at Risk.* Unpublished doctoral dissertation, DePaul University, 1991.

37. Jackson, Thomas. "A University Athletic Department's Rape and Assault Experiences," *Journal of College Student Development* 32 (January 1991), pp. 77–78.

Melnick, Merrill. "Male Athletes and Sexual Assault," *Journal of Physical Education, Recreation and Dance* 63 (May-June 1992), pp. 32–35.

38. Neimark, Jill. "Out of Bounds: The Truth About Athletes and Rape," *Mademoiselle* (May 1991), pp. 198, 244.

39. Gail Abarbanel quoted in Neimark, "The Truth About Athletes and Rape," p. 198.

40. Collison, Michelle. "Increase in Reports of Sexual Assaults Strains Campus Disciplinary Systems," *Chronicle of Higher Education* (May 15, 1991), pp. A29–A30.

41. Lenihan, Genie O., et al. "Gender Differences in Rape Supportive Attitudes Before and After Date Rape Education Intervention," *Journal of College Student Development* 33:4 (July 1992), pp. 331–38.

Martin, Patricia Yancey, and Robert A. Hummer. "Fraternities and Rape on Campus," *Gender and Society* 3:4 (December 1989), pp. 457–73.

Ellis, David. "Setting New Goals for the Greek System," *Educational Record* 70:3–4 (Summer-Fall 1989), pp. 48–53.

Status of the College Fraternity and Sorority, 1990. Bloomington, IN: Center for the Study of the College Fraternity, 1990.

Harrison, Patrick J., Jeanette Downes, and Michael D. Williams. "Date and Acquaintance Rape: Perceptions and Attitude Change Strategies," *Journal of College Student Development* 32 (March 1991), pp. 131–39.

42. Holland, Dorothy C., and Margaret A. Eisenhart. *Educated in Romance: Women, Achievement and College Culture.* Chicago: University of Chicago Press, 1990.

43. Fleming, Jacqueline. *Blacks in College*. San Francisco, CA: Jossey-Bass, 1984.
44. Vetter, Betty M. *Professional Women and Minorities: A Manpower Data Resource Service*, ninth edition. Washington, DC: Commission on Professionals in Science and Technology, March 1991.
45. Weiss, Catherine, and Louise Meling. "The Legal Education of Twenty Women," *Stanford Law Review* 40:5 (May 1988), p. 1313.
46. Weiss and Meling, "The Legal Education of Twenty Women," p. 1322.
47. Weiss and Meling, "The Legal Education of Twenty Women," p. 1333.
48. Weiss and Meling, "The Legal Education of Twenty Women," p. 1334.
49. Weiss and Meling, "The Legal Education of Twenty Women," p. 1336.
50. Weiss and Meling, "The Legal Education of Twenty Women," p. 1339.
51. Weiss and Meling, "The Legal Education of Twenty Women," p. 1344.
52. "A Review of Legal Education in the U.S." Chicago: American Bar Association, 1991.
    Torry, Sandra. "At Yale Law, a Gender Gap in Who Gets Clerkships Sparks Debate," *The Washington Post* (May 13, 1991), p. F5.
    Shultz, Marjorie Maguire. "The Gendered Curriculum: Of Contracts and Careers," *Iowa Law Review* 77 (1991), pp. 55–71.
53. "State Bar Report: Women Lawyers Bring Their Concerns to the Fore," *California Lawyer* (November 1989), pp. 99, 103–106.
54. Auster, Simon. "Human Context in Health Care: Adam and His Rib, a Bone of Contention in Medicine." Unpublished paper (March 27, 1991).
55. Grant, Linda. "The Gender Climate of Medical Schools: Perspectives of Women and Men Students," *Journal of the American Medical Women's Association* 43 (July-August 1988), pp. 109–10, 115–19.
    Marquan, J., K. Franco, and B. Carroll. "Gender Differences in Medical School Interviews." Paper presented at the 1988 conference, Association of American Medical Colleges. Reported in *AAMC Women in Medicine Update* 3 (Winter 1989), p. 3.
56. Kris, Kathryn B. "Developmental Strains of Women Medical Students," *Journal of the American Medical Women's Association* 40 (September-October 1985), pp. 145–48.

Tamburrino, Marijo B., Kathleen N. Franco, Cynthia L. Evans, and Patricia A. Seidman. "Finances: A Hidden Cost to Women Medical Students," *Journal of the American Medical Women's Association* 40 (September-October 1985), pp. 149–51.

Martin, Catherine A., Janie L. Jones, and Martha A. Bird. "Support Systems for Women in Medicine," *Journal of the American Medical Women's Association* 43 (May-June 1988), pp. 77–84.

57. "Women in Medicine Data Source," *American Medical Association*, 1992.

Moses, Yolanda T. *Black Women in Academe: Issues and Strategies*. Washington, DC: American Association of Colleges, Project on the Status and Education of Women, 1989.

Bickel, Janet. "Women in Medical Education: A Status Report," *New England Journal of Medicine* 319:24 (December 15, 1988), pp. 1579–84.

Titus-Dillon, Pauline, and Davis G. Johnson. "Female Graduates of a Predominantly Black College of Medicine: Their Characteristics and Challenges," *Journal of the American Medical Women's Association* 44 (November-December, 1989), pp. 175–82.

FACTS: Applicants, Matriculants and Graduates, 1986 to 1992. Washington, DC: Association of American Medical Colleges, October 1992.

58. Giacomini, M., P. Rozee-Koker, and F. Pepitone-Arreola-Rockwell. "Gender Bias in Human Anatomy Textbook Illustrations," *Psychology of Women Quarterly* 10:4 (1986), pp. 413–20.

Ehrenreich, B., and D. English. *Witches, Midwives and Nurses: A History of Women Healers*. Old Westbury, NY: Feminist Press, 1972.

Howell, M. C. "What Medical Schools Teach About Women," *New England Journal of Medicine* 291:6 (August 1974), pp. 304–7.

Scully, Diana, and P. Bart. "A Funny Thing Happened on the Way to the Orifice: Women in Gynecology Textbooks," *American Journal of Sociology* 78 (1973), pp. 1045–50.

Elder, R. G., W. Humphreys, and C. Laskowski. "Sexism in Gynecology Textbooks: Gender Stereotypes and Paternalism, 1978 through 1983," *Health Care for Women International* 9 (1988), pp. 1–17.

59. Ries, R. K., et al. "The Medical Care Abuser: Differentiated Diagnosis and Management," *Journal of Family Practice* 13 (1981), pp. 257–65.

Brownlee, Shannon with Elizabeth Pezzullo. "A Cure for Sexism," *U.S. News and World Report* (March 23, 1992), pp. 86–87, 90.

60. Fugh-Berman, Adriane. "Tales out of Medical School," *The Nation* (January 20, 1992), pp. 47, 54–56.

    Glazer, Susan. "Are Medical Schools Sexist?" *The Washington Post* (February 18, 1992), pp. 10–12.

61. *Sexual Harassment Survey*: Madison, WI: Commission on Women's Issues, University of Wisconsin-Madison, Center for Health Sciences, 1987.

    Dickstein, Leah J., and Allison Batchelor. "A National Survey of Women Residents and Stress." Paper presented at the Annual Meeting of the American Medical Women's Association, Los Angeles, California, October 1989.

    Baldwin, Jr., Dewitt C., Steven Daugherty, David Baron, and Edward Eckenfels. "Student Perceptions of Mistreatment and Harassment During Medical School: A Survey of Ten Schools." Unpublished manuscript cited in Julie Kuhn Ehrhart with Bernice Sandler, *Rx for Success: Improving the Climate for Women in Medical Schools and Teaching Hospitals*. Washington, DC: Project on the Status and Education of Women, Association of American Colleges, May 1990.

62. Herman, Robin. "Sex Stereotypes in Medicine: Even Women at the Top of the Profession Report Harassment," *The Washington Post* (February 16, 1993), p. 7.

    Leatherman, Courtney. "Stanford Said to Ask Physician to Quit Neurosurgery Post," *Chronicle of Higher Education* (March 4, 1992), p. A17–A18.

    Cannon, Lou. "Surgeon's Sexism Charge Hits Nerve in Profession," *The Washington Post* (June 23, 1991), p. A3.

63. Herman, Robin. "Surgeon Denied Promotion Files Suit, Accusing Children's Hospital of Sexism," *The Washington Post* (February 5, 1993), p. D5.

64. Preven, D. W., and K. Kachur. "Interviewing Skills of First-Year Medical Students," *Journal of Medical Education* 61 (1986), pp. 842–44.

    Plauche, W. C., and J. M. Miller, Jr. "Performances of Male and Female Students in an Obstetrics and Gynecology Clerkship," *Journal of Medical Education* 61 (1986), pp. 323–25.

65. Roman, Monica. "Commentary: Woman, Beware: An MBA Doesn't Mean Equal Pay," *Business Week* (October 29, 1991), p. 57.

Pennar, Karen. "Commentary: Women Are Still Paid the Wages of Discrimination," *Business Week* (October 28, 1992), p. 35.

66. Rosen, Benson, and Thomas H. Jerdee. "Sex Stereotyping in the Executive Suite," *Harvard Business Review* (March-April, 1985), pp. 45–58.

Martell, Richard F. "Sex Bias at Work: The Effects of Attentional and Memory Demands on Performance Ratings of Men and Women," *Journal of Applied Social Psychology* 21 (December 1991), pp. 1939–60.

Janman, Karen. "One Step Behind: Current Stereotypes of Women, Achievement, and Work," *Sex Roles* 21:3–4 (August 1989), pp. 209–30.

67. "Labor Force, Employment, and Earnings," *Statistical Abstract of the U.S.* Washington, DC: Bureau of the Census, U.S. Department of Commerce, 1992, pp. 392–94.

King, Mary C. "Occupational Segregation by Race and Sex, 1940–88," *Monthly Labor Review* (April 1992), pp. 30–37.

"Salary Survey, 1993," *Working Woman* (January 1993), pp. 39–43.

Nelson-Horchler, Joani. "The Best Man for a Job Is a Man!" *Industry Week* (January 7, 1991), pp. 50–52.

68. Tannen, Deborah. *You Just Don't Understand: Women and Men in Conversation*. New York: William Morrow, 1990.

Dovideo, John, et al. "The Relationship of Social Power to Visual Displays of Dominance Between Men and Women," *Journal of Personality and Social Psychology* 5:2 (1988), pp. 233–42.

Carli, Linda L. "Gender Differences in Interaction Style and Influence," *Journal of Personality and Social Psychology* 56:4 (1989), pp. 565–76.

Lakoff, Robin. *Talking Power: The Politics of Language in Our Lives*. New York: Basic Books, HarperCollins, 1990.

69. Morin, Richard. "Female Aides on Hill: Still Outsiders in a Man's World," *The Washington Post* (February 21, 1993), pp. A1, A18–A19.

8. The Miseducation of Boys

1. Safir, Marilyn, Rachel Hertz-Lazarowitz, Shoshana BenTsui-Mayer, Haggai Kupermintz. "Prominence of Girls and Boys in the Classroom: Schoolchildren's Perceptions," *Sex Roles* 27:9–10 (1992), pp. 439–53.

Bentsvi-Mayer, Shoshana, Rachel Marilyn Hertz-Lazarowitz,

and P. Safir. "Teachers' Selections of Boys and Girls as Prominent Pupils," *Sex Roles* 21:3–4 (1989), pp. 231–45.

2. Adler, Patricia, Steven Kless, and Peter Adler. "Socialization to Gender Roles: Popularity Among Elementary School Boys and Girls," *Sociology of Education* 65:3 (July 1992), pp. 169–87.

3. Smith, C., and B. B. Lloyd. "Maternal Behaviour and Perceived Sex of Infant," *Child Development* 49:4 (1978), pp. 211–14. Discussed in Askew, Sue, and Carol Ross, *Boys Don't Cry: Boys and Sexism in Education.* Philadelphia: Open University Press, 1988.

4. Condry, John C., and David F. Ross. "Sex and Aggression: The Influence of Gender Label on the Perception of Aggression in Children," *Child Development* 56:1 (1985), pp. 225–233.

5. Tillman, Linda, Linda McDonald, Renee Brickner, and C. Jeffrey Dykhuizen. "The World of Young Boys," *Independent School* (Fall 1992), pp. 29–32.

6. Berman, P. "Young Children's Responses to Babies: Do They Foreshadow Differences Between Maternal and Paternal Styles?" In Fogel, A., and G. F. Melson (eds.), *Origins of Nurturance: Developmental, Biological, and Cultural Perspectives on Caregiving.* Hillsdale, NJ: Lawrence Erlbaum Associates, 1986.

7. Tavris, Carol. *The Mismeasure of Woman.* New York: Simon and Schuster, 1992, pp. 63, 261–62.

8. Thorne, Barrie. *Gender Play: Girls and Boys in School.* New Brunswick, NJ: Rutgers University Press, 1993, pp. 97–101.

9. Stockard, Jean, and M. M. Johnson. "The Social Origins of Male Dominance," *Sex Roles* 3:2 (April 1979), pp. 199-218.

   Hort, Barbara, I. Faggot, and Mary Driver Leinbach. "Are People's Notions of Maleness More Stereotypically Framed Than Their Notions of Femaleness," *Sex Roles* 23:3–4 (August 1990), pp. 197–212.

10. Martin, Carol Lynn. "Attitudes and Expectations About Children with Nontraditional and Traditional Gender Roles," *Sex Roles*, 22:3–4 (1990), pp. 151–65.

11. Best, Raphaela. *We've All Got Scars: What Boys and Girls Learn in Elementary School.* Bloomington, IN: Indiana University Press, 1983.

12. Office for Sex Equity in Education, Michigan Department of Education, "The Influence of Gender-Role Socialization on Student Perceptions: A Report Based on Data Collected from Michigan Public School Students" (revised June 1990).

13. Miedzian, Myriam. *Boys Will Be Boys.* New York: Doubleday, 1991.

14. Best, *We've All Got Scars*, pp. 74, 75.

15. Messner, Michael. "Boyhood, Organized Sports, and the Construction of Masculinities," *Journal of Contemporary Ethnography* 18 (January 1990), pp. 416–44.
16. Coleman, James. *The Adolescent Society: The Social Life of the Teenager and Its Impact on Education*. New York: Free Press, 1961.
17. Eder, Donna, and Stephen Parker. "The Cultural Production and Reproduction of Gender: The Effect of Extracurricular Activities on Peer-Group Culture," *Sociology of Education* 60:3 (July 1987), pp. 200–13; quote from p. 206.
18. Adler, Patricia, Stephen Kless, and Peter Adler. "Socialization to Gender Roles: Popularity Among Elementary School Boys and Girls," *Sociology of Education* 65:3 (July 1992), pp. 169–87; quote from p. 174.
19. Adler, Kless, and Adler, "Socialization to Gender Roles," p. 172.
20. Eder, Donna. "The Cycle of Popularity: Interpersonal Relations Among Female Adolescents," *Sociology of Education* 58:3 (July 1985), pp. 154–65.
21. Lewis, William D. "The High School and the Boy," *Saturday Evening Post* (April 6, 1912), pp. 77–78.
22. Berkowitz, Steve. "High School Stars Learn the Score," *The Washington Post* (July 24, 1992), pp. A1, A2.
23. Snyder, Eldon E., and Elmer Spreitzer. "High School Athletic Participation Related to College Attendance Among Black, Hispanic, and White Males: A Research Note," *Youth and Society* 21:3 (March 1990), pp. 390–98.
24. Berkowitz, "High School Stars Learn the Score," pp. A1, A2.
25. Tyack, David, and Elisabeth Hansot. *Learning Together: A History of Coeducation in American Schools*. New Haven, CT: Yale University Press, 1990, pp. 155, 157.
26. Keller, Arnold Jack. *A Historical Analysis of the Arguments for and Against Coeducational Public High Schools in the United States*. Unpublished doctoral dissertation, Columbia University, New York, 1971, pp. 323–24.
27. Tyack and Hansot, *Learning Together*, p. 157.
28. New York City Report for 1909, p. 475. Quoted in Tyack and Hansot, *Learning Together*, p. 193.
29. Male Teachers' Association of New York City. "Are There Too Many Women Teachers?" *Educational Review* 28 (1904), pp. 98–105. Quoted in Tyack and Hansot, *Learning Together*, p. 159.
30. Sexton, Patricia. "Are Schools Emasculating Our Boys?" *Saturday Review* (June 19, 1965), p. 57.

31. Sexton, Patricia. *The Feminized Male: Classrooms, White Collars and the Decline of Manliness*. New York: Random House, 1969.

32. Bly, Robert. *The Pillow and the Key: Commentary on the Fairy Tale of Iron John, Part One*. St. Paul, MN: Ally Press, 1987, p. 17.

33. Bly, Robert. *When a Hair Turns Gold: Commentary on the Fairy Tale of Iron John, Part Two*. St. Paul, MN: Ally Press, 1988, p. 15.

34. Interview quotes from NBC's "Dateline" and the "Sally Jesse Raphael Show."

35. DePalma, Anthony. "Picture a Men's College Circa '56; That's Wabash," *The New York Times* (April 22, 1992), p. B8.

36. The discussion of VMI and The Citadel is based on the following sources:

    "Cadet Claims Shooting Probe Was Inadequate," *Charleston Post-Courier* (January 1, 1993), pp. 1A, 13A.

    Hackett, George, and Mark Miller. "Manning the Barricade," *Newsweek* (March 26, 1990), pp. 18–20.

    Harris, John F., and Joan Biskupic. "High Court Rebuffs VMI Appeal," *The Washington Post* (May 25, 1993), pp. A1, A7.

    Reilly, Rick. "What Is The Citadel?" *Sports Illustrated* (September 14, 1992), pp. 70–74.

    "Is VMI Getting Soft? School's Changes Displease Alumni," *The Washington Times* (September 13, 1992), p. A11.

37. "Arrow in Skull, Man Lives," *The Washington Post* (May 6, 1993), p. A18.

38. Brophy, Jere, and Thomas Good. "Feminization of American Elementary Schools," *Phi Delta Kappan* 54 (1973), pp, 564–66.

    Sadker, Myra, and David Sadker. *Sex Equity Handbook for Schools*. New York: Longman, 1982.

39. Kessler, R., and J. McRae. "Trends in the Relationship Between Sex and Psychological Distress, 1957–76," *American Sociological Review* 46 (1981).

    McLanahan, S. S., and J. L. Glass. "A Note on the Trend in Sex Differences in Psychological Distress," *Journal of Health and Human Stress* 2 (1976).

40. Sadker, David, and Myra Sadker, updated by Mary Jo Strauss. "The Report Card #1: The Cost of Sex Bias in Schools and Society." Distributed by the Mid-Atlantic Equity Center, Washington, D.C., and the New England Center for Equity Assistance, Andover, Massachusetts, 1989.

41. Duke, D. L. "Who Misbehaves? A High School Studies Its Discipline

Problems," *Educational Administration Quarterly* 12 (1976), pp. 65–85.

Office for Civil Rights. *1986 Elementary and Secondary Civil Rights Survey, State and National Summary of Projected Data.* Washington, DC: U.S. Department of Education, 1988.

42. Kimbrell, Andrew. "A Time for Men to Pull Together," *Utne Reader* (May-June 1991), pp. 66–75.

Watts, W. David, and Loyd S. Wright. "The Relationship of Alcohol, Tobacco, Marijuana, and Other Illegal Drug Use to Delinquency Among Mexican-American, Black, and White Adolescent Males," *Adolescence* 25:97 (Spring 1990), pp. 171–81.

43. Unpublished data of the National Center for Health Statistics, Public Health Service, U.S. Department of Health and Human Services, 1986.

"Death Rates from Accidents and Violence: 1970 to 1985," *Statistical Abstract of the United States, 1988.* Washington, DC: Bureau of the Census, U.S. Department of Commerce, 1988.

Poinsett, Alvin. "Why Our Children Are Killing One Another," *Ebony* 43 (December 1987).

Children's Defense Fund. *The State of America's Children: 1992.* Washington, DC: Children's Defense Fund, 1992.

44. Pleck, Joseph, and Robert Brannon (eds.). "Male Roles and the Male Experience," *Journal of Social Issues* 34 (1978), pp. 1–4.

Komarovsky, M. *Dilemmas of Masculinity: A Study of College Youth.* New York: Norton, 1976.

Sadker and Sadker, *Sex Equity Handbook for Schools.*

45. Lester, David. *Why People Kill Themselves: A 1990s Summary of Research Findings on Suicide Behavior,* third edition. Springfield, IL: Charles C. Thomas, 1992.

Maris, R. W. *Pathways to Suicide: A Survey of Self-Destructive Behaviors.* Baltimore, MD: Johns Hopkins Press, 1981.

46. Dewart, J. (ed.) *The State of Black America, 1989.* Washington, DC: National Urban League, 1989.

Garibaldi, Antoine M. *Educating Black Male Youth: A Moral and Civic Imperative.* New Orleans: Orleans Parish School Board, 1988.

Collison, Michelle N.-K. "More Young Black Men Choosing Not to Go to College," *Chronicle of Higher Education* 34:15 (December 9, 1987), pp. A1, 26–27.

Gibbs, Jewelle Taylor (ed.). *Young, Black, and Male in America: An Endangered Species.* Dover, MA: Auburn House, 1988.

47. Whitaker, Charles. "Do Black Males Need Special Schools?" *Ebony* (March 1991), pp. 17–18, 20.
48. Simons, Janet M., Belva Finlay, and Alice Yang. *The Adolescent Young Adult Fact Book*. Washington, DC: Children's Defense Fund, 1991.

    Children's Defense Fund. *The State of America's Children: 1992*, p. 52.
49. Lawton, Millicent. "Two Schools Aimed for Black Males Set in Milwaukee," *Education Week* X:6 (October 10, 1990), pp. 1, 8.
50. Dunkel, Tom. "Self-Segregated Schools Seek to Build Self-Esteem," *The Washington Times* (March 11, 1991), pp. E1–2.
51. Clark quoted in Whitaker, "Do Black Males Need Special Schools?" p. 18.
52. Leff, Lisa. "Maneuvering to Win Young Minds, P. G. School Chess Club Teaches Boys Self-Discipline, Self-Esteem," *The Washington Post* (May 17, 1993), pp. A1, A3.
53. Rotundo, E. Anthony. *American Manhood*. New York: Basic Books, 1993, p. 291.
54. Cramer, Robert Ervin, et al. "Motivating and Reinforcing Functions of the Male Sex Role: Social Analogues of Partial Reinforcement, Delay of Reinforcement, and Intermittent Shock," *Sex Roles* 20:9–10 (1989), pp. 551–73.

Osborne, R. W. "Men and Intimacy: An Empirical Review." Paper presented at the American Psychological Association, San Francisco, California, 1991.

9. Different Voices, Different Schools

1. Minnich, Elizabeth K. *Transforming Knowledge*. Philadelphia: Temple University Press, 1990, p. 39.
2. Gilligan, Carol. *In a Different Voice*. Cambridge, MA: Harvard University Press, 1982, p. 6.
3. Quoted in Faludi, Susan, *Backlash: The Undeclared War Against American Women*. New York: Crown, 1991, p. 328.
4. Gilligan, *In a Different Voice*, p. 173.
5. *Vogue* review quoted on book jacket of Gilligan, *In a Different Voice*.
6. Faludi, *Backlash*, p. 325.
7. Luria, Zella. "A Methodological Critique," *Signs: Journal of Women in Culture and Society* 11 (Winter 1986), p. 316–21.

8. Maccoby, Eleanor. "Gender and Relationships," *American Psychologist* 45:4 (1990), p. 513–20.

9. The research pointing to sex similarity in moral reasoning is extensive:

   Boldizar, Janet, Kenneth Wilson, and Deborah Kay Deemer. "Gender, Life Experiences, and Moral Judgment Development: A Process-Oriented Approach," *Journal of Personality and Social Psychology* 57:2 (1989), pp. 229–38.

   Donenberg, Geri, and Lois Hoffman. "Gender Differences in Moral Development," *Sex Roles* 18:11–12 (1988), pp. 701–17.

   Galotti, Kathleen. "Gender Differences in Self-Reported Moral Reasoning: A Review and New Evidence," *Journal of Youth and Adolescence* 18:5 (1989), pp. 475–88.

   Galotti, Kathleen, Steven Kozberg, and Maria Farmer. "Gender and Development Differences in Adolescents' Conceptions of Moral Reasoning," *Journal of Youth and Adolescence* 20:1 (1991), pp. 13–30.

   Pratt, Michael, Gail Golding, William Hunter, and Joan Norris. "From Inquiry to Judgment: Age and Sex Differences in Patterns of Adult Moral Thinking and Information-Seeking," *International Journal of Aging and Human Development* 27:2 (1988), pp. 109–24.

   Tsalikis, J., and M. Ortiz-Buonafina. "Ethical Beliefs, Differences of Males and Females," *Journal of Business Ethics* 9 (1990), pp. 509–17.

   Walker, Lawrence. "Sex Differences in the Development of Moral Reasoning: A Critical Review," *Child Development* 55:3 (1984), pp. 677–91.

   Walker, Lawrence. "A Longitudinal Study of Moral Reasoning," *Child Development* 60 (1989), pp. 157–66.

   Walker, Lawrence, Brian de Vries, and Shelley Trevethan. "Moral Stages and Moral Orientations in Real-Life and Hypothetical Dilemmas," *Child Development* 58 (1987), pp. 842–58.

10. Tavris, Carol. *The Mismeasure of Woman.* New York: Simon and Schuster, 1992.

11. Maccoby, "Gender and Relationships," pp. 513–20.

12. Carli, Linda. "Gender, Language, and Influence," *Journal of Personality and Social Psychology* 59:5 (1990), pp. 941–51.

13. Eagly, Alice, and Wendy Wood. "Explaining Sex Differences in Social Behavior: A Meta-Analytic Perspective," *Personality and Social Psychology Bulletin* 17:3 (1991), pp. 306–15.

14. Tavris, *The Mismeasure of Woman.*

Lakoff, Robin. *Talking Power.* New York: Basic Books, Harper-Collins, 1990.

Moore, Dwight, and Beth Haverkamp. "Measured Increases in Male Emotional Expressiveness Following a Structured Group Intervention," *Journal of Counseling and Development* 67 (1989), pp. 513–17.

15. Keller, Arnold Jack. *A Historical Analysis of the Arguments for and Against Coeducational Public High Schools in the United States.* Unpublished doctoral dissertation, Columbia University, New York, 1971.

16. Tyack, David, and Elisabeth Hansot. *Learning Together: A History of Coeducation in American Schools.* New Haven, CT: Yale University Press, 1990, p. 46.

17. Fairchild, J. "The Joint Education of the Sexes," *Pennsylvania School Journal* 1 (January 1853), p. 314.

18. "Female Education," *New York Teacher* 2 (January 1854), p. 97.

19. Brown, J. H. "Remarks on the Coeducation of the Sexes," *Pennsylvania School Journal* 3 (September 1854), pp. 120–22.

20. Thompson, James, and James Wickersham. "The Coeducation of the Sexes," *Pennsylvania School Journal* 3 (July 1854), p. 89. Quoted in Keller, *A Historical Analysis of the Arguments for and Against Coeducational Public High Schools*, p. 137.

21. "Description of a Good School," *Common School Journal* 8 (December 1, 1846), p. 357. Quoted in Keller, *A Historical Analysis of the Arguments for and Against Coeducational Public High Schools*, p. 156.

22. Charlestown, Massachusetts. *Reports Made to the School Committee of the City of Charlestown, Massachusetts, for a Separation of the Sexes in the Howard School.* Boston: Tuttle and Dennett, 1848. Quoted in Keller, *A Historical Analysis of the Arguments for and Against Coeducational Public High Schools*, p. 160.

23. Clarke, Edward. *Sex in Education; Or, A Fair Chance for Girls.* Boston: Houghton Mifflin, 1874.

24. Hall, Stanley G. *Adolescence: Its Psychology and Its Relations to Physiology, Anthropology, Sociology, Sex, Crime, Religion, and Education.* New York: D. Appleton, 1905.

25. Hall, *Adolescence*, p. 640.

26. Dewey, John P. "Is Coeducation Injurious to Girls?" *Ladies' Home Journal* (June 11, 1911), pp. 60–61.

27. Goodsell, Willystine, quoted in Keller, *A Historical Analysis of the Arguments for and Against Coeducational Public High Schools*, p. 333.

28. Lyles, Thomas. "Grouping by Sex," *National Elementary Principal* 46:2 (November 1966), pp. 38–41.

29. Hollinger, Debra (ed.). *Single-Sex Schooling: Perspectives from Practice and Research*. Washington, DC: Office of Educational Research and Improvement, Department of Education, 1993.

The following studies document gains that girls make in single-sex schools:

Cairns, Ed. "The Relationship Between Adolescent Perceived Self-Competence and Attendance at Single-Sex Secondary School," *British Journal of Educational Psychology* 60:3 (1990), pp. 207–211.

Carpenter, Peter, and Martin Hayden. "Girls Academic Achievements: Single Sex Versus Coeducational Schools in Australia," *Sociology of Education* 60:3 (July 1987), pp. 156–67.

Finn, Jeremy. "Sex Differences in Educational Outcomes: A Cross-National Study," *Sex Roles* 6:1 (1980), pp. 9–26.

Foon, Anne. "The Relationship Between School Type and Adolescent Self-Esteem, Attribution Styles, and Affiliation Needs: Implications for Educational Outcome," *British Journal of Educational Psychology* 58 (1988), pp. 44–54.

Hamilton, Marlene. "Performance Levels in Science and Other Subjects for Jamaican Adolescents Attending Single-Sex and Co-Educational High Schools," *International Science Education* 69:4 (1985), pp. 535–47.

Jimenez, Emmanuel, and Marlaine Lockheed. "Enhancing Girls' Learning Through Single-Sex Education: Evidence and a Policy Conundrum," *Educational Evaluation and Policy Analysis* 11:2 (Summer 1989), pp. 117–42.

Lee, Valerie, and Anthony Bryk. "Effects of Single-Sex Secondary Schools on Student Achievement and Attitudes," *Journal of Educational Psychology* 78:5 (1986), pp. 381–95.

Lee, Valerie, and Marlaine Lockheed. "The Effects of Single-Sex Schooling on Achievement and Attitudes in Nigeria," *Comparative Education Review* 34:2 (May 1990), pp. 209–31.

Lee, Valerie, and Helen Marks. "Sustained Effects of the Single-Sex Secondary School Experience on Attitudes, Behaviors, and Values in College," *Journal of Educational Psychology* 82:3 (1990), pp. 578–92.

Riordan, Cornelius. *Girls and Boys in School: Together or Separate*. New York: Teachers College, Columbia University, 1990.

Rowe, Kenneth. "Single-Sex and Mixed-Sex Classes: The Effects of Class Type on Student Achievement, Confidence, and Participation in Mathematics," *Australian Journal of Education* 32:2 (1988), pp. 180–202.

Steedman, Jane. "Examination Results in Mixed and Single-Sex Secondary Schools." In Reynolds, David (ed.), *Studying School Effectiveness.* London: Farmer Press, 1985.

Trickett, Edison, Penelope Trickett, Julie Castro, and Paul Schaffner. "The Independent School Experience: Aspects of the Normative Environments of Single-Sex and Coed Secondary Schools," *Journal of Educational Psychology* 74:3 (June 1982), pp. 374–81.

30. Johnson, Robert. "A Brave New World," *Independent School* 52:1 (Fall 1992), pp. 57–58; quote from p. 58.

31. Yankelovich, Shulman. *Girls' School Alumnae: Accomplished, Distinguished, Community-Minded.* National Coalition of Girls Schools, 1990.

32. The following studies suggest benefits for students who graduate from women's colleges:

Astin, Alexander. *Four Critical Years.* San Francisco, CA: Jossey Bass, 1977.

Elliott, Mary. *Women's Perceptions of the Classroom Environment at a Women's University and a Coeducational University.* Unpublished doctoral dissertation, Texas Woman's University, 1991.

Oates, Mary, and Susan Williamson. "Women's Colleges and Women Achievers," *Signs: Journal of Women in Culture and Society* 3:4 (1978), pp. 795–806.

Smith, Daryl. "Women's Colleges and Coed Colleges: Is There a Difference for Women?" *Journal of Higher Education* 61:2 (1990), pp. 181–97.

Tidball, Elizabeth. "Perspective on Academic Women and Affirmative Action," *Educational Record* (Spring 1973), pp. 130–35.

Tidball, Elizabeth. "Women's Colleges and Women Achievers Revisited," *Signs: Journal of Women in Culture and Society* 5:3 (1980), pp. 504–10.

Tidball, Elizabeth. "Baccalaureate Origins of Entrants into Medical Schools," *Journal of Higher Education* 56:4 (1985), pp. 385–402.

Tidball, Elizabeth. "Baccalaureate Origins of Recent Natural Science Doctorates," *Journal of Higher Education* 57:6 (1986), pp. 606–20.

Tidball, Elizabeth. "Women's Colleges: Exceptional Conditions,

Not Exceptional Talent, Produce High Achievers." In Pearson, Carol, Donna Shavlik, and Judith Touchton (eds.), *Educating the Majority: Women Challenge Tradition in Higher Education*. New York: Macmillan, 1989.

Tidball, Elizabeth, and Vera Kistiakowsky. "Baccalaureate Origins of American Scientists and Scholars," *Science* 193 (August 1976), pp. 646–52.

33. Sebrechts, Jadwiga. "The Cultivation of Scientists at Women's Colleges," *Journal of NIH Research* 4 (June 1992), pp. 22–26.

34. Conroy, Mary. "Single-Sex Schools," *New Woman* (September 1990), p. 146.

35. Hollinger, Moore, Piper, and Schaefer, *Single-Sex Schooling*. See the studies listed as documenting a single-sex advantage for girls. These same studies show more ambiguous findings concerning boys' schools.

36. Foon, Anne. "The Relationship Between School Type and Adolescent Self-Esteem, Attribution Styles, and Affiliation Needs: Implications for Educational Outcome," *British Journal of Educational Psychology* 58 (1988), pp. 44–54.

Hamilton, Marlene. "Performance Levels in Science and Other Subjects for Jamaican Adolescents Attending Single-Sex and Co-Educational High Schools," *Science Education* 69:4 (1985), pp. 535–47.

37. Lee, Valerie, Helen Marks, and Tina Byrd. "Sexism in Single-Sex and Coeducational Secondary School Classrooms," *Sociology of Education* (July 1993).

38. Tannen, Deborah. *You Just Don't Understand: Women and Men in Conversation*. New York: William Morrow, 1990, p. 251.

39. Hall, G. Stanley. "The Question of Coeducation," *Muncey's Magazine* 35 (February 1908), p. 589.

40. Hawley, Richard. "About Boys' Schools: A Progressive Case for an Ancient Form," *Teachers College Record* 92:3 (Spring 1991), pp. 433–44.

41. Barringer, Felicity. "Banning of Women at Military College Is Upheld," *The New York Times* (June 18, 1991), p. A10.

Lewis, Neil. "Court Tells Virginia to Give All Access to Military Training," *The New York Times* (October 6, 1992), p. A17.

42. Welch, Katherine. *Sex Differences in Language and the Importance of Context: An Observational Study of Classroom Speech*. Unpublished undergraduate thesis, Yale University, 1984.

43. "Separate but Better: Is Coeducation Bad for Girls?" *Los Angeles Weekly* (September 1991), pp. 13–19, 21, 24.

44. Stowe, Lawrence. "Should Physics Classes Be Single Sex?" *Physics Teacher* 6 (September 1991), pp. 380–81.

    Rubenfeld, Mona, and Faith Gilroy. "Relationship Between College Women's Occupational Interests and a Single-Sex Environment," *Career Development Quarterly* 40:1 (September 1991), pp. 64–70.

45. Rosenthal, R., and D. Rubin. "Further Meta-Analytic Procedures for Assessing Cognitive Gender Differences," *Journal of Educational Psychology* 74:5 (1982), pp. 708–12.

10. The Edge of Change

1. A few months after this event, an article appeared in a professional journal that was a description of the presentation and the ensuing confusion. The title captured the event: "Feminist vs. Principals; Result: A Draw at NAESP Convention," *Phi Delta Kappan* 55:2 (October 1973), p. 127.

2. Rosenthal, Robert, and Lenore Jacobson. *Pygmalion in the Classroom: Teacher Expectations and Pupils' Intellectual Development.* New York: Holt, Rinehart and Winston, 1974.

3. Kuebli, Janet, and Robyn Fivush. "Gender Differences in Parent-Child Conversations About Past Emotions," *Sex Roles* 27:11–12 (1992), pp. 683–98.

4. Siegal, Michael. "Are Sons and Daughters Treated More Differently by Fathers Than by Mothers?" *Developmental Review* 7 (1987), pp. 183–209.

5. Children's rooms were first analyzed for toy content in 1975 when the researchers found highly stereotyped playthings. In 1990, fifteen years into the gender revolution, another team of researchers found that little had changed.

    Rheingold, H. L., and K. V. Cook. "The Contents of Boys' and Girls' Rooms as an Index of Parents' Behavior," *Child Development* 46:2 (1975), pp. 459–63.

    Pomerleau, Andree, Daniel Bolduc, Gerard Malcuit, and Louise Cossette. "Pink or Blue: Environmental Gender Stereotypes in the First Two Years of Life," *Sex Roles* 22:5–6 (1990), pp. 359–68; quote from p. 365.

6. Schwartz, L. A., and W. T. Markham. "Sex Stereotyping in Children's Toy Advertisements," *Sex Roles* 12:1–2 (1985), pp. 157–70.

7. Raty, Hannu, and Leila Snellman. "Does Gender Make Any Difference? Common-Sense Conceptions of Intelligence," *Social Behavior and Personality* 20:1 (1992), pp. 23–34.

8. Yee, Doris, and Jacquelynne Eccles. "Parent Perceptions and Attributions for Children's Math Achievement," *Sex Roles* 19:5–6 (1988), pp. 317–34.

    Lummis, Max, and Harold Stevenson. "Gender Differences in Beliefs and Achievement: A Cross-Cultural Study," *Developmental Psychology* 26:2 (1990), pp. 254–63.

    Baker, David, and Doris Entwisle. "The Influence of Mothers on the Academic Expectations of Young Children: A Longitudinal Study of How Gender Differences Arise," *Social Forces* 65:3 (March 1987), pp. 670–94.

9. Olszewski-Kubilius, Paula, Marilynn Kulieke, Bill Shaw, and Gordon Willis. "Predictors of Achievement in Mathematics for Gifted Males and Females," *Gifted Child Quarterly* 34:2 (Spring 1990), pp. 64–71.

10. Houser, Betsy, and Chris Garvey. "Factors That Affect Nontraditional Vocational Enrollment Among Women," *Psychology of Women* 9 (1985), pp. 105–17.

    Coats, Patricia, and Steven Overman. "Childhood Play Experiences of Women in Traditional and Nontraditional Professions," *Sex Roles* 26:7–8 (1992), pp. 261–71.

11. Weitzman, Lenore, Deborah Eifler, Elizabeth Hokada, and Catherine Ross. "Sex Role Socialization in Picture Books for Preschool Children," *American Journal of Sociology* 77:6 (May 1972), pp. 1125–50.

12. Williams, J. Allen, Jo Etta Vernon, Martha Williams, and Karen Malccha. "Scx Role Socialization in Picture Books: An Update," *Social Science Quarterly* 68:1 (March 1987), pp. 148–56.

    McDonald, Scott. "Sex Bias in the Representation of Male and Female Characters in Children's Picture Books," *Journal of Genetic Psychology* 150:4 (December 1989), pp. 389–401.

    Bigler, Rebecca, and Lynn Liben. "The Role of Attitudes and Interventions in Gender-Schematic Processing," *Child Development* 61 (1990), pp. 1440–1452.

13. Stulberg, Lisa. *Still Teaching Sexism: An Ethnographic Analysis of Gender Dynamics in Three Elementary Schools.* Harvard University Honors Thesis, March 1992, p. 79.

14. This essay, written by Jackie Sadker, won first place in the National Women's Hall of Fame Essay and Poster Contest, Intermediate Division, in 1986.

15. For research summaries on the effect of reading material on development of nonsexist attitudes, see:

Sadker, Myra, and David Sadker. *Year 3: Final Report: Promoting Effectiveness in Classroom Instruction.* Washington, DC: National Institute of Education, 1984.

Sadker, Myra, David Sadker, and Susan Klein. "The Issue of Gender in Elementary and Secondary Education." In Grant, Gerald (ed.), *Review of Research in Education*, vol. 17. Washington, DC: American Educational Research Association, 1991, pp. 269–334.

Scott, K. "Effect of Sex-Fair Reading Materials on Pupils' Attitudes, Comprehension and Interests," *American Educational Research Journal* 23:1 (1986), pp. 105–16.

16. Sadker, Myra, and David Sadker. *Final Report: Project Effect (Effectiveness and Equity in College Teaching).* Washington, DC: Department of Education, 1986.

Sadker, Myra, and David Sadker. "Confronting Sexism in the College Classroom." In Gabriel, Susan, and Isaiah Smithson (eds.), *Gender in the Classroom: Power and Pedagogy.* Chicago: University of Illinois Press, 1990, pp. 176–87.

17. Webb, Noreen. "Sex Differences in Interaction and Achievement in Cooperative Small Groups," *Journal of Educational Psychology* 76:1 (1984), pp. 33–44.

18. Lockheed, Marlaine. "Reshaping the Social Order: The Case of Gender Segregation," *Sex Roles* 14:11–12 (1986), pp. 617–28.

19. Strang, Dorothy. "Sketches and Portraits," *Independent School* 52:1 (Fall 1992), pp. 19–26; quote from p. 20.

20. Hendrick, Joanne, and Terry Stange. "Do Actions Speak Louder Than Words? An Effect of the Functional Use of Language on Dominant Sex Role Behavior in Boys and Girls," *Early Childhood Research Quarterly* 6:4 (1991), pp. 565–76.

21. For an excellent discussion of parents raising a highly capable female student, see Finkel, David, "The Wiz." *The Washington Post Magazine* (June 13, 1993), pp. 8–13, 22–27.

22. Sittenfeld, Curtis. "A Sexist Peace: Why I Gave Up the Good Fight for Feminism at Groton," *The Washington Post* (May 30, 1993), pp. C1–C2.

Recommended Reading

Wonderful Women and Resourceful Girls: Books for Children to Grow On[*]

"Why are all the heroes boys?" a girl asked her mother recently. In answer to that question, we recommend the following books. From preschool to elementary school to middle school, from picture books to fantasy to historical fiction, these books offer girls strong role models. During the past decade there has been an explosion in the number of books with strong female characters at their center, so this list focuses mostly on recent publications. There are so many more we could have included, but this list is a place to begin.

Picture Storybooks

Adoff, Arnold. *In for Winter, Out for Spring*, illustrated by Jerry Pinkney. Harcourt Brace Jovanovich, 1991.

Allard, Harry, and James Marshall. *Miss Nelson Has a Field Day*, illustrated by James Marshall. Houghton Mifflin, 1985.

Andersen, Hans Christian. *The Snow Queen*, illustrated by Susan Jeffers. Dial, 1989 (1982).

Anholt, Catherine, and Laurence Anholt. *Twins, Two by Two*. Candlewick, 1992.

Ault, Mary Jane. *Peeping Beauty*. Holiday, 1993.

Bang, Molly. *Delphine*. Morrow, 1988.

Bemelmans, Ludwig. *Madeline*. Viking, 1962 (1939).

Blegvad, Lenore. *Anna Banana and Me*, illustrated by Erik Blegvad. Margaret K. McElderry, 1985.

Booth, Barbara. *Mandy*. Lothrop, Lee and Shepard, 1991.

Brown, Don. *Ruth Law Thrills a Nation*. Ticknor & Fields, 1993.

Browne, Eileen. *No Problem*, illustrated by David Parkins. Candlewick, 1993.

[*] Age levels are approximate—so much depends on the individual child.

Burningham, John. *Come Away from the Water, Shirley*. Harper, 1977.

Butterworth, Nick. *Amanda's Butterfly*. Delacorte, 1991.

Clifton, Lucille. *Three Wishes*. Viking, 1976.

Cole, Babette. *Princess Smartypants*. Putnam, 1986.

Cooney, Barbara. *Miss Rumphius*. Viking, 1982.

Demarest, Chris L. *No Peas for Nellie*. Macmillan, 1988.

Dorros, Arthur. *Abuela*, illustrated by Elisa Kleven. Dutton, 1991.

Eisenberg, Phyllis Rose. *You're My Nikki*, illustrated by Jill Kastner. Dial, 1992.

Ernst, Lisa C. *Miss Penny and Mr. Grubbs*. Bradbury, 1991.

Fitzgerald, Howard. *Aunt Flossie's Hats (and Crab Cakes Later)*, illustrated by Julie Vivas. Clarion, 1991.

Forest, Heather. *The Woman Who Flummoxed the Fairies*, illustrated by Susan Gaber. Harcourt Brace Jovanovich, 1990.

Fox, Mem. *Koala Lou*, illustrated by Pamela Lofts. Harcourt Brace Jovanovich, 1989.

——. *Possum Magic*, illustrated by Julie Vivas. Harcourt Brace Jovanovich, 1990

Garland, Michael. *My Cousin Kate*. Crowell, 1989.

Gerrard, Roy. *Jocasta Carr, Movie Star*. Farrar, Straus & Giroux, 1992.

Havill, Juanita. *Treasure Nap*, illustrated by Elivia Savadier. Houghton Mifflin, 1992.

Hayes, Sarah. *Mary Mary*, illustrated by Helen Craig. Margaret K. McElderry, 1990.

Hazen, Barbara Shook. *Mommy's Office*. Atheneum, 1992.

Henkes, Kevin. *Chrysanthemum*. Greenwillow, 1991.

——. *Sheila Rae, the Brave*. Greenwillow, 1987.

Hilton, Nette. *A Proper Little Lady*, illustrated by Cathy Wilcox. Orchard, 1989.

Hoffman, Mary. *Amazing Grace*, illustrated by Caroline Binch. Dial, 1991.

Holleyman, Sonia. *Mona the Vampire*. Delacorte, 1991.

Hopkinson, Deborah. *Sweet Clara and the Freedom Quilt*, illustrated by James Ransome. Knopf, 1993.

Isadora, Rachel. *"No, Agatha!"* Greenwillow, 1980.

Johnson, Angela. *Tell Me a Story, Mama*, illustrated by David Soman. Orchard Book, 1989.

Jonas, Ann. *The Trek*. Morrow, 1985.

Keats, Ezra Jack. *Maggie and the Pirates*. Four Winds, 1979.

Kesselman, Wendy. *Emma*, illustrated by Barbara Cooney. Doubleday, 1980.

Le Guin, Ursula. *A Ride on the Red Mare's Back*, illustrated by Julie Downing. Orchard, 1992.

Little, Jean. *Jess Was the Brave One*, illustrated by Janet Wilson. Viking, 1991.

Lotz, Karen. *Can't Sit Still*, illustrated by Colleen Browning. Dutton, 1993.

Luenn, Nancy. *Nessa's Fish*, illustrated by Todd Waldman. Atheneum, 1990.

McCully, Emily Arnold. *Mirette on the High Wire*. Putnam, 1992. Caldecott Medal.

McKissack, Patricia. *Flossie and the Fox*, illustrated by Rachel Isadora. Dial, 1986.

McPhail, David. *Annie & Co.* Henry Holt, 1991.

Mahy, Margaret. *Keeping House*. Margaret K. McElderry, 1991.

Mansell, Dom. *My Old Teddy*. Candlewick, 1991.

Merriam, Eve. *Mommies at Work*. Simon and Schuster, 1989 (1961).

Mosel, Arlene. *The Funny Little Woman*, illustrated by Blair Lent. Dutton, 1972. Caldecott Medal.

Munsch, Robert. *The Paper Bag Princess*, illustrated by Michael Martchenko. Toronto: Annick, 1980.

Nash, Ogden. *The Adventures of Isabel*, illustrated by James Marshall. Little, Brown, 1991.

Ochs, Carol Partridge. *When I'm Alone*, illustrated by Vicki Jo Redenbaugh. Carolrhoda Books, 1993.

Paterson, Katherine. *The King's Equal*, illustrated by Vladimir Vagin. Harper-Collins, 1992.

Pinkwater, Daniel. *Aunt Lulu*. Macmillan, 1988.

Ringgold, Faith. *Aunt Harriet's Underground Railroad in the Sky*. Crown, 1992.

Rockwell, Harlow. *My Doctor*. Macmillan, 1973.

Sendak, Maurice. *Outside Over There*. Harper, 1981.

Springer, Margaret. *A Royal Ball*, illustrated by Tom O'Sullivan. Bell, 1992.

Steig, William. *Brave Irene*. Farrar, Straus & Giroux, 1986.

Townson, Hazel. *What on Earth . . . ?*, illustrated by Mary Rees. Little, Brown, 1991.

Trivas, Irene. *Annie . . . Anya: A Month in Moscow*. Orchard Books, 1992.

Turkle, Brinton. *Rachel and Obadiah*. Dutton, 1978.

Waddell, Martin. *The Tough Princess*, illustrated by Patrick Benson. Philomel, 1986.

Walsh, Jill Paton. *When Grandma Came*, illustrated by Sophy Williams. Viking, 1992.

Wells, Rosemary. *Noisy Nora*. Dial, 1973.

Williams, Jay. *Petronella*, illustrated by Friso Henstra. Parents' Magazine Press, 1973.

——. *The Practical Princess*, illustrated by Friso Henstra. Parents' Magazine Press, 1969.

——. *The Silver Princess*, illustrated by Friso Henstra. Parents' Magazine Press, 1971.

Williams, Vera B. *A Chair for My Mother*. Greenwillow, 1982.

——. *Three Days on a River in a Red Canoe*. Greenwillow, 1981.

Winthrop, Elizabeth. *Maggie and the Monster*, illustrated by Tomie de Paola. Holiday, 1987.

Yolen, Jane. *The Emperor and the Kite*, illustrated by Ed Young. Philomel, 1967.

——. *The Girl Who Loved the Wind*, illustrated by Ed Young. Crowell, 1972.

Traditional Literature/Folktales

Aardema, Verna. *Borrequita and the Coyote*, illustrated by Petra Mathews. Knopf, 1991. Picture book.

Bierhorst, John. *The Woman Who Fell from the Sky: The Iroquois Story of Creation*, illustrated by Robert A. Parker. Morrow, 1993. Picture book.

de Paola, Tomie. *The Legend of Bluebonnet: An Old Tale of Texas*. Putnam, 1983. Picture book.

Goble, Paul. *The Girl Who Loved Wild Horses*. Bradbury, 1978. Caldecott Medal. Picture book.

Grifalconi, Ann. *Darkness and the Butterfly*. Little, Brown, 1987. Sequel: *Osa's Pride*, 1990. Picture books.

Grimm Brothers. *The Seven Ravens*, translated by Elizabeth Crawford, illustrated by Lizbeth Zwerger. Morrow, 1981. Picture book.

Hooks, William. *The Three Little Pigs and the Fox*, illustrated by S. D. Schindler. Macmillan, 1989. Picture book.

Lacapa, Michael. *Antelope Woman: An Apache Folktale*. Northland, 1992. Picture book.

Lesser, Rika. *Hansel and Gretel*, illustrated by Paul Zelinsky. Putnam, 1984. Picture book.

Mills, Lauren. *Tatterhood and the Hobgoblins: A Norwegian Folktale*. Little, Brown, 1993. Picture book.

Minard, Rosemary. *Womenfolk and Fairy Tales*. Houghton Mifflin, 1975. 7–10 years.

San Souci, Robert. *Cut from the Same Cloth: American Women of Myth, Legend, and Tall Tale*. Philomel, 1993. All ages.

Sherman, Josepha. *Vassilisa the Wise: A Tale of Medieval Russia*, illustrated by Daniel San Souci. Harcourt Brace Jovanovich, 1988. Picture book.

Stamm, Claus. *Three Strong Women: A Tall Tale from Japan*, illustrated by Jean and Mou-sein Tseng. Viking, 1990. Picture book.

Wahl, Jan. *The Cucumber Princess*, illustrated by Caren Cafaway. Stemmer, 1981. Picture book.

Wolkstein, Diane. *The Magic Wings: A Tale from China*, illustrated by Robert A. Parker. Dutton, 1983. 6 to 9 years.

Yolen, Jane. *Tam Lin*, illustrated by Charles Mikolaycak. Harcourt Brace Jovanovich, 1990. Picture book.

Young, Ed. *Lon Po Po: A Red Riding Hood Story from China*. Philomel, 1989. Picture book.

Contemporary Realistic Fiction

Ada, Alma Flor. *My Name Is Maria Isabel*, translated from the Spanish by Ana M. Cerro. Atheneum, 1993. 8 to 11 years.

Bauer, Joan. *Squashed*. Delacorte, 1992. 12+ years.

Blume, Judy. *Otherwise Known as Sheila the Great*. Dutton, 1972. 9 to 12 years.

———. *Starring Sally J. Freedman as Herself*. Bradbury, 1977. 9 to 12 years.

———. *Tiger Eyes*. Bradbury, 1981. 12+ years.

Bond, Nancy. *Country of Broken Stone*. Atheneum, 1980. 11+ years.

Boyd, Candy Dawson. *Breadsticks and Blessing Places*. Macmillan, 1985. 10+ years.

Byars, Betsy. *The Pinballs*. Harper, 1977. 10 to 12 years.

Cameron, Eleanor. *That Julia Redfern*. Dutton, 1982. Other books about Julia include *A Room Made of Windows*, Little Brown, 1971; *Julia and the Hand of God*, Dutton, 1977; *Julia's Magic*, Dutton, 1984; and *The Private Worlds of Julia Redfern*, Dutton, 1988. 9 to 12 years.

Castaneda, Omar S. *Among the Volcanoes*. Lodestar Books, 1991. 12+ years.

Cleary, Beverly. *Ramona the Pest*. Morrow, 1968. Sequels: *Ramona the Brave*, 1975; *Ramona and Her Father*, 1977; *Ramona and Her Mother*, 1979; *Ramona Quimby, Age 8*, 1981; *Ramona Forever*, 1984. 8 to 12 years.

Cleaver, Vera, and Bill Cleaver. *Where the Lilies Bloom*. Lippincott, 1969. Sequel: *Trial Valley*, 1977. 11+ years.

Conford, Ellen. *And This Is Laura*. Little, Brown, 1977. 8 to 11 years.

——. *Jenny Archer*. Little, Brown, 1987. Sequels: *A Case for Jenny Archer*, 1988; *Jenny Archer, Author*, 1989; *Jenny Archer to the Rescue*, 1990; *A Job for Jenny Archer*, 1990; *Can Do, Jenny Archer*, 1991. 7 to 10 years.

Fitzhugh, Louise. *Harriet the Spy*. Harper, 1964. 9 to 12 years.

George, Jean Craighead. *Julie of the Wolves*. Harper, 1972. Newbery Medal. 12+ years.

——. *The Talking Earth*. Harper, 1983. 11+ years.

Greene, Constance. *Isabelle the Itch*. Viking, 1973. Sequel: *Isabelle Shows Her Stuff*, 1984. 8 to 12 years.

Guy, Rosa. *The Music of Summer*. Delacorte, 1991. 12+ years.

Hamilton, Virginia. *Zeely*. Macmillan, 1967. 10 to 12 years.

Henkes, Kevin. *Words of Stone*. Greenwillow, 1992. 10+ years.

Higginsen, Vy, and Tonya Bolden. *Mama, I Want to Sing*. Scholastic, 1992. 12+ years.

Ho, Minfong. *Rice Without Rain*. Lothrop, 1988. 12+ years.

Knudson, R. R. *Zanballer*. Harper, 1972. Sequels: *Zanbanger*, 1977; *Zanboomer*, 1978. 11+ years.

Konigsburg, E. L. *From the Mixed-up Files of Mrs. Basil E. Frankweiler*. Atheneum, 1967. Newbery Medal. 9 to 12 years.

——. *Jennifer, Hecate, Macbeth, William McKinley, and Me, Elizabeth*. Atheneum, 1967. 8 to 12 years.

Lee, Marie G. *Finding My Voice*. Houghton Mifflin, 1992. 12+ years.

Lowry, Lois. *Anastasia Krupnik*. Houghton Mifflin, 1979. Sequels: *Anastasia Again*, 1981; *Anastasia at Your Service*, 1982; *Anastasia, Ask Your Analyst*, 1984; *Anastasia on Her Own*, 1985; *Anastasia Has the Answers*, 1986; *Anastasia's Chosen Career*, 1987; *Anastasia at This Address*, 1991. 8 to 12 years.

Lutzeier, Elizabeth. *The Wall*. Holiday, 1991. 10+ years.

MacLachlan, Patricia. *The Facts and Fictions of Minna Pratt*. Harper, 1988. 8 to 12 years.

Mazer, Norma Fox. *Silver*. Morrow, 1988. 12+ years.

Moore, Yvette. *Freedom Songs*. Orchard, 1991. 12+ years.

Murrow, Lisa. *Dancing on the Table*. Holiday, 1990. 8 to 12 years.

Naidoo, Beverly. *Journey to Jo'Burg*. Lippincott, 1986. Sequel: *Chain of Fire*, 1989. 11+ years.

Naylor, Phyllis Reynolds. *The Agony of Alice*. Atheneum, 1985. 9+ years.

——. *Josie's Trouble*. Atheneum, 1992. 8 to 12 years.

Paterson, Katherine. *Jacob Have I Loved*. Harper, 1980. Newbery Medal. 11+ years.

——. *The Great Gilly Hopkins*. Crowell, 1978. 10+ years.

Pullman, Philip. *The Broken Bridge*. Knopf, 1992. 12+ years.

Rylant, Cynthia. *Missing May*. Orchard, 1992. Newbery Medal. 11+ years.

Seabrooke, Brenda. *The Bridges of Summer*. Cobblehill, 1992. 10+ years.

Siskind, Leda. *Hopscotch Tree*. Bantam, 1992. 9 to 12 years.

Snyder, Zilpha Keatley. *The Egypt Game*. Atheneum, 1967. 9 to 12 years.

——. *Libby on Wednesday*. Delacorte, 1990. 9 to 12 years.

Soto, Gary. *The Skirt*. Delacorte, 1992. 7 to 10 years.

Spinelli, Jerry. *There's a Girl in My Hammerlock*. Simon and Schuster, 1991. 10+ years.

Thesman, Jean. *The Rain Catchers*. Houghton Mifflin, 1991. 12+ years.

Voigt, Cynthia. *Homecoming*. Atheneum, 1981. Sequels: *Dicey's Song*, 1983, Newbery Medal; *Seventeen Against the Dealer*, 1985. 11+ years.

———. *Izzy Willy-Nilly*. Atheneum, 1986. 12+ years.

Williams, Vera B. *Scooter*. Greenwillow, 1993. 6 to 8 years.

Woodson, Jacqueline. *Last Summer with Maizon*. Delacorte, 1990. Sequel: *Maizon at Blue Hill*, 1992. 10+ years.

Wrightson, Patricia. *The Sugar-Gum Tree*. Viking, 1991. 7 to 10 years.

Yep, Laurence. *Child of the Owl*. Harper, 1977. 12+ years.

Historical Fiction

Avi. *The True Confessions of Charlotte Doyle*. Orchard, 1990. 11+ years.

Blos, Joan N. *A Gathering of Days: A New England Girl's Journal, 1830-32*. Scribners, 1979. Newbery Medal. 9 to 12 years.

Brennan, J. H. *Shiva: An Adventure of the Ice Age*. Lippincott, 1989. Sequels: *Shiva Accused*, HarperCollins, 1991; *Shiva's Challenge*, HarperCollins, 1992. 10+ years.

Brink, Carol Ryrie. *Caddie Woodlawn*. Macmillan, 1936. Newbery Medal. 9 to 12 years.

Burnett, Frances Hodgson. *The Secret Garden*. Lippincott, 1938. 8 to 12 years.

Choi, Sook Nyul. *Year of Impossible Goodbyes*. Houghton Mifflin, 1991. Sequel: *Echoes of the White Giraffe*, 1993. 12+ years.

Dalgliesh, Alice. *The Courage of Sarah Noble*. Scribners, 1954. 7 to 10 years.

Fleischman, Paul. *The Borning Room*. Harper, 1991. 11+ years.

Greene, Bette. *The Summer of My German Soldier*. Dial, 1973. 12+ years.

Hautzig, Esther. *The Endless Steppe: Growing Up in Siberia*. Crowell, 1968. 12+ years.

Hesse, Karen. *Letters from Rifka*. Henry Holt, 1992. 9 to 12 years.

Highwater, Jamake. *Legend Days*. Harper, 1984. 12+ years.

Ho, Minfong. *The Clay Marble*. Farrar, Straus & Giroux, 1991. 12+ years.

Hudson, Jan. *Dawn Rider*. Scholastic, 1990. 11+ years.

Keehn, Sally. *I Am Regina*. Philomel, 1991. 12+ years.

Konigsburg, E. L. *A Proud Taste for Scarlet and Miniver*. Atheneum, 1973. 11+ years.

Lowry, Lois. *Number the Stars*. Houghton Mifflin, 1989. Newbery Medal. 9 to 12 years.

Lyons, Mary. *Letters from a Slave Girl*. Scribners, 1992. 12+ years.

MacLachlan, Patricia. *Sarah, Plain and Tall*. Harper, 1985. Newbery Medal. 8 to 12 years.

Moskin, Marietta. *I Am Rosemarie*. Harper, 1972. 10+ years.

O'Dell, Scott. *Island of the Blue Dolphins*. Houghton Mifflin, 1960. Newbery Medal. 10+ years. See all other books O'Dell has written.

Olson, Arielle North. *The Lighthouse Keeper's Daughter*, illustrated by Elaine Wentworth. Little, Brown, 1987. 5 to 8 years.

Paterson, Katherine. *Lyddie*. Dutton, 1991. 11+ years.

Pullman, Philip. *The Ruby in the Smoke*. Knopf, 1987. Sequels: *Shadow in the North*, 1988; *The Tiger in the Well*, 1990. 12+ years.

Rappaport, Doreen. *Trouble at the Mines*. Harper, 1987. 9 to 12 years.

Reiss, Johanna. *The Upstairs Room*. Crowell, 1972. 12+ years.

Rinaldi, Ann. *A Ride into Morning*. Harcourt Brace Jovanovich, 1991. 12+ years.

——. *A Break with Charity*. Harcourt Brace Jovanovich, 1992. 12+ years.

Snyder, Zilpha Keatley. *And Condors Danced*. Delacorte, 1987. 9 to 12 years.

Speare, Elizabeth George. *The Witch of Blackbeard Pond*. Houghton Mifflin, 1958. Newbery Medal. 12+ years.

Taylor, Mildred. *Roll of Thunder, Hear My Cry*. Dial, 1976. Newbery Medal. Sequels: *Let the Circle Be Unbroken*, 1981; *Road to Memphis*, 1990. 11+ years.

Taylor, Mildred. *Song of the Trees*. Dial, 1975. 7 to 10 years.

Uchida, Yoshiko. *Journey to Topaz: The Story of the Japanese-American Evacuation*. Scribners, 1971. 9 to 12 years.

Wilder, Laura Ingalls. *Little House in the Big Woods*. Harper, 1932. Sequel: *Little House on the Prairie*, 1935. 7 to 11 years.

Yep, Laurence. *The Star Fisher*. Morrow, 1991. 10+ years.

Yolen, Jane. *The Devil's Arithmetic*. Viking Penguin, 1990. 9 to 12 years.

Fantasy and Adventure

Alcock, Vivien. *The Monster Garden*. Delacorte, 1988. 10+ years.

Alexander, Lloyd. *The Illyrian Adventure*. Dutton, 1986. Sequels: *The El Dorado Adventure*, 1987; *The Drackenburg Adventure*, 1988; *The Jedera Adventure*, 1989; *The Philadelphia Adventure*, 1990. 10+ years.

Chetwin, Grace. *Child of the Air*. Bradbury, 1991. 10+ years.

Conrad, Pam. *Stonewords*. Harper, 1990. 10+ years.

Gregory, Philippa. *Florizella and the Wolves*. Candlewick, 1991. 8 to 11 years.

Hamilton, Virginia. *Sweet Whispers, Brother Rush*. Philomel, 1982. 12+ years.

Hilgartner, Beth. *A Necklace of Stars*. Little, Brown, 1979. 10+ years.

Hurmence, Belinda. *A Girl Called Boy*. Clarion, 1982. 8 to 11 years.

Jacques, Brian. *Mariel of Redwall*. Philomel, 1992. 10+ years.

L'Engle, Madeleine. *A Wrinkle in Time*. Farrar, Straus & Giroux, 1962. Newbery Medal. Sequel: *A Wind in the Door*, 1973. 10+ years.

McCaffrey, Anne. *Dragonsong*. Atheneum, 1976. Sequel: *Dragonsinger*. Atheneum, 1978. 10+ years.

McKinley, Robin. *Beauty: A Retelling of the Story of Beauty and the Beast*. Harper, 1978. 12+ years.

——. *The Blue Sword*. Greenwillow, 1982. 12+ years.

——. *The Hero and the Crown*. Greenwillow, 1985. Newbery Medal. 12+ years.

Mahy, Margaret. *The Changeover*. Viking, 1974. 12+ years.

——. *Dangerous Spaces*. Viking, 1991. 10+ years.

O'Brien, Robert C. *Z for Zachariah*. Atheneum, 1975. 12+ years.

Peck, Richard. *The Dreadful Future of Blossom Culp*. Delacorte, 1983. Other books about Blossom include *The Ghost Belonged to Me*, Viking, 1975; *Ghosts I Have Been*, Viking, 1977; and *Blossom Culp and the Sleep of Death*, Delacorte, 1986. 12+ years.

Pierce, Tamora. *Alanna: The First Adventure*. Athenuem, 1983. Sequels: *In the Hand of the Goddess*, 1984; *The Woman Who Rides Like a Man*, 1986; *Lioness Rampant*, 1988. 11+ years.

——. *Wild Magic: The Immortals*. Athenuem, 1992. 10+ years.

Reiss, Kathryn. *Time Windows*. Harcourt Brace Jovanovich, 1991. 10+ years.
Root, Phyllis. *The Listening Silence*. HarperCollins, 1992. 8 to 12 years.
Voigt, Cynthia. *Jackaroo*. Atheneum, 1985. 12+ years.
White, E. B. *Charlotte's Web*. Harper, 1952. 8+ years.
Wrede, Patricia. *Dealing with Dragons*. Harcourt Brace Jovanovich, 1990. Sequel: *Searching for Dragons*, 1991. 12+ years.
Wrightson, Patricia. *A Little Fear*. Atheneum, 1983. 8 to 12 years.

Biography

Adler, David. *A Picture Book of Anne Frank*, illustrated by Karen Ritz. Holiday, 1993. 4 to 8 years.
——. *A Picture Book of Eleanor Roosevelt*, illustrated by Robert Casilla. Holiday, 1991. 4 to 8 years.
——. *A Picture Book of Florence Nightingale*, illustrated by John and Alexandra Wallner. Holiday, 1992. 4 to 8 years.
——. *A Picture Book of Harriet Tubman*, illustrated by Samuel Byrd. Holiday, 1992. 4 to 8 years.
Anderson, William. *A Biography of Laura Ingalls Wilder*. Harper, 1992. 8 to 12 years.
Archer, Jules. *Breaking Barriers: The Feminist Revolution from Susan B. Anthony to Margaret Sanger to Betty Friedan*. Epoch Biographies, Viking, 1991. 12+ years.
Ayer, Eleanor H. *Margaret Bourke-White: Photographing the World*. Dillon, 1992. 9 to 12 years.
Balducci, Carolyn Feleppa. *Margaret Fuller: A Life of Passion and Defiance*. Barnard Biography series, Bantam, 1991. 12+ years.
Bernstein, Joanne E., and Rose Blue, with Alan Jay Gerber. *Judith Resnik: Challenger Astronaut*. Lodestar, 1990. 10+ years.
Blos, Joan. *The Heroine of the* Titanic*: A Tale Both True and Otherwise of the Life of Molly Brown*, illustrated by Tennessee Dixon. Morrow, 1991. 6 to 9 years.
Briggs, Carole S. *At the Controls: Women in Aviation*. Lerner, 1991. 10+ years.
Brooks, Polly Schoyer. *Beyond the Myth: The Story of Joan of Arc*. Harper, 1991. 12+ years.
Carpenter, Angelica Shirley, and Jean Shirley. *Frances Hodgson Burnett: Beyond the Secret Garden*. Lerner, 1990. 9 to 12 years.
Cleary, Beverly. *A Girl from Yamhill: A Memoir*. Dell, 1988. 12+ years.
Dash, Joan. *The Triumph of Discovery: Women Scientists Who Won the Nobel Prize*. Messner, 1991. 12+ years.
Ferris, Jeri. *Native American Doctor: The Story of Susan LaFlesche Picotte*. Carolrhoda Books, 1991. 9 to 12 years.
Fritz, Jean. *The Double Life of Pocahontas*. Putnam, 1983. 9 to 12 years.
Frank, Anne. *The Diary of a Young Girl*. Doubleday, 1952. 12+ years.
Giblen, James Cross. *Edith Wilson: The Woman Who Ran the United States*. Women of Our Times series, Viking, 1992. 7 to 10 years.
Gleasner, Diana C. *Breakthrough: Women in Science*. Breakthrough Biography series, Walker, 1983. 11+ years.
Greenfield, Eloise. *Mary McLeod Bethune*, illustrated by Jerry Pinkney. Crowell, 1977. 6 to 8 years.

——. *Rosa Parks*, illustrated by Eric Marlow. Crowell, 1973. 6 to 8 years.

Griffin, Judith Berry. *Phoebe and the General*, illustrated by Margot Tomes. Coward, McCann & Geoghegan, 1977. 7 to 10 years.

Hyman, Trina Schart. *Self-Portrait: Trina Schart Hyman*. Harper, 1989 (1981). 9 to 12 years.

Johnston, Norma. *Louisa May: The World and Works of Louisa May Alcott*. Four Winds, 1991. 11+ years.

Kent, Deborah. *Jane Addams and Hull House*. Cornerstones of Freedom series, Children's Press, 1992. 9 to 12 years.

Kittredge, Mary. *Barbara McClintock*. Chelsea, 1991. 9 to 12 years.

Little, Jean. *Little by Little*. Viking Kestrel, 1987. 10+ years.

Lyons, Mary E. *Sorrow's Kitchen: The Life and Folklore of Zora Neale Hurston*. Scribners, 1990. 12+ years.

McGovern, Ann. *The Secret Soldier: The Story of Deborah Sampson*. Four Winds, 1987 (1975). 8 to 12 years.

McKissack, Patricia C., and Frederick McKissack. *Madam C. J. Walker: Self-Made Millionaire*. Great African Americans series, Enslow, 1992. 6 to 9 years.

—— *Sojourner Truth: Ain't I a Woman?* Scholastic, 1992. 6 to 9 years.

Meltzer, Milton. *Dorothea Lange: Life Through the Camera*. Viking, 1985. 8 to 11 years.

Meyer, Susan E. *Mary Cassatt*. First Impressions series, Abrams, 1990. 12+ years.

Naylor, Phyllis Reynolds. *How I Came to Be a Writer*. Aladdin, 1987 (1978). 9 to 12 years.

Nichols, Janet. *Women Music Makers: An Introduction to Women Composers*. Walker, 1992. 12+ years.

O'Kelley, Mattie Lou. *From the Hills of Georgia: An Autobiography in Paintings*. Atlantic Monthly Press, 1983. 4 to 8 years.

Oneal, Zibby. *Grandma Moses: Painter of Rural America*. Women of Our Times series, Viking, 1986. 7 to 10 years.

Parker, Steve. *Marie Curie and Radium*. Harper, 1992. 8 to 12 years.

Quackenbush, Robert. *Stop the Presses, Nellie's Got a Scoop!: A Story of Nellie Bly*. Simon, 1992. 9 to 12 years.

Rappaport, Doreen. *Living Dangerously: American Women Who Risked Their Lives for Adventure*. Harper, 1991. 9 to 12 years.

Rubel, David. *Fannie Lou Hamer: From Sharecropping to Politics*. History of the Civil Rights Movement series, Burdett, 1990. 10+ years.

Sadler, Catherine Edwards. *Sasha: The Life of Alexandra Tolstoy*. Putnam, 1982. 10+ years.

Saunders, Susan. *Margaret Mead: The World Was Her Family*. Women of Our Time series, Viking, 1988. 7 to 10 years.

Sheafer, Silvia Anne. *Women of the West*. Addison-Wesley, 1980. 12+ years.

Shuker, Nancy. *Maya Angelou: Genius!* The Artist and the Process series, Burdett, 1991. 12+ years.

Sills, Leslie. *Inspirations: Stories About Women Artists*. Albert Whitman, 1989. 9+ years.

Stanley, Diane, and Peter Vennema. *Good Queen Bess: The Story of Elizabeth I of England*. Four Winds, 1990. 6 to 9 years.

Stanley, Fay. *The Last Princess: The Story of Princess Ka'iulani of Hawaii*, illustrated by Diane Stanley. Four Winds, 1991. 6 to 9 years.

Stevens, Bryna. *Frank Thompson: Her Civil War Story*. Macmillan, 1992. 10+ years.

Toll, Nelly. *Behind the Secret Window: A Memoir of Hidden Childhood*. Dial, 1988. 10+ years.

Turner, Robyn Montana. *Georgia O'Keefe*. Portraits of Women Artists for Children series, Little, Brown, 1991. 4 to 8 years.

———. *Frida Kahlo*. Portraits of Women Artists for Children series, Little, Brown, 1993. 4 to 8 years.

———. *Mary Cassatt*. Portraits of Women Artists for Children series, Little, Brown, 1992. 4 to 8 years.

———. *Rosa Bonheur*. Portraits of Women Artists for Children series, Little, Brown, 1991. 4 to 8 years.

Uchida, Yoshiko. *The Invisible Thread: A Memoir by the Author of* The Best Bad Thing. Messner, 1991. 9 to 12 years.

Wade, Mary Dodson. *Amelia Earhart: Flying for Adventure*. Gateway Biography series, Millbrook, 1992. 9 to 12 years.

Wadsworth, Ginger. *Rachel Carson: Voice for the Earth*. Lerner, 1992. 10+ years.

Zhensun, Zheng, and Alice Low. *A Young Painter: The Life and Paintings of Wang Yani—China's Extraordinary Young Artist*. Scholastic, 1991. 9 to 12 years.

Miscellaneous

Cole, Joanna. *The Magic School Bus Inside the Earth*. Scholastic, 1987. Sequels: *The Magic School Bus at the Waterworks*, 1988; *The Magic School Bus Inside the Human Body*, 1989; *The Magic School Bus Lost in the Solar System*, 1990; *The Magic School Bus on the Ocean Floor*, 1992. (Science) 4 to 8 years.

Ness, Evaline (ed.). *Amelia Mixed the Mustard and Other Poems*. Scribners, 1975. (Poetry) All ages.

Saxby, Maurice. *The Great Deeds of Heroic Women*. Peter Bedrick, 1990. (Mythology/History) 12+ years.

Thomas, Marlo, Gloria Steinem, and Letty Cottin Pogrebin. *Free to Be You and Me*. McGraw-Hill, 1974. All ages.

Vare, Ethlie Ann, and Greg Ptacek. *Mothers of Invention*. Morrow, 1988. (Science) 10+ years.

Index